D0850135

JACOB'S YOUNGER BROTHER

JACOB'S YOUNGER BROTHER

Christian-Jewish Relations
after Vatican II

Karma Ben-Johanan

THE BELKNAP PRESS OF
HARVARD UNIVERSITY PRESS

Cambridge, Massachusetts
London, England

2022

FIRST PRINTING

An earlier version of this book was first published as *A Pottage of Lentils: Mutual Perceptions of Christians and Jews in the Age of Reconciliation* (Hebrew) by Tel Aviv University Press, 2020.

Library of Congress Cataloging-in-Publication Data
Names: Ben Johanan, Karma, author.
Title: Jacob's younger brother : Christian-Jewish relations after Vatican II / Karma Ben-Johanan.
Other titles: Nezid ʻadashim. English
Description: Cambridge, Massachusetts : The Belknap Press of Harvard University Press, 2022. | An earlier version of this book was first published as A Pottage of Lentils: Mutual Perceptions of Christians and Jews in the Age of Reconciliation (Hebrew) by Tel Aviv University Press, 2020.—Title page verso | Includes bibliographical references and index.
Identifiers: LCCN 2021039009 | ISBN 9780674258266 (cloth)
Subjects: LCSH: Catholic Church—Relations—Judaism. | Christianity and other religions—Judaism—History. | Judaism—Relations—Christianity—1945– | Reconciliation—Religious aspects—Catholic Church. | Reconciliation—Religious aspects—Judaism. | Religious pluralism—Catholic Church. | Religious pluralism—Judaism.
Classification: LCC BM535 .B44513 2022 | DDC 296.3/96—dc23
LC record available at https://lccn.loc.gov/2021039009

To Tomehr, with love

Contents

Note on Translation and Transliteration

Quotations from the Hebrew Bible are from *The Holy Scriptures According to the Masoretic Text,* published in 1917 by the Jewish Publication Society of America, Philadelphia. New Testament quotations are from the New Revised Standard Version Bible, © 1989 National Council of the Churches of Christ in the United States of America. Used by permission. All rights reserved worldwide.

For citations from the Talmud, I relied on *The Babylonian Talmud: Translated into English with Notes, Glossary, and Indices* (London: Soncino Press, 1935–), with minor adaptations.

For translations of the works of Maimonides, I have followed the Yale edition where possible (*The Code of Maimonides,* 14 vols., Yale Judaica Series [New Haven: Yale University Press, 1949–]). Where translations from the Yale series were not available (such as for the *Book of Science*), I relied on Chabad's translation, with my own adaptations (https://www.chabad.org /library/article_cdo/aid/682956/jewish/Mishneh-Torah.htm). In the case of the *Laws of Idolatry,* I turned to the translation available in Michael Walzer, Menachem Lorberbaum, Noam J. Zohar, and Ari Ackerman, eds., *The Jewish Political Tradition,* vol. 2, *Membership* (New Haven: Yale University Press, 2003), 480–482, with some adaptations.

All other translations, except where otherwise indicated, are my own.

For transliteration from Hebrew, I have followed the guidelines established by the Academy of the Hebrew Language in 2011 (https://hebrew-academy .org.il/wp-content/uploads/taatik-ivrit-latinit-1-1.pdf), with the exception that common nouns are styled in lowercase.

JACOB'S YOUNGER BROTHER

Introduction

The events of the twentieth century shook Western civilization to its core. The ruin of two world wars—especially the horrors of World War II, with its ideologically justified bloodshed and institutionalized slaughter of those regarded as Others, perpetrated by the very paragons of high European culture—had left Europe reeling from a sense of moral failure. The cultural achievements of the century before had all too easily given way to barbarity. Regard for the Other became the cornerstone of the West's attempt to rebuild a moral foundation and redefine its values. Where universal reason, progress, and objective truth had once commanded center stage, the protagonists in the postwar period were now pluralism and the discourse of human rights.

In view of the iniquities that had defiled Europe, the Holocaust in particular, the Christian world had to contend with difficult and penetrating questions: Why had the Christian churches failed to save Europe from the abyss of cruelty? Had they fallen prey to secular regimes, or had Europe's Christian legacy itself sown the seeds of destruction? Was it even possible to "speak theology" after such a catastrophe, or was it better to finally depart from doctrinal obsessions? In the latter half of the twentieth century, Western Christianity grappled with the ethical challenge posed by—to use Emmanuel Levinas's words—the face of the Other.

Yet those same Others—that is, the Jews—were also called on to adjust to the new ethical challenge that had crystallized in response to their torment. Which face should Jews present to the West, with its new moral sensibilities?

Must that face remain anguished and subjugated, or was it now permissible to bare some teeth? And when facing their own Others—when facing Christians—must Jews assimilate the West's new ethical imperative and play by the rules formulated by those who had only yesterday been their murderers? Would the Jews embrace the lessons that had been learned from their own torment, or would they refuse, once again, to participate in the Western project, reluctant to adopt the new gospel of reconciliation as their own?

Jacob's Younger Brother focuses on the relation to the Other as a key component in the consolidation of religious identities in the second half of the twentieth century. It concentrates on mutual perceptions of Christians and Jews after they rose from the debacle of the world wars and reorganized themselves in a postmodern, multicultural, and liberal reality in which Jews have become sovereign in their own state and the Catholic Church has largely accepted the separation of church and state and withdrawn from many of its historical political aspirations.

It is in this context that the book discusses the religious literatures of two specific communities: the Roman Catholic community and the Orthodox Jewish community. Under the term *Roman Catholic,* I subsume the Christian communities that see themselves as subject to the spiritual authority of the pope. Under the term *Orthodox Jewish,* I subsume a diverse group of Jewish communities (from Modern Orthodox to ultra-Orthodox) that regard themselves as faithful representatives of Jewish tradition and as having an obligation to preserve it, especially through their commitment to halakha—the evolved (and evolving) body of laws, derived from the written and the oral Torah, that guide Jewish life and religious observance.

I chose to focus on these communities for several reasons. First, they have tremendous influence on contemporary religious identities. The Catholic Church is one of the most influential religious institutions in the world, and Jewish Orthodoxy fills a crucial role in defining Jewish identity for Jews both inside and outside the Orthodox community. In Israel, it holds a hegemonic position.

Second, there is a prominent common denominator that makes looking at these otherwise so different communities together eye-opening: Orthodox Jewish and Catholic leaders negotiate their traditions in the modern setting in a similar way. Unlike other Christian and Jewish denominations that often openly reject significant swaths of their traditions that are incompatible with contemporary value systems, Orthodox rabbis and Catholic priests and theologians define themselves as fully obligated to maintain the entire scope of their religious heritage. They can resort only to reinterpretation, not rejection.

Finally, the Christian-Jewish dialogue of recent decades is often represented by the images of a cardinal in a red cape and a bearded Orthodox rabbi—probably because these two specific communities symbolize "thick," traditional religious identities and are associated in Western memory with the historical Christian-Jewish rivalry that the contemporary phase of modernity seeks to solve. The problematization of this image—of religious tradition as the arena of conflict and of contemporary dialogue as this conflict's ultimate overcoming—is one of the objectives of this book.

The choice to focus on Catholic Christianity and Orthodox Judaism does not imply that Orthodox Jewish and Roman Catholic mutual perceptions are the only factors that define the direction of the Christian-Jewish relationship today, nor that these communities are more important than others. There are other fascinating and lively aspects of this relationship that are worthy of their own research.

This work focuses on the relations between Jews and Christians in the age of reconciliation. More specifically, it concentrates on the time between the Second Vatican Council's declaration *Nostra Aetate* (1965) and the resignation of Pope Benedict XVI (2013).[1] Nevertheless, several sections of the book are dedicated to earlier periods in the twentieth century, revolving especially around the immediate aftermath of the Holocaust and the foundation of the State of Israel. Developments that occurred later than 2013 are discussed only briefly, in the Epilogue. In the fourth paragraph of *Nostra Aetate,* the Catholic Church turned its back on its anti-Jewish heritage and paved the way toward rapprochement between the church and the Jewish people. The political independence of Jews in Israel has also removed many of the problems that characterized Christian-Jewish coexistence in the past. Yet these fundamental changes have not rescinded the ambivalence that has characterized the Christian-Jewish relationship throughout history. For many Catholics, the reconciliation with the Jews caused a theological avalanche and disorder. For many Orthodox Jews, the demand to adapt themselves to the conciliatory perceptions of Christians seemed to be another attempt to force a Christian agenda and a Christian timetable on them, this time with a liberal flavor. The process of reconciliation led, in both cases, to complex consequences. This book inquires into the elements that constitute the Christian-Jewish rapprochement of recent decades and the identity transformations that that rapprochement has demanded from each of the parties.

The book examines the discourse within each of the religious communities with respect to the other—that is, what Orthodox Jewish rabbis tell Jews about Christianity, and what Catholic theologians and priests tell Christians about Judaism. This focus reveals layers within the Christian-Jewish relationship that do not find expression in the explicit interreligious dialogue that is currently taking place between Jewish and Christian official representatives and that is careful about political correctness. I am interested mainly in the closed conversations in which one community discusses the other without diplomatic considerations.

To describe these internal discourses within both faith communities, I analyze a diverse body of sources that spans magisterial pronouncements, official declarations, journal articles, well-known halakhic rulings, and obscure internet discussions. I evaluate the texts not according to their official standing but according to the weight they carry in Catholic and Orthodox Jewish discourses as a whole. This strategy is central to the book, since it brings to the surface the tensions between what is done and thought officially and what is done and thought unofficially, a tension that is present in both communities' preoccupations with the relationship between them.

I do not pretend to cover the entire set of opinions of all Orthodox Jewish and Catholic thinkers on the issue. My objective in writing this book was to extract dominant trajectories out of a vast mixture of diverse phenomena. Moreover, I dedicate particular attention to the aspects of Orthodox Jewish and Catholic reciprocal perceptions that have remained underexplored in contemporary scholarship. My assumption is that the fruitful and overt dialogue that has been taking place between Orthodox Jewish rabbis and Catholic priests and theologians in the last decades is already known to the reader. The book thus seeks to bring to the surface precisely the points of resistance to Christian-Jewish dialogue, especially within the Orthodox Jewish world, and the sophisticated means by which the deepest questions raised by reconciliation are avoided, especially within the Catholic world. In other words, this book is about the problems of rapprochement and not about its successes.

The book, then, tells two different stories, a Catholic one and an Orthodox Jewish one, that progress in parallel and often with the agents of each group being unaware of the details of the other story. Part I deals with the way in which Catholic theologians and church officials have treated the Christian-Jewish relationship after the Holocaust, in particular after the Second Vatican Council.

As an introduction to Part I, Chapter 1 begins by examining the Catholic position on Jews from the early centuries of Christianity to the Holocaust. It connects the transformations in the church's attitude toward Jews and Judaism in the twentieth century with the transitions in the church's attitude toward modernity in general. It then analyzes the "Jewish section" of *Nostra Aetate* and the theological challenges it posed for postconciliar Catholicism.

Chapter 2 discusses the way theologians and clergy attempted to deal with Jewish matters in the first two decades after the council (1965–1985) and the complex implications that the discourse on Jews and Judaism had for the self-conception of the church, for Roman Catholic identity, and for Catholic theology as a whole. This chapter focuses on the efforts of theologians to reimagine early Christianity as constituting a continuation of Judaism rather than a rupture with it, on the position of the church on post-crucifixion Jews, and on the theological meaning of the Holocaust and the State of Israel. The chapter also discusses the question of the Jews' salvation and whether the church should be proactive in converting them. I argue that the theological discussion during these years posed a threat to the stability of the Catholic tradition, caused inner-Catholic polarization, and was often at odds with Jewish sensibilities. For these reasons, it did not maintain the same level of vitality in the following decades.

Chapter 3 deals with the turn in the ecclesiastical position regarding Jews and Judaism during John Paul II's pontificate, from 1978 to 2005. The first decades after the council had been characterized by a vibrant and poignant debate on theological matters, and John Paul II was concerned that theological adjustments instigated after Vatican II were hasty and might place the very foundations of the church at risk. Taking a conservative turn, he preferred to block further theological attempts to redefine Christian faith and to shift the conciliation between Christians and Jews to what he perceived to be a more effective and less risky platform. John Paul II availed himself of grand historical gestures that left their imprint on both Jews and Christians while circumventing the debate on doctrinal issues. The chapter thus explains the enigmatic tension between John Paul II's doctrinal conservativeness and his pastoral progressiveness in the realm of Christian-Jewish relations.

Chapter 4 addresses the position of Joseph Ratzinger on Jews and Judaism in his capacities as a theologian, as a cardinal serving as John Paul II's right-hand man (1981–2005), and as Pope Benedict XVI (2005–2013). Whereas Catholic discourse in the era of John Paul II had shunted aside the heavy theological issues in favor of grand gestures, Ratzinger grappled with these issues directly, to the displeasure of many Jews and liberal Catholics. This chapter examines the public discourse surrounding Ratzinger's actions and writings as a way to understand the deep tensions prevailing in the Catholic community regarding Jews and Judaism, the church's self-perception, and its conception of history. I argue that Ratzinger's attempts to theologically systematize the Christian-Jewish relationship were largely experienced as harmful by Christians and Jews alike, both of whom preferred to avoid head-on theological polemics and to pursue their dialogue in non-theological terms.

Part II focuses on Orthodox Jewish rabbis and Torah scholars' perceptions of Christianity after the Holocaust and the founding of the State of Israel, as reflected in rabbinic commentaries, halakhic tractates, and theological discussions. Chapter 5 addresses the variety of halakhic traditions and rabbinical theologies pertaining to Christianity from its beginnings to late modernity. Chapter 6 deals with contemporary halakhic discussions of Christianity and Christians; it points to a distinct halakhic turn in recent decades, over the course of which more moderate or tolerant positions on Christianity were marginalized and the halakhic perception of Christianity became increasingly inimical. Chapter 7 is devoted to a discussion of Christianity in religious Zionist circles affiliated with the theological school of Rabbi Abraham Isaac Kook and his son, Rabbi Zvi Yehuda Kook. It also brings to light an intense theological discourse among the Kooks' Francophone disciples, who imported their acquaintance with French philosophy and Catholic theology into Kookist thought to develop a sophisticated anti-Christian dialectic of history. These discussions within the Kooks' school, which has greatly developed in recent decades, attempt to revitalize the ancient anti-Christian polemics from late antiquity to medieval times. Chapter 8 is devoted to the internal controversies within the Orthodox Jewish community on the issue of interfaith dialogue with Christians, mostly taking place within Modern Orthodox circles in the United States and their extension in Israel. The chapter concludes with a discussion of the official dialogue that has been conducted between the Vatican and the Chief Rabbinate of Israel since the year 2000.

My intention is not to take sides or provide moral evaluations. This book was written from the point of view of a historian, not a partner in Christian-Jewish dialogue. From this perspective, I am looking into the paradoxes, asymmetries, and discrepancies of the Christian-Jewish relationship in its new garb and exploring how the two groups are adapting themselves to the postwar era of interfaith encounters.

With its gradual withdrawal from anti-Jewish perceptions, the Catholic Church sought to put an end to a long tradition of exploiting Judaism to meet Christianity's needs, especially that of maintaining Christianity's hegemony. Drawing on Susannah Heschel's metaphor, this move can be understood as a process of decolonization of Judaism, which is now entitled to its own self-definition.[2] Yet it can also be seen as a new attempt to reappropriate Judaism for the benefit of the changing cultural and political needs of Catholicism in the postwar era. To put it differently, contemporary Catholic theologians and church officials strive to dissolve the asymmetrical power relations in which the Jews have been the subordinated victims of the superior Christian religion for generations and to replace them with a relationship of dignity in which both parties have equal standing. Nevertheless, the Catholic-Jewish dialogue itself remains a Christian initiative dictated by Christian moral standards, adapted to Christian political sensibilities, and inaugurated at the very moment in which much of the tension of Christian-Jewish coexistence in the West had already been resolved, because Europe had lost most of its Jews through their destruction in the Holocaust. In this sense, Christian-Jewish dialogue preserves the imbalance in power relations, albeit in a conciliatory form and within a different world order.

The Orthodox Jewish response to the rapprochement initiative, as described in this book, corresponds to the Christian ambivalence with an ambivalence of its own. On the one hand, Orthodox rabbis and Torah scholars are embracing this long-awaited moment of self-definition, in which they can shed the customs imposed on them by Christian constructions and meet Christians as equal partners. Yet many of them experience the interreligious dialogue in itself as a construction of this kind, in that it instrumentalizes Jews as witnesses to Christianity's new progressive faith. The invigorated hostility found in parts of contemporary Orthodox Jewish literature toward Christianity represents an attempt to reappropriate Judaism to Judaism's own needs. Nevertheless, this reappropriation is done precisely through the conflictual subjectivity of the colonized, who continue to imagine themselves through the internalization of the Christian gaze and cannot give up vengeful acts of (literary) violence.[3] Instead of joining the flow of Christian-Jewish dialogue, many Orthodox currents have reverted to those old anti-Christian traditions that were most offensive to Christians and that were used against them during various anti-Jewish campaigns throughout the ages. Paradoxically, this sort of resistance to the Christian conciliatory initiative preserves Christian-Jewish rivalry and could raise precisely the kind of hostility from which Jews (and Christians) have sought to release themselves. This complicated dynamic is the prism through which I attempt to analyze the Christian-Jewish reconciliation of recent decades.

The Christian-Jewish relationship is so deeply marked by a history of struggle and abuse that it could not be expected to be completely mended, purified of ambivalence, and cleansed of resentment—certainly not in a few decades. Yet *Jacob's Younger Brother* does not end with a pessimistic conclusion regarding Christian-Jewish rapprochement. The unresolvable tensions do not dominate the Christian-Jewish relationship in its entirety. They are confined to specific realms of writing and thinking, to the doctrinal and halakhic cores of the respective traditions. Halakha and theology are where the demons abide, those demons that stubbornly resist supersession. This, however, is not because these realms are inherently irrational and frenzied, but precisely the opposite; it is because these are the realms that are less tolerant of contradictions, equivocal arguments, and loose ends and compromises. Perhaps there is no better alternative than a peaceful coexistence with those demons. Yet in other realms of human activity, whether religious or secular, new horizons of exchange, even of friendship, have been opened.

PART I

Judaism in
Catholic Theology

1

Historical and Theological Transitions

In order to evaluate the theological and practical transitions in the Catholic Church's attitude to Jews and Judaism after Vatican II, we need some historical background. This chapter offers a concise overview of the evolution of Catholic teaching on the Jews through the centuries. The scholarly literature focusing on the place of Jews in Catholic theology is extremely rich, and I will discuss here only those points that are especially helpful for the central discussion of this book, on post–Vatican II perceptions. Following a brief historical overview, the second section discusses the modern turn within the Catholic Church, as this provides an essential context to the church's discussion of Jews and Judaism both at the council and in its aftermath. Section 3 focuses on how the church coped with modern antisemitism and the Holocaust, which served as the immediate background to the doctrinal turn with regard to Jews and Judaism in the 1960s. Section 4 focuses on the "Jewish section" in *Nostra aetate,* particularly on the theological deliberations that stood behind its formulation.

A Brief Historical Survey

For hundreds of years, Christian tradition was inherently ambivalent toward Judaism, and attitudes were often blatantly hostile. This charged tradition was based on a specific hermeneutical system of reading the New Testament and on the conviction that an unbridgeable rift separated Christianity from Judaism.

However, the biblical basis for this traditional hermeneutical position has been deeply contested in the past few decades. Biblical studies and historical scholarship on the first centuries CE have introduced a paradigm shift in the understanding of early Christian texts. At the heart of this transformation is the scholarly effort to contextualize the New Testament in its original historical milieus. Beginning in the 1970s (with some precedents before that time), historians have been attempting to ground Jesus and his disciples in the historical context of Second Temple Judaism.[1] Similarly, the "new perspective on Paul" has allowed scholars to recover Paul's Jewish convictions and sensibilities and challenge the common presumption that he had an anti-Jewish agenda.[2] This anchoring of the New Testament within the Jewish context of its time has in turn called for an examination of the origins of traditional anti-Jewish readings of Scripture that assume a clear-cut separation between Judaism and Christianity. Accepting that Christianity and Judaism were not separate and were certainly not opposed to each other at the very beginning, scholars have begun to look for a later moment of separation, no longer viewing the antagonism between Judaism and Christianity as a timeless historical fact. Recent studies on the parting of the ways between Judaism and Christianity challenge the historical beliefs about an early separation and depict a much longer and more complex process than had previously been assumed, at times pushing the "final" departure to the ninth century.[3]

These projects of contextualization recover a Jewish landscape that was shared by Jews who followed Jesus and Jews who did not and reveal a complex entanglement of Jewish and Christian identities in the Roman Empire of the first centuries CE. Apart from the transparent historical logic of relocating Christianity within Judaism, this scholarly trajectory has also had the added value of questioning the allegedly inherited anti-Jewish characteristics of early Christian texts and stripping the interfaith hostility from these texts. If the scientific focus of the nineteenth and early twentieth century's historical, biblical, and philological scholarship was the dejudaization of Christianity (a scientific effort which was intertwined with an antisemitic worldview), the scientific focus of contemporary scholarship is precisely the opposite: by regarding the separation between Judaism and Christianity as a much later construction, contemporary scholars see early Christianity as mainly a Jewish phenomenon.

This scholarly trajectory is made possible by the Christian-Jewish post-Holocaust process of rapprochement, a process that freed scholars to study sources without assuming a clear-cut separation between the two traditions.[4] Nevertheless, the historiographical transformation is not just the fruit of the process of Christian-Jewish reconciliation; it also nourishes and facilitates it. The tools that scholars offer for reading and interpreting religious sources often serve the religious communities themselves by providing, in John Gager's words, "a new set of images" that "may have a liberating effect not only on scholars, with their specialized concerns, but also on the culture of which they are a part."[5] In other words, the scholarly reform and the religious reform of Christian-Jewish relations are closely intertwined. In this chapter I will briefly describe the new scholarly paradigms and the evolution of traditional perceptions that they seek to challenge, since an acquaintance with these traditions is necessary for understanding the current reform in Christian-Jewish relations.

Many Gospel passages describe quarrels and strife between Jesus and his disciples and other Jewish groups such as the Pharisees, the Sadducees, and the scribes (or sometimes the Jews in general, as we often find in John). These Jewish communities are presented as faithless, blind God-haters, stubborn and callous (John 12:37–40; Matt. 13:13–14, 19:8; Mark 10:5; Acts 7:51), sycophantic hypocrites (Matt. 15:7), sons of serpents (Luke 3:7), devil spawn who want to kill the Messiah (John 8:37–44), and informers and murderers (Acts 7:52). Famously, the Jewish crowd demands that Pilate crucify Jesus (John 19:6–7), calling out "His blood be on us and on our children!" (Matt. 27:25), a cry that was used by Christians over the centuries as evidence for the collective and transgenerational Jewish guilt for the crucifixion.

Before the latter half of the twentieth century, such passages were largely read as supporting the idea of a split between Judaism and Christianity that emerged from Jesus's critique of the ossified Judaism of his time, a split that deepened after his crucifixion and resurrection. Notwithstanding Jesus's ethnic affiliation to the Jewish people (an affiliation that was contested only by certain Nazi-inclined theologies in the twentieth century), Jesus and his disciples were seen as harbingers of a new religious community, a new affiliation, and a new gospel that were essentially different from those of Judaism. In other words, the New Testament, with regard to its relationship with Judaism, was traditionally read—by both Jews and Christians—as an anti-Jewish text.

Contemporary scholars, seeking to depart from this tradition, read the New Testament as a Jewish text written (mainly) by Jewish authors and reflecting (mainly) intra-Jewish controversies, conflicts, and sensibilities.

Instead of assuming a dichotomy between the "new" message of Christianity and the "old" ways of Judaism, these scholars point to the diversity of Jewish ideas and practices in the Roman Empire, a diversity that is also reflected in New Testament texts.

A similar dynamic is reflected in the reading of Paul's epistles. As the man who undertook the mission of spreading Christ's Gospel among the gentiles, Paul has been traditionally perceived as the founder of Christianity as an independent religion fundamentally different from Judaism. He has also been considered as the father of "replacement theology," or "supersessionism," that is, the perception that the Christian Church had replaced the Jewish people as God's chosen people. Many of Paul's statements have been interpreted, from the second century on, as a solidified and systematic approach to Judaism as an obsolete religion: his apparent polarization between the letter and the spirit, between the "old" covenant, which was made with the Jewish people according to the flesh and written in stone, and the "new covenant," which was written "on tablets of human hearts" (2 Cor. 3:3–6); his discussion of the "spiritual" affiliation with the seed of Abraham through faith rather than through heredity, the flesh, and the keeping of the commandments (Rom. 9:7); his critique of the overwhelmingly prominent preoccupation with the law, that is, with the observance of the Torah's commandments (Rom. 2:25–29, 3:9, 4:16, and 5:20–21; Phil. 3:2–10; and elsewhere); and his reference to the law as a prelude to the new covenant, such that the law now lost its justification (Gal. 3:24–26). The church, as opposed to the obsolete synagogue, was presented as the true heir of biblical promises. Moreover, Paul's depiction of the veil that covers Jews' eyes when they are reading their scriptures (2 Cor. 3:13–18) became for later Christians a paradigmatic prism through which to understand Judaism—as blind and stubborn, refusing to concede the true spiritual significance of the Bible and adhering, instead, to the literal interpretation of the law, as slaves to the written word, to this world and its rules.

Many of the components of this Pauline picture have been contested in the past five decades, with a new intuition that is often traced back to Krister Stendahl's seminal article "The Apostle Paul and the Introspective Conscience of the West."[6] Stendahl argued that the popular reading of Paul, which has far-reaching implications for Christian-Jewish relations, is an anachronistic projection of Martin Luther's sensibilities onto the Pauline sources. Reading Paul "in the framework of late medieval piety," which has roots in Augustine's reading of Paul, leads to a false understanding of Paul's attitude to the law as a component in the drama of the individual conscience—a component that must be overcome on the way to "justification by faith," just as Judaism, by analogy, must be overcome by Christianity. Paul, according to Stendahl, was in fact "grappling with the question about the place of the Gentiles in the Church and in the plan of God, with the problem Jew / Gentiles or Jewish Christians / Gentile Christians, which had driven him to that interpretation of the Law which was to become his in a unique way."

This change of framework was adopted by prominent Pauline scholars, who introduced a paradigmatic shift in the reading of Paul. Instead of seeing Paul as a convert from Judaism to Christianity, such scholars stress the continuity of Paul's Jewish affiliation and the conversion as his taking up his mission to the gentiles. Scholars may argue about the precise understanding of Paul's differentiation between Jews and gentiles or about the universality of his critique of the law, but the main pillars of the new paradigm are shared by many.[7] In addition to this new trajectory, as we shall see in later chapters, Paul's discussions of Israel in Romans 9–11 are no longer regarded as an appendix to his other interventions but as the paradigmatic key to understanding his perception of Judaism.

A strong ambivalence toward Judaism, based on how the New Testament was read, characterizes the early Christian literature that was written during the long process of the crystallization of Christianity. Both proto-orthodox and heterodox Christian authors have often deliberated on the relationship between the Christian Gospel and Jewish tradition and sought to differentiate between them. The second-century Marcion of Sinope, who made an immense contribution to the process of the canonization of the Christian scriptures, claimed that the Hebrew scriptures, in whole or in part, express a materialistic conception of religion that is incompatible with the spiritual love of Jesus and Paul.[8] The Hebrew books were written under the inspiration of the God of the Jews, an inferior material God, who completely differs from the spiritual God of the new gospel. Marcion was of the opinion that Christians should adhere to only some parts of the New Testament (Paul's epistles and the Gospel according to Luke) as scripture.

The proto-orthodox approach of the church fathers was different. The church rejected Marcion's position as heresy (144 CE) and sanctified the Hebrew Bible as part of the Christian canon. It adopted the Jewish scriptures but extensively reinterpreted them in allegorical fashion as prophecies about Christ and the end of days. The church fathers considered the problem to be not the Hebrew Bible (or its author) but its Jewish commentators. Anti-Jewish literature (*adversus Judaeos*), which was mostly based on the interpretation of sections from the Old Testament, was a widespread patristic genre.[9] The Hebrew Bible was cited as evidence of the history of Jewish treacherousness, and it already presaged, according to Christian tradition, the future replacement of the Jewish people with the congregation of gentiles, which was, in the language of Justin Martyr, *verus Israel*—the true Israel.

After the Christianization of the Roman Empire, this conception of Judaism became an orthodox Christian position. The fact that Christianity became the religion of the empire and was disseminated among many nations was perceived as the realization of the prophecies about the founding of the kingdom of God. The church of the gentiles was thus proven to be the true church. The Jews remained an empty vessel, and their messianic hopes for a political and religious hegemony were forever repudiated.

Yet contemporary scholarship complicates the uniformity of this historical picture, which focuses mainly on the writings of the church fathers. Instead of assuming the emergence of Christianity out of Judaism during the first or second century at the latest, contemporary scholars maintain that such a separation was alien to the context of the Roman Empire in late antiquity and to the plethora of identities inhabiting it.[10] Not only should the final separation between the two religious communities be dated to a much later period, but even the idea of differentiating Jewish ideas and affiliations from Christian ones is a later construction. As Daniel Boyarin argued while comparing rabbinic sources and patristic heresiologies, Judaism and Christianity were defined during the struggle of various identity options over the right to declare what should be regarded as orthodoxy. In this process, not only were Christianity and Judaism separated from each other; they were also "invented" as religions.[11] Drawing on postcolonial studies, scholars have argued that sources from late antiquity which seem to clearly define Jewish and Christian identities should be read "against the grain," as reflecting the motivations of the authors (which eventually became hegemonic) and not as depicting the objective historical reality, which is often very different.[12]

In the evolution of the Christian tradition's attitude to Judaism in late antiquity, a unique place is reserved for Augustine. Despite writing within the hostile *adversus Judaeos* tradition, Augustine developed a theological justification for the existence of Jews within Christian society (a "defense of Jews and Judaism," in Paula Fredriksen's words), a justification that was applied in

Europe throughout most of the Middle Ages.[13] In evaluating the historical persistence of the Jews in a Christian world, even though they murdered Christ and rejected his gospel, Augustine concluded that Jews survive because their existence is beneficial to the church; their blind adherence to the Old Testament and their refusal to understand its true significance are evidence that the texts, which every reasonable person can see presage the coming of Christ, were not faked by Christians. To the contrary, the greatest enemies of the Christians testify to the reliability of the texts. Augustine also thought that the miserable status of the Jews represented the just wages of those who reject Christ and indicated that the divine prophecies of success were intended not for them but for Christians. It was therefore fitting to humiliate the Jews and deride them, but they should not be physically harmed or killed, nor should they be forbidden from observing their ritual laws, for they should be allowed to fulfill their role as witnesses.[14]

Augustine's theological justification enabled the Jews of Europe to live in relative safety among their Christian hosts up until the twelfth century and even to enjoy a certain measure of religious tolerance. Following Gregory I in the sixth century, the popes of the Middle Ages issued papal bulls (*sicut Judaeis*) that safeguarded the status of Jews in Christian lands and prohibited harming Jews, taking their property, intervening in their religious rituals, or forcing them to convert.[15] The popes also determined that the Jews had to retain their inferior status vis-à-vis their Christian neighbors and that they should be humiliated and constrained in various ways. The protection of church authorities allowed Jews to exist (sometimes even thrive) within Christian society. They were the only minority that had such a status, while other religious minorities did not survive.

The coexistence of Jews and Christians encountered a crisis beginning in the eleventh century. The call to unify Europe under the cross raised questions about the status of marginal groups within Christian society. Institutional persecutions of heathens, Jews, homosexuals, and other groups defined as deviant began.[16] The fast integration of the Jews within the new market economy as moneylenders generated increasing hostility among the Christian masses. During the First Crusade, the Crusaders wished to first settle accounts with the enemies of Christ at home, so they slaughtered Jews on the way to the Holy Land (during the Rhineland Massacres of 1096). Other Jews were forcibly baptized.

In the twelfth century, Christian scholars began to display a deep interest in post-biblical Jewish tradition, and in particular in the Talmud, which until that time had not been part of the anti-Jewish polemic. The "discovery" of the Talmud by Christians brought a deterioration in their attitude; if in the early Middle Ages the Jews were perceived as worthy of tolerance thanks to the positive theological role accorded them by Augustine, it seemed that the unwritten contract with them had now been undermined. Augustinian tolerance was based on the idea that the Jews blindly cleaved to the Old Testament and did not veer right or left from their misguided apprehension of it. The revelation that the Talmud had replaced the Old Testament as the central sacred text in the religious lives of Jews undermined the theological justification for the tolerance displayed toward them.[17]

The increasing familiarity of Christians with the Jewish tradition exacerbated the relationship between the two communities. At first, it was Jewish converts who exposed the "secrets" of the Talmud; at a later stage, Christians of non-Jewish descent also began learning Hebrew and Aramaic so as to be able to efficiently dispute the Talmud. In his essay *Pugio Fidei* (written around 1280), the Spanish Dominican Ramon Martí translated sections of the Talmud into Latin, thereby making Jewish sources more accessible to Christian polemical writers and preachers, enabling them to sharpen their attacks against Judaism. Christian scholars also strove to use the Talmud to convert Jews to Christianity by proving Christian truths from within it.[18]

Because the Jews had betrayed their role as historical "fossils" (and were, in fact, considered heretics who denied Old Testament Judaism), Judaism began to be perceived as a redundant and ungrateful religion. This "breach of contract" removed some of the most effective theological safeguards from the Jews. The question of the need for Jews (or in any case, such a large number of Jews) became a recurring motif in Christian discussions, and in several cases, the Christian authorities reached the conclusion that it would be better to expel them. This process took place simultaneously with an increase in the gravity of the accusations directed at Jews as a consequence of various developments within the faith of the Christian community. The more the Passion of Christ and the emotional identification with it became central to the religious fervor of the time, the more the Jews' betrayal of Jesus and his torture and crucifixion became tangible and poignant in the Christian mind, exacerbating the enmity toward Jews within both the church hierarchy and popular culture. Moreover, from the twelfth century onward, the Jews began to be portrayed as malevolent rather than as simply mistaken. An increasing number of church officials no longer accused them of blindness to Jesus's messianism but of an attempt to destroy him even though they were aware of his true nature.[19]

The perception of Jews as deliberate traitors, along with the emphasis on the Passion, found expression in blood libels. During the twelfth century, stories began to appear accusing Jews of cruel murders of Christian children for ritual purposes, of cannibalism (in particular the use of Christian blood in the making of matzos), and of the desecration of the Eucharist. In these supposed acts of murder and cruelty, the Jews purportedly re-created the crucifixion with their young victims. Attributing the abuse of the Eucharist to them shows that they were perceived as being well aware that the sacramental bread became the body of Christ during communion and that they were reconstructing the crucifixion not because they lacked faith, but with full awareness of their deeds.[20]

The Fourth Lateran Council (1215) issued an order to coerce the Jews to wear an identifying patch.[21] The instructions of the council were implemented to one extent or another in England, France, Italy, and Germany. Spanish legislation also required Jews to differentiate themselves from the Christian population by means of a unique garment. Expulsions of the Jews from France, England, and parts of Germany during the twelfth and thirteenth centuries were often justified in terms of the need to protect Christian society from the injurious influence of Jews.[22]

The concern that Christian society would be "contaminated" by Jews grew stronger as the number of converts to Christianity among the Jews increased. The problem was particularly dire within the Iberian Peninsula, where as a consequence of a series of massacres that began around 1391 (the Seville Massacres), tens of thousands of Jews were forcibly baptized, and others joined the Christian Church out of fear and desperation. Another wave of conversions took place after the Disputation of Tortosa (1413–1414), which was perceived by both Christians and Jews as a Jewish defeat. At first, the Spanish Christians perceived the mass conversion of Jews as a miracle of divine providence. However, Christian society subsequently became troubled by a sense that the new converts had remained too Jewish. The new Christians were perceived as a threat to the spiritual health of the Christian community. Many of the conversions either were forced or were made out of considerations of benefit, and deep suspicions arose regarding their authenticity.[23] The conversion of Jews gradually came to be perceived as useless in purifying the Jews from their deeply rooted hatred of Christianity. New laws were needed to distinguish between new and veteran Christians.[24]

According to the concept of *limpieza de sangre* (blood purity), which became widespread in Spain and Portugal, newly baptized Christians and their offspring were regarded as pseudo-Jews until the fourth generation.[25] The Inquisition in Spain and Portugal took steps to punish the *conversos* who had secretly returned to Judaism and to distinguish between true Christians and impostors. Converts caught in heresy were burned alive. The Jews were ultimately expelled from Spain in 1492 and were forcibly converted in Portugal in 1497.

The events in Spain and Portugal followed in the wake of similar events, such as the expulsion of the Jews from England (1290), France (1394), and parts of Germany (1347–1450). By the end of the fifteenth century, western Europe had been emptied of most of its Jews. Some of them moved to the lands of Islam; others found refuge in eastern Europe—in Poland and Lithuania. They were, however, allowed to remain in the Papal States and in certain parts of Germany.

Sixteenth-century popes imposed severe restrictions on the Jews who had remained in central and western Europe and treated them with suspicion. During the Counter-Reformation, the church was busy with its own self-definition in the face of a plethora of heterodoxies and heresies. In this context, the church reopened the discussion of the status of Jews and Judaism in Catholic doctrine.[26] The effort to convert the Jews was now defined as one of the hallmarks of Christianity. The Jews were still tolerated, but the justification for it became the expectation of their ultimate conversion, which would herald the parousia.[27] The Jews were forced to live in ghettos, suffered economic embargos, and had their books censored or burned. They were recurrently banished and restored to various locations in Europe, exposed to blood libels and persecutions.

Jews residing in Protestant lands did not fare much better. Martin Luther called for merciless persecution of the Jews—to burn their synagogues, impose harsh economic restrictions against them, and exile them from Christian lands. Luther attacked the Catholic Church as "Judaizing" and identified its excessive emphasis on rituals with Jewish legalism. He compared his struggle with the Catholic Church to Paul's struggle with Rabbinic Judaism.[28] The Lutheran doctrine of justification by faith alone reinforced the vision of Judaism as a legalistic faith, which is the very opposite of Christianity—the religion of grace. At the same time, the Lutheran doctrine that accorded supreme authority to the Bible in all matters of ritual and doctrine generated a deep interest in Old Testament studies among Protestants, often in the original Hebrew. Protestant Hebraism expanded throughout the sixteenth and seventeenth centuries, and Christian scholars became well versed in Jewish literature.[29]

Once Enlightenment ideas of universal rights and religious tolerance became more widespread in the eighteenth century, the state of the Jews who remained in the West gradually improved. Enlightened rulers allowed Jews from eastern Europe to settle in central and western Europe. They were accorded unprecedented rights and had a chance to attempt to become integrated within the surrounding society. At the same time, European society in the age of Enlightenment was not without its religious residues, and the ancient ambivalence surrounding the Jews continued to exist and even took on new forms. There were those who viewed the assimilation of Jews— whether via the baptismal basin or otherwise—as a move that would benefit society as a whole. Others did not believe that Jews would be able to cast off their Jewish nature, even if they were to convert to Christianity; they thought that a rapid and successful integration of the Jews in modern Europe would be harmful to European society. Even though emancipation was quickly instituted in many European countries (France, the Netherlands, Belgium, England, Germany, Italy, Switzerland), it also gave rise to considerable resistance and hostility toward the Jews.

The Catholic Church and Modernity

In the course of the eighteenth century, the legacy of Catholicism became a symbol of the ancien régime, of outmoded values, superstitions, the oppression of the human spirit, and the suppression of reason, perceived as the antithesis of all that was modern and enlightened. The Catholic Church generally maintained a defensive position vis-à-vis modernism. In 1869, Pope Pius IX convened the First Vatican Council to contend with the problems of modernism (with particular emphasis on the rise of rationalism, liberalism, and materialism) and to establish an appropriate doctrinal Catholic response.[30] To bolster papal authority against the tempests of the era, the council announced the dogma of papal infallibility (*infallibilitas*) that applied whenever the pope established doctrines concerning morality and faith for the church.[31] The council was interrupted by the Savoy conquest of Rome and was never resumed, but the struggle of the church against modernism continued. In 1879, Leo XIII issued an encyclical titled *Aeterni Patris,* in which he warned against the dangers of secularization and modernization and called on the Catholic intellectual world to intensify its engagement with medieval scholasticism as a fitting response to the new philosophy.[32] The next pope, Pius X, maintained the same line as his predecessor and declared modernism to be "the compendium of every heresy" (*omnium haereseon conlectum*).[33] In 1910, the same pope imposed an oath against modernism (*Sacrorum Antistitum*) on the entire ecclesiastical hierarchy (priests and theologians included). One of the oath's paragraphs included a commitment to abstain from the historical-critical approach to biblical studies, which had become immensely popular in non-Catholic intellectual circles. These papal declarations directed Catholic theology toward deep engagement with medieval scholasticism and the development of the neo-Thomist school. Following the prohibition against engaging with Scripture in any way that departed from the traditional ecclesiastical prism, many Catholic thinkers refrained from biblical studies, and the discipline was left largely in the hands of their Protestant peers.

A new theological trend that deviated from the anti-modernism of Leo XIII and Pius X first became evident during the 1930s and 1940s, mainly in Germany and France, where voices began protesting against limiting theological engagement solely to neo-Thomist thought, claiming that it did not provide sufficient spiritual nourishment.[34] The critics wanted to "return to the sources"—termed *ressourcement* in French—to re-engage with the church fathers, liturgy, and Scripture. They wished to open themselves to a theological dialogue with the surrounding world and developed a theological perspective that was more attentive to history and to the subjective turn in modern philosophy. The work of these theologians, who did not necessarily view themselves as an organized group, was soon given the derogatory label of "*la nouvelle théologie*" (the "New Theology") by their neo-Thomist rivals, who claimed that rather than returning to any sources, these "New Theologians" were making up a new tradition. The "new" voices continued to reverberate on the margins of the Catholic intellectual world during World War II and became widespread within a younger generation of theologians from that period. Pius XII criticized them scathingly during the 1950s and accused them of modernism, but their ideas gradually began to percolate into the Catholic mainstream.[35]

In 1943, Pius XII instigated a revolution in the church's position on Scripture when he issued the encyclical *Divino afflante spiritu*, which called for translations of Scripture into the vernacular directly from the source languages (Hebrew and Greek), to take the place of the Latin translations that had been widespread in the Catholic world up to that time. Moreover, he permitted the application of the historical-critical method, so long as the church's sacred traditions were taken into account. This encyclical opened the door for the participation of Catholic theologians in Bible studies and for Catholic engagement with Scripture in general. Even though Pius XII objected to the modernist trends of the New Theologians (in an encyclical entitled *Humani Generis,* which he issued in 1950 and in which he reconfirmed Catholic reservations toward modernism), his "loosening of the reins" in regard to biblical studies nevertheless empowered the New Theologians and shifted them from the margins to the mainstream. These trends had a crucial impact on the crystallization of a new Catholic doctrine regarding Judaism, as eventually formulated in Vatican II's *Nostra aetate.*

The Catholic Church perceived itself to be relatively stable at the end of World War II with Pius XII at the rudder, since the main agents of destruction, Nazi Germany and Stalin's USSR, had distanced themselves from religion. Nevertheless, there was an increasing sense in certain Catholic circles that without revisiting its values and institutions, the church would fail to provide a significant spiritual alternative for contemporary Europe. In view of the general upheaval in post–World War II Europe, many Catholics felt that the time had come to reexamine the relationship of the church with the surrounding world, as well as its role within it. The newly elected pope, John XXIII, shared these sentiments and believed that the church needed an "update"—aggiornamento—that would allow it to respond to the spirit of the times.[36] A short time after his ascension to the Holy See, John XXIII announced his intention to convene an ecumenical council that would "open the windows of the church" and bring in fresh air.

Vatican II opened in October 1962 and closed at the end of 1965. More than two thousand bishops gathered in St. Peter's Basilica, along with hundreds of professional theologians who served as expert consultants (*periti*). The bishops discussed drafts that were prepared for them by special committees, and they were able to consult the various theological specialists who accompanied them. These experts often represented the new theological trends. The council ultimately approved four constitutions, three declarations, and nine decrees. These documents transformed the church's agenda in both a practical and a doctrinal sense.

The Church, Antisemitism, and the Holocaust

Many Catholics in twentieth-century Europe identified with the nationalist sentiments that had characterized their countries since the previous century. In some of these countries, Jews were seen as a foreign element, both religiously and nationally. On the other hand, Catholics were members of a transnational church that espoused equality among all those accepting the Catholic faith. The German brand of racist nationalism was irreconcilable with this worldview. Accordingly, the Catholic Church was principally opposed to the racist theories of nineteenth- and twentieth-century Europe. Nevertheless, in practice, there were many Catholic thinkers who sought to integrate racist and ecclesiastical doctrines and saw no conflict between them, while others were opposed to some parts of the racist worldview but adopted others.

The Catholic establishment's opposition to racist doctrines was not informed by ideological pluralism or inspired by compassion for Jews.[37] The church's old and deep-seated hostility toward Jews made its relations with Nazi antisemitism ambivalent. While many Catholics chose not to identify with Nazism and were even persecuted by the Nazis, the distinction between Nazi antisemitism and old-fashioned Christian anti-Judaism was not always clear-cut. Indeed, several scholars argue that the very attempt to make such a distinction is anachronistic and designed to absolve the church of its responsibility.[38] In the 1930s and early 1940s, some Catholics felt that the Nazis' treatment of the Jews was legitimate and that it was only right to discriminate against them and humiliate them as Christ killers whose perfidy posed a constant threat to the Christian community. Some felt that the Nazis' antisemitic acts were a proper punishment for the Jews' cardinal sin and that in a certain sense, the Nazis were doing God's work. Others recoiled at Nazi savagery, but to many of those, this was only a question of degree; they were not fundamentally opposed to anti-Jewish policies.

Among those who sought to distinguish between Catholic and Nazi antisemitism, it was often believed that only mass conversion would save the Jews from the divine punishment meted out by their persecutors. Some Catholics who were opposed to Nazi antisemitism sought to remedy the Jewish "problem" by evangelization. Had the Christians made a real effort to convert the Jews, they argued, such terrible cruelty could have been avoided.[39] Members of Amici Israel believed that to open the Jews' hearts to Christianity, the Catholic Church should improve its attitude toward them;

they asked Pope Pius XI to modify the Good Friday Prayer for the Jews' conversion by removing the word *perfidis* (literally, "faithless," but understood as "traitors"). Changing Christian attitudes to Jews for the better, they argued, would lead to a Jewish change of heart and conversion.[40]

The view of conversion as the panacea for racist antisemitism was also prevalent among the most outspoken opponents of antisemitism in the 1930s and 1940s, including the French philosopher Jacques Maritain, American theoretician Waldemar Gurian, Austrian American theologian John M. Oesterreicher, and German theologian Karl Thieme.[41] In point of fact, before World War II, we would be hard pressed to find representatives of a Catholic approach completely free of ideas that are now often considered anti-Jewish.[42] The Jews were not at the center of the Catholic Church's agenda either before or during the war. Nazism was considered a form of paganism, substituting the nation for a god, that should be vehemently rejected regardless of the Jewish question. In his 1937 encyclical to German bishops, *Mit brennender Sorge* (With burning concern), Pius XI explicitly denounced racist Nazi ideology as contravening the basic tenets of Christianity, without any reference to Jews or antisemitism. Pius XII, who denounced racism (albeit not unequivocally), seemed to assume that the public understood that his words referred to the Nazi treatment of Jews, despite not mentioning them by name.[43]

During the Holocaust, there were Catholic friars and priests who helped Jews hide in convents throughout Europe out of a deeply held sense that Christianity required them to love their neighbor. Indeed, many Christians hid and helped save Jews, often risking their own lives in the process.[44] Many others, however, collaborated with the Nazis in exterminating Jews even without sharing the Nazis' racist doctrines.[45]

The church's official position was cautious, as suggested by numerous studies on Pius XII. Before his election as pope, Eugenio Pacelli had served as the Vatican secretary of state, in which capacity he concluded the Reichskonkordat, the 1933 treaty between Germany and the Catholic Church that was designed to protect the latter's religious freedom. The agreement put an end to the Catholics' opposition to Nazi authorities and obliged them not to take steps against Nazi policies. As pope, beginning in March 1939, Pacelli did his utmost not to upset the delicate balance between the church and the Reich and maintained diplomatic relations with the Nazis throughout the war. His protests against Nazism were cautious and limited, whether because he feared for the church, because he preferred Nazism to Communism, or for other reasons. When he sought to act for the Jews, he did so quietly, under the Nazis' radar.[46] The church's voice did not resonate clearly and unequivocally when the Jews of Europe were murdered.

As Nazi cruelty toward Jews intensified, however, some Catholics who were opposed to antisemitism felt a more urgent need to redefine the church's attitude to Jews and to clearly distinguish it from racist antisemitism. The blows meted out to the Jews were seen as having a theological significance that exceeded the "appropriate" punishment for their sins. Why was it that the children of Israel had to suffer so? What was the meaning of this indescribable suffering in the divine plan? For many Catholic believers, the Jews' suffering held a profound symbolic significance that attested not to the wrath of God but to the exact opposite. Jacques Maritain, for example, likened the Final Solution to the crucifixion; it testified to the divine choice of the Jewish people as those whose fate was the closest to that of the Jewish messiah crucified at Golgotha.[47] Upon their collective crucifixion, claimed Maritain, the Jews were finally reunited with their messiah. The Nazis were not simply mass murderers. They directed their evil specifically toward God's chosen people, thereby acting as the re-murderers of Christ himself. The Final Solution was seen as proof that the Jews' historical role was not over and that in some mysterious way, they continued playing the role of the chosen ones.[48] However, while the war was raging, such theological reflections were entertained by only a tiny minority of Catholic intellectuals.

In the immediate aftermath of the war, Catholics tended to consider themselves victims of Nazism and did not feel responsible for the rise of Nazi antisemitism.[49] Only a handful of intellectuals and theologians began to reconsider Christianity's treatment of the Jews in light of the Holocaust. Nevertheless, as part of the general atmosphere of building bridges and recovering from the disasters of the war, attempts were made to reconcile Christians and Jews. One of the first conferences dedicated to the Christian responsibility for antisemitism and the Holocaust was the Seelisberg Conference, held in Switzerland in 1947, where Jews, Protestants, and Catholics discussed the role of Christian doctrines in the development of antisemitism in Europe and considered proposals for their revision. The conference discussions revolved around nineteen points proposed by French historian and Holocaust survivor Jules Isaac, who subsequently played a key role in bringing the Jewish question to the attention of Pope John XXIII.[50] The participants formulated ten points, now considered the first fruits of postwar Christian-Jewish dialogue, addressing the Jewish origins of Jesus and the apostles and the need to avoid presenting the Jews in a negative light. They also stated that not all Jews were complicit in the crucifixion and that the responsibility for it is shared by all humankind.

Although overt hostility toward Jews disappeared from the postwar Catholic discourse for obvious reasons, it was not replaced by any theological discussion seeking to revise church perceptions of the Jews or interfaith relations, and any such initiatives remained isolated. Even after John XXIII declared his intention to convene an ecumenical council, only a few of the proposed agendas he received from churchmen related to Jews.[51] In reformulating the church's approach to the Jews, the pope relied on a handful of scholars and theologians, mostly converts to Christianity, who represented no significant Catholic community. These converts, who were personally familiar with the role of the Other in the Catholic Church, were responsible for the new Catholic doctrine, and as convincingly argued by John Connelly, without them, the church would never have found the language to talk about Jews in the post-Holocaust world.[52]

The Second Vatican Council's Declaration on the Jews

In 1960, Pope John XXIII met with Jules Isaac, who presented to him his writings on the concept of "the teaching of contempt" (*l'enseignement du mépris*), the tradition of anti-Jewish Christian teachings that Isaac identified as the root of modern antisemitism.[53] This meeting is considered decisive in shaping the pope's decision to formulate a declaration on the Jews. Long before the meeting, Angelo Giuseppe Roncalli, the future John XXIII, had shown sensitivity to the Jews' fate and did much to save Jews during the war as Pius XII's apostolic delegate to Turkey and Greece.[54]

Immediately after becoming pope in 1958, John XXIII deleted—as part of the liturgical observance of Christ's Passion—the offensive words *perfidis* and *perfidiam* ("perfidious" and "perfidy," literally, "faithless" and "faithlessness") from the Good Friday Prayer for the Jews. These were the very words that Amici Israel had sought to remove in the 1920s.[55] Subsequently, the pope appointed Cardinal Augustin Bea, a German biblical scholar and Pope Pius XII's personal confessor, to head the newly formed Secretariat for Promoting Christian Unity to prepare the groundwork for the ecumenical council's discussion of the Jews. Bea had been acquainted with the new Catholic discourse on the Jews of a decade earlier, in the course of his work in the Congregation for the Doctrine of Faith (the papal committee in charge

of Catholic doctrine issues, formerly known as the Supreme Sacred Congregation of the Holy Office and historically known as the Inquisition). He
appointed a subcommittee on the church's relation to the Jews whose members included Augustinian friar and New Theologian Gregory Baum (son
of a Jewish mother and Protestant father who had converted to Catholicism);
Catholic theologian and convert Monsignor John Oesterreicher; and Bene-
dictine friar Leo von Rudloff, who, like Oesterreicher, was well versed in the
theological rethinking of Judaism.[56] Subsequently, other priests joined the
work on the document, most notably Johannes Willebrands, Bea's secretary
who in 1969 replaced him as president of the Pontifical Council for Promoting Christian Unity; Anton Ramselaar, cofounder of the Dutch Catholic
Council for Israel together with Miriam Rookmaaker van Leer; and Dominican friar Yves Congar, a leading French New Theologian who would become
one of the most influential figures in the council.[57]

Updating the Catholic language about the Jews was an obvious necessity
in view of the widespread embarrassment over the Holocaust. However, it
was not easy for the institutional church to turn its back on ancient theological traditions. The so-called Jewish document (*Decretum de Iudaeis*)
quickly turned out to be one of the most controversial issues in Vatican II.
It was edited, shortened, rejected, re-edited, appended to another declaration (about ecumenism), and then moved to still another (on the church's
relations with non-Christian religions); some even considered including it
in a third declaration (about the church; and indeed, *Lumen Gentium* contains a short discussion of the issue).[58] It attracted considerable media attention and caused a political storm before being finally accepted by the
council fathers in the fourth article in the 1965 "Declaration on the Relation
of the Church to Non-Christian Religions" (*Nostra aetate*), by a huge majority of 2,312 to 88.

The chief task for the document's formulators was to distance Catholic
doctrine on the Jews from antisemitism. Isaac's portrayal of Nazi antisemitism as evolving from traditional Christian perceptions required a response.
The church had to be absolved of anti-Judaism by presenting this notion as
contradictory to its true spirit. Yet the council fathers were torn between their
honest desire to be morally "up to date" and their profound loyalty to Catholic tradition. Oesterreicher and Bea were well aware that many of the
bishops were concerned about the tremendous transformation proposed in
the document. Accordingly, Oesterreicher presented the inevitable move as
a *ressourcement*, a return to deeper and more ancient traditional layers aban-

doned through the generations only to be rediscovered.[59] And in response to recurring attempts to remove the document from the council's agenda, Bea argued that the document had to struggle with the impression that the Catholic tradition was anti-Jewish or congruent with antisemitism and reveal its true approach. This was no small task, as Catholic tradition was replete with anti-Jewish sentiments. Consequently, the document's formulators chose to rely almost exclusively on Romans 9–11.

Paul opens chapter 9 of Romans with an unprecedented expression of love for his people: "I have great sorrow and unceasing anguish in my heart. For I could wish that I myself were accursed and cut off from Christ for the sake of my own people, my kindred according to the flesh" (Rom. 9: 2–3). In chapter 11, he warns his followers, who are likened to branches from a wild olive tree grafted onto a well-cultivated tree, not to look down on the Jews: "Do not boast over the branches. If you do boast, remember that it is not you that support the root, but the root that supports you" (Rom. 11:18). This statement was interpreted by the declaration's formulators as a warning against antisemitism.

It is reasonable to assume that most of the council's participants agreed with Bea regarding the need to "love" the Jews, if only out of commitment to the doctrine of Christian love. The question was what such love meant in theological terms. The major problem the church coped with in this context was the deicide teaching, which held the Jews collectively responsible for the crucifixion. As already mentioned, this teaching was also fundamental to historical Christian hostility toward Jews, often motivating Catholics to attack them.[60] It was also used as a rationalization for some Catholics' identification with modern antisemitism.

The subcommittee adopted a number of strategies to contend with the deicide issue. First, they argued, Christ's first followers were Jews, and it would therefore be inaccurate to hold *all* Jews responsible for his death; only the Sanhedrin and its subordinates were to blame. Second, many Jews lived outside Palestine at the time and were entirely unaware of what transpired there. The third argument was more strictly theological: Jesus took it upon himself to suffer and die to atone for the sins of all humanity; hence the responsibility for the crucifixion lies with everyone, not to mention the fact that Christ forgave his tormentors on the cross.

Not everyone agreed. The deicide charge was so integral to European Catholicism that early in the process of formulating the declaration, even Bea suggested that it was the cry of "all" the Jewish people—"His blood be on us and on our children!" (Matt. 27:25)—that doomed Jerusalem. However, Oesterreicher insisted that the Jerusalem crowd in Matthew was not representative of all the Jews. Oesterreicher's efforts to denounce the deicide teaching are clearly evident in the declaration's second draft, which explicitly warns against blaming an entire people (in the past as well as in the present) for the killing of Christ and against calling the Jews "Christ killers."[61]

Some bishops claimed that it was not permitted to revise a doctrine explicitly articulated in the Scriptures. Joseph Ratzinger (the future Pope Benedict XVI), who served as an expert advisor at the council, testified to Congar that Pope Paul VI himself was convinced of the Jews' collective guilt and was opposed to revising a doctrine so deeply entrenched in Catholic tradition.[62] Correspondingly, in the spring of 1964, conservative bishops supported by the Curia shortened the draft without Bea's and the Secretariat's knowledge—probably with Paul VI's tacit approval—and sought to attach it as an appendix to the declaration on the church, without any reference to the deicide charge but with the express hope for the Jews' conversion.[63]

Soon, however, the substance of the new draft was leaked to the press, which was already aware of the previous one. The fathers of the council feared that omitting the Jews' expiation from the accusation of deicide, having already appeared in a previous draft, would indicate that the church was unwilling to discard the infamous doctrine.[64] Eventually, Bea himself attacked the doctrine at the council, based on the arguments the subcommittee had put forth, and secured overwhelming support. The condemnation of the deicide teaching was consequently included in the final document, although the explicit term was omitted.

Nevertheless, the idea that the Jews killed Christ was part and parcel of an entire conceptual system for rationalizing the Jews' ongoing denial of Christ. It was emblematic of the Jews' continued rejection of the very messiah whose coming they had prophesied. Accordingly, the deicide teaching was central to replacement theology, or supersessionism, according to which the divine election of Israel was transferred from Israel "of the flesh" to the Christians, the gentiles who, in accepting the belief in Jesus Christ, had become Israel "of the spirit"—superseding the children of Abraham. Replacement theology was fundamental to the church's self-perception and its reading of Scripture.

It was fairly easy for the church to pay homage to its ancient Jewish heritage. The transition from perceiving Christianity as an abrupt denunciation of the Jewish legacy to perceiving it as Judaism's finest fruit was relatively

easy to digest. It was clear to all that the church owed a special debt of gratitude to the people who had given it the Old Testament and Christ according
to his flesh, a debt that by extension was owed also to its modern descen-
dants. Accordingly, the final version of Article 4 reads:

> The Church . . . cannot forget that she received the revelation of the Old
> Testament through the people with whom God in His inexpressible
> mercy concluded the Ancient Covenant. Nor can she forget that she
> draws sustenance from the root of that well-cultivated olive tree onto
> which have been grafted the wild shoots, the Gentiles.
>
> The Church keeps ever in mind the words of the Apostle about his
> kinsmen: "theirs is the sonship and the glory and the covenants and the
> law and the worship and the promises; theirs are the fathers and from
> them is the Christ according to the flesh" (Rom. 9:4–5), the Son of the
> Virgin Mary. She also recalls that the Apostles, the Church's mainstay
> and pillars, as well as most of the early disciples who proclaimed Christ's
> Gospel to the world, sprang from the Jewish people.[65]

The argument regarding the ancient Jews' legacy is clearly foremost in the
article dedicated to the Jews in *Nostra aetate,* and it still remains the most
consensual among the arguments presented in the document, despite the fact
that its theological implications have not been thoroughly or conclusively
thought out. It was far more difficult to frame a positive view of the Jews *in
the present,* given the fact that they had rejected Christ and clung to their
fossilized religion without grasping its true significance. Though the final
document avoids this question of post-crucifixion Judaism almost entirely,
the council fathers engaged in a heated debate on that matter.[66] One solution proposed was to refer to contemporary Jews in strictly humanitarian
terms and consider them a nation among nations, relinquishing any specific
theological conception of Judaism. Indeed, some participants—such as Jean
Daniélou, as well as Bea himself when he started working on the document—
reasoned that the church had to denounce hatred of the Jews just as it had
to denounce hatred of all human beings. Attempts by council members to
change the document's title to "On Jewish Religion" or proposals to integrate
the discussion of the Jewish people into the discussion of others, such as the
Armenian people, articulated the same concern. According to this view, the
experiences of Jews in the present lacked a uniquely religious dimension

relevant to the Jews as a *people,* since Jewish peoplehood had lost its religious substance after the crucifixion.

However, ignoring the Jewish present as having any religious substance could be construed as clinging to supersessionism, as it implicitly suggested that the Jews had lost their unique status and historical role. From this perspective, it was necessary to try to formulate a doctrine that would endow contemporary Jewish existence with religious meaning. Indeed, traditional Catholic theology held a unique place for the Jewish religion within the divine plan. Nevertheless, those traditional accounts of post-crucifixion Judaism were hard to mobilize for the sake of purging anti-Judaism from Christianity, since they were themselves replete with anti-Jewish notions. The Augustinian doctrine of Jews as witnesses to the faith (which had ensured their survival in medieval Christian society) was no longer acceptable because it sentenced them to eternal exile (and was now counterfactual to the establishment of the State of Israel) and misery (a view that became unsustainable after Auschwitz) due to their obstinacy and blindness. An alternative justification for the continued historical existence of the Jews had to be found without countenancing their persistent rejection of Christ, which was not an issue that could simply be ignored.

Based on Romans, some of the drafters of the "Jewish document" argued that the Lord never stopped loving the Jews, even after the crucifixion: "I ask, then, has God rejected his people?" Paul asks rhetorically at the beginning of chapter 11. "By no means! I myself am an Israelite, a descendant of Abraham, a member of the tribe of Benjamin. God has not rejected his people whom he foreknew" (1–2). Later in the chapter, Paul refers to the Jews as a people who still enjoy God's favor, despite having rejected the Gospel: "As regards the gospel they are enemies of God for your sake; but as regards election they are beloved, for the sake of their ancestors"; most importantly, he adds: "for the gifts and the calling of God are irrevocable" (28–29). According to Connelly, the conciliar declaration's drafters chose to use this Pauline statement to claim that the Jewish people are still the chosen people in a certain sense; despite their sins, the Lord remains loyal to his own promise to them. Thus, the declaration's paraphrasing of Paul hints at the continuous value of the Jews' covenant with God: "Nevertheless, God holds the Jews most dear [*adhuc carissimi*] for the sake of their Fathers; He does not repent of the gifts He makes or of the calls He issues—such is the witness of the Apostle."[67] Through this interpretation, Paul's words provide an authoritative justification for discarding replacement theology and formulating a new doctrine according to which the Jewish people are not accursed, but still loved by God.[68] As argued by Joseph Sievers, this interpretation of Paul was almost unprecedented in Catholic history. Throughout the generations, most theologians and exegetics interpreted Romans 11:29 as referring to all chosen ones, including both Jews and gentiles, rather than to the Jewish people as a whole. Others reasoned that God indeed does not repent of his gifts, but the addressee may change; that is, having rejected divine grace, the Jews were superseded by the gentile church. Still other exegetes did, however, interpret the verse as referring to the Jewish people. Although they reasoned that the Jews were rejected by God in the present, like branches torn from the olive tree on which the wild olive branches had been grafted in their stead, in the future, they would return, "for God has the power to graft them in again" (Rom. 11:23). According to this last reading, the Jews' graceless present is contained within historical parentheses stretching between their glorious past, as described in the Old Testament, and their glorious future, when they shall accept Christ and be redeemed as had been promised. This was the most "pro-Jewish" interpretation available in the pre–*Nostra aetate* tradition.[69]

Thus, the drafters of Article 4 of *Nostra aetate* sought to interpret Paul as conveying the message that the Jews are still beloved by God—that even their present is not graceless. Yet what is the meaning of this grace? Are the Jews worthy of it even during the (admittedly extended) hiatus between their rejection of Christ and their acceptance of him at the end of time? Do they follow God's will even now? Is their refusal therefore meaningless?

The declaration provides no answer to these questions. The Jewish refusal could not be completely circumvented, but the drafters clearly avoided discussing its implications: "Jerusalem did not recognize the time of her visitation, nor did the Jews in large number, accept the Gospel"; however, the declaration continues, they are beloved by God by virtue of their forefathers (see Rom. 11:28). The authors also avoided reference to any rivalry between the two "Israels," and only a single phrase suggests any tension between the Jews' election and the church's subsequent status: "Although the church is the new people of God, the Jews should not be presented as rejected or accursed by God, as if this followed from the Holy Scriptures."[70] Thus, one part of the Pauline dichotomy (the Jews' rejection by God) was omitted, while the other was retained (the church is the new Israel).

In fact, beyond stating that the Jews were still beloved by God and that the council sought to foster mutual understanding and respect, the declaration did not provide any real answer to the question of the Jews' current status.[71] And although the Holocaust had been the primary motivation for composing the "Jewish document" (and its spirit clearly hovers over it), it is not mentioned explicitly.[72] The absence of the Jewish present from the declaration had obvious political and diplomatic reasons.[73] The fear lest it be interpreted as supporting the State of Israel and the Zionist project made the discussion of contemporary Jews highly charged. Indeed, Arab leaders had warned the council participants to avoid any special treatment of the Jews. In a conciliatory response, Bea clarified that the church would remain strictly apolitical, as is explicitly stated in the declaration itself (in a notion that could hardly be understood outside the political context in which it was formulated): the church's rejection of hatred is moved "not by political reasons but by the Gospel's spiritual love."[74] The political angle, however, does not make the theological difficulty redundant. What was at stake was the theological meaning of post-crucifixion Jewry: What religious significance should the church attach to contemporary Judaism? This issue remained unresolved not only in *Nostra aetate* but also in the Catholic discourse of the following decades.[75]

Apart from the conundrum of the Jewish present, the Jews' future also posed a significant challenge to Catholics and represented an issue just as controversial as the deicide charge. According to Catholic tradition, the Jews were expected to accept the faith in the eschatological future and be redeemed—as Christians. The Jewish final conversion was a pivotal doctrine that provided some justification for their ongoing existence. Upon their return to the fold, the salvation process would be completed and Christianity's superior virtue proven for all time. Moreover, Catholic scholars' opposition to Nazi antisemitism before and during World War II largely relied on the argument that Jews could be redeemed by converting, while the Nazi position left them no possibility of denouncing their Judaism, and certainly not of salvation. Catholics had been praying for the Jews' conversion for centuries, and they considered this hope a distinct form of Christian love. The surprising insight that Jews considered the Christian mission as the complete opposite of love, which was one of the revelations of the Christian-Jewish dialogue in the post-Holocaust era, sounded foreign and disconcerting to Catholic ears.

The first draft of the declaration had voiced the eschatological hope for the Jews' conversion explicitly and powerfully. "The Church believes," it read, "in the union of the Jewish people with herself as an integral part of Christian hope. . . . The Church believes . . . with the apostles that at the time chosen by God, the fullness of the sons of Abraham according to the flesh will finally attain salvation (cf. Rom 11:12, 26). Their reception will be life from the dead (cf. Rom 11:15)."[76] However, it soon turned out that this point was the most strenuously rejected by the very Jews that the church had wanted to appease. Thus, the messianic hope for the Jews' conversion was scrapped in the second draft in favor of the abstract statement that Christ unified Jews and Christians with his love, but it resurfaced in the shortened draft of spring 1964 (the same one that abandoned the denial of the deicide charge): "It is also worth remembering that the union of the Jewish people with the church is part of the Christian hope. Therefore, following the teaching of the Apostle Paul (cf. Rom 11:25), the church waits with unshaken faith and deep longing for the entry of that people into the fullness of the people of God established by Christ."[77]

Shortly after this shortened draft was leaked to the press, Rabbi Abraham Joshua Heschel, one of the Jews who had the strongest influence on the drafting of the declaration, published an emphatic response in *Time* magazine that unsettled the council fathers. In early September 1964, he wrote that this phrasing amounted to "spiritual fratricide" and that he was "ready to go to Auschwitz any time, if faced with the alternative of conversion or death."[78] Heschel further warned that Jews worldwide would be deeply disappointed and aggrieved if, so shortly after the Holocaust, the Vatican conveyed this message of conversion. He also emphasized that the annihilation of the Jews was the responsibility of a fundamentally Christian civilization. Later on, he would meet with Pope Paul VI—himself a supporter of the Jews' evangelization—and leave a lengthy theological memorandum on Bea's secretariat desk.[79]

Following these public storms, the bishops decided to remove the controversial text from the draft. Nevertheless, the eschatological question could not remain unresolved. The magic formula was finally found by Oesterreicher, who, at this point in his career, was keenly aware of Jewish sensitivities. He replaced the church's "deep longing" for conversion with a vague eschatological hope for a future time when the nations would be united in God's worship, without referring to the exact nature of that shared worship. The biblical text Oesterreicher chose to rely on was the same verse in the book of Zephaniah that Maimonides used in the *Mishneh Torah* (his codification of halakha) to describe the appropriate role of Christianity and Islam in the history of salvation.[80] The final version of the declaration read, "In company with the Prophets and the same Apostle, the church awaits that day, known to God alone, on which all peoples will address the Lord in a single voice and 'serve him shoulder to shoulder' (Zeph. 39)."[81] This deliberate vagueness (the day is "known to God alone") suggests that it is for God to fulfill the prophecy as he should see fit. This ambiguous messianic vision enabled a broad range of stakeholders to accept the declaration. Indeed, the use of the Old Testament phrasing mollified the Jews (including Heschel), as it voiced their own hope, without converting it into concepts they could not identify with. Moreover, the Maimonidean echo—whether known to the drafters or not—even suggested the possibility that it would be the Christians who would eventually convert, rather than the Jews. Conversely, conservative Catholics were not required to relinquish their hope of unifying humanity under the true faith, although this faith was not explicitly named.

According to Oesterreicher, the formula left open two possibilities for a Catholic reading of the Pauline statement "And so all Israel will be saved" (Rom. 11:26). One possibility was that the Jews' change of heart would precede their salvation, while the other was that divine grace would be revealed unconditionally.[82] In other words, Zephaniah's messianic hope enabled Catholic interpreters to consider the Jewish existence without (at least conscious) faith in Christ as invaluable to the divine scheme of salvation.

This reading, however, suggests that the church actually has no role to play in mediating the Jews' salvation. In that respect, it challenges a pivotal Catholic doctrine, according to which the church is the exclusive and universal vessel leading humanity to Christ (*extra ecclesiam nulla salus*). Does God's ongoing election of the Jewish people mean that they need not be included in the new chosen people, the church, to be saved? Are these two separate chosen peoples destined to be redeemed in two different ways—before finally reuniting?

The question of the eschatological future thus became a direct extension of the issue of the Jewish present. The denial of supersessionism required a conception of the ongoing election of the Jewish people. This in turn challenged the church's view of itself as the chosen people and called for a reformulation of the relationship between it and the Jewish people, one that would clarify its priority—if any—over the Jews and whether Jews need the church to be saved (now or in the end of time). In other words, the church was also called upon to examine the implications of changing its relation to the Jews for its claim to universal mediation of salvation. Even if it gave up on proselytizing them in practice, the question remained wide open on the theoretical level.

Vatican II reopened all the major questions about Jews and Judaism for theological discussion. In its discussion of the past, the council renounced the deicide charge, emphasized the common heritage of Jews and Christians, and reaffirmed the Jewishness of Jesus and the apostles. Nevertheless, apart from those expressions of family-like proximity to the Jewish people, the declaration did not investigate the theological implications of this perception of the church's past for its self-definition and doctrine. With regard to the present, the council opened the question of the role of post-crucifixion Jews in the history of salvation, and the question regarding Judaism's religious value. It was no longer possible to see the suffering of the Jews and their exile as a punishment and as evidence of Christianity's victory. To what, then, does their persistent survival throughout their turbulent history (including the Holocaust and the founding of the State of Israel) testify? Finally, there was the eschatological question. If the Jews did not murder Christ, were not punished or rejected by God until the end of history, and were not replaced by the church, does this imply that they, alone of all other peoples, do not need the church to achieve salvation? Where do the Jews stand in relation to the church's universal vision, which is at the heart of its self-perception as God's chosen people? These questions were waiting for post-conciliar theologians to grapple with.

2

After Vatican II

The Second Vatican Council closed in late 1965. It was now time for the church to interpret and assimilate its conclusions and heritage. The overall evaluation of the council varied with its exegetes. Some saw it as a healthy and indispensable move that freed the church from inertia and turned it into a spiritual force relevant in the modern world. For others, it wreaked havoc by causing a rupture in the Catholic tradition and introducing the modern heresy so often warned against by the popes of the nineteenth century. Only marginal extremist groups wholly rejected the authority of the council.[1] Most Catholics were busy limiting or expanding its implications for the life of the church, in accordance with the beneficial or injurious effects they ascribed to it.

After Vatican II was adjourned, a new multilingual theological journal called *Concilium* was launched by some of the theologians who had been most influential in the council's discussions, as a platform for pursuing its theological project.[2] In 1969, the International Theological Commission (ITC) was established—a group of thirty theologians subject to the Congregation for the Doctrine of the Faith (CDF)—both to disseminate the magisterium's ideas and to counsel the magisterium on theological matters. Many hoped that the ITC would also convey the voices of theologians from the Catholic periphery to the church's center, in Rome. These are but two manifestations of the ongoing theological thriving after Vatican II and the desire to continue the productive cooperation between leading theologians and church leaders during the council's discussions.

However, over the course of the 1970s, the rift between conservatives and liberals within the Catholic Church deepened, especially regarding the significance and implications of Vatican II. Paul VI was attacked from the left and the right, the left objecting to his conservative positions on such issues as contraceptives and family planning, the right objecting to the far-reaching reforms that he introduced into Catholic liturgy.

Disagreements appeared even among the theological circles that represented the living spirit of the council. Some considered that the drive to continue extending John XXIII's aggiornamento would fill the faithful with doubts regarding the essential positions of the church and its mission in the world. It seemed that the "updated" church adopted modern individualism in almost all areas, empowering every person to decide things independently. The ITC lost some of its innovative energy, as it was joined by an increasing number of conservative theologians who wished to curtail the commission's critical task vis-à-vis the CDF—the very task for which it had been convened. Liberal theologians—Karl Rahner among them—ultimately left the commission.

Stunned by Catholic believers' apparently becoming enraptured with the student uprisings of spring 1968, and suspicious of the progressivism that had become widespread in theological circles, some of the most prominent reformers of Vatican II came to identify with conservative positions. In 1972, Joseph Ratzinger, Henri de Lubac, Hans Urs von Balthasar, and others withdrew from the editorial board of *Concilium* and established an alternative journal, *Communio: Internationale Katholische Zeitschrift,* which quickly became a prominent voice in the Catholic world. This journal strove to restore the spirit of Catholicism and the legacy of the council by means of *ressourcement,* a return to the sources, instead of constant innovation. The founders believed that a correct reading of Vatican II required that it be perceived in continuity with Catholic tradition rather than as a revolution (as it was presented both by adamant traditionalists and by progressivists).

The church's position on Jews and Judaism was central to the interpretation of Vatican II, as it touched on a long list of key issues, such as the church's position regarding its past, modern biblical studies, religious freedom, other religions, and more. To a significant degree, the changes that *Nostra aetate* initiated in regard to Judaism became emblematic of Vatican II as a whole; in the two decades succeeding the council, virtually every prominent Catholic theologian wrote something about Judaism, whether a few paragraphs, a whole book, or an entire oeuvre.

The question of the extent to which Christian doctrine was responsible for the growth of modern antisemitism was construed as a test case for a more comprehensive issue: Was it possible to apply a process of *ressourcement* to "cleanse" Catholic tradition of erroneous interpretations and injustices that had accrued to it over the generations, or were the ethical issues so deeply entrenched in Catholic tradition that it would be better to completely disavow the problematic doctrines and set out on a new path? These discussions focused on the entire temporal-theological continuum of Christian-Jewish relations: the past (the Jewish roots of Christianity); the present (the status of the Jews in the divine plan of salvation after the crucifixion); and the future (the question of the salvation of the Jews and the preparation for it).

The Past: Rethinking Christianity's Jewish History

The greatest theological interest with regard to the Jews in the years following the council focused on the Jewish historical context in the emergence of Christianity. The theological turn to the Jewish past of Christianity was first and foremost a consequence of the permission that had been given to Catholics to engage in academic biblical studies, first by Pius XII (1943) and subsequently by Vatican II (in *Dei verbum*). As Balthasar wrote a few years before the council, it was by virtue of having pulled the carpet out from under the traditional idea of the Bible's divine origins that modern biblical studies showed Christians the depth of their debt to Jewish tradition. The new conception, wherein scriptures were intimately associated with the human beings who experienced the revelation and put it into writing, made it clear to Catholics that one could not make such a clear-cut distinction between the Old Testament and the people who had brought it to the world.[3] Modern biblical studies reminded the church, as expressed in *Nostra aetate*, "that she draws sustenance from the root of that well-cultivated olive tree onto which have been grafted the wild shoots, the Gentiles."[4]

Based on modern biblical studies, Catholic theologians argued for a profound similarity between the soteriological, apocalyptic, and eschatological conceptions of the ancient church and conceptions that were widespread among certain groups in the divided Judaism of the Second Temple era and were typical of the spiritual turmoil of the time.[5] The discovery of the Dead Sea Scrolls at Qumran between 1946 and 1956 was considered key evidence that even before the time of Jesus, Jewish denominations had expressed ideas that were very close to those that would eventually be considered part of the

Christian "revolution."[6] The harsh references to Jews in the New Testament were now regarded as differences of opinion between brothers in faith rather than as a paradigmatic schism that turned Judaism into an empty vessel. The new position was that the apostles were not only Jews by descent but that they had never intended to renounce their Judaism. Their admonishments toward their Jewish brethren were themselves Jewish in style and, if anything, articulated their love of their people and the urgency they sensed in preparing the children of Israel for messianic times. Peter never blamed "the Jews" for rejecting the Gospel, but only the Jerusalemites, the Sanhedrin, and those who followed the Sanhedrin's authority. Luke (23:27, 35, 47–49) and Mark (11:7–10) were well aware of the fact that the masses who followed Jesus were made up of lower-class Jews.[7] Even John, who used a generalizing language and directed his prophecies of destruction toward the entire Jewish people, was, according to Gregory Baum, "a Jewish prophet, speaking the idiom of Qumran, boiling with rage and indignation at the leaders of the synagogue for having so tragically misled his own beloved people."[8] Sweeping statements that could not be explained as internal differences of opinion among the Jews were often interpreted as later additions that, despite being included in the Gospel, were representative not of Jesus's period but of later times. As the Commission for Religious Relations with the Jews (CRRJ) stated, "It cannot be ruled out that some references hostile or less than favorable to the Jews have their historical context in conflicts between the nascent Church and the Jewish community. Certain controversies reflect Christian-Jewish relations long after the time of Jesus."[9]

This new historical reading, which anchored the New Testament in Second Temple Judaism, gave central place to the rereading of Paul. "Who could have been more Jewish than Paul?" wondered Baum. "And who could have been more proud of his Jewishness?"[10] Traditionally considered the most virulent critic of Judaism and the uncontested father of replacement theology, the apostle was now read as a Jewish theologian who criticized Judaism from within rather than calling for its abolition.[11] Paul's attitude toward the law—that is, the Torah—was seen as complex and as much more positive than in the past: "There was not the slightest shade of an anti-nomian in Paul," claimed Baum.[12] Paul's arguments against the Jews—often seen as quite sweeping—were said to be the result of his persecution by his brethren rather than reflecting a negative attitude toward the Jews as a whole.[13] His admonitions did not weaken his conviction that "he is called by God to love them [the Jews] and to identify himself with Israel." Indeed, Paul was ready to make "every sacrifice to endure every tribulation, for the sake of his nation [*dei propri connazionali*], 'For I could wish that I myself were accursed and cut off from Christ for the sake of my own people, my kindred according to the flesh' [Romans 9:3]."[14]

Jesus, too, was now construed as a Jew not only according to the flesh but also in spirit. Theologians began reading him as someone for whom "to be a Jew was not some sort of garment that one could simply cast aside, but part of his very essence."[15] Jesus was "a man of his times and environment in the fullest sense of the word—a man of first-century Jewish Palestine, sharing its anxieties and hopes."[16] "His Scriptures, his worship and his prayers were all Jewish."[17] Jesus was an observant Jew. He never downplayed the value of the Torah but only criticized narrow interpretations of it.[18] Moreover, he felt particularly close to the Pharisees and criticized them much as they criticized themselves.[19] "Jesus," writes Clemens Thoma, "as a so-called 'transgressor of the Law' . . . does not exist!"[20] More than anything else, Catholic theologians cited Jesus's words in the Sermon on the Mount as reflecting his true position on Judaism: "Do not think that I have come to abolish the law or the prophets; I have come not to abolish but to fulfill" (Matt. 5:17).[21] Some even argued that Jesus himself understood his mission in Jewish terms. Even his relationship with God was experienced in a "Jewish" form, or as Schillebeeckx put it, he had a profound "Abba experience" with the Lord.[22] Many theologians consulted Jewish scholars who could shed light on the Jewish aspects of Christian faith. Joseph Klausner, Schalom Ben-Chorin, Geza Vermes, Leo Baeck, David Flusser, and others are quoted repeatedly as authorities on Jesus's Judaism.[23] Finally, the rabbinical Midrash was considered essential for the exegesis of the New Testament.[24] As summed up by Hans Küng, "The Jew particularly could help the Christian to conduct the *discussion* on Jesus afresh."[25]

All of this was unprecedented. Until that time, the church seemed to have little need for Jewish experts or experts on Judaism to explain its faith. Yes, Jesus was flesh and blood, but because of his divine nature, he was different—by definition—from any other person. To a great extent, Jesus was everyman, because the importance of the incarnation lay in the bond it created between God and humanity. His particularity as a Jew was, if anything, secondary; Christ materialized as a Jew to allow the children of Israel, the chosen people, the right of first refusal. Since they had rejected the redemptive truth offered to them, they were superseded. The children of Israel "according to the flesh" could not be the source of correct interpretation of Christ. Precisely the opposite.

The Jewish issue was, needless to say, but one aspect of the many theological questions that were raised with the entrance of critical biblical studies to the Catholic mainstream. For many liberal Catholic scholars, the historical-critical method was a means for instigating far-reaching changes in doctrine and in the self-conception of the church in view of the ethical, political, and intellectual issues that characterized their generation. Some of them associated the contextualization of the origins of Christianity in its historical milieu with the marginalization of post-biblical doctrines, in particular the Trinitarian and Christological doctrines of the church fathers and the councils. The attempt to return to the foundational moments of Christianity was naturally associated in their minds with a peeling away of the layers that had accumulated over those initial moments, which had dictated to future generations how to view them. Catholic tradition was now perceived not only as an obstacle blocking the way of authentically "touching" Christian sources (in a way that obviously echoed the Protestant conceptions that had given rise to the critique of the Bible in the first place) but also, to a great extent, as the main cause of the ethical distortions of Christianity over history. The attempt to trace the sources of Christianity also led to a demand for rectification—a demand to restore its ethical crown in a way that would correspond to the sensitivities of liberal theologians in the post-council era.

The theological approach to Judaism reflected these trends; the discourse on Judaism was, to a great extent, more about them than it was about Judaism. Theologians were all in favor of rejuvenating the lost kinship between Christians and Jews, but they were in disagreement as to who was to blame for having deviated from it. The more theologians identified themselves as progressive or liberal, the more they criticized post-biblical Catholic doctrines as responsible for the development of supersessionist attitudes and traditions hostile to Judaism. Some of them even demanded that the church go further than it did in *Nostra aetate* and explicitly withdraw from the post-biblical theological traditions related to Judaism, as a pre-condition for the annulment of replacement theology and crystallization of the church's identity as a more tolerant and less dogmatic entity.

The most scathing critique directed at Catholic doctrine in regard to the Jews was that of the American theologian Rosemary Ruether, who published her book *Faith and Fratricide: The Theological Roots of Anti-Semitism* in 1974. Ruether viewed the Jewish roots of Christianity not as evidence of any fundamental amity between Christians and Jews but rather as the obverse. Hatred for the Jews lay at the very core of Christian doctrine—within the scriptures themselves, and even more so in Christology, in the claim of Christ's divinity.

Ruether rejected the prevalent view that antisemitism was a pagan legacy rather than a Christian invention. She argued that the traces of pagan hatred of Jews in anti-Jewish Christian literature are negligible. Christian hatred of Jews relied on different foundations.[26] She agreed that the Christian-Jewish polemic was initially a quarrel among siblings, but she claimed that this was not enough to relieve the church of its responsibility for antisemitism. To the contrary, it was the fact that the conflict arose out of an inheritance feud over the divine promise in the Jewish scriptures that made it so bitter and prolonged. Christianity's anti-Judaism, argued Ruether, developed side by side with the Christological reading of the Bible. At the heart of the quarrel between the two Jewish groups lay Jesus's messianism—the conceptualization of him as the realization of the Jews' hopes and the fulfillment of divine promises. Jesus's disciples sought proof of their conception in the Hebrew scriptures and began interpreting it in contemporary terms. Early Christians interpreted references in the Hebrew scriptures to the enemies of the Messiah as connoting the enemies of the Gospel—the Jews (or rather their leaders, the priests and scribes) who rejected Christ's prophetic call for repentance while he was still alive and who refused to identify him as the Messiah after his death.[27] In other words, "the Jews'" rejection of Christ became part of the prophetic drama identified by the early Christians in the Hebrew scriptures. Overcoming Jewish perfidy and murderousness were, so they believed, central to Jesus's messianic mission. Hatred for the Jews was thus built into the Christological reading of scripture; in Ruether's words, Christian anti-Judaism is "the left hand of Christology."[28]

Since Christology was the problem, Ruether proposed to radically revise it. She argued that the most dangerous idea, on the basis of which Christian antisemitism developed, was the concept of the resurrection. Thus, Christianity had to abandon the historicity of that concept and declare, together with the Jews, that in the deepest sense, the Messiah has not yet come. For too long, she added, Christians had confused their earthly kingdom with the eschatological kingdom of God. Their historical victory celebrations—upon the Christianization of the Roman Empire or, alternatively, of the missionary success in the colonialist period—made them forget that redemption was not yet complete and that Christ was destined to return. Now that Christendom had fallen, Christianity had to learn how to reconsider itself as a

"Diaspora religion."[29] Ruether does not state explicitly that Christ did not rise from the dead but refers to the resurrection as an "experience" of his believers, as a "decision of faith," and so on.[30] For her, the resurrection is but a symbol for the hope that good will overcome evil, but this expression of hope does not support the argument that it has already been realized in Christ or that it can be expressed exclusively in his name.[31]

Ruether's radical thesis received unlikely support from Baum, who, as mentioned earlier, had played a key role in drafting *Nostra aetate*. Baum confessed that in the past, he had believed that the hostile passages in the New Testament were directed specifically at the Jews of Jesus's time and that it was only subsequent Christian exegesis that directed them against the entire Jewish people. Now, less than a decade after the publication of *Nostra aetate*, Baum felt that antisemitism was more deeply rooted in Christian tradition than he had dared think—that it was already planted in Scripture rather than in its subsequent readings. Baum felt unable to justify the revision of the doctrine on Judaism as *ressourcement*, because he now realized that the sources themselves were suffused with anti-Judaism.

Specifically, the declaration's attempt to "mobilize" chapters 9–11 of Romans to counterbalance all expressions of hostility against the Jews in the New Testament seemed disingenuous to Baum. Paul himself, he argued, was the architect of the Christology that was the foundation of replacement theology:

> Paul himself, from whom Vatican II has taken its language about Israel's ongoing election, had no intention whatever of recognizing Jewish religion as a way of grace. Israel had become blind, according to Paul; it was a way of death, of spiritual slavery. Despite this blindness, the apostle taught, God did not permit Israel to disappear; the election remained with it, not however as a source of present grace, but as a divine promise guaranteeing the conversion of the Jews at the end of time and their integration into the Christian Church, the one true Israel. All attempts of Christian theologians to derive a more positive conclusion from Paul's teaching in Romans 9–11 (and I have done this as much as others) are grounded in wishful thinking.[32]

Baum concluded that *Nostra aetate* provided no more than a cosmetic sheen to Catholic doctrine. He demanded that the church fundamentally renounce the idea of its exclusiveness, which denied Jews the possibility of salvation without conversion to Christianity.

Baum and Ruether thus raised the alarming prospect that Christianity could not be rid of its hostility to the Jews without revising, even to a certain extent rescinding, the core pillars of Christianity. They believed that the past could not be reinterpreted and that the church had no choice but to openly turn its back to it. The two thinkers went much further than the church could afford to go, however, and their path led to a dead end. Nevertheless, many shared the suspicion that Christology—and especially dogmatic formulations of Christology—was indeed inextricably tied to the darkest and most hostile elements of Christian tradition.

In his book *Jesus: An Experiment in Christology* (1974), the prominent Belgian theologian Edward Schillebeeckx proposed to examine Christology in terms of its historical origins rather than through the dogmatic retrospection of Catholic tradition. Schillebeeckx's book was among the most influential theological publications in the Catholic world during the 1970s.

Schillebeeckx claimed that both Christ and his disciples understood his gospel through the Jewish terminological and symbolic system of meaning. Even the crucifixion and resurrection were consistent, he argued, with contemporary Jewish ideas. The Judaism of the Second Temple period was rich in a variety of messianic concepts that were intuitive rather than formulated in coherent philosophical language and that existed side by side and influenced each other. As time passed, significant parts of the Jewish messianic heritage of the first Christians were marginalized to enable the church to construct its distinct "Christian" identity instead of the multiple ideas and trends that had initially characterized it. After the New Testament was canonized, the multiple Christologies current among first-century believers underwent a gradual standardization process that culminated, in 325 CE, with the dogmatization of a single Christology—that based on the Gospel of John—in the Council of Nicaea.[33] The Christians' need to ward off attacks by the Jews on the one hand and by the pagans (and their Greco-Roman philosophical heritage) on the other made them commit to an increasingly well-defined dogma. Just as the Christian Jews had experienced Jesus in life and death within the conceptual framework of their Jewish culture, so did the Christian gentiles experience him within the framework of Hellenistic thought.[34] With time, the Greek worldview against which the non-Jewish Christians grappled became predominant, and the Jewish exegetic options were forgotten.[35]

According to Schillebeeckx, the dogmas formulated at Nicaea and Chalcedon (451 CE) do not represent the richness embodied in the living memory of Jesus of Nazareth. They express certain horizons delimited by the cognitive and linguistic tools used to fashion them. Schillebeeckx maintained that cultural context transforms how we think and conceive of everything, including God.[36] Because Christ's mission draws its validity and significance from its contemporary cultural context, how can it be discussed as a universal and eternal truth? Finding an appropriate way of bringing Christ's particularity as a specific historical figure and his universal salvation message to terms with one another is thus seen by Schillebeeckx as Christianity's major challenge. Accordingly, formulaic declarations of faith are detrimental to the historicity and particularity of Jesus as a person in the fullest sense of the word, as one who inhabited particular cultural and linguistic conditions; indeed, Schillebeeckx believed that the Enlightenment—with its abstract universalism—also falls into the same trap.[37] It is the Christians' duty to reintroduce particularism into universalism rather than allow it to become blurred within rationalistic abstractions and ontological claims. The church must maintain the living presence of Christ despite the storms of time, because this presence—in all its particularity—is the true key to Christian universalism.

It is implicit in Schillebeeckx's book that the church had not remained completely loyal to the living memory of Jesus. To return to the primal experience of the encounter with Christ, one must place ecclesiastical traditions formulated in the most important ecumenical councils in church history in parentheses. Although Schillebeeckx tried to avoid a frontal attack against central Catholic doctrines, that was the upshot of his book, which marginalized later ecumenical traditions in view of new research findings garnered from biblical studies. This undermining of the authority of tradition was one of the major reasons that the church had prohibited the use of the methods of historical criticism for so long.

Schillebeeckx, however, was not alone. Hans Küng's *On Being a Christian* (*Christ Sein*) was published in the same year as Reuther's and Schillebeeckx's books. Küng's book made extensive use of the historical-critical method, and it too sought to temporarily suspend "Christology from above" to rediscover "Christology from below," that is, to reconstruct "something like the perspective of the first disciples of Jesus." Küng argued that this perspective was in fact that of "the questioning person of today, the historical difference, of course, being taken into account."[38] Küng contrasted the early "Jewish"

Christianity of the first Christians, which he considered to be more flexible and open, with the dogmatic Christianity of church traditions, which he found to be both ahistorical and authoritarian.[39] In the short chapter that he devoted to Jews and Judaism in this book, he, like Schillebeeckx and Reuther, utilized the early Christian "Jewish" perspective as a model for skepticism and healthy spiritual flexibility (appropriate for modern believers), as contrasted with more dogmatic positions:

> Who is Jesus? More than a prophet? More than the law? Is he even the Messiah? A Messiah crucified in the name of the law? Must the discussion come to a complete end at this point? Here perhaps the Jew could help the Christian to conduct the discussion on Jesus afresh . . . , not from above, but *from below.* This would mean that we too would consider Jesus today from the standpoint of his Jewish contemporaries. Even his Jewish disciples had to start out first of all from Jesus of Nazareth as man and Jew and not from someone who was already obviously the Messiah or still less Son of God. It is only in this way that they could raise at all the question of the relationship of Jesus to God. . . . If in what follows we start out from Jesus of Nazareth as man and Jew, we shall be able to go *a good part of the way together* with an unbiased Jew. And it may be that in the end the final decision for or against Jesus will yet look rather different from what the long Jewish-Christian dispute might have led us to expect. . . . At a time of fundamental reorientation of the relationship between Christians and Jews, we shall have to remain open to all future possibilities.[40]

Küng claimed that to fully understand the acts and words of Jesus, one must remove one's dogmatic spectacles and examine them within their original historical context. Walking in the footsteps of Jesus is a better way of being a Christian than developing doctrines around Jesus. Such an approach naturally gives rise to a fellowship with Jews and Judaism, thanks to Jesus's love for them and the fact that Jesus himself was a Jew.[41]

At the beginning of the 1980s, the German theologian Johann Baptist Metz, a pioneer of liberation theology, published a number of works on the implications of the Holocaust for Catholic theology.[42] "Can our theology before and after Auschwitz remain unchanged?," asked Metz.[43] "It is not a matter of a revision of Christian theology with regard to Judaism," he argued, "but a matter of the revision of Christian theology *itself.*"[44] This is

possible only if it faces the Jews as subjects living in time rather than regarding Judaism as an object to be appropriated and theologically system-
atized. The Holocaust is a clear indication of Christianity's profound indifference to history, which makes it a "bourgeois religion" brimming with
self-content. This, argued Metz, is evidenced in the fact that in the Catholic
theology "which in my eyes was the best of that time," "Auschwitz was not
mentioned."[45]

After Auschwitz, Christianity was compelled to face history again and be
concerned by it. To do so, it had to refer to the Jewish messianism of the
Gospels (and turn its back somewhat on its Pauline version). Based on a dialogue with Martin Buber's *Two Types of Faith,* Metz wrote:

> Christian theology after Auschwitz must stress anew the Jewish dimen-
> sion in Christian beliefs and must overcome the blocking-out of the
> Jewish heritage within Christianity. This thesis does not merely want
> to bring back into the memory of Christian theology the Jewish exis-
> tence of Christ himself. It aims at the Jewish-originated form of the
> Christian faith. . . . . This kind of Christology is not primarily formed
> in a subjectless concept and system, but in discipleship stories. [It]
> stands against that kind of Christianity which considers itself as a kind
> of religion of victors—with a surplus of answers and a corresponding
> lack of passionate questions. . . . It is the Jewish-formed synoptic
> manner of believing which calls our attention to the fact that the Chris-
> tian belief is a sensuous happening, a happening of the senses which
> cannot be simply spiritualized [into purely a faith of attitude]. Haven't
> we been confronted for a long time by the danger of total spiritualiza-
> tion and inferiorization of evangelical contents and imperatives? . . .
> How would it otherwise be possible that Christian theologians, for ex-
> ample, can say that we, the Christians, are the "real" religion of exile,
> the "real" religion of the diaspora, of the painful dispersion in the world.
> Can such a statement be defended in the face of Jewish experience
> through the centuries?[46]

Metz tied the historicity of the Holocaust together with that of the New
Testament; after the Holocaust, Christians must revert not only to the historical memory of their Jewish roots but also to Christ's disciples' experience of Jewish faith, an experience that was essentially grounded in history rather than in theological abstractions. Christianity has forgotten its

concrete Other, as a lived reality. Returning to Christianity's Jewish roots
therefore should renew Christianity's ability to experience an immediate
encounter with reality in general, an ability immanently related to the encounter with Jews (both past and present)—the ultimate victims of Christian spiritualization.

For Ruether, Baum, Schillebeeckx, Küng, and Metz, the turn to Judaism
was intertwined with the historical turn in Catholic theology and with challenging the authority of dogmatic tradition. The encounter with the Jews
was an important catalyst for theologians who discovered, in the words of
the theologian Eva Fleischner, "a new willingness . . . to reexamine even the
most fundamental Christian dogmas and to relativize doctrinal formulas,
knowing that they can never contain adequately, once and for all, divine revelation."[47] Instead of statements formulated as ahistorical truths devoid of
context or any contact with a tangible Other, these "progressive" theologians
strove to reformulate the Christian Gospel as a creed that does not demand
hermetic ownership of truth or salvation but is open to skepticism of its own
certainties through its dynamic experience of the world. "Jewish" Christianity, as they imagined it, thus became the symbol of an updated Catholic
theology—a postcolonial pluralistic theology with historical sensibilities that
was not indifferent to the suffering of others and was willing to criticize itself on the political, spiritual, and intellectual levels. Judaism was a symbol
of progressivism.

Thus, the return to Christianity's Jewish origins involved, at the same time,
a break with tradition. The theologians behind this movement may have
explicitly made the connection between these two trends, but even without
bold statements, it appears that the theological discourse on Jews and Judaism tended to minimize the importance of central Catholic doctrines,
including those that had to do with Christ as the second person in the trinity,
or with his divinity in general, while avoiding discussion of the far-reaching
doctrinal implications of such a shift. Theological dialogue between Jews and
Christians aspired to root itself within (historical) common ground rather
than (dogmatic) differences. In this regard, the conciliatory theological approach of the Catholic Church toward the Jews increasingly interfaced with
the (originally Protestant) split between the historical Jesus and the Jesus of
faith. This split also provided a convenient platform for Jewish scholars,
who could now easily participate in the discourse surrounding the historical Jewish Jesus while firmly rejecting the Jesus of ecclesiastical tradition.

Consequently, Christian-Jewish dialogue was pulled in more historical and less theological directions, while traditional doctrines remained outside the discourse and were even perceived as threatening.

The Present: Post-Christum Jews and the History of Salvation

The church had declared that it cherished the biblical people of Israel, as well as the Judaism of the Second Temple within which Jesus lived. Following Vatican II, Paul's admonition "Do not boast over the branches. If you do boast, remember that it is not you that support the root, but the root that supports you" (Rom. 11:18) was read as a commandment to revere the Jews out of respect for the Jewish roots of Christianity. At the same time, the turn of the church to its Jewish origins to establish a continuous affinity between itself and post-crucifixion Jews demanded an explanation. An appreciation of the Old Testament and of the Jewish people before the rejection of Christ was one thing. Contemporary Jews, however, constituted a far greater theological challenge.

In Paul's parable, post-crucifixion Jews are not considered to be part of the "root"; rather, they are branches cut off so that the branches of the wild olive, the gentiles, may be grafted onto the root in their place: "if some of the branches were broken off, and you, a wild olive shoot, were grafted in their place to share the rich root of the olive tree" (11:17). The branches were cut off the sacred root because they rejected Jesus—"because of their unbelief" (11:20). How, then, did theologians conceive of the Catholic doctrine's approach to the branches—that is, to Jews who had rejected the Gospel? Did the church still consider them "broken off" the tree, in Paul's words? And if they were, from exactly what were they broken? The covenant? Divine grace? Salvation? What is the link between the church and contemporary Jews, apart from the fact that the Christians may not boast against them? How did leading theologians treat the implications of the Jewish rejection of Christ without slipping into anti-Judaism?

The authors of the fourth section of *Nostra aetate* were deeply troubled by the question of the theological status of contemporary Jews. (The very motivation of the church to address this issue arose directly from the impact that the Holocaust had made on the Catholic world.) It soon became evident that the issue was too loaded and complex to be addressed within *Nostra aetate* itself, and the authors therefore ultimately settled on an extremely minimalist statement: "God holds the Jews most dear for the sake of their Fathers; He does not repent of the gifts He makes or of the calls He issues—such is the witness of the Apostle" (paraphrasing Rom. 11:29, 9:4–5). This statement did not explain the implications of divine love and nonrepentance for the history of actual Jews, and it explicitly refrained from raising the question of the link between the rejection of the Gospel and the fate of the Jews throughout history.

This was a sensitive issue for a number of reasons, first and foremost because the Jews' rejection of Christ constituted the linchpin of traditional replacement theology; following their rejection (of which deicide was the ultimate expression), the Jews lost their status as the chosen people and were doomed to eternal damnation, as manifested in their many sufferings in the course of history. The Holocaust made it clear that this perspective seriously undermined theodicy, because the punishment befalling the Jews was so atrocious that it vilified God's own morality. This was one of the factors that motivated the church to withdraw from its traditional teachings on Jews and Judaism as far as possible in Vatican II.

Traditional doctrines did give the Jews a role in the history of salvation, by constituting them as witnesses to the faith through their suffering. Rejecting this tradition without suggesting an acceptable substitute for it would have deprived the Jews of their role in the history of salvation, a conclusion that would undermine the clear aims of the doctrinal reform, since the implication was that the Jewish people who had a role before the crucifixion lost their status after it. Thus, a doctrinal vacuum in regard to contemporary Jews became impossible, for the very negation had theological implications. It therefore behooved Catholic theologians not to reject the doctrine of the unique role of contemporary Jews in its entirety but rather to update it.

A coherent approach seemingly required abandoning the conception of a break in the historical continuum of the Jewish people by arguing that this nation had remained faithful to its God since the days of the Bible, and in that context, its refusal to acknowledge Christ also expressed faith rather than betrayal—just as the Jews had always claimed. This conclusion was obviously too extreme, however. First, it failed to coincide with Paul's testimony that the branches (Israel of the flesh) had indeed been removed from the tree, even if only temporarily. Second, it deeply undermined the position of the church as the mediator of salvation. A handful of liberal theologians may have toyed with these ideas, but it was taken as a given that they would not enter the consensus. "It is not possible for us [Christians] to see in contemporary Israel the people of God in the same way that Israel was the people of God before Christ," wrote Jean Daniélou in 1967.[48] Even theologians who agreed that the Jews were not to blame for the crucifixion and are still beloved by God were not willing to forget that the Jews refused to accept Christianity—which for these theologians was the true religion. It became necessary to develop an approach that would recognize the rejection of the Gospel by the Jews and define its implications, while also assigning a positive role to contemporary Jews.

The careful way to do so was to affirm that post-crucifixion Jews did have a role in the history of salvation but to keep that role a "mystery." This was the approach adopted by *Nostra aetate,* which allowed the church to live with the contradiction between Jewish rejection of the Gospel and the Jews' continuing status as God's chosen people, without insisting on solving it. In his book *La chiesa e il popolo ebraico,* Cardinal Bea explained that the Jewish rejection of Christ was an event with historical implications but that these implications are in no way linked to any punitive divine intervention in the history of the Jews; punishment does not befit God, and the Jews themselves do not deserve it:

> It was not God, then, who rejected his people. . . . It is not God who rejects and suddenly, without more ado, sends down the lightning of his punishments. He continues to hold out the good news of salvation, even at the cost of the suffering and persecution of his messengers, but through an unhappy chain of circumstances, the members of the Jewish people again and again reject the Gospel until at last, respecting man's freedom, God sends his messages elsewhere.[49]

Rather than write of the Jewish refusal of Christ and its consequences in terms of sin, punishment, and rejection, Bea constructed it almost in terms of a botched choice: the Jews rejected the Gospel (without a collective blame put on their shoulders, as it was only "an unhappy chain of circumstances"), but God remained faithful to them. God does not hate them, insisted Bea in his interpretation of Romans 11:28 ("As regards the gospel they are enemies of God for your sake; but as regards election they are beloved, for the sake of their ancestors"). Rather, "He hates their repudiation of the Gospel [*odia il loro ripudio del Vangelo*]."[50] Divine grace was never taken from them, even if it is not as available to them as it was during the lifetime of Jesus.

However, Bea admitted that the status of the Jewish people *did* change when they rejected Christ, claiming that from that time on, it "is no longer the people of God in the sense of an *institution for the salvation of mankind* [instituzione di salvezza per l'umanità]":[51]

> The reason for this, however, is not that it has been rejected, but simply that its function in preparing the kingdom of God terminated with the advent of Christ and the founding of the Church. From then on, the nature of the people of God and the way of becoming incorporated into it changed completely: the "people of God" of the New Testament is no longer confined to a single people and is no longer propagated by descent according to the flesh but by faith. All this, however, does not in fact imply the disavowal of the election of "Israel according to the flesh."[52]

Bea emphasized God's continued choosing of "Israel according to the flesh," but as in *Nostra aetate,* he refrained from clarifying the significance of this "chosenness" and how it manifests itself. He avoided the seemingly consequential challenge of tracking the manifestations of this status in the actual history of the Jews. Rather, Bea chose to remain faithful to the ahistorical spirit of *Nostra aetate*'s fourth article, which avoided any explicit discussion of the Holocaust and the State of Israel despite the direct influence of these events on its composition.

Other theologians were not content to relegate the role of the Jews in salvation history to a "mystery." They believed that contemporary Jewish history presented such clear religious hints that it was impossible to refrain from trying to interpret it in theological terms. Moreover, in the absence of a theological interpretation of the history of the Jewish people, the church fell under the suspicion that it was, in fact, incapable of ascribing any positive significance to the actual existence of the Jewish people but could only encapsulate the Jews once more—as figures lacking any significance in the present—within brackets that extended from the crucifixion to the very end of history.

The Holocaust as a Theological Category

The Holocaust was a natural candidate for theological examination for two reasons. The first reason was a general Christological one: the Passion of Christ had made human suffering into a deeply significant Christian category, and therefore historical manifestations of suffering were naturally in-

terpreted in the light of Christian doctrine. The second reason was more specific: Jewish suffering had been perceived as significant within the context
of salvation history since ancient times and was therefore a recognized theoretical category.

Catholic thinkers who pioneered the doctrinal shift vis-à-vis Judaism had
begun discussing the theological implications of the persecutions of the Jews
as far back as the late 1930s. They continued to view Jewish suffering as religiously significant, as in the past, but this significance gradually lost its negative connotations (the Jews were persecuted because God hates them) and
assumed positive ones (the Jews were persecuted because God loves them).
The Jews' suffering began to be conceived not as the manifestation of a divine
curse but as a deep expression of their closeness to God. It was now thought
that because they were God's chosen people, the persecuted Jewish masses
were doomed to re-create the drama of Golgotha.[53]

However, as far as these preconciliar thinkers were concerned, this positive reinterpretation of Jewish suffering in no way obviated the contention
that by rejecting their Messiah, the Jews had indeed brought suffering upon
themselves. In other words, according to this conception, the Jews, beloved
of God, were indeed punished for having rejected the Messiah, even though
their punishment was not an expression of divine hate. Jacques Maritain,
for example, explained that in order to correctly perceive the "punishment"
of the Jewish people for rejecting the Messiah, one must replace the "legal
anthropomorphism" of the Western conception of punishment with a conception of punishment more like the law of karma. God is not some external
judge who applied the law to mankind by fitting the punishment to the crime;
rather, sin is likened to a tree that naturally bears the fruit of punishment.
By choosing the world over God, the Jews were trapped in the world they
had chosen; that is, their choice fulfilled their wish in a horrifying way. And
yet, despite Israel's betrayal, it is "ever awaited by the Bridegroom, who has
never ceased to love her."[54] Daniélou, too, considered in 1963 that even
though the Jews were not collectively responsible for the crucifixion, their
rejection of the Messiah had marked their fate "with a mysterious sign."[55]

Like his French colleagues, Hans Urs von Balthasar was also involved
during the early 1960s in an attempt to settle the seeming contradiction between the continuing loyalty of God to the Jews and the teaching affirming
that the Jews paid with their suffering for their refusal to recognize him. According to Balthasar, "The greatest tragedy in the history of Christian theology" was interpreting the divine rejection of the Jews who had refused to

acknowledge Christ in eschatological rather than historical terms.[56] The Jews who disavowed Christ were indeed rejected by God on the historical level, and their rejection had a role to play in the history of salvation.[57] The condition of the Jewish people reveals that divine providence operated in history as concurrent reprobation and election. The historical destiny of Israel and the church was a direct continuation of the Old Testament narrative in which Isaac and Ishmael, Jacob and Esau, Moses and Pharaoh—light and darkness, spirit and flesh, choice and rejection—were the two sides of God's single plan for human history, a plan whose purpose was salvation for all. Just as in the past Israel had bathed in light while the gentiles wallowed in darkness, the opposite was now true. It is especially because of this that Christians should not "boast over the branches":

> Never are the elect granted any sort of right over those blinded, no spiritual right either to lord it over them in their humiliation, no right to mockery, revenge, persecution, anti-Semitism. The shadow cast over Israel by God comes from God. It is the shadow of God himself, given solely as a mirror for those entered into the light, to make them realize the darkness from which they themselves came and into which they fall back if they "puff themselves up"; to show them that they must ascribe their election solely to grace; and finally, to illustrate the indissoluble union and destiny binding those in darkness and those in the light.[58]

In this paragraph, which was written about four years before *Nostra aetate,* Balthasar attempted to update traditional ecclesiastical doctrine in a way that would preserve its principles while cleansing it of hostility toward the Jews. He demanded that Christians construe Jewish blindness as a paradoxical indicator of a shared fate rather than alienation, without realizing that these very categories embody considerable enmity. Contemporary Jews, according to Balthasar, were still "blind in the mirror" and still fulfilled the function of witnesses to the Christian faith in accordance with the Augustinian model (which requires them to suffer in order to testify that God has now chosen the gentiles).

As I shall subsequently show, ideas of this kind became largely irrelevant following Vatican II. The ambivalence rooted in the Jewish rejection of Christ was gradually phased out from the discourse on Jews, which became exclusively positive. Few Catholic thinkers persisted in discussing this unpleasant matter after 1965, and their musings were eventually pushed out of the discourse. Maritain, three years before his death, was one of them:

> And wounded love [the love of God to the Jews who turned away from Him] has formidable ways of not making itself importunate. It is enough for it to not intervene, and to wait. . . . To be loved by God can mean to have to sweat blood. *It is the love of God to the Jewish people* which abandoned it during centuries to the abominable treatments of the Gentiles,—we are the blindest of the blind if we do not understand this. And this love is always there, the Jews can count upon it. He watches always over His people, He weeps for it and with it, He will pull it always from the worst steps. He will strengthen it always. To tell the truth this people carries in its own manner the Cross of Jesus, by enduring in its unconquered soul all the affliction of the world and bending its shoulders under all the burdens, *in order to survive.*[59]

Balthasar, too, did not substantially withdraw from his supersessionist positions after Vatican II and continued to express his amazement over the persistence of the Jews in history: "The fact that Israel survives Christ and continues to exist in history beside the church remains a mystery that cannot be unveiled," he wrote in 1978.[60]

The Jewish rejection of Christ continued to preoccupy Balthasar, especially in view of the development of a Christian-Jewish dialogue in directions that blurred the deep distinctions between the two religions. In the third volume of his renowned *Theo-Drama* series, Balthasar followed Karl Barth (whose theology of the Jewish people was distinctly ambivalent) in emphasizing that the continuous choice of God in the Jews does not lessen the seriousness of their refusal to accept Christ, nor does it cancel the fact of divine rejection:[61]

> We must agree with Karl Barth when he says that there is only one People of God, consisting of Synagogue and Church together. But if we are to define the relationship of each part to the other, it is not enough, on the one hand, to establish areas of agreement between them—for example, that both are still journeying toward their ultimate fulfilment . . . , proceeding toward the same Redeemer and Judge, that both have the same Old Testament Scriptures in common, and so forth—and, on the other hand, to raise only secondary differences, for the purpose

of promoting Jewish-Christian dialogue. The breach between the two "parts" is based on their Yes or No to what the Christian Church ultimately is; Israel has refused to acknowledge this reality as its own fulfilment. . . . Then, with Karl Barth, we shall say that Israel and the Church represent two sides of the one redemptive mystery of the cross: the side of judgment and the side of grace. . . . We can liken the two "peoples" to the two malefactors and say that the crucified Jesus, with his hands outstretched to both of them, expresses his solidarity both with the one turned toward him and with the one turned away from him.[62]

Balthasar viewed post-crucifixion Jews as distant from God by their own choice but close to God by God's choice. Their privileges were all void, yet divine grace continued to dwell over them in a way that was significant but different from in the past:

What is simply beyond our concepts is this: on the one hand, Israel's privileges are obsolete, empty shells; but, on the other, they are instituted by God's faithfulness with a view to their fulfilment, and as such they *do* have theological substance; at the very least they are filled with God's present and abiding faithfulness. . . . The exile would not be a *privatio* unless the special relationship persisted between the One-who-forsakes and the forsaken nation. . . . Here we have something positive immanent in something that is negative; this cannot be dissolved away: it is a characteristic of the entire existence of post-Christian Israel.[63]

In the period during which they were written, these insights were an exception that proved the rule. Maritain had a respectable place as one of the architects of the doctrinal change in regard to the Jews during the 1930s, 1940s, and 1950s, but in the course of the first decade following Vatican II, many of his positions on the subject were outdated. Balthasar's conception of Judaism also failed to gain currency, even though he was without doubt one of the most influential theologians in Catholic discourse at the time. For mainstream postconciliar Catholic thought, any view of the Jewish people as rejected, even if it was by their own choice, became unthinkable, even when amended and even though it was espoused by important theologians. Any link between Jewish suffering and divine punishment or rejection (even in its moderate versions) were forcefully denied.[64]

The fate of ideas associating Jewish persecutions with the crucifixion was another matter. After cleansing their doctrine of such motives as rejection and punishment, many agreed with Maritain and his early colleagues that Auschwitz testified to God's love for his people. "In Jesus is the Jewish existence before God 'summarized' in a focal point," claimed Franz Mußner.[65] Moreover, "Israel," he wrote, "has not ceased, even post-Christum, to be, through its unheard of sufferings, together with Christ, the reconciling 'Servant of God' for the sins of the world."[66] "What the Christian can truly say," claimed Marcel Dubois, "is that to the eye of faith, Jesus fulfils Israel in her destiny of the Suffering Servant, and that Israel, in her experience of solitude and anguish, announces and represents even without knowing it the mystery of the Passion and of the Cross."[67] The similarity between Auschwitz and the crucifixion was conceived as almost self-evident: "A believing Christian should not find it so very difficult to interpret the sacrifice of the Jews during the Nazi terror," explained Clemens Thoma. "His thoughts should be turned toward Christ to whom these Jewish masses became alike, in sorrow and death. Auschwitz is the most monumental sign of our time for the intimate bond and unity between the Jewish martyrs—who stand for all Jews—and the crucified Christ, even though the Jews in question could not be aware of it."[68] It would be against reason to ignore this affinity: "How is it possible not to be struck by the resemblance of these two countenances?" wondered Dubois.[69] "We must believe that all the suffering of Israel, persecuted . . . because of its Election, is part of the Messiah's suffering," explained Jean-Marie Lustiger. "Otherwise, God himself would appear incoherent regarding his promise to Israel."[70]

It soon became evident, however, that Christian willingness to assign a theological role of redeeming suffering to the Jewish people, creating an affinity between the Holocaust and the crucifixion, was abhorred by many Jews. Unlike Marc Chagall, Jules Isaac, Morris Samuel, and other Jews who had themselves related the suffering of the Jewish people to the Passion of Jesus in previous decades, Jewish thinkers who contemplated the Holocaust during the 1970s and 1980s were less sympathetic, to say the least, to such Christological analogies. Catholic scholars and church officials who sought ways to establish dialogue with actual Jews discovered that their good intentions of updating their doctrine regarding contemporary Jews caused great discomfort to those very Jews themselves: "The Cross has always been described as a voluntary act on the part of God and his Son," John Pawlikowski wrote, reflecting the Jewish criticism of the comparison. "Auschwitz was neither voluntary nor redemptive in any sense. Here Emil Fackenheim's contention that to assign any form of *meaning* to the Holocaust is blasphemy must be safeguarded at all costs."[71] "It is blasphemy, in the words of Abraham Heschel, to look for meaning in the Holocaust," wrote Eva Fleischner. "If Jews that have lived through Auschwitz can find no meaning in it . . . , it is perhaps a warning to the Christian not to find meaning too easily."[72] "How can one compare the Holocaust with the Cross!" cried Dubois. "The Cross brandished in the pogroms by murderers, and, for so many Jews, the symbol of intolerance, oppression, and hatred!"[73]

But for many Christians, the comparison was too valuable to completely relinquish: "May my Jewish friends pardon me if here I seem to annex to the Passion of Christ an ocean of suffering whose abyss they alone know," continued Dubois. "Yet . . . the transcendent intelligibility of the Holocaust can be granted only by light from above, and for us Christians that light passes through the mystery of Golgotha."[74]

One way or another, many theologians now realized that it was not enough to avoid accusing the victim. While it settled Christian theological difficulties, it was offensive to the Jews, with whom the church wished to reconcile. Comparing the Passion of Christ with the Holocaust not only injured the historical sensibilities of many Jews but also gave rise to an immoral position vis-à-vis suffering in general, since it gave priority to the sanctification of suffering rather than taking any tangible action to prevent it, as eloquently explained by Metz: "We refuse to interpret the suffering of the Jewish people as part of the history of salvation. Under no circumstances will we mystify this suffering! We encounter in this suffering only the mystery of our own insensitivity, the mystery of our [Christians'] own apathy, not the traces of God."[75]

The State of Israel as a Theological Category

The theologization of the Holocaust was thus problematic with regard both to the moral implications of the doctrine and to the tensions that it evoked between Catholics and Jews. One of the most bothersome consequences of this debate was the fact that it gave rise to something that most of the Catholic intelligentsia did not want to engage with. In the same way that Catholic thinkers found it difficult to resist the temptation of discussing the theological implications of the Holocaust despite Jews' protests, they exerted considerable effort to avoid any theological discussion of the Jewish state, even though Jews beseeched them to do so. Precisely because of the intensive engagement with Jewish suffering, this asymmetry unavoidably gave rise to the question of whether the Jews were forced to suffer in order to be acknowledged by Christians as religiously significant. How else could one explain the enthusiastic adoption of the Holocaust as a theological category alongside the decisive rejection of any theological significance ascribed to the founding of the State of Israel in the divine plan? Did the discussion of one event as "a sign of the times" not necessitate a discussion of the other? Moreover, how could the church claim that it took the self-perceptions of the Jews seriously if it disregarded the State of Israel? If Catholics thought that the covenant between the Jewish people and God still existed, was it not more plausible to identify that covenant in the national resurrection of the Jews in the Holy Land than in their destruction in Europe?

Vatican II was determined to differentiate between its reconceptualized attitude to the Jews and any expression of politics: "the Church, . . . moved not by political reasons but by the Gospel's spiritual love, decries hatred, persecutions, displays of anti-Semitism." The final version put the seal to a long list of clarifications provided by Cardinal Bea, who reiterated throughout the council's discussions that the formulators of the document addressing the Jews only viewed the issue from its religious aspects and that no political significance should be ascribed to it.[76]

Bea's comments were certainly necessary to appease the bishops in the Arab world whose objection to the formulation of the declaration stemmed precisely from a concern that it would be perceived as taking a side in the Israeli-Arab conflict. However, the church's avoidance of any recognition of the founding of the State of Israel emerged from a combination of political pressures and theological considerations. The insistence on avoiding a political stance on this matter coincided with a tradition of church neutrality and its intentional abstention from clear political identifications (as formulated also in the conciliar constitution *Gaudium et Spes*). The church's firm ties with the European rulers now lay in the distant past, and its assumption of a neutral position made it easier for the church to cope with the frequent political upheavals that characterized the modern age.[77] It should be remembered that even in the course of World War II, the pope did everything in his power to maintain political neutrality, sustaining criticism from both sides.

After the war, the concern over adopting a political position became even stronger; once becoming acquainted with the messianic fervor that accompanied both Nazism and communism, scholars and clergy became doubly eager to remove the religious aspirations of the church from the political realm. They validated the traditional Augustinian distinction between political history and salvation history in order to distinguish between the church, as a super-national spiritual community, and worldly national communities, and between the hope of salvation in the next world and any political type of aspiration for redemption.

In their aversion to political messianism, some Catholic thinkers even drew inspiration from the Jewish resistance to the Christological conception that the world has already been redeemed with the coming of Christ and preferred to emphasize, along with the Jews, that full redemption was yet to come. Ironically, this enthusiasm over the Jewish postponement of the Messiah to the future took place at the very moment that Jewish denominations were beginning to develop renewed enthusiasm for the possibility of political messianism here and now.[78] The Jewish state came into being precisely when the church was making tremendous efforts to disengage from its ties to worldly power. The State of Israel constituted a Jewish effort to be rid of the (alleged or real) historical-political disengagement of the Jews and replace it with earthly power. Not only did the Jews suddenly become a sovereign political entity, but, as was becoming increasingly evident, this was an entity that had inherited from European politics the volatile mix of secularism (or seeming secularism), the adoration of power, and utopianism, a mix that in the second half of the twentieth century gave rise to acute allergic reactions on the part of the church in particular and the liberal West in general. At the very point in time that the church learned to retreat from its political demands, to distance itself from the mundane and postpone salvation once more to the end of history, the Jews rediscovered the redemptive value of worldly power and identified the "surplus spirituality" that had characterized them in the past as a disease for which power was the cure.[79]

Moreover, the logic of Augustine's critique of the mixing of earthly history and the history of salvation, a critique which the church made use of in the aftermath of World War II, was intimately (though probably not consciously) intertwined with the rejection of Jewish political theology (as the church traditionally understood it). The Christian tradition often viewed the exile of the Jews and the destruction of Jerusalem as evidence that the Jewish interpretation of scripture was erroneous, for the prophecies of the Jewish prophets had not come true for the "Israel of the flesh" in the earthly manner to which the Jews aspired.[80] Augustine and other early theologians viewed the dispersion of the Jews within the (Christian) world as evidence that their hopes for salvation, for the renewal of their political autonomy in the Holy Land, and for the construction of the Third Temple were unfounded. The Christian rejection of the political after World War II was thus, implicitly, also a form of admission that the church had erred in "Judaizing" its political theology, contaminating the spiritual with the political in its years of hubris.

In this respect, both Zionism and the post–Vatican II "aggiornamented" church each fulfilled (mutatis mutandis) its traditional role in the ancient Christian-Jewish polemic; the former yearned for political redemption and celebrated its worldly power, while the latter demanded that a distinction be made between matters of redemption (unto God) and matters of politics (unto Caesar).

The significance of this state of affairs was that it became impossible, at least on the part of the church, to differentiate between a theological position vis-à-vis the Jews and a political one, since that very distinction served the church in the past as a theological weapon to be used in the context of polemics that were always political and theological at one and the same time. Not taking a stand was therefore perceived by many—both Jews and Christians—as in fact legitimizing the church's traditional anti-Jewish attitudes. Some interpreted the silence of the church in regard to the Jewish state in light of the cold shoulder that Pius X had given Binyamin Zeev Herzel when the latter asked for his support for Zionism in 1907: "The Jews have not acknowledged Our Lord, and so we cannot acknowledge the Jewish people."[81]

In other words, where the State of Israel was concerned, the church found itself in a quandary. Any objection to the Jewish state on theological grounds was out of the question, since it re-created the logic of the rejected replacement theology; any support of the state for theological reasons would be a blatant breach of the distinction between theology and politics and the principle of political neutrality, while a nontheological position vis-à-vis Jewish politics conflicted with tradition. As summed up by Edward Flannery as far back as 1958, "Are we at all justified in regarding an apparently purely political fact with the eyes of the theologian? Perhaps this question is best answered by reversing it: is it possible to view Israel in any other way?"[82]

How did Catholic thinkers cope with this bind before Vatican II? In a short article published in 1957, Yves Congar (one of the more prominent representatives of the *nouvelle théologie*) attempted to affirm the theological significance of Jewish history, but without ascribing messianic meaning to the State of Israel that would contradict Christian doctrine: "God did not deliver his People that they might plant vineyards in the Holy Land instead of

making bricks in Egypt," wrote Congar. "He did not liberate Israel for liberation's sake."[83] The possibility that the State of Israel itself constituted a realization of the visions of the prophets (a possibility obviously entertained
by a not inconsiderable number of Jews) stood in blatant conflict with Christian theology. The founding of the State of Israel was a secular event, not a
messianic phenomenon. (Congar emphasized that Orthodox Judaism also
viewed things in a similar manner.)

But did this mean that the State of Israel was completely devoid of any
significance in the plan of salvation? Such a conception could not be reconciled with the doctrinal certainty that, in Congar's words, "Christians cannot
look at Israel from a purely secular point of view, for they must see Israel as
an essential part of God's plan for men." But was the founding of the State
of Israel a merely insignificant detail in the divine plan (as would have been
the founding of a Jewish center in Eastern Europe instead of the Middle
East), or an event with theological significance? Congar attempted to reconcile these possibilities by stating that "restoration to the Land of Promise,
even though under secular auspices, *may* well be a *distant* preparation of the
whole people for the final encounter with grace."[84] Congar also wrote:

> It is conceivable that some day the Jews will hold the Old City of Jeru-
> salem. They will hold the site of the Temple. Naturally they will not con-
> tinue to lament at the Wailing Wall as they did under the Turks. The
> question of the restoration of the cult will arise. This is practically im-
> possible to solve. Will animal sacrifices be restored? Certainly not. . . .
> So the Mosaic Law will have to be re-interpreted in the light of the find-
> ings of Jewish and Christian scholars through the ages: the difficult
> question of cult, the function of the Temple itself, and the Priesthood
> which no longer exists. . . . At the moment when the Jewish people find
> themselves on the horns of this dilemma and seek for a solution, the
> confrontation with grace will take place. According to St Paul the sole
> purpose of the Law was to bring men to the realization that it cannot
> be observed in its fullness, and that man can only be justified by the
> grace of Jesus Christ. This is the impasse to which we may expect the
> restoration of Israel will lead.[85]

According to Congar, the unprecedented resemblance of the State of Israel to the realization of the ancient Jewish dream of rebuilding the temple
and renewing worship there might finally open the eyes of the Jews and make

them realize the senselessness of this dream and how inappropriate it is for modern times (for otherwise, why would the renewal of animal sacrifices in the temple be implausible?).

Edward Flannery, another influential figure in the area of Christian-Jewish relations at that time, adopted Congar's conclusions: "The disillusionment . . . can only grow with time; eventually it may force them [the Jews] to weigh reality against promise and lead them to a new search," which will ultimately lead to the long-awaited acknowledgment of Christ.[86]

Maritain, who was less cautious than Congar and Flannery, insisted that the Jews had an absolute right to the Land of Israel:

> [It] is the sole territory, considering the entire spectacle of human history, that it is absolutely, *divinely* certain that a people has an uncontestable right to. Because the people of Israel is the only people in the world to which a land, the land of Canaan, was given by the true God . . . , and what God has given once, is given for good.[87]

Just as Maritain viewed the Holocaust as a mass crucifixion, so he identified the Jewish state as a resurrection; he expressed great enthusiasm over events in Israel, and he too, like his peers, saw these events as preparatory to the imminent return of Jesus. "Are we not allowed to think," he wrote in 1964, "that in fact Israel, without even knowing it, is approaching the great day which, according to Saint Paul, would be for the world a resurrection from the dead?"[88] Maritain even advised Muslims to relinquish their claim to the Land of Israel because of the divine promise to Israel.[89]

These ideas indicate that the clear distinctions that we currently make between the attitude to the State of Israel by Catholic Christians and by Evangelical Christians—who are pining for the building of the Third Temple under the kingdom of the Antichrist in the State of Israel as a vital stage in the program of salvation—were not always so self-evident. There were those among Catholic theologians, too, who thought that one should take the "worldly" religiousness of the Jews "to its extreme" before they would be able to open their eyes to the truth.[90]

Thus, between the founding of the State of Israel and Vatican II, Catholic thinkers wishing to ascribe religious significance to the State of Israel in the spirit of Christian-Jewish friendship did so by including the State of Israel within the Christian messianic metanarrative. In the same way that the extermination of the Jews was perceived, before Vatican II, as a divine tactic aimed at opening the eyes of the Jews to Christ, so these thinkers hoped that the Jewish state would accomplish the same end. As time passed, however, it became evident that the idea that the State of Israel could serve to open Jewish eyes was no less scandalous than the idea that the Holocaust was a device within the Christian program of salvation. Most Catholic thinkers thought that it would be preferable to postpone the issue of Jewish conversion to "a day known only to God," as stated by *Nostra aetate,* and to disassociate the question of the Jewish present and its theological significance from the issue of the messianic future. However, without the Christological-eschatological option, the problem of the theological meaning of the State of Israel kept reappearing.

One form of coping with the problem attempted by the church was to ignore the State of Israel, thereby avoiding from the outset the entanglements it created between the political and the theological. This was the approach adopted by Paul VI in his historic visit to the Holy Land in 1964, when he intentionally chose to enter Israel not through Tel Aviv or Jerusalem but rather through Meggido, which did not symbolize Jewish sovereignty over Israel (and is tied in Christian theology with the Apocalyptic battle [Revelation 16:16]) and for which choice the chief Sephardic rabbi, Yitzhak Nissim, refused to greet him.[91] *Nostra aetate* also took this approach, as did the first document of the CRRJ in 1974, "Guidelines and Suggestions for Implementing the Conciliar Declaration 'Nostra Aetate' no. 4," which made no mention of the Jewish state at all. This was quite an embarrassing omission, especially in the context of the statement made in the document that "Christians must therefore strive to . . . learn by what essential traits the Jews define themselves in the light of their own religious experience."[92] In 1974, when this document was published, there was no doubt that the State of Israel certainly constituted an "essential trait" of the Jewish religious experience.

A complete omission, then, turned out to be problematic. Attempts were made to acknowledge the theological significance ascribed by Jews to the Land of Israel and to the State of Israel without expressing Christian identification with this theological position. Both theologians and clergy were willing to recognize the "Land of Israel" as a legitimate theological category but felt deep ambivalence toward the interpretation that was predominantly popular within Jewish circles, which sanctified the State of Israel as the only mediator of traditional Jewish attachment to the Land of Israel. While empathy for the religious-political tendencies of the Jews was considered positive, both theologians and clergy were careful not to adopt them as their own.

"Christians must take into account the interpretation given by Jews to their ingathering around Jerusalem, which, according to their faith, is considered a blessing," wrote the French bishops in a statement issued in 1973. However, the bishops were quick to warn against any hasty conclusions: "Today more than ever, it is difficult to pronounce a well-considered theological opinion on the return of the Jewish people to 'its' land." And subsequently: "Christians must not be carried away by interpretations that would ignore the forms of Jewish communal and religious life, or by political positions that, though generous, are nonetheless hastily arrived at."[93] The American bishops expressed similar sentiments in a 1975 statement:

> In dialogue with Christians, Jews have explained that they do not consider themselves as a church, a sect, or a denomination, as is the case among Christian communities, but rather as a peoplehood that is not solely racial, ethnic or religious, but in a sense a composite of all these. It is for such reasons that an overwhelming majority of Jews see themselves bound in one way or another to the Land of Israel. Most Jews see this tie to the land as essential to their Jewishness.

This was followed, again, by an immediate warning against over-identification with any particular Jewish interpretation of that "bond":

> Whatever difficulties Christians may experience in sharing this view they should strive to understand this link between land and people which Jews have expressed in their writings and worship throughout two millennia as a longing for the homeland, holy Zion. Appreciation of this link is not to give assent to any particular religious interpretation of this bond. Nor is this affirmation meant to deny the legitimate rights of other parties in the region, or to adopt any political stance in the controversies over the Middle East, which lie beyond the purview of this statement.[94]

In "Notes on the Correct Way to Present the Jews and Judaism in Preaching and Catechesis in the Roman Catholic Church," issued by the CRRJ in 1985, the authors wrote that "Christians are invited to understand this religious attachment [of Jews to the Land of Israel] which finds its roots in Biblical tradition"; but, they added, "without however making their own any particular religious interpretation of this relationship."[95]

Thus, Christians were exhorted to "take into account," "understand," "recognize," "acknowledge," and "esteem" the position of the Jews vis-à-vis the Land of Israel but were warned not to "judge," "get swept away," "agree with," "approve," or "adopt" it. There were those who expressed an agnostic position toward the theological value of political events: "It is an essential question," admitted the French bishops, "whether or not the ingathering of the dispersed Jewish people—which took place under pressure of persecution and by the play of political forces—will despite so many tragic events prove to be one of the final ways of God's justice for the Jewish people and at the same time for all the nations of the earth."[96] Others, however, refused to even consider such a possibility: "A Christian theologian of Judaism . . . must not disregard the existence of the state of Israel, which is of existential significance not only to the citizens of that state but to Jews everywhere," wrote Clemens Thoma. "Yet," he added, "neither Christians nor Jews should glorify the state; . . . Bible verses [should not] be drawn upon in a fundamentalistic way to defend the state of Israel. Neither romantic nor nostalgic, neither sacral nor eschatological nor theocratic ideas are appropriate."[97]

The CRRJ stated that "the existence of the State of Israel and its political options should be envisaged not in a perspective which is in itself religious, but in their reference to the common principles of international law."[98] From a purely humanitarian point of view, "the conscience of the world community cannot refuse the Jewish people, who had to submit to so many vicissitudes in the course of its history, the right and means for a political existence among the nations," as phrased by the conference of French bishops.[99] From a theological point of view, however, as Ignace de la Potterie and Bernard Dupuy made clear in 1973, "It would not be going too far to assert that [the return of part of the Jews to the Land of Israel] has caught the Christian mind at a disadvantage," because "in Christian theology, the theme of the land retains a properly religious sense only to the extent that it is understood in a spiritual and eschatological sense."[100]

Catholic thinkers were thus cognizant of the inherent tension between Jewish and Christian conceptions. "The collapse of Christendom and the founding of Israel, then, provide Christians and Jews with a new historical situation from which to rethink their relationship," wrote Ruether. At the very point that the church began to internalize what it should have learned many years before, she continued, and "think of itself as a Diaspora religion," "the Jewish people . . . have taken a giant leap against all odds and against their two thousand years of urban Diaspora culture, and founded the state of Israel."[101] Or, as the reform rabbi Jacob Petuchowsky told his Catholic colleagues, "The creation of the State of Israel has taken place at the very time that Christianity is no longer as sure as it had been for centuries that the church herself is still *in* the world":

> Christian states have been secularized. Christian belief is widely rejected, even in the so-called Christian world. And within an ever shrinking world, Christians have discovered that they are far from being the majority of the world's total population. Indeed, Christians are beginning to find out that, within the total world picture, they represent the kind of minority that Jews used to represent within Christian society. The Church had discovered that she, too, is in *galuth,* "in exile"—a discovery which may well have been one of the driving considerations that made the Church willing to engage in the current stage of the Christian-Jewish dialogue.[102]

The State of Israel did not coincide with the historical horizon that was gradually opened before the church, nor with what the church wanted to learn from the Jews. However, Mußner wondered, was this particularly not characteristic of the Jewish people, who had defied any attempt to neatly conceptualize history since time immemorial? The Jews had always made the categorization and abstraction processes of the West more difficult because they functioned as witnesses to the "concreteness of salvation history," which can neither by abstracted nor spiritualized. He therefore claimed:

> The state of Israel . . . is more than a merely profane historical givenness; rather, it is an indication of the leading of Israel by God who through the Old Testament prophets spoke of the restoration of Israel. . . . The existence of the Jew does not allow a merely profane view of history to be cultivated; rather, the Jew is the continuing witness to the concreteness of salvation history, its real relationship to history.[103]

In this way, Mußner provided an apologetic response to the reservations of Catholic Christianity against viewing the Israeli political establishment as a stage in the program of salvation. John Oesterreicher directly attacked the Christian reluctance to read theological meaning into the historical and the political:

> In view of Israel's quite unlikely history, it is fair to assume that her success is not all together due to the cunning of her statesmen, the

superior strategy of her generals, the bravery of her soldiers, and the steadfastness of her citizens. Rather was it the "outstretched arm" (Ex 6:6) of the Lord which once more rescued His people. For the theologian, Israel's future cannot be a mere political problem. Heaven forbid that he allows the cry "politics!" to prevent him from taking a stand. . . . I, at least, cannot see how the renewal of the land could be anything to the theologian but a wonder of love and fidelity, how the reborn State could be anything but a sign of God's concern for His people. . . . If God entered history, a Christian cannot but get involved in the struggle of men to make the societies they live in more human and thus more worthy of His name. Even less can he stand aloof as God's chosen people wrestles to lead a life of dignity.[104]

Post–Vatican II theologians vacillated between an aversion to the messianic interpretation that many Jews had given to the State of Israel and the feeling that the recent events in the Holy Land were so miraculous that it would be futile not to see them as part of salvation history. They oscillated between a vision of the Jews as *the* victims of Western nationalism—which was now perceived as satanic—and their perception of them as its implementers. They wavered between an aversion to nationalism and feelings of guilt over that very aversion when directed toward Jews, between doubting their own tradition and feeling a sense of mixed wonder and distaste toward the Jewish people.[105]

The Jews were supposed to serve as a symbol and paragon for the tolerant, compassionate, and inclusive church of the post-national era, a church that had taught itself to accept the Jewish (forced) relinquishment of worldly power as a model worthy of emulation. Instead, Jews moved in the opposite direction and whole-heartedly supported the very things whose antithesis they were supposed to symbolize—worldly power, nationalistic characteristics, and a fusion of religion, ethnicity, and politics.[106]

The Future: Mission and Salvation for the Jews

The last question that remained open with regard to the Jews after Vatican II was how they might be saved. This was among the most contentious issues in the course of the council's debates surrounding the "Jewish document," and a different response was provided in each draft. In response to the considerable ire expressed by the Jews toward the formulations included in the various drafts, the council fathers chose to omit from the final version of *Nostra aetate* any mention that the Jews would be required to join the church or acknowledge Christ as a precondition to their salvation. "In company with the Prophets and the same Apostle," stated the declaration, "the church awaits that day, known to God alone, on which all peoples will address the Lord in a single voice and 'serve him shoulder to shoulder.'"[107] The events that would lead to this messianic future remained obscure—but another facet of the mystery of Israel.

Like the other issues that perturbed Catholic theologians with regard to the Jews, this issue, too, was the subject of extensive debates that far exceeded the Catholic focus on Judaism, for it also concerned the salvation of all those who were not Catholic. In one of the most dramatic turns it instituted in its attempt to establish new relationships with the surrounding world, Vatican II greatly tempered the meaning of the ancient doctrine whereby "there is no salvation outside the church," renewing discussions of ecclesiology, soteriology, and missiology.[108] In the Second Vatican Council's documents *Lumen gentium* and *Unitatis redintegratio,* the council fathers displayed a willingness to drop the identification of Christ's church solely with the Catholic Church and to recognize non-Catholic Christian congregations as its partners, at one level or another, and as means to salvation.[109]

The possibility of being saved without being Christian at all was a more complex matter. Unlike non-Catholic Christians, members of other religions do not share baptism with the church or faith in Christ—conditions that were deemed to be necessary for salvation at the Council of Trent in the sixteenth century. However, the council made some implicit allowances for the salvation of the believers of non-Christian religions, too, even if they did not officially join the church.[110]

By interiorizing the challenge of a pluralist society and the fact that the full conversion of humanity to Christianity did not appear to be imminent—or perhaps because dooming most of humanity to hell now seemed "disproportional"—the council expressed an unprecedented positive regard for other religions.[111] In addressing non-Christian religions, the council fathers drew on the ancient idea of "seminal rationalities" (*rationes seminales*) that God had sown within the human race before the logos had incarnated in Jesus. The church fathers had used this term to explain their particular appreciation of a specific cultural legacy—that of Greek philosophy, which was part of a pagan civilization. They viewed these seeds of truth and morality as a preparation for the Gospel (*praeparatio evangelica*), as means that had prepared the hearts for the acceptance of Christ, in whom they assumed their full significance.[112] In line with this tradition, Vatican II had declared that "the Catholic Church rejects nothing that is true and holy in these religions," as stated in *Nostra aetate*, but rather, "she regards with sincere reverence those ways of conduct and of life, those precepts and teachings which . . . often reflect a ray of that Truth which enlightens all men."[113] According to *Ad gentes* 9, "Whatever truth and grace are to be found among the nations" constitute "a sort of secret presence of God." Moreover, all human beings are part of the divine plan, and "all men are called by the grace of God to salvation" (*Lumen gentium* 13). Or, in the phrasing of *Gaudium et Spes* 22, "We ought to believe that the Holy Spirit in a manner known only to God offers to every man the possibility of being associated with this paschal mystery."[114]

However, the fact that each and every human being is bestowed with God's grace and that the religions contain seeds of truth that are also a consequence of grace does not mean that their believers do not need the church for their salvation. According to Catholic dogma, all grace is mediated through Christ and draws its recipients to be saved in Christ. "Christ . . . has established His Body which is the church as the universal sacrament of salvation."[115] "Established by Christ as a communion of life, charity and truth, it is also used by Him as an instrument for the redemption of all."[116] Thus, divine grace is inextricably linked to the church. In other words, even those who are not officially members of the church must be connected to it by some mystic fashion in order that they be saved. Does this mean that they must desire to formally join the church or at least believe in Christ? The council did not express any explicit position in this regard and only noted that "those who have not yet received the Gospel are related *in various ways* to the people of God."[117]

According to *Lumen gentium*, the most significant connection between the church and those outside it is that which exists between the church and the Jews: "In the first place we must recall the people to whom the testament and the promises were given and from whom Christ was born according to the flesh. On account of their fathers this people remains most dear to God, for God does not repent of the gifts He makes nor of the calls He issues." *Lumen gentium* adds and enumerates members of other religions who are "connected" to the church via less binding ties and announces that "Divine Providence [does not] deny the help necessary for salvation from those who, without blame on their part, have not yet arrived at an explicit knowledge of God and with His grace strive to live a good life."[118]

As these statements show, the authors of the constitution on the church refrained from fixing a specific interpretation of the doctrine that the church is the universal sacrament of salvation and did not explain the actual implications of this dogma for the accessibility of salvation to people who are neither Christian believers nor have ever been a part of the Christian congregation.[119] At the same time, this constitution ipso facto established that it was not necessarily required to explicitly state one's belief or to be baptized in order to be saved. Its wording gave rise to the impression that sometimes goodwill, even without any awareness that it derives from Christ, may suffice. According to Francis Sullivan, the church had exchanged its exclusive formulation, "There is no salvation outside the Church," for an inclusive one, "The Church is the universal sacrament of salvation," a formulation that encompasses—at least potentially—the entire human race.[120]

However, the opening of salvation to non-Christians raised several questions. First, if most of humanity can receive divine grace and be saved without even becoming aware of the Christian Gospel, does this not make the church's missionary work completely redundant, or at least call for its redefinition? What then is the role of the church in the salvation of non-Christians? Second, even though Vatican II respected other religions as containing seeds of truth, it was not clear if such religions played any role in their believers' progress toward salvation, or if those of their believers who were destined for salvation could be saved regardless of their religion. Does the church credit the conscious actions of other religions as means to salvation? And if so, how do these religions view the church, as the universal salvation mediator?

These issues led to stormy disagreements in the immediate aftermath of the council. Missionaries and church officials feared that the more "liberal" interpretation of the council's documents would pull the rug out from under the church's uniqueness as a "universal sacrament of salvation," and, most important, from under its missionary project. As explicated by the apostolic exhortation *Evangelii nuntiandi,* distributed in 1975, Paul VI shared the concerns that the mission would lose its justification and therefore attempted to provide a more conservative interpretation of the conciliar documents where the issue of salvation was at stake, an interpretation that would refrain from radicalizing the council's statements on the matter:

> We should know how to put aside the excuses which would impede evangelization. The most insidious of these excuses are certainly the

ones which people claim to find support for in such and such a teaching of the Council. Thus one too frequently hears it said, in various terms, that to impose a truth, be it that of the Gospel, or to impose a way, be it that of salvation, cannot but be a violation of religious liberty. Besides, it is added, why proclaim the Gospel when the whole world is saved by uprightness of heart? We know likewise that the world and history are filled with "seeds of the Word"; is it not therefore an illusion to claim to bring the Gospel where it already exists in the seeds that the Lord Himself has sown?[121]

According to Paul VI, even if God were capable of saving everyone, including those who have not yet heard the good news, this does not imply that Christians may become lax in their missionary obligations. It is their mission to declare the tidings of Christ and his kingdom to all of humanity, just as it is the right of humanity to hear the Gospel: "God can accomplish this salvation in whomsoever He wishes by ways which He alone knows. And yet, if His Son came, it was precisely in order to reveal to us, by His word and by His life, the ordinary paths of salvation."[122] Paul VI was an enthusiastic supporter of interfaith dialogue. However, in his position regarding the divine qualities of other religions, he was cautious not to interpret the council in a way that went too far, in his opinion, in breaking with previous church teachings on the issue:[123]

> Even in the face of natural religious expressions most worthy of esteem, the Church finds support in the fact that the religion of Jesus, which she proclaims through evangelization, objectively places man in relation with the plan of God, with His living presence and with His action. . . . In other words, our religion effectively establishes with God an authentic and living relationship which the other religions do not succeed in doing, even though they have, as it were, their arms stretched out towards heaven.[124]

These issues, which greatly occupied church leaders and Catholic theologians in the first decades following the council, bore a particular flavor where the Jews were concerned. This was primarily because, as noted in *Lumen gentium*, the Jewish religion, among all the non-Christian religions, was the closest to Christianity. Paul VI could say that all other religions were human artifacts, but there was no argument that the Jewish religion was based on an authentic experience of revelation, which made it a preferred candidate as a means of salvation outside the church. In view of this, one may interpret the apostle Paul's statement that "And so all Israel will be saved" (Rom. 11:26) as pertaining to Judaism as an institution capable of bringing salvation to the Jews in a "special way" that does not require joining the church.[125] Is the fact that the Jews persevered in their belief despite hundreds of years of Christian evangelization not an intimation that God is interested in leaving them in their Jewishness and that it would therefore be better to let them be?[126]

The possibility that the Jews may be saved without having to convert to Christianity—perhaps even without having to explicitly acknowledge Christ—found expression in the new prayer for the Jews composed in the context of Vatican II's liturgical reform (1970). This prayer was a new version of the ancient liturgy for Good Friday—Prayer for the Conversion of the Jews (*Oratio pro conversione Iudaeorum*), which was considered one of the most salient expressions of the anti-Jewish tradition of the church and included several expressions that are currently perceived as part of "replacement theology."

The traditional prayer (as it was read since the Council of Trent and up to 1959) explicitly stated that the Jews must acknowledge Christ to be saved:

> Let us pray also for the faithless Jews: that Almighty God may remove the veil from their hearts; so that they, too, may acknowledge Jesus Christ our Lord. . . . Almighty and everlasting God, from whose mercy not even the treachery of the Jews is shut out: pitifully listen to us who plead for that blinded nation, that opening at last their eyes to the true light, which is Christ, he may dispel the darkness in which they are shrouded.[127]

The prayer was reformulated following Vatican II. Its name was changed from Prayer for the Conversion of the Jews to Prayer for the Jews, and its content was also overhauled:

> Let us pray for the Jewish people, the first to hear the word of God, that they may continue to grow in the love of his name and in faithfulness to his covenant. Almighty and eternal God, long ago you gave your promise to Abraham and his posterity. Listen to your Church as we pray that the people you first made your own may arrive at the fullness of redemption. We ask this through Christ our Lord. Amen.[128]

As its new name indicates, the prayer contains no expectation of conversion, not even for a change of heart (which is the other "inner" meaning of the Latin word *conversio*). It does not confront the question directly, but it can certainly give the impression that all the Jews have to do is remain faithful to their God and the covenant he made with them, and their eventual salvation will be assured. This is not explicitly stated, but the text of the prayer implies that Jews can be saved through their Jewishness and that they are therefore exempt from joining the church. Indeed, the prayer's supplication on behalf of the Jews is brought before Christ—the lord of salvation—but unlike the traditional text, which included such utterances as "may acknowledge Jesus Christ our Lord" and "opening at last their eyes to the true light, which is Christ, he may dispel the darkness," the new text makes no mention of any acknowledgment of Christ by the Jews. This liturgy thus supports the wider interpretation of *Nostra aetate* (the interpretative option promoted by Oesterreicher) that exempts the Jews from consciously and explicitly acknowledging Christ as a precondition to their salvation.

Yet the prayer for the Jews did not settle the matter, for Paul himself had emphasized that the salvation of the Jews was contingent on their "not persist[ing] in unbelief" (Rom. 11:23) and that "hardening" shall persist "until the full number of the Gentiles has come in" (Rom. 11:25); that is, he prima facie made the future of the Jews contingent on their acceptance of Christ.

At the same time, even the more enthusiastic supporters of the mission to the Jews were forced to admit that past experience indicated that the dissemination of the Gospel among the Jews was often carried out in dubious fashion and with limited success. As Jews often reminded their new friends, they did not take a kind view of the attempts to convert them. Jews viewed the Christian mission as an exceedingly violent and abusive act. There were therefore some Catholic theologians who thought that for pragmatic reasons, it would be better to cease all attempts to bring the Jews to Jesus. Even if the Jews had to undergo conversion (whether through an external act of religious conversion or through an inner acknowledgment of Christ) in order to be saved, history indicated that rather than bringing them closer to Christianity, the mission had caused them an aversion to it. As of now, the task of the church was to amend itself so that the Jews would no longer feel so alienated toward it. Jean-Marie Lustiger, for example, claimed that "in our time of history, it is not our task to exhort Israel [to convert]."[129] In his opinion, the Jews will only recognize their connection to the church when "the Christian ceases to appear as a vital threat, someone who wants to divert Israel of its own destiny, to kill or persecute it, and instead becomes, for Israel, a sign of the superabundant blessing of God."[130]

The church made an effort to formulate an official position on these questions in the first document published by the CRRJ in 1974. On the one hand, this document sought to restrain the openness expressed in the council's statements and the subsequent Prayer for the Jews, while on the other hand, it attempted to contend with the grave marks that the Christian missionary legacy had left on Christian-Jewish relations:

> In virtue of her divine mission, and her very nature, the Church must preach Jesus Christ to the world. Lest the witness of Catholics to Jesus Christ should give offence to Jews, they must take care to live and spread their Christian faith while maintaining the strictest respect for religious liberty in line with the teaching of the Second Vatican Council. They will likewise strive to understand the difficulties which arise for the Jewish soul—rightly imbued with an extremely high, pure notion of the divine transcendence—when faced with the mystery of the incarnate Word. While it is true that a widespread air of suspicion, inspired by an unfortunate past, is still dominant in this particular area, Christians, for their part, will be able to see to what extent the responsibility is theirs and deduce practical conclusions for the future.[131]

This document made clear to its Catholic readers that they were not exempt from witnessing their faith to the Jews, while at the same time it explained that this was a sensitive matter that should be handled with care, taking due note of the criticism against past missionary activities among the Jews, as well as clearly accepting the liberal conception of freedom of religion.

The CRRJ continued to debate the mission to the Jews in the following years as well. One of the most well-known discussions of the issue was a lecture by Tommaso Federici, who served as a consultant to the CRRJ, given at the sixth conference of the International Catholic-Jewish Liaison Committee in 1977. Although the Catholic Church considered neither Federici nor his lecture authoritative, this lecture turned out to be influential in the decades to come. In this lecture, which followed an extensive dialogue with Jewish representatives over a number of years, Federici claimed that the respect of Vatican II for freedom of religion necessitated the limitation of the means available to the church in influencing others as it attempted to spread its message in the world, and in particular where the Jews were concerned:

> The Church thus rejects in a clear way every form of undue proselytism. This means the exclusion of any sort of witness and preaching which in any way constitute a physical, moral, psychological or cultural constraint on the Jews, both individuals and communities, such as might in any way destroy or even simply reduce their personal judgment, free will and full autonomy of decision at the personal or community level. Also excluded is every sort of judgment expressive of discrimination, contempt or restriction against the Jewish people as such, and against individual Jews as such or against their faith, their worship, in general, and in particular their religious culture, their past and present history, their existence and its meaning. . . . Any action is rejected which aims to change the religious faith of the Jews, whether groups, minorities or individuals, by offering more or less overt protection, legal, material, cultural, political, and other advantages, on educational, social, or other pretexts.[132]

Federici adopted such a wide interpretation of the concept of "religious coercion" that it was difficult to understand the conditions under which missionary activities targeted at Jews would not be injurious. After all (as argued by the leader of Modern Orthodoxy in America, Rabbi Joseph B. Soloveitchik, discussed further in Chapter 8), one cannot clear the residues of past and present coercion from Christian-Jewish dialogue. Almost any encounter between Jews and Christians can be interpreted as involving some kind of pressure on the part of Christians. Moreover, the demand that the Christian message be completely cleansed of "every sort of judgment expressive of discrimination, contempt or restriction against the Jewish people as such, and against individual Jews as such or against their faith, their worship, in general, and in particular their religious culture, their past and present history, their existence and its meaning" was extremely broad, at least so long as the church continued to view itself as having provided humankind with an innovation, as compared with the Judaism from which it sprang. Indeed, Federici stated that "consequently, attempts to set up organizations of any sort . . . for the 'conversion' of Jews must be rejected."[133] In other words, Federici called for the dissolution of all institutional aspects of the mission to the Jews. Instead, he suggested, Christians would do better to thoroughly study "the history of Israel . . . , the existence, the history and the mission of Israel, her survival in history, her election and call, and her privileges which are recognized by the New Testament. . . . What the Jews have to say must be listened to."[134]

Federici identified with Paul VI's dilemma of "how to reconcile respect for individuals and civilizations and sincere dialogue with them . . . with the universality of the mission entrusted by Christ to the Church."[135] Nevertheless, while Paul VI emphasized the universality of the Christian Gospel and the supremacy of the Catholic Church over other human institutions as the mediator of salvation, Federici emphasized the truth value that the church found in other religions, a truth that allows the church to perceive interfaith dialogue as contributing first and foremost to its own conversion rather than (just) as a means for reaching out to those who do not believe in Christianity. Each side in the dialogue with the Jews was therefore supposed to remain faithful to its own belief and testify to that belief in front of the other, "avoiding any form of relativism and syncretism which would try artificially to join together irreconcilable elements" and utilizing the encounter "to discover new dimensions and values in one's own faith and that above all one learns to love one's faith in humility . . . by seeing the 'treasures God has distributed among men' (*Ad gentes* 11)."[136]

Federici's lecture was not accepted as an official position at this point, but in practice, his approach was adopted by leading theologians and church officials, who encouraged Catholics to avoid institutionalized missionary work among Jews. At the same time, the tension between the nature of Christian testimony in the context of interfaith dialogue and the possible role of Catholics in bringing Jews closer to the true faith remained unresolved.

Contra Federici's liberal theological emphases and his inclusive reading of the council's declarations (and *Lumen gentium* in particular), the CRRJ (to which Federici was a consultant) reemphasized the exclusive elements in Catholic doctrine and the actions that it behooved the church to take by virtue of the superiority of its faith over all others. The document "Notes," published by the CRRJ in 1985, limited the interpretative possibilities in regard to the salvation of the Jews even more than a previous one ("Guidelines and Suggestions," published in 1974) and directly addressed the issue of the need for church mediation. With reference to the paragraph quoted above from "Guidelines and Suggestions," the new document stated:

"In virtue of her divine mission, the Church," which is to be "the all-embracing means of salvation" in which alone "the fulness of the means of salvation can be obtained" (*Unitatis Redintegratio* 3), "must of her nature proclaim Jesus Christ to the world" (cf. *Guidelines*, I). Indeed, we believe that it is through Him that we go to the Father (cf. Jn 14:6). . . . Jesus affirms . . . that "there shall be one flock and one shepherd." Church and Judaism cannot then be seen as two parallel ways of salvation, and the Church must witness to Christ as the Redeemer for all, "while maintaining the strictest respect for religious liberty in line with the teaching of the Second Vatican Council (*Dignitatis Humanae*)" (Guidelines I).[137]

In contrast to Federici's lecture and the 1974 "Guidelines" issued by the CRRJ, "Notes" is less focused on "the difficulties which arise for the Jewish soul" as it stands before the Christian message and places a greater emphasis on the church's universal duties, which include the Jews as well.[138] However, this continued to be an unresolved dilemma even among the representatives and the consultants of the CRRJ, as is clearly evidenced by the CRRJ's latest document, "The Gifts and the Calling of God Are Irrevocable" (2015), which officialized Federici's position by formally declaring the church's abstention from institutionalized missionary activity among Jews. "The Gifts," however, does not provide a theological reason for this abstention, and therefore leaves the theological question still unanswered.[139]

The post–Vatican II debate on the mission to the Jews vacillated between two positions, thereby reflecting the general discontent that prevailed in the Catholic intellectual world in regard to the question of the salvation of non-Christians, the role of the church as a mediator of salvation, and the legitimate tools at its disposal to fulfill that mission. It was obvious to all that the nature of the testimony to the Jews—as to the entire world—required updating and adjustments, but there was no consensus as to the extent of the doctrinal and practical changes that this would entail or how they should be brought about. As I will show in the next chapters, the argument reignited among theologians and clergy in the 2000s.

The church's position regarding Judaism lay at the very core of the theological renaissance of the two decades that followed Vatican II and was characterized by a plurality of voices, courageous reexamination of the boundaries of tradition, and intense debates between different factions. Yet the more penetrating the debate became, the more numerous were the issues that seemed beyond resolution, and even too sensitive to touch upon. At first, difficult themes such as God's response to the Jewish refusal of Christ were pushed out of the discussion. These were later joined by the theological meaning of the Holocaust, and its shadow, the theological meaning of the State of Israel. And finally came the uncomfortable question of mission, which heavily divided liberal Catholics from conservatives and seemed to cause an unresolvable tension between Christians and Jews.

This state of affairs gradually changed when John Paul II was elected pope. In the course of the 1980s, independent Catholic theologians no longer viewed the relations between the Jews and the church as a matter central to Catholic theology, and the theological wings of the discussion were clipped. The discussion of Christian-Jewish relations continued to evolve in the hands of a few theological experts on the topic, yet it was no longer an integral part of the general Catholic intellectual landscape. This did not mean that the process of reconciliation between the two religions was abandoned; it continued to evolve, but along other lines, not as strongly reliant on a revision of Christian doctrine.

3

John Paul II and Christian-Jewish Reconciliation

A decade and a half after the historic reconciliation initiative of Vatican II, the church was torn between two contradictory trajectories. On the one hand, theologians and church officials were eager to cleanse their tradition of hostility and befriend the Jewish people. On the other hand, the costs of this conciliatory approach were very high; a dose of ambivalence toward Judaism turned out to be fundamental to the Catholic tradition. But the fact that the theological discussion of Jews and Judaism threatened to undermine essential Catholic doctrines was not the only problem. Apparently, Jews were themselves often discontent with the new theological trajectories. Was a fundamental doctrinal revision indeed the best means to deepen the process of Christian-Jewish rapprochement?

Pope John Paul II was well aware of this tension. He was a conservative leader, a man of doctrine. He feared threatening the balance of the Catholic community with far-reaching reforms. Nevertheless, reconciliation with the Jews was a high priority for him, and he attributed a deep symbolic meaning to it. In this chapter, I will show how John Paul II handled this tension through transforming the essence and the focus of the Catholic-Jewish relationship. Unlike his predecessors, who focused above all on revising theological perceptions of the Jews, John Paul II sought rapprochement with the Jews not through systematic intellectual discussion but through acts and gestures, personal meetings, diplomatic contacts, and the creation of shared memories. These gestures allowed John Paul II to maintain his conservative theological convictions and not negotiate them in the interreligious realm, while presenting an extremely progressive line toward Judaism in the non-theological realm. Understanding John Paul II's legacy as consisting of two separate, parallel trajectories of discourse (that is, the theological and the symbolic) can also solve the alleged contradiction between his general conservativeness and his progressiveness in Christian-Jewish matters. It is not that John Paul II excused his conservative approach and his Christocentric perceptions when approaching the Jews. Rather, his progressiveness appears on a different level, purposely separated from the doctrinal realm. Even though this pope's gestures often entailed theological overtones that may have been at odds with his explicit theological agenda, he was careful not to affirm (or negate) these overtones in his doctrinal and theological statements. Though John Paul II's intention was to guard doctrine and theology against those whom he perceived as their opponents, this move also caused a certain overshadowing of the importance of theology to Christian-Jewish relations altogether and blurred the theological tensions that remained unaddressed.[1]

To place this transformation in the broader context of John Paul II's pontificate, I will first discuss John Paul II's confrontation with postconciliar theologians in matters that do not pertain directly to the Christian-Jewish relationship. I will then present his parallel strategies of consolidating a firm doctrinal line, on the one hand, and replacing theology with an alternative medium through which to communicate with the world, and especially the world outside the Catholic Church, on the other. Next, I will focus on the symbolic use he made of the Christian-Jewish rapprochement in the framework of his program for the restoration of Europe and the introduction of Catholicism as a cultural and moral position befitting the needs of the time, throughout his pontificate. Finally, I will describe how John Paul II, in the last fifteen years of his pontificate, adopted and made use of a system of Jewish symbols and how he came to be regarded as the greatest friend of the Jewish people of all popes in history.

Combatting Theologians

When Karol Józef Wojtyła, the archbishop of Kraków, was elected pope in 1978, the Catholic community around the world was in a state of perplexity. The trajectories introduced by the Second Vatican Council were tearing it from within. Many believers experienced a growing alienation from tradition and distanced themselves from the church. Some felt that the church had been secularized, and their faith in the hierarchy and its stability was shaken. Others celebrated Vatican II's reforms and called to broaden them further.

John Paul II set himself a goal of putting an end to the confusion. He frequently reaffirmed his commitment to the legacy of Vatican II and quoted from its documents; nevertheless, his interpretation of the council's statements was often limiting. Uneasy with the way "progressive" Catholic theologians had interpreted it, John Paul II consistently presented the council as continuing church tradition rather than breaking from it.[2] The theologians' role was, for him, to serve the magisterium by protecting and safeguarding the revelation entrusted to the church.[3]

On Christmas Eve of 1979, about a year after Wojtyła assumed the papacy as John Paul II, the distinguished Catholic theologian Edward Schillebeeckx (a Belgian Dominican) was summoned by the Congregation for the Doctrine of the Faith (CDF) to an unofficial hearing on the supposedly unorthodox positions enunciated in his 1974 book *Jesus: An Experiment in Christology*. The main charge was that Schillebeeckx had renounced the Council of Chalcedon.[4] At the same time, the CDF forbade another well-known theologian, Hans Küng, from continuing to refer to himself as a Catholic theologian (he went on writing and publishing successfully under the title of "ecumenical" theologian).[5] The symbolic effect of this simultaneous assault against two of the Catholic world's leading theologians was amplified by harsh criticism against the Jesuit order, the elite of Catholic intelligentsia, many of whose members were represented in the church's progressive movement. The most significant struggle against disfavored theological experiments during John Paul II's pontificate was directed toward "liberation theology," a progressive Catholic theological current that became extremely popular from the 1960s to the 1980s, in particular in South America.[6] This movement was led mainly by Jesuits who sought to bring about radical sociopolitical reforms grounded in a worldview that combined Christological ideas of social justice with Marxist ideas. The pope's profound personal disdain of communism and his distrust of overly independent theological initiatives led him to exert the full authority of his position to suppress liberation theology.

The official charged with implementing this policy throughout most of John Paul II's years as pope was Joseph Cardinal Ratzinger, the future Pope Benedict XVI.[7] Ratzinger, who headed the CDF from 1981 to 2005, was deeply concerned by what he identified as an absence of theological discipline. As far as he was concerned, there were too many Catholic thinkers deciding for themselves what was true and what was not in the Catholic faith.[8] Despite vehement criticism by some former friends (such as Karl Rahner), who considered his stringency to be excessive, Ratzinger kept reining Catholic intellectuals in, curtailing their freedom considerably and contributing to the decline in the stature of theology in the post–Vatican II church—even though he was a deeply devoted (and innovative) theologian himself. Ratzinger's term as prefect of the CDF involved about a hundred "silencings" of theologians. New appointees to theology and philosophy faculties in Catholic universities and seminaries were required to sign an oath of allegiance. The result of all these was a rift between the Catholic intelligentsia and the Vatican.[9]

Prima facie, the curtailment of the theologians' academic freedom was mainly directed at liberal theology, while conservative theology in the spirit of Ratzinger and John Paul II was able to continue to thrive. John Paul II adopted Hans Urs von Balthasar as his protégé, for example, and his work in the area of sexuality and marriage was lauded. The pope himself devoted time to developing a theology of the body that was also intended to fortify the traditional institutions of the family. He published an extremely large number of encyclicals, in which he tirelessly insisted on the importance of mission, on the centrality of the church, and on Christ as the sole and universal savior.

Yet outside of the doctrinal realm and parallel to his efforts to stabilize doctrine and unify the church around an authoritative theological line, the pope was also invested in promoting radical reforms in the church's communication both with its own members and with non-Catholics. In this realm of his activity, John Paul II introduced bold changes, which often pointed in an entirely different direction from his theology. He dumbfounded the world when he invited Catholics to fast along with Muslims on the last day of Ramadan in 2001, when he knelt in prayer with the Anglican archbishop in the Anglican Canterbury Cathedral in 1982, and, above all, when he convened, in the autumn of 1986, a "World Day of Peace" in Assisi, during which religious leaders of diverse convictions prayed in each other's company. Many Catholics argued that these gestures made the impression that all religions (including sheer idolatry) were to the pope equal means to salvation. Even if he himself offered "conservative" explanations for his own radical gestures, these gestures spoke for themselves and showed the world that theological differences were not that important after all (this critique was also voiced by Cardinal Ratzinger, who later ceased the Assisi prayer when serving as Pope Benedict XVI).[10] Nevertheless, there was no overt contradiction between John Paul II's official theology and the implicit theology that resonated from his other activities, precisely because his pastoral gestures were not theologically articulated. The language of the pope was thus traditional and authoritative at the same time that it was equivocal and vague.

However, it was not only when he sought to introduce progressive reforms but also when he acted as a conservative to bolster the authority of the pope and of the church hierarchy that John Paul II often introduced changes outside the theological realm. He encouraged charismatic, conservative, and popular Catholic communities. He cultivated the worship of the popular stigmatist Italian Capuchin saint Padre Pio (beatified in 1999 and canonized in 2002), whose case raised grave suspicions and was heavily criticized by Pope John XXIII. John Paul II preferred conservative Catholic communities and orders (such as Opus Dei) over groups considered more elitist (such as the Jesuits), and he made it clear that when reforms were needed, charisma was preferred to intellectual inquiry, community cohesion to critical reflection, and gestures to words.

John Paul II thus worked in two parallel trajectories. While holding to a steadfast conservative position on the doctrinal level, he carried out his revolutions "under cover," preferring to avoid any explicit expression of the tension between official ideology, as encoded in doctrinal formulations, and the unexpressed ideology that arose from his gestures.[11] This double effort of John Paul II to preserve Catholic doctrine and protect conservative theology on the one hand and to introduce radical changes on the pastoral and practical levels on the other seemed to stem from a sense that at this stage of history, the potential harm of theological reforms outweighed their benefits. The tendency to "correct" what had been painstakingly built over millennia seemed to John Paul II both reckless and risky. Moreover, in a postmodern world addicted to televised gestures and sound bites, *any* theology, be it left-wing or right-wing, with its hard-to-understand technical jargon and emphasis on philosophical distinctions that most believers found meaningless, only pushed believers away instead of attracting them. The pope's goal was to bring the masses back to the church, and he believed that this end would be more easily accomplished through symbols and gestures than through theological sophistry. In many matters, John Paul II defended theology by diverting attention away from it without impairing its doctrinal content. A decade into his long pontificate, it was already clear to all that the theological renaissance generated by Vatican II was over. Theology was no longer a major avenue for renewing church life or reexamining its relations with the world. It was important mostly to signify to the world that the church remained faithful to itself and did not surrender to passing fashions.

Christian-Jewish Reconciliation in the 1980s

Research on John Paul II tends to emphasize the personal history of this pope as a crucial catalyst for his commitment to reconciling the church with the Jews.[12] Indeed, in his youth, Karol Wojtyła had friendship ties with Jews, ties that undoubtedly influenced his opinions. As a young seminarian, he personally witnessed the Holocaust (his hometown, Wadowice, was located less than twenty miles from Auschwitz), and it left a deep impression.[13]

However, John Paul II's position on the Jews cannot be exhausted by reference to personal tendencies or memories, for it is obvious that he also understood the bond between the church and the Jewish people as a symbol of something far greater, and he carefully wove his personal ties with Jewish friends into his narrative of the Polish people, the story of the church in the modern era, and the story of Europe as a whole. Throughout his long pontificate, John Paul II made considerable efforts to connect the increasingly secularized modern culture with its religious roots and to present the Catholic faith as a worthy antidote to the ills of a civilization that had been trampled down by a series of godless ideologies, from Nazism and communism to materialism and individualism. He presented the Christian Gospel as the fount from which human rights arise and as the surest means to protect those rights. To propose Catholicism as a relevant alternative for postwar Europe, it was necessary to convince the world that the cause of the continent's calamities was not its Christian heritage but rather the turning away from that heritage. In the Jewish context, John Paul II attempted to interpret the annihilation of European Jewry as the monstrous fruit of a civilization that had lost its faith.

John Paul II worked to achieve this end by means of a series of symbolic gestures and dramatic verbal statements. The first significant reference that this pope made to the destruction of European Jewry was in the course of his historic visit to Auschwitz in 1979. This visit, which is perceived as a milestone in Polish history and as an important achievement in John Paul II's struggle against communism, took place against the background of a struggle between various parties over the legacy and meaning of Auschwitz.[14] The death camp was deeply significant to the Polish people, who had been conquered and tortured by the Nazis and now suffered under a communist regime. World interest in the camp was also gradually increasing, along with references to Auschwitz as the main site in which the destruction of European Jewry took place.[15]

John Paul II wove the competing narratives together as he presented Poland and the entire world with his own interpretation of the site. He prayed in the starvation cell of the Polish Franciscan priest Maximilian Kolbe, a prominent leader of the Polish church during the interwar period who had been murdered in Auschwitz in 1941 and had been beatified in 1972. (Kolbe's service for the church included supervision of a popular Catholic newspaper that had published antisemitic articles, a matter that John Paul II chose to overlook.) John Paul II used Kolbe's figure to lend Auschwitz a dimension of Christian martyrdom, epitomizing the triumph of human dignity and Christian love over the murderous oppression of apostate regimes—the Nazi regime explicitly, and the communist one implicitly—as an expression of the denial of faith in both God and humankind.[16]

However, John Paul II did not restrict his utterances to the Polish context, declaring in the course of his visit to the camp:

> I have come to pray with all of you . . . and with the whole of Poland and the whole of Europe. Christ wishes that I, who have become the Successor of Peter, should give witness before the world to what constitutes the greatness and the misery of contemporary man, to what is his defeat and his victory. I have come and I kneel on this Golgotha of the modern world. . . . I kneel before all the inscriptions that come one after another bearing the memory of the victims of Birkenau in languages: Polish, English, Bulgarian, Romany [he enumerates the nineteen languages in which the site's commemoration inscriptions are written].[17]

Auschwitz was thereby ascribed a universalist meaning, as expressed in the many languages that told its story. Of the nineteen languages that he enumerated, however, the pope chose to highlight three: Polish, Hebrew, and Russian. As to the Hebrew inscription, he said:

This inscription awakens the memory of the People whose sons and daughters were intended for total extermination. This People draws its origin from Abraham, our father in faith (cf. Rom 4:12) as was expressed by Paul of Tarsus. The very people that received from God the commandment "Thou shalt not kill," itself experienced in a special measure what is meant by killing. It is not permissible for anyone to pass by this inscription with indifference.[18]

By pausing to contemplate the Hebrew inscription, John Paul II identified the singularity of the Jewish history of Auschwitz, which cannot be simplistically universalized. Pondering the significance of the site, the pope chose to emphasize the particular fate of Auschwitz's Jews as a central thread in his universal narrative. His words and gestures were perceived as liberating for the Polish people and empowering for the Catholic community, while at the same time intensifying and accelerating the transformation of the camp into the ultimate and universal symbol of evil. Yet John Paul II also presented Auschwitz as a metonym for the Holocaust of the Jewish people, identifying the specific tragedy of the Jews, and also naming them as Abraham's children along with their Christian counterparts. This focus on the Jewish victims of Auschwitz became increasingly salient in Western thought and culture over the course of the 1980s. The attention given to the unique Auschwitz experience of the Jews by the leader of the Catholic Church was unusual for its time, especially when the audience numbered in the hundreds of thousands.[19] However, John Paul II embedded Jewish suffering within a Christian metanarrative that begins in suffering and ends in salvation, within "this Golgotha of the modern world."

This duality crops up again and again in John Paul II's many references throughout the 1980s to the destruction of European Jewry.[20] The pope repeatedly stresses that without losing anything of its uniqueness, the tragedy of the Jews finds its meaning within the Christian narrative. "The terrible experience" of the Holocaust, which revealed that the Jews "continue [their] particular vocation, showing [themselves] to be still the heirs of that election to which God is faithful," calls us "to commit ourselves to a shared effort of all people of good will to renew 'a civilization of love' here in Europe, inspired by the best Jewish and Christian ideals," he stated in a 1987 address.[21] "And as the two parts of the Bible are distinct but closely related, so are the Jewish people and the Catholic Church," he declared in a speech before the

Anti-Defamation league in 1984.[22] Most importantly, he remarked in 1980, paraphrasing the Epistle to the Romans,

> The first dimension of this dialogue, that is, the meeting between the people of God of the old covenant never revoked by God and that of the new covenant, is at the same time a dialogue within our Church, that is to say, between the first and second part of her Bible. . . . A second dimension of our dialogue—the true and central one—is the meeting between present-day Christian Churches and the present-day people of the Covenant concluded with Moses.[23]

These statements, and especially the declaration according to which the old covenant ("concluded with Moses") was never revoked by God, were pregnant with theological associations. Yet what did John Paul II exactly mean when he said that? Referring to Moses, the pope seemed to imply that it was the Sinai covenant that remained valid. Did this mean that he viewed the Sinai covenant as a soteriological covenant, implying that observing the commandments is a valid means to salvation? Did John Paul II seek to declare that Jewish law leads to salvation without faith in Christ? This possibility was at odds with the pope's multiple statements about the uniqueness of the church and about Jesus Christ as the sole savior of mankind, such as in his encyclical *Redemptoris missio*.[24] Yet John Paul II never refuted other theological interpretations when directly addressing Jews or when discussing Christian-Jewish relations. He did not spell out the theology implied by his words but rather allowed its overtones to echo freely. As far as he was concerned, the critical point was to present the church as a sister to the Jews in their suffering rather than as an accomplice to the crimes against them: "The threat against you was also a threat against us," he declared in Warsaw in 1987. "It was you who suffered this terrible sacrifice of extermination," he continued, "also for the others who were meant for extermination like you."[25] "The dreadful face of a world without, and even against God is revealed here," he said in a sermon in Vienna in 1988, "[a world] whose intentions of extermination were openly directed against the Jewish people, but also against the faith of those who worship the Jew, Jesus of Nazareth, the Savior of the world."[26]

In 1989, at the Vatican, he declared:

> The new paganism and the systems related to it were certainly directed against the Jews, but they were likewise aimed at Christianity, whose

teaching had shaped the soul of Europe. In the people of whose race "according to the flesh, is the Christ" (Rom. 9:5), the Gospel message of the equal dignity of all God's children was being held up to ridicule.[27]

For John Paul II, the fateful bond between Jews and Christians is what gave the Jewish tragedy its significance as a redeeming message of vital importance for all of Europe:

> Faith tells us that God does not desert the persecuted, but rather reveals himself to them and by it enlightens that people [the Jews] on the way to salvation. This is the teaching of Holy Scripture, this is revealed to us in the Prophets, in Isaiah and Jeremiah. In this faith, the common heritage of both Jews and Christians, are the roots of Europe's history. For us Christians, every human suffering finds its ultimate meaning in the Cross of Jesus Christ. However, this does not hinder us, but urges us to sympathize much more in solidarity with the deep wounds which were inflicted on the Jewish people in the persecutions, especially in this century, due to modern anti-Semitism.[28]

John Paul II's historical-theological narrative echoed the arguments raised by the pioneers of the Christian-Jewish turn of the 1940s and 1950s: since the Jews were no longer perceived as the crucifiers of Jesus, but to the contrary, as his closest kinsmen, the murderousness toward them was now construed to have emerged from their persecutors' deep anti-Christian drive to crucify Christ. Thus, Christian antisemitism became impossible by definition. This theological position, already stressed by the council, was expressed by John Paul II in a variety of ways, which transformed it from an apologetic argument into the existential-religious experience of many Catholics vis-à-vis the Jewish people. The Christian-Jewish connection was an important foundation in John Paul II's plan to restore Europe to the tradition of its fathers.

In the same way that John Paul II used the figure of Maximilian Kolbe to charge recent Polish history with religious significance, so did he use two other extraordinary figures—Edith Stein and Jean-Marie Lustiger—to symbolize the Christian-Jewish connection that linked the annihilation of the Jews with the cross and marked the appropriate horizon for Europe. Stein was a German-born Jewish philosopher who converted to Christianity and became a Carmelite nun by the name of Theresa Benedicta of the Cross. Stein, who continued to view herself as a daughter of the Jewish people

even after her conversion, was captured by the Gestapo and murdered in
Auschwitz as a Jew. In the course of his visit to the camp in 1979, John Paul II
mentioned Stein's death alongside that of Kolbe. Despite the fact that, unlike Kolbe, Stein did not willingly sacrifice her life but was murdered because
of her Jewishness, John Paul II described her death as a martyrdom, which
endowed her with "triumph" (that is, salvation). In 1987, John Paul II beatified Stein and called her "a daughter of Israel [*eine Tochter Israels*]" who died
"for the sanctification of God's name" with her people.[29] Stein was canonized in 1998, and in 1999, John Paul II declared her a patron saint of Europe.

Jean-Marie Lustiger was born Aron Lustiger in 1926 to a Jewish family
from Poland.[30] In 1940, he was baptized into Catholicism, to the displeasure
of his parents. In 1942, while he, his sister, and his father found sanctuary in
the south of France, his mother was deported from Paris and ultimately murdered in Auschwitz.[31] Lustiger was ordained a priest in 1954 and subsequently nominated by John Paul II as the bishop of Orléans in 1979, as the
archbishop of Paris in 1981, and as a cardinal in 1983. "The Jewish cardinal,"
who was deeply detested by progressive forces in the French church, defined
himself as a Jew who reached "accomplishment" thanks to his Catholic faith.
Lustiger often claimed that he felt he was not forsaking his Judaism with his
attraction to Christianity but rather discovering its true significance.[32]

Lustiger wished to resurrect the first-century church of the circumcised
(*ecclesia ex circumcisione*), which had lived harmoniously with the church of
the gentiles (*ecclesia ex gentibus*) but had disappeared with the increase in
the hostility between the religions. He repeatedly claimed that Christianity
was not supposed to be the religion of the gentiles that had replaced the religion of the Jews, but rather that there was room for both Jews and gentiles,
one alongside the other within the church of the Messiah.[33] While he echoed
Balthasar, Jacques Maritain, and others who had written on the subject in
earlier periods, Lustiger claimed that antisemitism emerged because Christians of pagan origin (that is, those who joined the church from among the
gentiles) grew envious of the Jews for having been chosen before them and
attempted to establish themselves as sole inheritors rather than as partners
of their elder brothers.[34] He claimed that the pagan temptation to be rid of
Judaism began from Marcion's call in the second century to be rid of the Old
Testament and ended in the Protestant theology that attempted to detach
Jesus from the Jewish people and view him as a member of the Aryan race.[35]
In other words, Lustiger viewed antisemitism as an idolatrous invasion into
Christianity, alien to the spirit of Christianity itself. The continuity between

Judaism and Christianity was thus destroyed not by the Catholic Church but by its enemies. Luther and Hitler were the architects of antisemitism (and Marx too, despite being Jewish!), for the essence of antisemitism is denial of Israel's divine election. It was they who had created the divide between the two religions and wished to erase God himself by erasing his chosen people—both conceptually and physically—from the face of the earth.[36]

Yet the Christian-Jewish theology that was reflected in Lustiger's life story was far more important than his intellectual cogitations on the issue. Stein and Lustiger, two converted Jews who felt a deep sense of solidarity with their kindred, demonstrated the insistence of the church that, exactly like them, it had never forsaken the Jews or its Jewish past but rather had charged its Jewish legacy with a new soteriological significance. A nun who shared the fate of her siblings in Auschwitz and a Jewish cardinal who lost his mother there, Stein and Lustiger linked the Holocaust and the cross through their Judeo-Christian life stories.

John Paul II's Judeo-Christian symbolic system provided an apt illustration of the theological claim that the attitude of Catholic Christianity toward Judaism was one of "fulfillment" rather than "replacement" (in accordance with Matt. 5:17). Instead of formulating the new paradigm via theological arguments, John Paul II formulated it performatively. However, this dramatic treatment of the Holocaust by the pope had contradictory consequences. On the one hand, papal attention boosted the global importance ascribed to the preservation of the memory of the Holocaust and the struggle against antisemitism in a way that probably far exceeded what theological arguments could have achieved. On the other hand, the highly public symbolic expropriation of the Holocaust to incorporate it into a Catholic historical metanarrative of a "Judeo-Christianity" gave rise to bitter antagonism over many years and created obstacles to Christian-Jewish reconciliation. Had John Paul II been content with statements and sermons, his attitude toward the Jews might have been less controversial than it ultimately became. The celebration of Mass under the shadow of a huge cross at "the world's greatest Jewish graveyard," however, was another matter. So, too, was the veneration of Kolbe and Stein, which many Jews perceived as the dubious adulation of an antisemitic priest and a *meshumedet* (the derogatory term for a convert to Christianity, parsed from the word *shemad*, "destruction"). When directed at the Holocaust, the embrace of the Jews by the Catholic Church since *Nostra aetate* was perceived as suffocating. As we have seen, theologians were well aware of this tension, and many of them had already abstained from theologizing the Holocaust in this way. Yet John Paul II's grand gestures brought to the surface what had passed with relatively little remonstration on the theological level. The ambivalence that broke through John Paul II's gestures evoked increasing disfavor within the Jewish world, which, like the church, was also busy reconstructing its attitude to its European past.

This Jewish disapprobation found its most significant expression in the protracted dispute over the Carmelite convent at Auschwitz. On August 1, 1984, a dozen or so Carmelite nuns established themselves at the "Theater," the building that had been used by the Nazis to store the poisonous gas Zyklon B (at Auschwitz I). A large cross was erected in the garden of the building. The entire matter became publicly known only a year later, following distribution in Belgium of a leaflet titled "Help a Church in Need."[37] The leaflet attempted to raise funds for the Carmelite convent, which was to be dedicated to the pope.[38] Jewish organizations and leaders throughout the world vehemently protested the founding of the convent. In 1986, a delegation of Jews met with Catholic Church officials (Cardinal Lustiger among them) to discuss the issue, and in 1987 it was agreed that the convent would be transferred to an adjacent location, outside the camp, within two years.[39]

When the two years elapsed and the convent was still in place in 1989, the protests were renewed with increased vigor. Rabbi Avraham Weiss and his students from Riverdale, New York, protested in front of the convent and even climbed the garden wall—an action that ended in a physical clash with the convent employees and exacerbated the conflict even more.[40] Cardinal Glemp, the primate of the Polish Catholic Church, claimed that the protesters intended to murder the nuns and complained that the Jews controlled the media.[41] The prime minister of Israel, Yitzhak Shamir, declared that all Poles suckle antisemitism with their mother's milk.[42]

Jewish protests over the Auschwitz convent were not all cut from the same cloth. Some called for violent action, while others demanded that the problem be solved entirely through diplomatic channels. Some thought that the camp should be "universalist" in nature and "void" of all religious attributes, while others considered a Star of David to be more appropriate than a cross.[43] One way or another, many argued that the fact that 90 percent of the victims of Auschwitz were Jews should be taken into consideration when discussing the commemoration of the site (or in the undiplomatic formulation of Adi Steg, then president of the Alliance israélite universelle, the Jewish people "have inalienable rights to Auschwitz").[44]

The poignant protest within the Jewish world brought to the surface the incompatibility of the Christian and the Jewish metanarratives: the former viewed Christians as siblings of the Jews in suffering and the Gospel as the realization of Judaism's hopes, while the latter viewed Christians as accomplices to Nazi crimes and the Nazis themselves as the executors of the ancient Christian hope for the annihilation of the Jewish people. In other words, while the church was largely occupied in distancing Christianity from antisemitism and binding Christians to the Jewish victims of the Holocaust, Jewish communities were largely occupied with binding Christians to antisemites, as perpetrators. This is how Dov Shilanski, a Knesset member on behalf of the Likud, presented the issue to the Knesset: "Our forefathers went through the seven gates of hell . . . and never in their lives did they convert or bow to the cross. Now, after they are dead, the symbol of their tormentors is to be placed on top of their tormented bodies. What they were unable to do to them while they were alive, they are coming now to do to them, spiritually, after their death."[45]

Thus, the memory games of the Polish church were perceived by many Jews as a symbolic extension of their physical extermination. The disregard of the Polish church for Jewish historical consciousness was experienced as contiguous with the extermination of the Jews. Again and again, Jewish thinkers, scholars, and leaders emphasized that setting up crosses and convents and a cult of martyrs did not make Auschwitz into a site of Christian salvation and love but rather effaced the uniqueness of Jewish suffering, which was not voluntary and was not sweetened in the memory of the survivors as a path to salvation. Some even complained that the very use of the English word *Holocaust* was tarnished by Christian conceptions that would endow the Jewish catastrophe with the flavor of an expiating sacrifice.[46]

The Catholic Church was expected to disentangle its narrative from the Jewish one and to relinquish its claim to be remembered as a victim of the Nazis, and even more so, to admit its share in the culpability of the aggressors. It was in this context that the dispute over the "silence" of Pius XII during the Holocaust became more pointed. Jews demanded that the church both give a historical accounting of its actions and be willing to perceive them on their own terms rather than as a chapter in the ecclesiastical narrative. In other words, once John Paul II began using Jews as a Christian symbol, Jews struggled to be the interpreters of their own history and negotiated resolutely for the use of symbols they claimed for themselves.

The dispute between the Carmelite nuns and the heads of the Polish church and Jewish representatives was intimately associated with the dramatic symbolism of the Polish pope's visit to Auschwitz in 1979 and therefore raised doubts about the sincerity of his efforts to reconcile with the Jewish people. A number of sermons that John Paul II gave over the course of the second half of the 1980s during the conflict over the convent were perceived by Jews as expressing agreement with pre–Vatican II replacement theology, which they had hoped had been relegated to the past.[47] In addition, the fact that the Vatican refused to recognize the State of Israel as a political entity was a further cause of outrage within the Jewish world, as it was interpreted as arising from anti-Jewish theological considerations.[48] The refusal to establish diplomatic relations with Israel was perceived as just another rejection of Jewish historical consciousness. The meeting of John Paul II with the chairman of the Palestinian Liberation Organization, Yasser Arafat, in 1982, and with the Austrian president, Kurt Waldheim, who was suspected of having participated in the deportation of the Balkan Jews during his service as a Wehrmacht officer, enhanced the tensions between the Vatican and the Jewish community.

John Paul II's efforts to allay the tension were also made via performative gestures rather than any theological argument. The most celebrated gesture he made in the course of this tense period was his historical visit to the Great Synagogue in Rome. Within the synagogue, after some words of thanks, the pope began by saying:

> I would like us to reflect together, in the presence of the Holy One—may He be blessed! (as your liturgy says)—on the fact and the significance of this meeting between the Bishop of Rome, the Pope, and the Jewish community that lives and works in this city which is so dear to you and to me. I had been thinking of this visit for a long time. . . . The heritage that I would now like to take up is precisely that of Pope John, who on one occasion, as he passed by here . . . stopped the car so that he could bless the crowd of Jews who were coming out of this very Temple. And I would like to take up his heritage at this very moment, when I find myself not just outside but, thanks to your generous hospitality, inside the Synagogue of Rome.[49]

In entering the synagogue, John Paul II signaled that he took seriously the plea of many Jews to be seen according to their own terms and not as an inner-Christian category. It was his appeal to this profound Jewish sensitivity that distinguished the enterprise of John Paul II from all other previous promoters of Christian-Jewish reconciliation. This gesture was so powerful that it made it easier for John Paul II to refrain from discussing, or to circumvent, the issues that he wished to avoid.

Previous drafts of his synagogue speech indicate that John Paul II deliberated whether to assume explicit responsibility for the role of Catholics in the fate of the Jews of Europe.[50] Yet these self-recriminations were omitted from the speech (it was not until the 1990s that John Paul II would make such explicit statements). Instead, John Paul II said:

> This gathering in a way brings to a close . . . a long period which we must not tire of reflecting upon in order to draw from it the appropriate lessons. Certainly, we cannot and should not forget that the historical circumstances of the past were very different from those that have laboriously matured over the centuries. The general acceptance of a legitimate plurality on the social, civil and religious levels has been arrived at with great difficulty. Nevertheless, a consideration of centuries-long cultural conditioning could not prevent us from recognizing that the acts of discrimination, unjustified limitation of religion freedom, oppression also on the level of civil freedom in regard to the Jews were, from an objective point of view, gravely deplorable manifestations. Yes, once again, through myself, the church, in the words of the well-known Declaration *Nostra Aetate* (no. 4), "deplores the hatred, persecutions and displays of anti-Semitism directed against the Jews at any time and by anyone"; I repeat: by anyone.[51]

John Paul II also refrained from referring to the State of Israel, despite the fact that Elio Toaff, Rome's chief rabbi, explicitly implored him to do so. Toaff mentioned the biblical promise given to the Jewish people that they will return to the Land of Israel and claimed:

> This Return is actually happening: the survivors of the Nazi death camps have found a refuge in the Land of Israel, and a new life of liberty and dignity that are gained anew [*riconquistata*]. It is for this reason that our rabbis named this return: "the beginning of the coming of the final redemption."[52] The return of the Jewish people to its land has to be acknowledged as a good and as an unequivocal achievement for

the world, because it preludes—according to the teaching of the prophets—the age of universal brotherhood for which all are hoping, and the redeeming peace that finds its certain promise in the Bible. The recognition of this irreplaceable function of Israel in the final plan of redemption which God has promised us cannot be denied.[53]

The pope, reported Riccardo Di Segni (Toaff's successor as Rome's chief rabbi), responded to these demands with a biblical reference: "For everything there is a season, and a time for every matter under heaven" (Eccl. 3:1).[54] At the high point of his synagogue speech, John Paul II said:

> The Church of Christ discovers her "bond" with Judaism by "searching into her own mystery" (cf. *Nostra Aetate* [Article 4]). The Jewish religion is not "extrinsic" to us, but in a certain way is "intrinsic" to our own religion. With Judaism therefore we have a relationship which we do not have with any other religion. You are our dearly beloved brothers and, in a certain way, it could be said that you are our elder brothers.[55]

Following the synagogue sermon, the expression *elder brothers* became paradigmatic for Christian-Jewish reconciliation, despite the fact that the expression itself was not only far from revolutionary but bore the explosive undercurrent of the Christian-Jewish competition over the identity of Jacob (the younger brother).[56] The link made by the pope between the firstborn and love gave this statement a new significance, as if the family relationship actually did produce fraternity rather than hostility.[57] This is an impressive example of the pope's choice to eschew semantics and rely on pragmatics instead. The context, the tone, the implications, and the emotional expression replaced theological work and left the most sensitive theological issues untouched.

Christian-Jewish Reconciliation in the 1990s

The theological discussions about the Jewish "refusal" of Jesus, the need to work for the Jews' conversion, or the question of the Jews' access to salvation outside the church through observing the mitzvoth (commandments), had given rise to firm and contentious positions. John Paul II let all this go. His expressions of fraternity were of another type—they did not test the mettle of central doctrines and traditions or the goodwill to reconcile with the Jewish people and reach an understanding with them.

One of the most prominent advantages of John Paul II's expressive style was that it could be adapted to circumstances without falling into contradictions. Such adaptations were made in the 1990s. Despite the evident success of the synagogue visit, the first decade of John Paul II's incumbency as pope ended in an atmosphere of hostility and suspicion. The Carmelite convent in Auschwitz remained in place despite the agreement that had been made, and the State of Israel continued to remain outside the agenda of the Holy See.[58] John Paul II was thus perceived at this stage as speaking with a forked tongue. On the one hand, he had expressed a desire to strengthen the ties of the Catholic Church with the Jewish world and give credence to the way in which Jews perceive themselves; on the other hand, he continued to ignore (Zionist) Jews' deepest identity demands (which were not so much theological as historical and political, touching the memory of the Holocaust and acknowledgment of the State of Israel).

After the fall of the Eastern Bloc—probably one of John Paul II's greatest aspirations since his election—the pope was able to increase the flexibility of his symbolic language and take it another step toward the Jewish world of meaning. His strategy in the 1990s was to shift emphasis from the Catholic metanarrative that maintained Christian-Jewish relations as an antithesis to atheism and paganism and to emphasize conversations with actual Jews instead. Rather than signal to the world and to the church that Judaism was "subsumed" within Catholic identity, the pope now placed the uniqueness of the Jewish experience at the center of his gestures. In other words, it was during the 1990s that John Paul II completed his about-face from focusing on Judaism "on the inside"—inside the Christian canon, inside the postconcilar polemics, and inside the array of forces that were contending over the future of Europe—to dealing with Jews "on the outside" who were largely unconcerned with these matters.

The main demand that Jewish representatives made on the Vatican was to sever the Gordian knot that church officials had created by attempting to tie Jews and Christians together as victims of the Nazis. When faced with the option of portraying Jews and Catholics as having been on the same side during the twentieth century, many Jews preferred to see themselves as standing alone against a non-Jewish world congealed into a single murderous mass. In this narrative, modern antisemitism was not an essentially different category from Christian anti-Judaism, and the Holocaust differed from previous persecutions only in scale; through this prism, the pistol that appeared in the first act, with the deicide charge, went off in the third act, with the Final Solution.

Just as the main Catholic narrative was significant within the ecumenical project for the moral and cultural rehabilitation of Europe, so the main Jewish narrative was essential for the Zionist project, in which the rejection of diasporic existence was incompatible with a conception of Europe as having a positive Judeo-Christian legacy. Those "bridging" figures that the pope had elevated—such as Franz Rosenzweig, Martin Buber, and Edith Stein—were largely pushed away from the Israeli project. More than seeing Christians as potential partners for the construction of a common civilization, Jews expected their Christian counterparts to justify Zionism and the State of Israel. The demand that the Vatican acknowledge the Jewish past in Europe as a past of persecution, often Catholic persecution, was intimately linked with the other demand presented by Jewish representatives—that the church recognize the State of Israel as the only possible alternative to a persecuting Europe. These demands were, in fact, two sides of the same coin.

Senior church officials gradually began conceding to these demands. In 1990, the Australian bishop Edward Cassidy, who had replaced Johannes Cardinal Willebrands as the head of the Commission for Religious Relations with the Jews (CRRJ), declared in a symposium convened in Theresienstadt that "the fact that anti-Semitism had found a place within Christianity calls for penitential acts."[59] Local bishop conferences (in Germany, France, Poland, the United States, and other places) issued apologies for the part played by their churches in the persecution of the Jews. The word *Holocaust,* which had gradually been phased out of Catholic discourse, was replaced with a transliteration of the Hebrew word *Shoah.* In 1993, the pope finally intervened and demanded that the Carmelite nuns leave the "Theater" at Auschwitz. At the end of that same year, in tandem with the popularity that the August 1993 Oslo Agreements bestowed on Israel (and perhaps also following the direct appeal of the then US president George Bush to John Paul II in December 1992), Yossi Beilin, the Israeli foreign minister, and Archbishop Claudio Maria Celli, the deputy chairman of the Vatican for relations with nations, signed a fundamental agreement between the State of Israel and the Holy See.[60]

In 1996, the American Jewish Committee appealed to the pope to issue an encyclical that would denounce antisemitism.[61] Shortly thereafter, the Vatican began work on the formulation of a document investigating the historical roots of antisemitism among Catholics. In 1998, on the eve of the millennium, the CRRJ published the official document "We Remember: A Reflection on the Shoah" ("Noi ricordiamo: Una riflessione sulla Shoah").[62]

This document, which was part of John Paul II's project of urging the Catholic world to repent for the sins of the past, was devoted to a detailed historical accounting of the behavior of the church during the Holocaust:

> Historians, sociologists, political philosophers, psychologists and theologians are all trying to learn more about the reality of the *Shoah* and its causes. Much scholarly study still remains to be done. But such an event cannot be fully measured by the ordinary criteria of historical research alone. It calls for a "moral and religious memory" and, particularly among Christians, a very serious reflection on what gave rise to it. The fact that the *Shoah* took place in Europe, that is, in countries of long-standing Christian civilization, raises the question of the relation between the Nazi persecution and the attitudes down the centuries of Christians towards the Jews.[63]

Without raising the complex theological issues of typology, of replacement and fulfillment, of preaching the Gospel to the Jews, or of their salvation with or without Christ, the authors of "We Remember" chose to focus on the practical manifestations of Christian hostility toward Jews throughout history, from the "disputes between the early Church and the Jewish leaders and people" after the crucifixion of Jesus through mobs' attacks on synagogues in late antiquity, the deportations and forced conversions of the Middle Ages, and finally, the legal discriminations against Jews in the eighteenth century. The authors did not hesitate to lay a heavy burden of responsibility on Catholics' shoulders for their bad attitude toward the Jews who lived among them:

> Despite that fact, Jews throughout Christendom held on to their religious traditions and communal customs. They were therefore looked upon with a certain suspicion and mistrust. In times of crisis such as famine, war, pestilence or social tensions, the Jewish minority was sometimes taken as a scapegoat and became the victim of violence, looting, even massacres.[64]

Nevertheless, the authors strove to be precise in their definition of the boundaries of this responsibility and made two important distinctions. First, in line with *Nostra aetate*, Article 4, they clarified once more that Christian hostility toward Jews *does not* stem from Scripture but only from a distorted interpretation of Scripture: "Despite the Christian preaching of love for all, even for one's enemies, the prevailing mentality down the centuries penalized minorities and those who were in any way 'different.'"

Second, alongside the assumption of responsibility for the hostility of Christians toward the Jewish people, the document's authors emphasized that the nature of Christian hostility differed from that of secular antisemitism, which had grown up from a background of modern nationalist and racist theories: "There began to spread in varying degrees throughout most of Europe an anti-Judaism that was essentially more sociological and political than religious."[65] And subsequently:

> Thus we cannot ignore the difference which exists between anti-Semitism based on theories contrary to the constant teaching of the Church on the unity of the human race and on the equal dignity of all races and peoples, and the long-standing sentiments of mistrust and hostility that we call anti-Judaism, of which, unfortunately, Christians also have been guilty. . . . At the level of theological reflection we cannot ignore the fact that not a few in the Nazi party not only showed aversion to the idea of divine Providence at work in human affairs, but gave proof of a definite hatred directed at God himself. Logically, such an attitude also led to a rejection of Christianity, and a desire to see the Church destroyed or at least subjected to the interests of the Nazi state. It was this extreme ideology which became the basis of the measures taken, first to drive the Jews from their homes and then to exterminate them. The *Shoah* was the work of a thoroughly modern neo-pagan regime. Its anti-Semitism had its roots outside of Christianity and, in pursuing its aims, it did not hesitate to oppose the Church and persecute her members also.[66]

This paragraph positions "We Remember" in the middle ground between the Christian narrative that identified Christians as brothers and sisters to Jewish suffering under the Nazis and the Jewish narrative that presented the extermination of the Jews as a common interest of Christians and Nazis. "We Remember" admits that Catholic Christians did not experience the Shoah and had themselves expressed hostility toward Jews, to the point of murder. At the same time, they were not Nazis themselves; they opposed the Nazis, and the Nazis persecuted them. The authors made a considerable effort to clarify that these distinctions were not made to absolve Christians of their responsibility but rather to clearly delineate its boundaries:

But it may be asked whether the Nazi persecution of the Jews was not made easier by the anti-Jewish prejudices embedded in some Christian minds and hearts. Did anti-Jewish sentiment among Christians make them less sensitive, or even indifferent, to the persecutions launched against the Jews by National Socialism when it reached power?

The document provides a complex response to this question:

Did Christians give every possible assistance to those being persecuted, and in particular to the persecuted Jews? Many did, but others did not. Those who did help to save Jewish lives as much as was in their power, even to the point of placing their own lives in danger, must not be forgotten. During and after the war, Jewish communities and Jewish leaders expressed their thanks for all that had been done for them, including what Pope Pius XII did personally or through his representatives to save hundreds of thousands of Jewish lives. Many Catholic bishops, priests, religious and laity have been honored for this reason by the State of Israel. Nevertheless, as Pope John Paul II has recognized, alongside such courageous men and women, the spiritual resistance and concrete action of other Christians was not that which might have been expected from Christ's followers. We cannot know how many Christians in countries occupied or ruled by the Nazi powers or their allies were horrified at the disappearance of their Jewish neighbors and yet were not strong enough to raise their voices in protest. For Christians, this heavy burden of conscience of their brothers and sisters during the Second World War must be a call to penitence. We deeply regret the errors and failures of those sons and daughters of the Church.[67]

"We Remember" elicited mixed responses. Several critics felt that the document was intended not so much to encourage the church to contend with its share in the Holocaust as to provide cover for the church to shirk its responsibility.[68] In particular, the fact that it mentioned the name of Pius XII only in a positive context (in his pushing for the saving of hundreds of thousands of Jews) without responding to the question of why the pope never publicly denounced the murder of the Jews drew considerable fire.[69] There were even those who claimed that the declarations of local bishop conferences displayed greater courage in their willingness to assume responsibility for the church's sins against the Jews, and that the document was a disappointment and a step backward.[70]

Yet even if the content of the various historical claims in "We Remember" was not in line with the prevailing Jewish historical account of the role of the church in the Holocaust, the very questions that the document posed reflected a willingness within the church to adapt its Holocaust discourse to the main concerns expressed by Jewish representatives. The very genre of the document and the main questions that guided it testify to a deep change in the way that church officials and representatives involved in dialogue with Jews approached their task. "We Remember" was fundamentally different from the two previous documents issued by the CRRJ ("Guidelines and Suggestions" from 1974 and "Notes" from 1985). These focused mainly on integrating the theological heritage of *Nostra aetate* into Catholic preaching, scriptural exegesis, sermons, and education and were intended primarily for the consumption of Catholic clergy. "We Remember" was directed not only inward but also outward, to Jewish eyes (it should be remembered that the document was written in response to a Jewish request), and its authors almost completely refrained from addressing theological issues (except for the argument regarding the secular-pagan nature of antisemitism). The document responded to the recurring demand of Jewish leaders that the church provide an accounting for its problematic past with the Jews. In this respect, in "We Remember," the CRRJ adopted its perception of the "Jewish view" as the criterion for examining the history of the relations between the church and the Jews, even if it did not necessarily identify with the Jewish claims. The church accepted the burden of proving that there was no continuity between its teaching and Nazi racism, a paradigmatic change when compared with the way this issue had been addressed in the past. Moreover, the authors had embedded, at the heart of their document, an expression of remorse, though this expression was not as encompassing as many Jews might have hoped. This was not another intra-Catholic theological document but an intercommunal historical one that was dedicated to a different set of problems.

The criticisms directed at "We Remember" were absorbed by the pope and his representatives. In the following years, instead of painstakingly defining the precise historical circumstances and insisting on forming the exact boundaries of the church's responsibility, the pope and his representatives placed expressing remorse to the Jews at the center of their endeavors, without splitting too many historical hairs.[71] The dry historical discourse and semi-academic texts were replaced with impressive religious events and the illustrious prayers of the pope himself. On the international Day of Pardon, conducted on March 12, 2000, the first Sunday of Lent, as part of the millennium celebrations, John Paul II held a special mass for repentance and absolution, where he and Cardinal Cassidy confessed "sins against the people of Israel."[72] Cardinal Cassidy opened the prayer with these words:

> Let us pray that, in recalling the sufferings endured by the people of Israel throughout history, Christians will acknowledge the sins committed by not a few of their number against the people of the Covenant and the blessings, and in this way will purify their hearts. [Silent prayer]

John Paul II then continued:

> God of our fathers, you chose Abraham and his descendants to bring your Name to the Nations: we are deeply saddened by the behavior of those who in the course of history have caused these children of yours to suffer, and asking your forgiveness we wish to commit ourselves to genuine brotherhood with the people of the Covenant. We ask this through Christ our Lord. Amen.[73]

Two weeks later, John Paul II went on a pilgrimage to the Holy Land. His visit was a grand demonstration of erudition in the Israeli-Jewish symbolic system and identification with it. John Paul II made an effort to persuade Israelis that he respected Jewish sovereignty. In contradistinction to Paul VI's visit to the region, this one was an official state visit; the pope did not limit himself to just the Christian sites but came to the Western Wall and respected Jewish customs by placing a note in a crack in the ancient wall. On that note, he wrote the text of his prayer on the Day of Pardon, with the request for forgiveness from God—without Cassidy's words and, most importantly, without the final sentence addressed to Christ, so as not to offend Jewish sentiments.

The high point of the trip was John Paul II's visit to the Yad Vashem Holocaust Museum in Jerusalem. "There are no words strong enough to deplore the terrible tragedy of the Shoah," he said there.[74] Paraphrasing *Nostra aetate*, he went on to denounce antisemitism but added a reference to Christian sins: "I assure the Jewish people that the Catholic Church, motivated by the Gospel law of truth and love, and by no political considerations, is deeply saddened by the hatred, acts of persecution and displays of antisemitism directed against the Jews *by Christians* at any time and in any place."[75]

This unequivocal expression of remorse proved a turning point in Jews' feelings toward the Catholic Church. The papal acknowledgment of the Holocaust involved more than moral commitment to the victims' memory. John Paul II officially recognized the raison d'être of the Jewish state. He was well aware of the implicit expectations the Jewish public held as he visited one of its holiest secular sites: to acknowledge the horror of the Shoah and apologize for Christian crimes of commission and omission that may have contributed, whether directly or indirectly, to the annihilation of European Jewry. During the ceremony, the audience heard how at the end of the war, the young Karol Wojtyła carried a labor camp survivor by the name of Edith Zierer in his arms to safety. Moreover, Jewish friends from Wadowice testified to his sincere sympathy for the Jews and his kindness to them—before, during, and after the war.

During his papal visit, John Paul II also made a point of initiating official dialogue between local representatives of the Holy See and the Chief Rabbinate. This, too, attested to his recognition of Jewish sovereignty and of Israeli institutions as partners for dialogue with the church.

These significant gestures, combined with John Paul II's extraordinary charisma, turned the visit to the Holy Land into a triumph. According to public opinion, within three short days, the pope seemed to have done more for Christian-Jewish reconciliation than had been accomplished in three decades of cautiously articulated statements.

By the end of John Paul II's pontificate in 2005, the relations between the Jews and the Catholic Church were, at least on the surface, better than ever. The sharp disputes among Catholic theologians had ebbed away, and no one continued to demand a radical doctrinal reform. The theological complexity of the relationship now interested only a handful of experts, most of them American theologians, while the friendly and semi-official dialogues between Jewish and Christian representatives were brought to the fore. The pope's moves transformed Christian-Jewish reconciliation from an effort of liberal reformers to one of mainstream Catholic conservatism; circumventing the sensitive theological questions, it was no longer a threat to conservative identity. On the contrary, Christian-Jewish rapprochement became one of its central markers, even if the exact contents of this Judeo-Christian heritage were not always clear. It seemed that both Jews and Catholics now saw eye to eye and agreed that the church's willingness to apologize for its historical wrongs was sufficient, even without exhausting the finer details of doctrine. The pope's statements about the Jews—particularly, referring to them as "the people of God of the old covenant never revoked by God" and stating, "You are our dearly beloved brothers, and in a certain way, it could be said, our elder brothers"—became the ultimate symbols of the new interreligious dialogue.[76] Powerfully symbolic, also, were the images of the pope leaning against the Western Wall or talking with the rabbis of Rome and Jerusalem.

The fact that the theological meaning of these statements remained inconclusive did not seem to bother anyone. It could even be said that it had been an advantage—that it strengthened the general sense that the church had resolved its doctrinal problems with Judaism to the point that it could now look squarely at flesh-and-blood Jews. It appeared that both Jews and Christians had agreed to abandon their complex theological polemics around the Jewish refusal to recognize Christ, divine election, the covenant, and salvation, and befriend each other on a human and diplomatic basis, with religious tradition adding an aspect of dignity to this setting, which largely transcended its original language. This abandonment was acceptable to the public opinion of both Jews and Christians. For the Jews, the theological discourse had always been alien, and they had always protested against their conversion into a theological category. For Christians, the theological discourse had been charged and traumatic, threatening the fragile balance between the existence of the church as an ethical entity in an enlightened world and its loyalty to a tradition that was often mired in contradictions.

4

Joseph Ratzinger and the Jews

Few of the theologians who "made" Vatican II were still active in the 1990s. Henri de Lubac and Yves Congar were very old, Karl Rahner and Hans Urs von Balthasar were dead, and Edward Schillebeeckx and Hans Küng were far from the Catholic mainstream. The dust of liberation theology had already settled, and just a few new stars were seen on the horizon of the Catholic intelligentsia. However, together with the Curia's methodical effort to stifle liberal global Catholic theology (out of fear of relativism, postmodernism, and the liberalization of theology), the church sought to cultivate a school of authoritative theology that would follow the magisterium's guidelines closely. One of the key members of this school was Joseph Ratzinger, in his work both as an independent theologian and as the prefect of the Congregation for the Doctrine of the Faith (CDF) from 1981 to 2005, where he presided over the church's theological policy. To a significant extent, Ratzinger was the last active representative of the theologians who had been influential at the council.

Because John Paul II shifted the center of gravity in relations with the Jews from the theological to the symbolic, the vibrant theological discourse in the church about Jews and Judaism in the preceding decades had significantly dwindled. Conversely, the focus on interfaith dialogue moved to the center.[1] In Europe and elsewhere, systematic theological debates were replaced by friendly, semi-intellectual dialogues between Christian officials (not only Catholic) and Jewish rabbis from various denominations. Many of these public dialogues were subsequently published in book form.[2]

It was precisely at this belated stage, after mainstream Catholic theology had largely abandoned it, that Ratzinger became involved in the theological discussion about the relations between the Jews and the church. Judaism had never been central to Ratzinger's theological work, which focused on the relations between faith and reason, Christology, ecclesiology, and liturgy. His study of Judaism had always been part of a broader discussion about the problems of faith in the modern and postmodern world. Nevertheless, he made a unique contribution to the theological discussion on Judaism. Precisely because he was not an active participant in interreligious dialogue, unlike most theologians who continued to write on Jews and Judaism in the mid-1980s and later, but was simply an important Catholic theologian, Ratzinger could demarginalize the discussion of Judaism and place it in the wider context of Catholic theology. Ratzinger's insights on this subject, as included in the trilogy he wrote as a pope, *Jesus of Nazareth,* reached an audience probably broader than that reached by any formal declaration ever published by the pontifical Commission for Religious Relations with the Jews (CRRJ).

Unlike John Paul II, Ratzinger did not have a special personal relation with Jews. The importance he attached to this issue emerged first and foremost from his struggle to connect the secularized West with its Christian roots by renewing theology and distilling doctrine. Because Christianity's roots were bound with Judaism, and the split between the two was the first in a long history of partitions, relations with Judaism were emblematic for the shaping of the relationship between Christianity and secular modern culture; reconnecting Christianity with its Jewish roots was paradigmatically important to reconnect modern culture with Christianity.

Ratzinger's stand on Judaism did not change significantly after his appointment to the papacy in 2005. His different hats often required, however, that he discuss the matter in different ways. This chapter follows Ratzinger's approach to Jews and Judaism in two sections, reflecting Ratzinger's guises as both theologian and church official. The first discusses Ratzinger's theology concerning Judaism and the Jews since he began writing on the subject. The second concerns major polemics around two official documents: *Dominus Iesus,* whose writing Ratzinger oversaw as prefect of the CDF, and the revised Good Friday Prayer for Jews in the Tridentine Rite, which he composed as Pope Benedict XVI. Ratzinger's last and most important contribution to the Catholic theology of Judaism appeared in an article he published in *Communio* in 2018. This contribution, which is beyond the historical scope of this book, is briefly discussed in the Epilogue.

Ratzinger's Hermeneutic Jews: Marcionism, Antisemitism, and the Christian Canon

The importance of Ratzinger's work on Jews and Judaism lies in the fact that he integrated the questions of Christian-Jewish relations into the wider landscape of Catholic theology. Nevertheless, this integration came at a cost, since Judaism often became a tool in the service of promoting other theological agendas. An example can be found in Ratzinger's preface to the Pontifical Biblical Commission (PBC) document *The Jewish People and Their Sacred Scriptures in the Christian Bible* (2002). As the head of the CDF, Ratzinger had also served as the president of the PBC and oversaw the writing of the document. *The Jewish People and Their Sacred Scriptures in the Christian Bible* deals with the Hebrew Bible and the Christian scripture and with the links between the Christian and Jewish hermeneutics.[3] As we shall see, there is a certain tension between the orientation of the document's main text and Ratzinger's preface, a tension that is instructive concerning Ratzinger's own interest in Christian-Jewish relations.

The PBC document attempts to update the church's exegetical method so as to remain faithful to the Catholic tradition while being free of the hostility toward Judaism that had accompanied it throughout the generations. The document, which is divided into three parts, explores the connection between the two testaments and the importance of the Old Testament and the Jewish tradition to the understanding of the New Testament; analyzes the ways in which the New Testament interprets and develops Old Testament themes Christologically; and finally, eases the tension embedded in certain New Testament statements regarding the Jews by anchoring them in Old Testament style and language.

One example of the document's movement in these directions is the argument that a Catholic reading of the New Testament as "fulfilling" the prophecies of the Hebrew Bible does not strip the stories of the Old Testament of their inherent value. The Catholic typological interpretation, according to the document, proposes a double reading of the Old Testament: reading it in light of the meaning it had when it was written, and rereading it in the light of Christ:[4]

> This new interpretation does not negate the original meaning. Paul clearly states that "the very words of God were entrusted" to the Israelites (Rm 3:2) and he takes it for granted that these words of God could

be read and understood before the coming of Christ. Although he speaks of a blindness of the Jews with regard to "the reading of the Old Testament" (2 Co 3:14), he does not mean a total incapacity to read, only an inability to read it in the light of Christ.[5]

It would be incorrect, according to the PBC document, to state that the Jews have failed to understand the meaning of the text; it would be more correct to say that Christians, through the perspective offered by the New Testament, have discovered a new meaning that had been concealed within it as a latent potential. Moreover, Christians are warned against reducing the message of the text to a salvation that has already been accomplished in Christ:

> Insistence on discontinuity between both Testaments and going beyond former perspectives should not, however, lead to a one-sided spiritu-alisation. What has already been accomplished in Christ must yet be accomplished in us and in the world. The definitive fulfilment will be at the end with the resurrection of the dead, a new heaven and a new earth. Jewish messianic expectation is not in vain. It can become for us Christians a powerful stimulant to keep alive the eschatological dimen-sion of our faith. Like them, we too live in expectation. The difference is that for us the One who is to come will have the traits of the Jesus who has already come and is already present and active among us.[6]

The reflective statement that *for the Christians,* he who is to come *bears Jesus's traits* betrays the caution with which the document approaches the sensitive matter of the Messiah's identity, thus striving to resolve the tension between the Jewish and Christian readings of the Old Testament:[7]

> Christians can and ought to admit that the Jewish reading of the Bible is a *possible* one, in continuity with the Jewish Sacred Scriptures from the Second Temple period, a reading analogous to the Christian reading which developed in parallel fashion. Both readings are bound up with the vision of their respective faiths, of which the readings are the result and expression. Consequently, both are irreducible.[8]

The statement that the Jewish reading is "a possible one" is, of course, equivocal. On the one hand, it could imply that a Jewish reading of the Bible can lead to salvation. On the other hand, it could suggest that this reading is simply coherent and reasonable given the Jews' fundamental assumptions. It may be that the document attempts to reject Paul's claim that the Jews are blind and hard of heart and to suggest that Jewish interpretation, even after the First Coming, is not essentially unfounded. Nevertheless, it is obvious that not every possible interpretation, as coherent as it may be, is redemptive. What value, then, does the Jewish traditional reading have for the Christians?

These few examples from the PBC document are reflective of its authors' goal to purge the Catholic exegesis of anti-Judaism, with the help of academic biblical studies. While taking up this task, they were careful not to make strong theological claims, and they purposely phrased the document in a way that would remain open to interpretation.

Ratzinger's interest in the PBC document, as reflected in his preface, was nourished by a different motivation. More than being keen on cleansing any animosity toward Jewish readings of the Old Testament from the Christian interpretation of Scripture, Ratzinger wished to defend the church's exegetical traditions against modern biblical scholarship, which attacked the Catholic typological and allegorical readings of the Old Testament as invalid. This framing enabled Ratzinger to transform the PBC document from a text defending the value of Jewish exegesis within the Catholic tradition to one defending Catholic exegesis within the setting of modern biblical scholarship. Instead of a document dealing with Christian-Jewish relations, the PBC document exemplified, for Ratzinger, how it was possible to use modern methods to research the Bible without giving up on a uniquely Catholic position.

To facilitate this change of focus, Ratzinger stressed the connection between anti-Judaism and the splitting of the New Testament from the Old Testament. Ratzinger emphasized the potential danger that biblical criticism, and the historical study of Jesus in particular, could lapse into "Marcionism."[9] He reminded his readers that the Lutheran biblical scholar Adolf von Harnack had turned Marcion into a hero and called on the Christian world to continue the mission begun but not completed by the Protestant Reformation, doing away with Catholic tradition in favor of a literal interpretation of the Scriptures. Ratzinger wrote:

> The triumph of historical-critical exegesis seemed to sound the death-
> knell for the Christian interpretation of the Old Testament initiated by

the New Testament itself. It is not a question here of historical details, as we have seen, it is the very foundations of Christianity that are being questioned. It is understandable then that nobody has since embraced Harnack's position and made the definitive break with the Old Testament that Marcion prematurely wished to accomplish. What would have remained, our New Testament, would itself be devoid of meaning. The Document of the Pontifical Biblical Commission introduced by this Preface declares: "Without the Old Testament, the New Testament would be an unintelligible book, a plant deprived of its roots and destined to dry up and wither."[10]

The church's decision to include the two testaments in its canon was therefore nothing less than existential. The Bible's allegorical interpretation was not just one of many options the church could have picked, Ratzinger argued, but the only one that gave the Christian Gospel its validity and authority. The man whose own personal spiritual path embodied this historical choice was Augustine of Hippo. In his *Confessions,* written in the closing years of the fourth century CE, Ratzinger reminds us, Augustine withstood the temptation of renouncing the salacious and strange biblical stories in favor of a gnostic, spiritual, and pure version of the Christian gospel.[11] Upon reading the Hebrew Bible, Augustine

> experienced a terrible disappointment: in the exacting legal prescriptions of the Old Testament, in its complex and, at times, brutal narratives, he failed to find that Wisdom towards which he wanted to travel. In the course of his search, he encountered certain people who proclaimed a new spiritual Christianity, one which understood the Old Testament as spiritually deficient and repugnant; a Christianity in which Christ had no need of the witness of the Hebrew prophets. Those people promised him a Christianity of pure and simple reason, a Christianity in which Christ was the great illuminator, leading human beings to true self-knowledge. These were the Manicheans.[12]

Only when Augustine found (through Ambrose) the interpretive key to the Old Testament "that made transparent the relationship of Israel's Bible to Christ" could he turn his heart to Christianity. His own personal salvation history, much like the church's, had to pass through the bumpy path of Jewish history, before the latter opened up to the gentiles and fulfilled its destiny in the crucifixion and resurrection of Christ.[13] Indeed, the formula proposed by Augustine to describe the relationship between the covenants was accepted as paradigmatic at Vatican II: "The New Testament be hidden in the Old and the Old be made manifest in the New."[14]

To defend against the secularization of the Gospel to the point of emptying it of all meaning, Ratzinger required the reaffirmation of the link between the two testaments and of the importance of the Old Testament for the Catholic worldview (and, if we are to read between the lines, in doing so, he also reaffirmed Augustine's reservations against the non-Christological—that is, the Jewish—reading of the Old Testament, with its "complex and, at times, brutal narratives"). The "pure" and "enlightened" Christianity that was offered to Augustine by the Manicheans anticipated the Enlightenment and the admiration of secular reason, thus placing Catholicism on the middle ground between the irrationality of a primitive religion (represented by the Old Testament) and the emptiness of secular reason (represented by Greek and Roman philosophy). The exegetical heritage of the church was therefore essential for the maintenance of a balance between these two poles.

In the wake of the Holocaust, Ratzinger wrote in his preface, the Christian world resonated with the question of whether the church needed to forsake the Old Testament that it had "monopolized" and leave it to the Jews. Ratzinger's implied answer to this question is that it is not the traditional Catholic interpretation of the Old Testament that is potentially antisemitic, but precisely the secular (originally Protestant) methods that carry such potential, while the traditional Christological holding together of the two testaments is what guards Christianity from lapsing into antisemitism. Thus, the secularizing attack that threatens the Catholic tradition by negating the unity of the testaments is in fact the root of antisemitism as well.

Interestingly, this inner-Christian debate about whether it is more pro-Jewish to leave the Old Testament inside the canon or to part ways with it is a reverse continuation of the second-century Christian debate on the Judaization of Christianity. As David Nirenberg pointed out, in the original debate between Marcion and the proto-Orthodox Justin Martyr, both sides—those who supported the canonization of the Hebrew scriptures and those who rejected it—blamed each other for "Judaizing."[15] For Marcion, it was the Hebrew scriptures that threatened the purity of Christianity by introducing foreign concepts into the Christian canon, while for Justin Martyr, it was precisely Marcion who was veering too close to the Jews in his overly "carnal" interpretation of the Jewish scriptures. For Justin Martyr, dualists like Marcion and the Jews were both blind to the true Christological meaning of the Hebrew scriptures. Nirenberg argues that although Judaism had an important rhetorical role in that intra-Christian second-century debate, in truth, it was a debate not about Judaism but about Christianity.

In his criticism of Protestant and modern trends of exegesis, Ratzinger made a similar rhetorical use of Judaism. Unlike Marcion and Justin Martyr, he did not blame his opponents for Judaizing. On the contrary; it was no longer Judaization that threatened Christian identity but *anti*-Judaism. Maintaining the Old Testament within the Christian canon was seen as evidence that the church was not anti-Jewish, rather than, as it was for Justin Martyr, evidence that the church was able to overcome its Jewish heritage. While Justin accused Marcion of Judaization, Ratzinger accused the modern "Marcionites" of anti-Judaism. Nevertheless, the Jews were no less rhetorical here than they were in the original second-century debate about the Christian canon, and the rhetorical instrumentalization of Judaism in the service of intra-Christian canonical debates remained intact.

In Ratzinger's other writings, this argument, which connects antisemitism to unorthodox Christian perceptions, is also applied in reverse: if renouncing the traditional link between Old and New Testaments was closely related to modern antisemitism, then antisemitism was essentially directed toward the Catholic faith. In betraying the shared heritage of Christians and Jews, present-day Harnack-style Marcionism directly attacked the divinity that ties both covenants together. Though it was sometimes disguised as Christian, antisemitism was in fact an atheistic or pagan sin directed not only against the Jews but against the church and even against God. Ratzinger's later controversial references to the Holocaust clearly echo this move: "The *Shoah* was perpetrated in the name of an anti-Christian ideology, which tried to strike the Christian faith at its Abrahamic roots in the people of Israel."[16] Or as he said as pope in his 2006 visit to Auschwitz, "By destroying Israel, by the *Shoah,* they ultimately wanted to tear up the taproot of the Christian faith and to replace it with a faith of their own invention: faith in the rule of man, the rule of the powerful."[17] Like John Paul II and his colleagues de Lubac, Balthasar, and Lustiger, Ratzinger viewed the hatred toward the people of Israel and the Old Testament as a profound hatred toward God himself, an attempt to murder him and erase his traces from history.[18]

Protestant Christianity, which turned its back on Catholic tradition, also sought to uproot Christianity's Jewish foundations by cutting off the link between the Old and New Testaments. This, Ratzinger implied, represents the same schismatic spirit that subsequently led German intellectual history to adopt the Nazi ideology and physically destroy Judaism. Ratzinger thus associated the "pro-Jewish," post-Holocaust theological trends that sought to rescue the Hebrew Bible from the monopolizing Catholic tradition with the historicist theological trends (which were distinctly anti-Jewish) that had preceded it. This line of thought emphasizes the importance of ancient Judaism for the preservation of Catholicism, identifies contemporary Jews with the Old Testament, and places the root of antisemitism outside of Catholic theology, and more precisely, within ancient heretical attitudes that reappeared in liberal Protestantism.

Ratzinger's preface to the PBC document makes clear that the reconciliation between Christians and Jews is not only about the Christian-Jewish relationship, which often plays but a small role in a bigger drama. On the one hand, seeing Christian-Jewish reconciliation as only a means for a greater purpose makes it less important. On the other hand, it is exactly the placement of this relationship in the greater quest for crystallizing modern Catholic identity that makes it important for Catholic theology and for the Catholic Church in general.

Christ's Reform: Defining Catholicism vis-à-vis Judaism, Protestantism, and Modern Secularism

Ratzinger's emphasis on the choice to maintain the Old Testament inside the Christian canon and on the strong connection between the project of the decanonization of the Old Testament and the attacks on the Jews did not mean that he sought to minimize the differences between the two faith systems. Ratzinger opens the first volume of *Jesus of Nazareth*, which he wrote while serving as Pope Benedict XVI, with a lengthy theological dialogue with a book by the Jewish scholar Jacob Neusner, *A Rabbi Talks with Jesus*, on Jesus's attitude to the Torah.[19] The pope's choice of conducting a theological dialogue with a scholar who can hardly be considered a religious authority was quite surprising, as was his extolling of Neusner's book as "by far the most important book for the Christian-Jewish dialogue in the last decade."[20] I believe that the reason Ratzinger was so impressed by Neusner's book had to do with the fact that Neusner stated in no uncertain terms that there was an unbridgeable gap between Judaism and Christianity, while most scholars chose to blur the differences by discussing only the common denominators.

In an imaginary dialogue with Jesus, Neusner takes on the role of a first-century Jew who listens to Jesus's preaching and considers whether to join his followers. Despite the profound and clear linkage Neusner's fictional character identifies between Jesus and the Jewish tradition, he finally decides to reject his preaching and remain with "the Eternity of Israel."[21] He makes that choice, so he argues, because of one innovation introduced by Jesus that was incompatible with Jewish heritage: the fact that Jesus places himself, in the first person, at the heart of his message.

In his own book, Ratzinger reconsidered the dialogue between Neusner's fictional character and Jesus from a Catholic point of view, while adopting Neusner's Christocentric conclusion to the full. Ratzinger delves deeply into the concept of Jesus's "fulfillment" of Israel's Torah. This fulfillment, argues Ratzinger, involves a profound inherent tension, since Jesus continued the Jewish tradition while at the same time annulling it. On the one hand, in his Sermon on the Mount, Jesus made it clear that he did not come to "abolish the law or the prophets" but "to fulfill. For . . . until heaven and earth pass away, not one letter, not one stroke of a letter, will pass from the law until all is accomplished" (Matt. 5:17–18). Soon enough, however, Jesus presents his own law as antithetical to Moses's law in a series of oppositions presented in a repetitive formula: "You have heard that it was said to those of ancient times . . . But I say to you . . ." (Matt. 5:21–22). Upon hearing him preach, "the crowds were astounded at his teaching, for he taught them as one having authority, and not as their scribes" (Matt. 7:28–29). According to Ratzinger, this astonishment was due to the fact that the Jewish audience realized that Jesus did not include his law within the Jewish interpretive tradition side by side with other interpreters but placed himself on the same level of authority as the lawmaker himself, who gave Israel the Torah.[22] Such self-reference could not be justified unless he truly had divine authority. Thus, according to Ratzinger, the only way of making sense of Jesus's Gospel was to consider his words as representing a divine "I." This way, Ratzinger sought to heal the rupture between the historical Jesus and the theological Christ of the Catholic tradition.[23] If Jesus was merely a liberal rabbi or reformer of Judaism, as is argued by many scholars who have espoused the return to the historical Jesus, then the authority he assumed in the Sermon on the Mount is scandalous.

One of the stories often cited in support of Jesus as a liberal reformer is that of his disciples plucking heads of grain on the Sabbath. When the Pharisees protested against this unlawfulness, Jesus replied, "The sabbath was made for humankind, and not humankind for the sabbath; so the Son of Man is lord even of the sabbath" (Mark 2:27–28). Ratzinger wrote as follows on the "liberal" interpretation of this story:

> It was, in fact, the Sabbath disputes that became the basis for the image of the liberal Jesus. His critique of the Judaism of his time, so it is said, was a freedom-loving and rational man's critique of an ossified legalism— hypocritical to the core and guilty of dragging religion down to the level of a slavish system of utterly unreasonable obligations that hold man back from developing his work and his freedom. It goes without saying that this interpretation did not favor a particularly friendly image of Judaism. Of course, the modern critique—beginning with the Reformation—saw in Catholicism the return of this supposedly "Jewish" element.[24]

Ratzinger makes clear that his Jesus is not a liberal Protestant. Jesus did not seek to make life easier for his disciples or to free them of the burden of the Torah (as many have interpreted Matt. 11:30: "For my yoke is easy, and my burden is light"). In fact, the strictness demanded by Jesus of his disciples was in no way less than that of the (other) Jews.[25] The sacred text refuses to adhere to the secularized moralistic interpretation; it demands, according to Ratzinger, a Christological one that places Jesus's divinity at the center of his reform of Israel's Torah. Ratzinger's Jesus *is* the law, the word of God made flesh. Hence, he calls himself, with full authority, lord of the Sabbath.

Nevertheless, the incarnation of the Torah in the flesh was not easy for the Jews to accept. Jesus's great innovation was not a smooth transition but a radical transformation that was, and still is, very difficult for the Jewish people. Elsewhere, Ratzinger likened the transition required of Judaism to the difficult labor of the woman of the apocalypse in Revelation 12. After much torment, the woman becomes "the new Israel, the mother of new peoples, and she is personified in Mary, the Mother of Jesus."[26] The Israelites found it difficult to accept Jesus because he forcefully opened up the nation's womb to give birth to God's "gift of universalism" to humankind. For the lord of Israel to become the light unto the nations, as prophesied in the Hebrew Bible, Judaism's ethnic, genealogical aspect had to be overcome: the Sabbath, the circumcision, and the blood relations among the Jews had united the people of Israel thus far; now, with the coming of Christ, they faced a radical shift.[27] This is why Paul was opposed to circumcising the gentiles and demanding that they follow the commandments; he realized that the coming of Christ prefigured a radical ethnosocial transformation, and he did not want to leave in place those orders designed to protect the boundaries of the Jewish nation.[28] Ratzinger clearly did not identify with the effort made by certain theologians and biblical scholars to fully bring Paul back to the fold of the Judaism of the Second Temple.

Neusner's fears of Jesus's undermining of the Jewish social order and blood ties and the stability of the community were therefore justified, according to Ratzinger. The universalization of Judaism is immanently bound up with this undermining. "Israel 'had to' see here something much more serious than a violation of this or that commandment, namely, the injuring of that basic obedience, of the actual core of its revelation and faith: Hear, O Israel, your God is One God."[29] Instead of the Jewish order unified by blood ties and the commandments, Christ starts a new family, unified by the spirit and focused on the cross.[30] In doing so, he fulfills Judaism's calling of being a light unto the nations, and brings Israel and the nations together as one family.

Jesus's transformation of the Torah is related to the most sensitive issue in Christian-Jewish relations, an issue Ratzinger avoided in his dialogue with Neusner: the continuity of God's covenant with Israel and, moreover, the status of the covenant concluded by Moses on Mount Sinai, that is, the status of the commandments as effective instruments for the salvation of the Jews. Ever since John Paul II said that the Jews were "the people of God of the old covenant never revoked by God" and related to them as "the present-day people of the covenant concluded with Moses," the status of the Sinai covenant quickly turned into a litmus test for the church's philosemitism.[31] John Paul II's expression remained open for interpretation, and it was impossible to know whether the pope meant to say that the Jewish law brings salvation or that the Sinai covenant maintains a different value, and if so, of what kind. Benedict XVI had said more explicit things on this issue; he also used the expression "the people of the Covenant of Moses" with reference to the Jews and underscored the validity of the eternal principles given by the Lord to his people on Mount Sinai.[32] And he made it clear that from the Jewish point of view, the law is the concrete manifestation of grace, the "visibility" of divine will in the world, which as such "gives the possibility of right living."[33] However, these statements, which clearly attach profound religious significance to the Jews' relationship with God even after the crucifixion, do not unambiguously validate the Sinai covenant. For Ratzinger, the Mosaic covenant in Sinai was the sensitive spot, where Jesus's transformation of the Torah charged the highest price from the Jewish people, since indeed some aspects in it became obsolete.

The incarnation does not revoke the old covenant, but it certainly changes it from within. It brings together all of Israel's rites and embodies them in a single point—Christ.[34] This transformation is not "spiritualization," as is often argued with reference to Paul's approach to the Torah, but represents instead the Torah's realization in the most concrete sense (a point that again hints at Protestantism's interpretation of Christianity and its relation to Judaism). All the aspects of the covenant of Sinai that have prevented it from being revealed in its fullest meaning to the nations are removed in the transformation stage. Divine will is one and immutable, but the instruments used by God to lead humanity to salvation vary; they become invalid after completing their mission. When the end is achieved, the means can be dispensed with.[35] Limited to the children of Israel, the Sinai covenant imposes laws whose nature is to change with time.[36] Eventually, it loses its validity as a spiritual and practical system and needs to be viewed (as soon as the correct interpretation—Christ—appears) as a prophetic covenant, a covenant of promise, at one with Abraham's. What remains eternally valid in it are only the universal and prophetic aspects and not all those laws required to maintain the Jews' existence throughout history. The Mosaic covenant is violated and eternal at the same time; it is included in the history of salvation together with God's other covenants with humanity: with Noah, Abraham, Jacob, David, and Jesus. Through all runs the thread of God's will to bind himself with love to the human race, the will ultimately embodied in the cross.

Thus, Ratzinger converted Paul's oppositional language to a softer one that emphasizes the intercovenantal continuity as representing an ongoing history of divine grace, without assuming a break between the dispensation of the law and the dispensation of grace. Nevertheless, he is far from offering the Jewish people a simple or uncritical message. Albeit in a subtle way, he does not hesitate to use the traditional supersessionist terminology: "The Sinai covenant is indeed superseded. But once what was provisional in it has been swept away we see what is truly definitive in it. So the expectation of the New Covenant, which becomes clearer and clearer as the history of Israel unfolds, does not conflict with the Sinai covenant; rather, it fulfills the dynamic expectation found in that very covenant."[37]

The incarnation revokes those laws that apply only to the Jewish people. Accordingly, to a certain extent, the universalization of the Torah involves a secularization of the sociopolitical order, as opposed to the Mosaic law, which had sanctified it and sought to perpetuate it through the commandments. The distinction offered by Ratzinger between the provisional and particular (revoked with the coming of Christ) and the eternal and universal (reassured by Christ) also represents a social revolution that grants the human race the blessed freedom of a secular realm. To return to his dialogue with Neusner:

> What is happening here is an extremely important process whose full scope was not grasped until modern times, even though the moderns at first understood it in a one-sided and false way. Concrete juridical and social forms and political arrangements are no longer treated as a sacred law that is fixed ad litteram for all times and so for all peoples. The decisive thing is [from Christ on] the underlying communion of will with God given by Jesus. It frees men and nations to discover what aspects of political and social order accord with this communion of will and so to work out their own juridical arrangements. The absence of the whole social dimension in Jesus' preaching, which Neusner discerningly critiques from a Jewish perspective . . . conceals an epoch-making event in world history that has not occurred as such in any other culture: The concrete political and social order is released from the directly sacred realm, from theocratic legislation, and is transferred to the freedom of man, whom Jesus has established in God's will and taught thereby to see the right and the good.[38]

This was Ratzinger's crucial point: by virtue of his divine authority, Jesus could perform a liberating act and create an amended secular world, grounded in universality and communality among humans and between them and God. To do so, a continuity between the Torah of Israel and the Torah of Christ had to be maintained, because that continuity was integral to Christ's authority. However, this continuity was not everything: the law had to be detached from the social order and spiritualized, so as to free humans from the risk of a totalitarian theocracy.

Ratzinger's discussion of Christian-Jewish relations was therefore directly relevant to his extensive and ongoing discussion of the relations between the church and modern secularism, a subject that preoccupied him over several decades. To him, the Enlightenment principles of freedom and universalism had to be anchored in the principle of obedience to God and delimited by a non-human criterion, so as not to slip down the relativist slope. Liberty had to be binding by divine law, for otherwise, humans would allow themselves to violate it, to relativize it, and eventually to revoke it. The liberty Jesus brings to humanity is in itself the embodiment of law, and it is won by obedience.

There is, once again, an analogy between Ratzinger's view of the Christian-Jewish relationship and his view of the relations between Christianity and the heritage of the Enlightenment.[39] Just as Christianity had to draw sustenance from the root of Judaism to retain its validity and authority, so did the Enlightenment need to stand on the foundations of Christianity; otherwise it would be cutting the branch it sits on. Godless liberalism is not truly valid, just as the Christian Gospel is invalid without the personal God of the Hebrew Bible, the lawmaker of the Ten Commandments.[40] The church, in other words, lies in the middle between Judaism and secularism and seeks to hold both their hands, to open up a liberated secular space, where Judaism saw only holiness bound by specific legal and social systems, without letting that space be completely cut off from the absolute, which gives it its boundaries and validity.

How Are the Jews to Be Saved? The Dispute over *Dominus Iesus*

In 2000, the CDF, headed by Ratzinger, published *Dominus Iesus,* a document that caused an intense conflict of opinions in the Catholic world and was widely considered as an obstacle for both ecumenical discourse and interreligious dialogue.[41] In it, the CDF formulated its position regarding the possibility of redemption outside the church, Christ's mystical body. To the indignation of many liberal Catholics worldwide, it seemed that *Dominus Iesus* went against the zeitgeist by reverting to the ancient rule of the church: *extra ecclesiam nulla salus*—there is no salvation outside the church.

Dominus Iesus provided the church's answer to the question resonating throughout the Catholic world ever since Vatican II. In the dogmatic constitution *Lumen gentium,* one of the more controversial documents published by the council, the church had touched on the question of salvation outside its boundaries. *Lumen gentium* significantly expanded the church's definition of the possibility of salvation.[42] Under certain conditions, the constitution suggested, non-Catholic Christians, followers of other religions, and even people who do not recognize God (through no fault of their own) can be saved. Only those who knowingly reject the Gospel cannot be saved.

This message, whatever its right interpretation, took the Catholic world by storm after Vatican II. The secessionist ultraconservative group that believed in sedevacantism (the idea that the Holy See is vacant because the current occupant is not a valid pope) viewed Article 8 (and 14–18) of the constitution as clear evidence that the church had embraced heresy, because it had renounced its exclusiveness as the true church. Conversely, leading liberal theologians such as the Brazilian Leonardo Boff, the Belgian Jacques Dupuis, and the Vietnamese American Peter Phan interpreted the constitution as affirming that other churches, in addition to the Catholic Church, could also be considered the embodiment of the church of Christ on Earth and even as affirming that followers of other religions could be saved through their faith, without the intercession of the Catholic Church or perhaps even without believing in Christ.[43]

The latter position was opposed by Cardinal Ratzinger and members of his circle, since it was the obvious representation of the new Catholic theology's contemptible relativist tendency. *Dominus Iesus* was written to disseminate the magisterium's stand on this issue against contemporary liberal publications and to accommodate *Lumen gentium* with the church's traditional position that "the Church of Christ . . . continues to exist fully only in the Catholic Church," even if certain manifestations of truth and grace may be found outside its walls. Quoting less controversial passages of *Lumen gentium, Dominus Iesus* states that the faithful *"are required to profess"* that the church is essential for salvation, and that Christ is its exclusive mediator.[44] Even those who profit from divine grace despite not being official and visible members of the Catholic Church are mysteriously connected to it and are granted grace by Christ: "It would be contrary to the faith to consider the church as *one way* of salvation alongside those constituted by the other religions, seen as complementary to the church or substantially equivalent to her."[45] Thus, Jesus's universality and exclusivity as the savior of humanity cannot be relativized:

> With the coming of the Saviour Jesus Christ, God has willed that the Church founded by him be the instrument for the salvation of *all* humanity. This truth of faith does not lessen the sincere respect which the Church has for the religions of the world, but at the same time, it rules out, in a radical way, that mentality of indifferentism "characterized by

a religious relativism which leads to the belief that 'one religion is as good as another.'"[46] If it is true that the followers of other religions can receive divine grace, it is also certain that *objectively speaking* they are in a gravely deficient situation in comparison with those who, in the Church, have the fullness of the means of salvation.[47]

The document ultimately incorporates interreligious dialogue itself into the church's mission to proclaim the Christian truth among the nations, stating that "*Equality,* which is a presupposition of interreligious dialogue, refers to the equal personal dignity of the parties in dialogue, not to doctrinal content, nor even less to the position of Jesus Christ."[48]

Many protested against the document's implications for the church's relation to Judaism. Shouldn't the readers of *Dominus Iesus* understand that Judaism, like other non-Christian religions, was "seriously" inferior to the Catholic Church and that the Jews had to convert, or at least believe in some way in Christ's salvific mission, in order to be redeemed? If anyone had sought to give the church's recurring statements regarding the Jews' ongoing covenant with God a soteriological interpretation, this document pulled the rug out from under them. Moreover, efforts by many theologians and priests to establish a dialogue with Jews had involved statements that they were not interested in baptizing them. The document's claims regarding the nature and purpose of interreligious dialogue, so they believed, compromised the entire Christian-Jewish dialogue enterprise. "I could not speak some of the language of *Dominus Iesus* with my dialogue partners," remonstrated theologian John Pawlikowski.[49] The theologian Mary Boys concurred: "The way of Torah certainly seems to me salvific for those who walk in it."[50] Jewish participants in Christian-Jewish dialogue felt that the document was "a public relations disaster of the first order."[51] Rabbi David Berger of Yeshiva University considered the document's position on interreligious dialogue cause enough to withdraw from it immediately.[52]

The theologian most alarmed by the publication of *Dominus Iesus* was Walter Cardinal Kasper, the newly appointed head of the CRRJ, who replaced Cardinal Cassidy. Kasper had been Ratzinger's rival for many years. As head of the CRRJ, he was required on many occasions to perform theological acrobatics to clear the waters muddied by Ratzinger.[53] The publication of *Dominus Iesus* was one of those occasions.

In a speech before the International Catholic-Jewish Liaison Committee in New York, Kasper contended that Judaism was not included in *Dominus*

Iesus's discussion of world religions. The document was written, he argued, to counter the threat of new-age relativistic theories "that deny the specific identity of Jewish and Christian religion, and do not take into account the distinction between faith as answer to God's revelation and belief as human search for God and human religious wisdom." Moreover, *Dominus Iesus* sought to defend "the specific revelation character of the Hebrew Bible" vis-à-vis the holy scriptures of other religions and "against theories claiming, for example, that the Holy Books of Hinduism are the Old Testament for Hindus." In other words, he explained, not only does the document not refer to Judaism as one of the world's religions, but it places Judaism and Christianity on the same level, as revelatory religions: "Against such theories we, as Jews and Christians, are on the same side, sitting in the same boat; we have to fight, to argue and to bear witness together. Our common self-understanding is at stake."[54]

To prove that the *Dominus Iesus* was indeed not directed at Jews, Kasper quoted a selection of statements by Pope John Paul II about the extraordinary relationship between Judaism and Christianity; Judaism, according to these quotes, is not seen by the church as a different religion, but rather as part of its own identity. He also quoted a statement by Ratzinger, published in *L'Osservatore Romano* several months after *Dominus Iesus* had been published, as evidence that Ratzinger himself sought to clarify that the contents of *Dominus Iesus* did not apply to the Jews (Ratzinger avoided any explicit reference to *Dominus Iesus* in that article).[55]

Kasper's most surprising move, however, touches directly on the soteriological validity of the covenant with the Jews:

> One of these questions is how to relate the covenant with the Jewish people, which according to St. Paul is unbroken and not revoked but still in vigour, with what we Christians call the New covenant. As you know, the old theory of substitution is gone since II Vatican Council. For us Christians today the covenant with the Jewish people is a living heritage, a living reality. There cannot be a mere coexistence between the two covenants. Jews and Christians, by their respective specific identities, are intimately related to each other. It is impossible now to enter the complex problem of how this intimate relatedness should or could be defined. Such question touches the mystery of Jewish and Christian existence as well, and should be discussed in our further dialogue. The only thing I wish to say is that the Document *Dominus*

Iesus does not state that everybody needs to become a Catholic in order to be saved by God. On the contrary, it declares that God's grace, which is the grace of Jesus Christ according to our faith, is available to all. Therefore, the Church believes that Judaism, i.e. the faithful response of the Jewish people to God's irrevocable covenant, is salvific for them, because God is faithful to his promises.[56]

In this bold move, Kasper reaffirmed the most radical interpretation of *Nostra aetate* as well as of Romans 11:29, one that understands the covenant with the Jews as completely obviating the need for conversion. In this text, not only does Jewish tradition have religious value, as also argued by Ratzinger, but it has salvific power. Judaism persists not only mysteriously and for vague reasons until all gentiles turn their hearts to the Messiah but also as a faithful response to a covenant with God that requires no fundamental correction—either by man or by God. Evidently, the Jews are doing God's will. Of course, the divine grace that continues to be bestowed on the Jewish people emanates from Christ, as does all divine grace; Jesus remains the only and the universal savior of the human race. However, he saves the Jews through Judaism, without requiring any Christian supplement to be "fully saved."

This interpretation makes the Jews an exception from the rest of humanity in that they do not require the Christian mission and evangelization. According to Kasper, the church avoids missionary work among the Jews not only for political reasons; the Jews simply do not have to be Catholic to be redeemed. Mission had been originally dedicated to converting pagans from idolatry to belief in "the true and one God, who revealed himself in the salvation history with his elected people. Thus mission, in its strict sense, cannot be used with regard to Jews, who believe in the true and one God."[57] The church's dialogue with the Jews is therefore situated on a different level from its dialogue with the rest of the human race.

Although theologically coherent, Kasper's position was certainly not concomitant with the approach taken by *Dominus Iesus,* as argued by both Berger and Boys.[58] Had the CDF's document meant to exclude the Jews, it could have stated so explicitly and could even have quoted—as Kasper himself did—a range of papal statements to support that view. Moreover, the only passage in *Dominus Iesus* that does refer to the Jews cautiously suggests that they, too, require mission and conversion:

It was in the awareness of the one universal gift of salvation offered by the Father through Jesus Christ in the Spirit (cf. Eph 1:3–14), that the first Christians encountered the Jewish people, showing them the fulfilment of salvation that went beyond the Law.[59]

Nevertheless, Kasper enjoyed enough authority in the Catholic Church for his words to gain a validity of their own, for even though they were not consistent with a literal reading of *Dominus Iesus,* they did not challenge it but only gave it a different interpretation. His speech became a fundamental document in the Christian-Jewish dialogue, and many kept returning to it as an authoritative source on the church's attitude toward the Jews.

What did Ratzinger think of Kasper's speech? First, it may be assumed that his hope that *Dominus Iesus* would unite theologians behind a single clear and consistent doctrine was largely shattered by that speech—at least as far as the Jewish context was concerned. Second, it is obvious that Ratzinger's stand on the question of the Jews' salvation was not identical to Kasper's. At about the same time *Dominus Iesus* was published, a book based on an interview with Ratzinger by German journalist Peter Seewald was published that included statements in a spirit completely different from those attributed to Ratzinger by Kasper, which had ostensibly been based on the article in *L'Osservatore Romano.*[60] It may be assumed that Kasper was well aware of the statements in Seewald's book but chose not to refer to them in his speech. In the interview with Seewald, Ratzinger said:

It is quite obvious that the Jews have something to do with God and that God has not abandoned them. And that is how the New Testament sees it, too. Paul says to us in the Letter to the Romans: In the end all of Israel will be brought home. It is another question, how far, with the rise of the Church—the people of God called from all peoples—and with the coming of the new covenant, life under the old covenant, a life that remains closed to the new covenant that comes from Christ, is still a valid way of life. . . . Of course, we can see that Israel still has some way to go. As Christians, we believe that they will in the end be together with us in Christ. But they are not simply done with and left out of God's plans; rather they still stand within the faithful covenant of God.[61]

In response to the interviewer's question about whether the Jews must recognize Christ to be saved, Ratzinger said:

That is what we believe. That does not mean that we have to force Christ upon them but that we should share in the patience of God. We also have to try to live our life together in Christ in such a way that it no longer stands in opposition to them or would be unacceptable to them. . . . It is in fact still our belief as Christians that Christ is the Messiah of Israel. It is in God's hands, of course, just in what way, when and how the reuniting of Jews and Gentiles, the reunification of God's people, will be achieved.[62]

Unlike Kasper, Ratzinger refused to give up on the exclusiveness of the Catholic Church as the instrument of full redemption; in other words, he included the Jews, at least in that sense, in the universal position formulated in *Dominus Iesus*. He also refused to abandon the demand that the Jews recognize Christ; in this, he adopted a significantly more conservative line—in interpreting *Nostra aetate*—than that which considered the salvation of the Jews as a purely unilateral act of grace requiring no action on their part. The validity of the covenant with the Jews thereby received a "classic" Pauline interpretation: God's loyalty to his gifts means that he will enable the Jews to be saved at the end of time despite their ongoing refusal to recognize him as the Christ.

Nevertheless, in continuation with Tommaso Federici's lecture from 1977, Ratzinger stated that there was no point in missionizing the Jews at this time in history. Moreover, he suggested that the Jews did have a religious role to play even in the present. Although the Christians are waiting for the Jews to recognize Christ as the son of God and reunite with them, for now, they must recognize them as God's witnesses, who are active at their side and carry a historical mission of their own, rather than forcing their reunification with the church.[63] The nature of the Jews' testimony did not remain a complete mystery for Ratzinger, and he enumerated its elements: "First, there is the Torah, the commitment to God's will and the establishment of his rule, his kingdom in this world. Secondly there is the hope, the expectation of the Messiah; the expectation, even the certainty, that God himself will step into this history and create justice—for the forms of justice we ourselves set up are very imperfect."[64] Even later on, as pope, Ratzinger continued to view the Ten Commandments, which come from "the Torah of Moses," as "a great ethical code for all humanity."[65] His words in *L'Osservatore Romano* as quoted by Kasper lend further support to this view.

Ratzinger, then, did believe that the Jews were situated on a different level from the rest of humankind, as they responded to the divine revelation documented in the Old Testament. This covenant was still valid, but it was transformed with the coming of Christ, a transformation that still awaited recognition by the Jews. Did this mean that the church had to act to convert the Jews? The answer to that question was not clear. Ratzinger referred to this matter explicitly only years later, as pope, following an additional, and more serious, controversy regarding his relation to Judaism, as we will see later in this chapter.

The Reverberations of the *Dominus Iesus* Controversy in the United States

The approach to the salvation of the Jews emerging from *Dominus Iesus* kept generating controversies between theologians and churchmen in the years to come. In the summer of 2002, representatives of the United States Conference of Catholic Bishops (USCCB)—the Bishops' Committee on Ecumenical and Interreligious Affairs—joined together with the National Council of Synagogues and published a document bearing the title "Reflections on Covenant and Mission," in which members of both parties expressed their opinions on the issue.[66] In the Catholic portion of the document, the authors repeated Cardinal Kasper's words, following the publication of the CDF's document, as clear and unequivocal testimony to the effect that the Jews may be granted salvation by virtue of their unique and ongoing covenant with God and that, therefore, the church does not encourage them to convert to Christianity. The Catholic Church, they declared, "must always evangelize and will always witness to its faith in the presence of God's kingdom in Jesus Christ to Jews and to all other people" and must accept individual converts of all religions, including Judaism, with love and openness, without violating their freedom of religion. "However," they continued, the Catholic Church "now recognizes that Jews are also called by God to prepare the world for God's kingdom. Their witness to the kingdom, which did not originate with the church's experience of Christ crucified and raised, must not be curtailed by seeking the conversion of the Jewish people to Christianity." Hence, when it comes to the Jews, and as stated in *Nostra aetate,* the church can only await the day, "known to God alone, when all peoples will call on God with one voice and serve him shoulder to shoulder."[67]

In stating its position on the nature of the interfaith dialogue with the Jews, the American committee expanded (following Kasper and Federici) the term *evangelization* to the point that it had very little to do with the explicit proclamation of Jesus Christ as the savior of the human race and could certainly not be reduced to the encouragement of new converts. The "evangelization" involved in the interreligious dialogue on the part of the Catholics was nothing but "a mutually enriching sharing of gifts devoid of any intention whatsoever to invite the dialogue partner to baptism."[68]

It did not take long before the American declaration was attacked as misleading, incorrect, and lacking authority. (Though it was not, strictly speaking, an authoritative document, it did go through the office of doctrine.) Leading conservative Avery Cardinal Dulles published a detailed response in the Catholic journal *America* in which he argued that the idea of excluding the Jews from evangelization (in the traditional sense of the term) was completely alien to the New Testament, as Peter stated clearly that all the house of Israel had to be baptized in the name of Christ for the remission of their sins (Acts 2:36–38), and Paul was willing to be accursed from Christ for the sake of converting his brethren according to the flesh (Rom. 9:3). The apostles themselves, wrote Dulles, "would be astonished to find that the present document, after posing the question whether Christians should invite Jews to baptism, leaves it open and unanswered."[69]

The reference to the Jewish people as having a permanent salvific covenant with God also seemed problematic to Dulles in light of the explicit statement in Hebrews that the new covenant made the first one "obsolete," and "what is obsolete and growing old will soon disappear" (Heb. 8:13). The promises of the old covenant were still in force, as Paul stated in Romans, but their enduring value only held so long as they were interpreted in the light of Christ. In any case, this did not mean that "Israel is already saved by adherence to the Sinai covenant," but that a day would come when it is saved through acceptance of Christ. Interpreting certain Pauline texts as though they suggested the existence of two parallel covenants ran counter to the explicit statements of other Pauline texts and was therefore incoherent. Dulles concluded his article with a sharp admonishment of his liberal colleagues as participants in interfaith dialogue who strive to avoid conflict at any cost: "It is of course desirable to ease tensions, but the avoidance of controversial points can easily lead to ambiguity and dissimulation. *Covenant and Mis-*

sion seems to imply that conversion to Christ, baptism and adherence to the church are no longer considered important for Jews."[70]

Dulles shared Ratzinger's commitment to express clear theological positions aligned with the church's comprehensive dogmatic approach, even if they were not always to everyone's liking. In this article—as well as in another written several years later—he contended that the magisterium's position on this matter was unequivocal, leaving no room for error.[71] John Paul II, he wrote, had made it absolutely clear that the word of God must be announced before all humanity, with no exception.[72] As argued in Chapter 3, I believe that the source of "ambiguity" (or "dissimulation," as flung by Dulles at fellow theologian Eugene J. Fisher) in the American bishops' position lies precisely in John Paul II's statements on the Jews, which were actually less unequivocal than Dulles would have us believe. It was John Paul II, in talking about the covenant that has never been revoked, who indirectly invoked the saving character of Judaism as a possible interpretation of Paul, or at least the assumption according to which the Jews receive Christ's grace even without consciously confessing him, through their faithfulness to Judaism. As we have seen, John Paul II purposely avoided systematic and clear theological statements and left behind a mist that allowed for various interpretations. Moreover, whereas in many areas the tone dictated from above was conservative, the Jewish area was one where it could be understood that the pope would welcome expansive interpretations. As elegant and daring as it was, Kapser's move largely followed in John Paul II's diplomatic footsteps in giving up on any attempt to systematize his position by bringing it to terms with contradictory texts in the scriptures, with contradictory statements by the pope, and with other relevant issues.[73] In other words, the disagreement lay not only in different positions on the salvation of the Jews, but also in how the relations with the Jews should be approached—whether from a conciliatory, diplomatic stance that left a lot of loose ends, or on the basis of systematic theological inquiry.

In 2009, the USCCB Offices of Ecumenical and Interreligious Affairs and of Doctrine published a "Note on the Ambiguities Contained in *Reflections on Covenant and Mission*," in which the USCCB realigned itself with Cardinal Dulles. The note explained that the original document was not official and did not represent the USCCB's formal position and therefore had not undergone the methodical editing process reserved for official documents. Because in the years following its publication some had referred to it erroneously as though it were an authoritative text—despite the fact that it contained "some statements that are insufficiently precise and potentially misleading"—some clarifications were in order.[74]

The clarification note reaffirmed that Judaism was situated on a level different from that of other religions because it had been founded on authentic divine revelation, but it qualified this affirmation with the caveat that it was "potentially misleading in this context to refer to the enduring quality of the covenant without adding that for Catholics Jesus Christ as the incarnate Son of God fulfills both in history and at the end of time the special relationship that God established with Israel." The core of Kasper's declaration, which referred to *post-crucifixion* Judaism as a religion leading to salvation, was replaced here by a statement regarding the value of *biblical* Judaism as a revelatory religion that could become salvific only by its transformation to the new covenant in Christ. The clarification note ultimately undermined Kasper's position by stating in no uncertain terms that "though Christian participation in interreligious dialogue would not normally include an explicit invitation to baptism and entrance into the church, the Christian dialogue partner is always giving witness to the following of Christ, to which all are implicitly invited."[75]

David Berger, who, as we have seen, had often served as the guardian of the Jewish dialogue partner in the face of Christian mission, formulated a sharply worded letter that was sent by the American Jewish Committee, the Anti-Defamation League, the National Council of Synagogues, the Orthodox Union, and the Rabbinical Council of America to the USCCB.[76] The letter argued that the statement in the clarification note regarding the Christian dialogue partners' implicit missionary intention made the intention explicit; moreover, it made the interfaith dialogue completely undesirable for Jews keen on avoiding apostasy.

It is worth mentioning that although the Jewish response was indeed sharp and all-encompassing, not all Orthodox Jewish representatives of the dialogue with Christians felt the same urgency about the USCCB's clarification note. After he was approached by a concerned, high-ranking Catholic official who came to seek his advice over the Shabbat table, Yehiel Poupko, a Modern Orthodox rabbi who represents the Jewish Federation of Chicago and the Chicago Jewish community in its relationship with the Christian Churches, attempted to lower the flames by telling his Jewish colleagues of the tireless effort made by church representatives to navigate between the doctrinal necessity of professing Christ as the universal redeemer and their respect for the integrity of the Jewish covenant:

The Church holds that all humanity needs Christ, and Jews are included in all humanity. On the other hand, by not actively seeking to bring the Jewish people to Christ, but by merely professing that as a belief and hope, the Church is communicating a message. It is as if the Church is saying to us as follows, "To be a Christian is to believe that everyone needs Christ. However, given the oppression of the Jewish people throughout history, to which the Church has contributed, culminating in the Holocaust, the Church does not have the active work of converting Jews as a top priority. It has other priorities that precede that."

Poupko argued that friendly gestures—such as John Paul II's visit to the Western Wall—constituted performative theology and were therefore able to mitigate doctrinal severity and to suspend the doctrine's unwarranted effects on Jewish lives. The fact that the doctrinal conversation still takes place within the Catholic community should not bother the Jewish dialogue partners as long as it does not have any harmful practical implications: "This is an internal debate within the Catholic Church. The debate surely affects us. What we can and should do is ask the Church to conduct this internal discussion in a manner that causes no harm to the Jewish people. To date, that is the case."[77]

Poupko's somewhat sober perspective did not alter the sense of alarm among the church hierarchy in America following the Jewish organizations' remonstration. In response to the reservations expressed by the letter from the Jewish organizations, the USCCB hastened to omit controversial passages from the clarification note and published a revised clarification note whose criticism of the original document was now so mild as to make the very need for a clarification unclear. Needless to say, the proliferation of clarifications ended up complicating things more than simplifying them. Once again, the church's doctrinal interest clashed with its interest in promoting Christian-Jewish dialogue, and once again, church officials preferred diplomacy to theology.

To conclude, *Dominus Iesus,* whose publication by the CDF had originally been intended to clarify the Catholic Church's position on the soteriological question, led to such an extensive and prolonged debate that it was simply impossible to tell what this position really was. Although Ratzinger had wanted to avoid ambiguous statements and to present a clear and consistent theological stand, and was willing to sacrifice political correctness in the process, his systematic theological thought ultimately yielded to the ambiguity and equivocation typical of the Catholic discourse on the Jews.

Every time he tried to clear the mist hanging over the remaining vague passages in the *Nostra aetate,* his statements created a commotion that undermined his intent, leaving insult and acrimony in the air, and no doctrinal stability.

The Dispute over the Good Friday Prayer for the Jews

The controversy around Ratzinger's activity as prefect of the CDF continued well into his term as Pope Benedict XVI. As part of his effort to heal the rift between the ultraconservative Catholic groups that seceded (or were excluded) from the church following Vatican II, Benedict XVI allowed, in the summer of 2007, more extensive use of the traditional Latin mass, which had been almost completely sidelined by the vernacular *Novus ordo* that had been widely adopted since the council's liturgical reform.[78] As mentioned earlier, the Good Friday Latin service included the traditional version of the Prayer for the Conversion of the Jews. One of the oldest in the Catholic liturgy, this prayer was considered an exceptionally flagrant manifestation of the church's anti-Jewish tradition and included several expressions strongly identified with replacement theology. The traditional prayer, used from the Council of Trent until 1959, was largely based on Paul's words:

> But their minds were hardened. Indeed, to this very day, when they hear the reading of the old covenant, that same veil is still there, since only in Christ is it set aside. Indeed, to this very day whenever Moses is read, a veil lies over their minds; but when one turns to the Lord, the veil is removed. (2 Cor. 3:14–16)

These verses had been paradigmatic of the traditional Catholic approach to the Jews prior to the turning point in *Nostra aetate,* which settled on Romans 9–11 as its theological prism on Judaism.

The prayer underwent significant revisions even before Vatican II. Jews and Christians had discussed its implications for their relations as early as the 1920s, when Amici Israel called on the church to omit the most controversial words—*perfidis* and *perfidiam.* Similar calls were voiced after the Holocaust. Although he refused to omit the offensive words, Pius XII did make it publicly clear that they needed to be interpreted literally, as connoting "lack of faith" rather than betrayal. Until that time, the prayer for the Jews did not include genuflection by the priest and the congregation, since this act was seen, in this context, as echoing the bowing of the Jews who mocked the crucified Christ (Matt. 27:29). For the first time, Pius XII added genuflection to the prayer, as was common in others, to tone down its anti-Jewish connotations.

Pius XII's successor, John XXIII, had omitted the words *perfidis* and *perfidiam* as early as 1959, before Vatican II was convened. As mentioned in Chapter 1, in 1970, as part of the council's liturgical reform, the new order of service included a new prayer for the Jews in the spirit of *Nostra aetate*. This new version does not echo 2 Corinthians and does not refer to perfidy, blindness, or darkness—it even avoids expressing the hope for the conversion of the Jews. It stresses the enduring validity of the Jews' covenant with God and proposes little more than strengthening that covenant, without stating explicitly how: "Let us pray for the Jewish people, the first to hear the word of God, that they may continue to grow in the love of his name and in faithfulness to his covenant."[79] This prayer may be easily interpreted as testifying to the Jewish people's fidelity to their covenant, and it certainly contains no allusion to "faithlessness" on the part of the Jews. The prayer for the full redemption of Israel "through Christ our Lord" also includes no expectation for Christ to be recognized by the Jews, leaving the soteriological question open.

In the summer of 2007, when Ratzinger, in his position as Pope Benedict XVI, allowed more extensive use of the traditional Latin mass, many Jews were concerned that this heralded a return to the traditional prayer in the Catholic liturgy (although the permission applied only to the 1962 version approved by John XXIII, in which the words *perfidis* and *perfidiam* do not appear). The Anti-Defamation League protested the decision, which it considered "a theological setback" and "a body blow to Catholic-Jewish relations."[80] In response, in 2008, the pope presented yet another version that was supposed to be included in the Latin mass instead of the traditional prayer. In this version, Benedict XVI returned to the traditional title, Prayer for the Conversion of the Jews, rather than the subtler title of the 1970 version, Prayer for the Jews. The 2008 Latin prayer reads as follows:

Let us also pray for the Jews: That our God and Lord may enlighten their hearts, that they may acknowledge Jesus Christ as the Savior of all men. Almighty ever living God, who will that all men be saved and come to the knowledge of the truth, graciously grant that all Israel may be saved when the fullness of the nations enters into your Church. Through Christ Our Lord. Amen.[81]

Rather than silencing the commotion, this new prayer only poured more fuel on the fire.[82] The pope had failed to consult with senior church officials responsible for relations with the Jews (such as Cardinal Kasper) before issuing the new version, and he did not attach any explanation to his decision or any interpretation of the prayer. The prayer was widely seen as representative of a trend reneging on the heritage of Vatican II and as highly offensive to Jews.[83] Some even feared that the pope intended to eventually replace the postconciliar version with his newly issued version. In response, Jewish representatives worldwide cancelled their participation in interreligious dialogue activities.[84]

The objections to the prayer may be broken down into three specific criticisms. The first argued that it called for renewed missionary activities among the Jews.[85] Although the prayer itself contained no reference to mission, the very reference to Christ as the universal savior of humankind, and in particular the Jews' need to have their hearts "illuminated," was interpreted as implying the need for their proselytization. The return of the old title—"for the Conversion of the Jews"—was interpreted by critics as a clear call for missionary activity (even though the prayer says nothing about missionary action on behalf of Catholics).

The second criticism was that the new prayer resonated with the original anti-Jewish version, since the reference to the Jews as requiring illumination was a variation on the "darkness" and "blindness" of 2 Corinthians, albeit in a positive articulation. At the same time, the key verses in Romans 9:4 ("They are Israelites, and to them belong the adoption, the glory, the covenants, the giving of the law, and worship, and the promises") and 11:29 ("for the gifts and the calling of God are irrevocable") are completely ignored in the prayer.[86] As opposed to the *Novus ordo* version, Benedict XVI's prayer insists that the Jews' faithfulness to God is defective, for otherwise they would not require illumination, let alone conversion.

The third point of criticism was that in legitimizing another prayer "for the Jews" alongside the 1970 version, Benedict XVI created a double theological standard in the Catholic Church's approach to Judaism.[87] Considering the pope's strenuous efforts to reunite the church behind a uniform theological standard, this argument did not lack irony.

High-ranking church officials acted quickly to clear the air, reinterpret the prayer, and explain the pope's position. As always, the first to assuage tensions was Walter Cardinal Kasper, who headed the CRRJ. Kasper argued that the severe Jewish reaction to the new version of the prayer was more emotional than rational and was due mainly to the residues of the past.[88] The very declaration of Christ as humanity's universal savior apparently should not have caused so much agitation, so long as it did not use or encourage "disdainful" language. Moreover, the prayer reiterated the articles of Catholic faith and did not require the Jews to recognize these articles as true.

In his interpretation of Benedict XVI's version of the prayer for the Jews, Kasper sought to anchor it in Romans 9–11 and thereby show that it was a direct extension of the heritage of *Nostra aetate,* no less than was the 1970 version. According to Kasper, the pope's prayer "starts from Chapter 11 of the Letter to the Romans, which is fundamental also for *Nostra Aetate.*" He continues:

> For Paul, the salvation of the Jews is an abysmal mystery of divine election through grace [11:5, 35]. God's gifts are without repentance, and God's promises to his people, despite their disobedience, have not been revoked [11:29]. Nevertheless, due to their faithlessness, God has hardened the hearts of the majority of His people, with the exception of a holy remnant [11:5, 25]. The hardening of the Jews' hearts brings salvation of the Gentiles. The wild branches of the Gentiles have been grafted into the holy root of Israel. However, God has the power to graft on again the branches that have been cut off [11:17–24]. When the fullness of the Gentiles enters into salvation, all Israel will be saved. Israel therefore remains the bearer of the promise and of the blessing [9:4].[89]

In fact, however, the only passage in Benedict XVI's prayer that is reminiscent of Romans is "grant that all Israel may be saved when the fullness of the nations enters into your Church," which echoes Romans 11:25–26: "A hardening has come upon part of Israel, until the full number of the Gentiles has come in. And so all Israel will be saved." As opposed to Kasper's argument, most scriptural resonances in the prayer are not from Romans, but neither are they from the highly controversial verses of 2 Corinthians (3:14–17). As Hans Hermann Henrix argues, the pope formulated the prayer based mainly on the universal Christological verses in Paul's epistles and elsewhere that refer to Christ as the savior of all humankind, the "light of the glorious gospel," whose glory shines in our hearts "out of darkness" (e.g., 2 Cor. 4:1–6; Eph. 1:18; Acts 4:12). These verses are not directly related to the unique status of Israel in the eyes of God or the plan of salvation. We may wonder why Benedict XVI chose not to rely on the significant verses from Romans so central to *Nostra aetate,* which have become the main prism for understanding relations with the Jews in the post–Vatican II era. However, it is difficult to view his version of the Good Friday Prayer as an attempt to reintroduce replacement theology through the back door.

Kasper also took issue with critics who saw the prayer as a call for evangelization. Based on Benedict XVI's echoing of Romans 11:25—the salvation of Israel after "the full number of the Gentiles has come in"—Kasper argued that the prayer postpones the Jews' conversion to the eschatological age, thus obviating the need for missionary work among the Jews within historical time. Indeed, it is the gentiles who require conversion, since the Jews' hardening of heart is supposed to be a blessing for them, as it gave them the gift of faith. Only after all the gentiles have entered Christ's church will there be such a time—at the end of time—when Christ will save Israel as well. Thus, Kasper interprets Benedict XVI's prayer as clear testimony to the church's renunciation of missionary work among the Jews, leaving their conversion to God alone.

Kasper's article does not refer to the prayer's explicit statement regarding the Jews' need to recognize Christ. He may have wanted to reopen the interpretive horizon of *Nostra aetate* on the soteriological issue (whether or not explicit recognition of Christ by the Jews is essential for their salvation), a horizon closed by Benedict XVI's version of the prayer.[90]

Kasper's position in the dispute over the Good Friday Prayer evinces a distinct shift from his position on *Dominus Iesus.* Though he mentioned the universality of Christ's grace in his comments on *Dominus Iesus,* too, his wording created an impression that the Jews' faithfulness to Judaism is a sufficient vehicle for salvation. This time, he made it explicit that the Catholic Church did believe that Christ was the exclusive savior of all humankind, "as Jews and Christians have the same master." The fact that the church did not pursue organized missionary activities among the Jews did not mean that "Christians must remain idle and do nothing." Certainly, Kasper continued, even today "they must testify to the richness and beauty of their belief in Jesus Christ. As did Paul as well." Although he reiterated that the covenant with the Jews had enduring validity, Kasper's words now made it clear that the old covenant was not sufficiently salvific without Christ. It appears that in the years that passed since the *Dominus Iesus* controversy, Kasper came closer to Ratzinger's direct theological attitude and chose to avoid any intimation that Judaism may be sufficient for redemption in and of itself.

Karl Cardinal Lehmann acted to calm heated spirits in Germany. Like Kasper, he believed that there was no justification for viewing Benedict XVI's prayer as encouraging missionary activity.[91] Conversely, the Austrian Cardinal Christoph Schönborn published a detailed article in the *Tablet* that declared that the church was indeed committed to evangelizing the Jews based on the Holy Scriptures and that such activity must not be delegitimized.[92] Instead of entertaining the theory of "two ways to salvation," which is "incompatible with the Catholic belief in one salvation in Jesus Christ," he proposed a "twofold way of bearing witness to the Gospel," grounded in Romans 1:16: "For I am not ashamed of the gospel; it is the power of God for salvation to everyone who has faith, to the Jew first and also to the Greek." Schönborn further argued that the church had apologized for forcing the Jews to convert in the past and that it now had to avoid it. Instead of an explicit call for proselytism, it had to proclaim the Gospel "in the most sensitive way, cleansed of all un-Christian motives. Prayer, the offering of life, tokens of unselfish love and above all recognition of Jewish identity should win 'the goodwill of the people' [Acts 2:47] . . . so that bearing witness to their faith in Christ . . . may be recognized by them [the Jews] as the fulfilment—and not as a denial—of the promise of which they are the bearers."[93] The view of Christianity as the fulfillment of Judaism was used here as a solution that enabled the Catholic Church to preserve its articles of faith vis-à-vis Judaism without giving up on the new awareness of the Jews' uniqueness as the people of the covenant and God's chosen children.

Why, then, did Benedict XVI choose to compose a new prayer rather than include the Latin version of the 1970 prayer in the traditional service? Would it not have been simpler to impose the postconciliar version on the Latin Mass? Diplomatically speaking, such a move would certainly have made his public relations work as pope much easier, despite perhaps leading to heated protests among conservatives favoring the purity of the Latin mass. Benedict XVI's choice to compose a new prayer himself is indeed surprising. It is reasonable to assume that he would not have done so had he not felt, at least to a certain degree, uneasy with the *Novus ordo* version. Reintroducing the Christological element to the prayer, emphasizing Christ's universalism as the savior of all humanity, and portraying Judaism as incomplete so long as it has not recognized Christ—all of these are consistent with his previous statements, before and after his election to the papacy. Nevertheless, there is no doubt that his quest for theological clarity proved problematic for his relations with real-life, contemporary Jews.

Two years after the publication of the new prayer, the pope made a direct statement regarding the conversion of the Jews. In the second book of his *Jesus of Nazareth* trilogy, Benedict XVI analyzed Romans 11:25–26, the same passage he had chosen to echo in the Good Friday Prayer for the Jews.[94] History, he argued in his interpretation of these verses, was "the time of the Gentiles," the time when the church spread its universal gospel among the nations, before the end. Missionizing among the gentiles was essential to propel history toward its telos. And what about evangelizing the Jews? According to Benedict XVI, "The beginnings of a correct understanding have always been there, waiting to be rediscovered, however deep the shadows [obscuring it]." He then turns to the advice that Bernard of Clairvaux gave to Pope Eugene III in the twelfth century, reminding him of his commitment to the apostates: Jews, Greeks, or other gentiles. Calling on the pope to once again spread God's word among the nations, Bernard wrote, "Granted, with regard to the Jews, time excuses you; for them a determined point in time has been fixed, which cannot be anticipated. The full number of the Gentiles must come in first. But what do you say about those Gentiles?"[95] Like Kasper, Benedict XVI entrusted Israel to God, in the assurance that the Jews "will be saved" once "the full number of the Gentiles has come in" (Rom. 11:25). For the time being, we may infer, there is no need to missionize the Jews.

Ultimately, Ratzinger's attempts to clear the waters he himself had muddied failed time after time. His theological clarifications did little to repair the damage caused by the Good Friday Prayer, and the other gestures of conciliation and friendship made in his last years as pope were unsuccessful. His visit to Israel in 2009, for example, was perceived by the local Jews as a public relations disaster. Although he did his best to follow in the footsteps of John Paul II's visit to the Holy Land, his reception was utterly different. Whereas John Paul II had befriended Jews as a child, Benedict XVI was remembered as a member of the Hitler Youth (albeit an unwilling one). In Yad Vashem, the Polish pope had met a survivor he himself had saved from death, while Benedict XVI did not seize the opportunity to refer to his own German background. Moreover, instead of talking about the part played by the Christian world in the crime against the Jews, as he was expected to, the pope gave an abstract intellectual speech about people's names.[96] The visit to the Western Wall was similarly a debacle; John Paul II had written a note asking for God's forgiveness for the suffering caused by Catholics to the Jewish people, while Benedict XVI wrote a prayer for peace. Precisely because of his personal history, the fact that he did not repeat the gesture by asking for forgiveness caused hurt and resentfulness.[97] His attempts to promote dialogue with the Jewish people, such as referring to the profound relation between Jews and Christians in his speech on Mount Nebo in Jordan, of all places, while facing Jerusalem, attracted little media attention. Above all, Benedict XVI lacked John Paul II's charisma, and the public—both in Israel and worldwide—was largely deaf to his theological finesse.

As a theologian, Ratzinger sought to promote the relations between the church and the Jewish people on the doctrinal and intellectual plane, in the spirit of the original project of Vatican II. He wanted to provide a clear answer to the questions raised by *Nostra aetate,* to anchor its new theological intuitions in the context of the Holy Scriptures, to cleanse the tradition of hatred of Jews without violating the articles of faith, and to provide the Catholic public with a clear and consistent doctrine on the Jews. The importance of Ratzinger's work in the Jewish context lay in his giving Article 4 of *Nostra aetate* a context that made it an organic part of Catholic tradition, preventing it from becoming an odd theological divergence from the mainstream of church teachings.

In the end, however, Ratzinger's contributions to the Christian-Jewish discourse came too late, after the sun of theology had already set and both Christians and Jews had turned to other avenues in their efforts to rehabilitate their relations. The global mainstream of Christian-Jewish dialogue had shown time and time again more sympathy for vague goodwill statements than for direct doctrinal assertions, which were often experienced as confrontational, even polemical.

By the time of Ratzinger's resignation from the papacy in 2013, not only was doctrine seen as less important than gestures of friendship and face-to-face dialogue, but it was often experienced as downright detrimental.

PART II

Christianity in Orthodox Jewish Thought

5

Christianity in the Jewish Tradition

Late Antiquity

Most of the testimonies available to us regarding the attitudes of Rabbinic Judaism to Christianity date back to the Middle Ages. The halakhic discussion of Christianity began in early medieval Ashkenaz, and the theological-polemical preoccupation with Christianity began in the same time period in Muslim countries, moving to Europe in the twelfth and thirteenth centuries. Jewish sources dealing with Christianity before this period, at least explicitly, are sparse and mainly consist of the marginal references to Jesus and Christianity that one finds in the Talmud and the book *Toledot Yeshu* (The history of Jesus), a collection of derogatory narratives on the life of Jesus, the earliest versions of which are dated to the seventh to ninth centuries CE.[1]

Scholars have traditionally tended to view this absence of Jewish reference to Christianity as indicating a lack of interest. According to this view, Jewish communities in late antiquity were relatively autonomous and religiously reclusive and were not bothered by the Christian presence, at least not enough to require particularly strenuous spiritual or halakhic efforts.[2] The most commonly used simile to explain the significant gap between the plethora of Christian sources dealing with Judaism and the paucity of Jewish sources dealing with Christianity during this period is that of a mother and daughter; the church, as the wayward daughter of Judaism, was required to define itself vis-à-vis the mother, while the mother herself was already fully formed at the time of her daughter's birth, so that her attitude toward the daughter was not an intimate part of her self-perception.[3]

It was therefore not until the Middle Ages that it became necessary for the Jews to find halakhic definitions for their relationships with the Christian majority within which they lived and to enter into a methodical theological debate with Christians. Scholars tended to construe the anti-Christian comments in the Talmud as "barbaric" and lacking in method.[4] However, in recent decades, a growing body of literature has begun to view the polemics of the Middle Ages as a development of more ancient anti-Christian traditions. Scholars suggest that anti-Christian sentiments are powerfully present beneath the surface of the Talmud, the Midrash, and the liturgy.[5] Extensive parts of the Passover Haggadah, for example, have been described by Israel Yuval as having incorporated a hidden anti-Christian polemic that corresponds with contemporary Christian sources and expresses the response of rabbinical authorities to the Christian eschatological narrative. The references to Christianity in the Talmud, which have also been perceived in the past as capricious attacks against it rather than as systematic polemics, are now viewed by contemporary scholars as constituting a fundamental critique of Christian dogma and an attempt to create an alternative for the Christian narrative.[6] According to Peter Schäfer, the references to Jesus in the Talmud may not be conducive to attempts to find traces of the historical Jesus (an attempt that historians of previous generations had already despaired of), but they do constitute important testimony to the intellectual and spiritual struggle of the rabbis against the emerging church.[7] Schäfer claims that the coarse descriptions of Jesus in the Talmud are not mere invectives; they are based on a thorough rabbinical acquaintance with the Gospels, with Christian doctrine, and with exegetical techniques. Using their knowledge of Christianity, the rabbis created the "Gospel according to the Talmud," an alternative narrative to the gospels provided in the New Testament.

Recent studies thus view the rabbinical struggle with Christianity as a fundamental and crucial element in the formation of Jewish identity in late antiquity and the beginning of the Middle Ages. These scholars believe that the image of the two religions as mother and daughter is inappropriate. They propose that a more fitting image would be the relationship between two sisters battling over the legacy of their mother, the ancient tradition of Israel.[8] Rabbinic Judaism and Christianity both crystallized in light of the destruction of the Second Temple in the year 70 CE. The two groups struggled to inherit the Temple Judaism that had been abruptly expunged from the world.

Both had a reasonable claim to view themselves as the legal inheritors of their mother.[9] Moreover, according to Yuval, the impact that Christianity had on Judaism was stronger than the impact that Judaism had on Christianity.[10] Rabbinic Judaism is thus conceived by contemporary scholars as a religious system that struggled with Christianity from the very outset and defined its identity through that struggle. The seemingly sporadic references to Christianity in the Talmud constitute, in this view, a fundamental critique of Christian dogma and an attempt to create an alternative to the Christian narrative.

The scholarly attitude to the *Toledot Yeshu* also changed, along with the attitude to the Talmudic discourse on Christianity. *Toledot Yeshu* extends the stories about Jesus scattered throughout the Talmud into a coherent and continuous narrative. The book was regarded until recently as a marginal and grotesque product of Jewish popular imagination. Today, however, some scholars claim that this was a book of great importance in the Jewish world of late antiquity and the early Middle Ages and that it might have originated in more elite circles, that is, in the Babylonian yeshivas.[11] The various versions of the text differ in language, style, and content, but they all display a clear narrative of contesting Christian principles of faith on a one-to-one basis—outlining a "counter-Gospel" to the Gospels while expressing deep scorn for the sacred precepts of Christianity.[12] *Toledot Yeshu* continues the hostile tradition of the Talmud toward Christianity and further develops it.

The Jewish tradition, then, was not totally indifferent to Christianity in late antiquity and the early Middle Ages. An anti-Christian tradition—whether influential or marginal—preceded both the halakhic discussion of Christianity and the later rabbinic polemic against it.

The Middle Ages

The controversy over the centrality of the Jewish struggle against Christianity within rabbinic literature is still unfolding, but it is hard to argue with existing evidence regarding the presence of a consistent anti-Christian perception within the Jewish tradition. Anna Abulafia argues that Jews used the *Toledot Yeshu* and the Talmud as a base for creating a medieval anti-Christian lexicon that replaced central Christian terms with alternative Jewish terms that expressed contempt and disgust. In this lexicon, the virgin birth is countered by the description of Jesus as a "bastard" (*mamzer*), the emblematic cross is replaced by Jesus's depiction as "the Hanged Man" (*HaTaluy*), the site of his purported resurrection is called a "trench" (*shuha*), and the baptismal waters are referred to as "the waters of the adulteress" (*mey sotah*) or "accursing waters" (*mayim me'arerim*), thereby echoing the conception of Mary as an adulteress. The Gospels themselves are designated by a pun signifying "pages of sin" (*Avon Gilyon* instead of *Evangelion*), and so on.[13]

Yuval has shown that Ashkenazi liturgy is rife with the eschatological expectation for the final destruction of the kingdom of Edom, that is, Christendom. The utter defeat sustained by Judaism following the destruction of the Second Temple made it difficult for Jews to uphold their faith in view of historical facts that seemed to indicate the justification of Christianity, and this, argues Yuval, was a main motive force in the rise of Jewish messianism, as Jewish apologists began deferring the triumph of Judaism to the messianic future.[14] The liturgical poets of Ashkenaz, who were surrounded by a Christian majority that strongly emphasized their subordinate position, hoped for a bloodbath that would put an end to the kingdom of Edom in its entirety, and sealed their liturgies with prophecies of destruction and doom for Edom.[15]

Jewish anti-Christian traditions were taken up a notch following the massacres of 1096 during the First Crusade. Many Ashkenazi Jews chose death at the hands of the Crusaders over baptism and conversion to Christianity. Moreover, some of them chose to commit suicide and even to murder their own children and family members to prevent conversion. This sweeping resistance to Christianity was not based on halakhic considerations, and, as shown by Chaim Soloveitchik, halakhic arbiters were obliged to rely on non-halakhic sources and insubstantial arguments to justify the non-halakhically sanctioned actions of these martyrs.[16] The widespread perception of these actions in the Ashkenazi community as exemplary acts of valor required rabbinical authorities to make special efforts to frame breaches of strong halakhic precepts against the taking of life as acts of courage rather than crimes.[17]

Alongside the revulsion toward Christianity, the chronicles of the 1096 massacres also evince the familiarity of Ashkenazi Jewry with Christian values and their assimilation of Christian ideas and the spiritual trends that characterized Christianity during the period that preceded the First Crusade.[18] In other words, the Jews had assimilated the Christian symbolic system and "converted" it for Jewish use against Christianity.[19]

While the emotional enmity toward Christianity in medieval Ashkenaz drew on ancient theological traditions that created a counter-position mirroring and subverting Christian theology, the halakhic view of Christianity developed as a response to the practical needs of the times. Halakhists were required to regulate the daily interactions of Jews with Christians and to make them permissible at a time when the Jewish dependency on the Christian majority was great. This dependency required great flexibility in interpreting Talmudic halakhic precepts that severely limited any commerce or contact between Jews and idolaters, running the entire gamut from strict endogamy to refraining from paying pagans on their feast days lest they thank their gods, thereby making the Jew who paid them an accomplice. The rabbis of Ashkenaz found a number of ways to allow Jews to form partnerships and do business with Christians, by distinguishing between Christians and the idolaters described in the Talmud.[20] The tenth-century halakhist Gershom ben Yehudah (Rabbenu Gerhsom) relied on a Talmudic statement that "the gentiles outside the land [of Israel] are not idolaters; they only continue the customs of their ancestors"; that is, their seemingly idolatrous rituals are based on the power of habit and tradition rather than religious fervor.[21] On the basis of this interpretation, Gershom determined that it was permissible to negotiate and trade with Christians on their holy days.[22] Rashi's statement in the eleventh century that "the Gentiles in this time are not well versed in the essence of idolatry" expresses a similar idea. As far as Rashi was concerned, most gentiles were members of the local laity who maintained objectionable practices without being aware of the deeper meaning of their actions.[23] Rashi transformed the Talmudic idea that distinguishes geographically between non-Jews in the Land of Israel and non-Jews outside the Land of Israel into a historical distinction between idolaters at the time of the Talmud and the gentiles of his own period, that is, Christians.[24]

Other halakhic exemptions were self-reflective in that they considered the pros and cons of enmity for the Jews themselves and ruled that one should live peaceably with Christians "for fear of enmity" (*mishum eyva*) and "for the sake of the ways of peace" (*mipney darkey shalom*); that is, certain activities were permitted out of concern that prohibiting them might enrage Christians and thereby put Jews at risk.[25]

One of the most well-known halakhic permissions of the Tosafists (medieval Ashkenazi rabbis who composed glosses on the Talmud) pertained to accepting the oath of a Christian in order to avert monetary loss to a Jew. This permission is ascribed to Rabbenu Tam of the twelfth century or, according to another source, to his contemporary Rabbi Isaac ben Samuel the Elder (HaZaquen). The Talmud forbids entering a partnership with a gentile because such a partnership might lead to the gentile's taking an oath on his idol, which could put the Jewish partner at risk of having enticed the gentile into practicing idolatry and thereby transgressing the Torah prohibition, "Make no mention of the names of other gods; they shall not be heard on your lips" (Exod. 23:13).[26] The prohibition against accepting an oath from a gentile placed Jews in a problematic position, since the oath was an accepted judicial method of obligating parties to negotiations. Rabbenu Tam justified accepting an oath from a Christian when the prohibition involved monetary loss for the Jew, on the basis of the principle of "rescuing from their hands" (*metsil miyadam*)—the principle that a Jew should save his fortune from the hands of gentiles.

The other justification that Rabbenu Tam provided is called *shittuf* (association) in halakhic jargon. According to this principle, the Christian believes in the true God, but associates "something else" (*davar a'her*) to it:

> In any case, in our times, everyone swears by their holiness and does not perceive it as divine, and although they mention heaven while intending something else [*davar a'her*], this is still not considered idolatry; and they do refer to the creator of the heavens, and even though they are associating God's name with something else [*davar a'her*], it is not found that it is prohibited to cause others to worship by means of association. And there is no putting an obstacle before them [in letting them swear by what might be considered as idolatry], since the sons of Noah have not been warned about that [association].[27]

What does "associating the name of heaven with something else" mean? The parallel text, attributed to Isaac ben Samuel the Elder, contains a more explicit explanation:

> They [the gentiles] swear by their scriptures, sacred to them, known as Evangelium, which they do not regard as deity, and although they mention the name of heaven, meaning thereby Jesus of Nazareth, they do not, at all events, mention a strange deity, and moreover, they mean thereby the maker of heaven and earth, too. And despite the fact that they associate the name of heaven with an alien deity, we do not find that it is forbidden to cause others [i.e., gentiles] to make such an association [*leshattef*]. Likewise, no transgression of the prohibition "Thou shalt not place a stumbling block before the blind" [Lev. 19:14] is involved, since such association [*shittuf*] is not forbidden to the sons of Noah.[28]

According to Jacob Katz, the first sentence makes it clear that the "sacred things" on which the Christian swears are not idols. The Christian swears on the New Testament, the *Avon Gilyon* in traditional Jewish terms. Isaac ben Samuel claimed that when a Christian takes an oath in the name of his God, he intends "the Creator of Heaven and Earth" and Jesus at one and the same time. Thus, association is construed as a mental mixing of belief in the true God and in an idol.

Here, Isaac ben Samuel contends with an additional problem: if the Christian believes in the true God and in Jesus at the same time, then he transgresses the Talmudic prohibition that "whoever associates the Heavenly Name with anything else [as co-deities] is utterly destroyed [lit., "eradicated from the world"], for it is written, He that sacrificeth unto any god, save unto the Lord alone, he shall be utterly destroyed (Exod. 22:19)."[29] Thus, a Christian swearing in heaven's name and in Jesus's name at the same time transgresses the prohibition on idolatry, and a Jew would be transgressing by leading the Christian to this sin. Isaac ben Samuel circumvents this problem by making an essentialist distinction between Jews and gentiles and stipulating that the sons of Noah—that is, gentiles—are not prohibited from such beliefs, so that at least within the specific context of accepting an oath, the belief in association does not breach the first and most important Noahide commandment, which is the prohibition on idolatry.[30] The Seven Laws of Noah are the only commandments in which Jewish tradition obligates the gentiles; therefore the gentiles who observe the seven Noahide laws are not regarded as transgressors. The laws against cooperating with idolaters do not apply to them. Thus, a Jew who causes a Christian to worship association through requiring his oath is not guilty of enticing a gentile to commit sin.

This theological waiver of *shittuf,* which absolves Christians of the sin of idolatry and thereby bypasses all the many strict halakhic laws that would have prohibited Jews from engaging with them, eventually became widespread, undergoing many transformations within Jewish tradition and giving rise to a number of controversies. Yet its medieval beginnings were quite modest, as were the other halakhic waivers developed for the same reason; it was a practical solution for the contingent needs of the time. The rabbis continued to see Christians as idolaters culturally and psychologically, however, even if halakhically they were exempted from that fault in order to allow Jews to negotiate with them.[31] The classic example is found in the words of Rabbenu Gershom, following the Talmudic statement quoted earlier, that "since 'the gentiles outside the Land of Israel do not worship idols,' *even though they do worship them,* it does not count as idolatry."[32] What began as a practical halakhic workaround would eventually develop into a full-blown theological position, as the idea itself (contrary to the position that empties Christians of agency and deep religious feelings) portrays them as people having a religious conception that has a true part (faith in the true God) and a false part (faith in Jesus). This deeper theological aspect eventually opened a way to exempt Christians from the category of idolaters as a matter of theological principle in the modern age.

The only halakhic thinker in the Middle Ages who attempted to go beyond the merely practical and change the halakhic status of Christians on the basis of a theological principle was the thirteenth-century Jewish scholar Menachem Meiri.[33] Meiri excluded both Christians and Muslims from the category of idolaters by inventing a new descriptive category for them, that of "nations restricted by the ways of religion."[34] Like Jews, claimed Meiri, Christians (and Muslims) are bound by their beliefs to ethical precepts. This common denominator was sufficient to justify placing Christians on the same level as Jews where their legal rights were concerned. Meiri interpreted the discrimination between Jews and gentiles found in halakha as arising from the moral depravity of idolaters rather than from affiliation with a non-Jewish group. Those "constrained by religion" adhere to fundamental moral values, while idolaters do not comply with such values.

Meiri refrained from any explicit discussion of Christian doctrine or ritual. He did not differentiate between true and false religions, as did Maimonides, nor did he distinguish between variants of monotheism. Rather, he focused on the common denominator of all Jews, Christians, and Muslims of his time: the civilizing impact of religious mores, which allows a shared public sphere and tolerance.

Meiri, however, in excluding Christians from the category of worshippers of idolatry as a matter of principle, was the exception among European halakhic arbiters. He had little impact on Christian-Jewish relations, as his halakhic works did not become part of the prevalent halakhic discourse.[35]

The anti-Christian polemical treatises composed by Jews in Europe during the Middle Ages were written in response to the pressure exerted by the mendicant orders, from the twelfth century on, to convert the Jewish community. European Jews imported their basic arguments from the Jewish philosophy that had developed in the Muslim world commencing from the tenth century.[36] The philosophical polemics against Christianity were a cornerstone of Muslim thought in the early Middle Ages. Jewish philosophers between the ninth and twelfth centuries took part in these polemics, siding with the Muslim call for a pure monotheism and attacking the doctrines of the Trinity and the incarnation.[37] The great twelfth-century halakhic sage Maimonides was aligned with the prevailing Muslim view that perceived Christianity to be a "defective" monotheism.[38] The several paragraphs that he devoted to the concept of the Trinity indicate a certain familiarity with this doctrine and with various Christian strategies of scripture interpretation that support it.[39] Maimonides also refuted Christian claims by relying on the Talmudic texts describing Jesus as the son of a Jewess and a Roman legionary born out of wedlock.[40] Following the Babylonian Talmud, Maimonides considered Jesus to have been indicted and tried by the Sanhedrin, which sentenced him to death for his crimes.[41]

Alongside his critique of central Christian doctrines, Maimonides incorporated Christianity into Jewish-centric theology, assigning it an eschatological role. According to Maimonides, God advances his plan of redemption in a natural way by gradually converting the hearts of humanity from idolatry to monotheism. The idolatrous nations resist this process with all their might and strive to defeat the Jewish people, who raise the banner of faith in the one true God. After they failed to physically destroy the people of Israel, the idolatrous nations became more sophisticated and, in their embodiment in the Greek and Roman Empires, attempted to defeat Judaism both on an intellectual level, through philosophy, and by outright religious suppression. When these strategies, too, eventually failed, the gentiles developed a third strategy to vanquish Judaism by artificially emulating it. Jesus claimed that he was realizing the prophecies of the Torah, but his interpretation of Torah contradicted the Jewish teachings that he purported to realize, thereby sowing confusion, doubt, and perplexity among the Jewish people. Christianity was thus construed by Maimonides as a mere ploy by idolaters, similar to Judaism only in external form, in the same way that an ape is only superficially similar to a human being.[42]

This crafty attack by the heathen nations against monotheists, however, was directed by providence against idolatry itself; despite its overt intentions, Christianity subtly fostered the monotheist idea among the nations, as Maimonides described at some length:[43]

Even though Jesus the Nazarene imagined himself to be the Messiah and was killed by the Rabbinic Court—Daniel had already prophesied his coming, as it is said: "The lawless among your own people shall lift themselves up in order to fulfill the vision, but they shall fail" (Dan. 11:14). Has there been ever a greater stumbling block than this? That all prophets prophesied that the Messiah shall redeem the people of Israel and save them and will gather their dispersed multitudes and strengthen their commandments; and this one led to the death of Israel by sword, and to the dispersion of their remnants and the replacement of the Torah, as well as led most of the world astray to worship a God other than the true God.

But the creator's thoughts—no human can conceive them, for our ways are not his ways and our thoughts are not his thoughts, and all these matters of Jesus the Nazarene, and those of the Ishmaelite who arose after him—are intended only to pave the way for the King Messiah and to amend the entire world to worship God together, for it is written: "I will change the speech of the peoples to a pure speech, that all of them may call on the name of the Lord and serve him with one accord" (Zeph. 3:9).

How? The world has already been filled with words of the Messiah and words of Torah and words of laws [mitzvoth], and these matters have spread to the farthest islands and among many coarse-hearted nations. . . . And when the true King Messiah shall stand in truth and will succeed and arise and rule, they shall immediately revert and realize that their ancestors had inherited lies, and that their prophets and ancestors had led them astray.[44]

In this greatly influential passage, Maimonides ascribes a clearly positive theological role to Christianity and Islam; these two religions serve providence to advance the divine plan for humanity.[45] This does not mean that Maimonides thought well of Christianity but only that he attributed to God the power to extract good from bad and to advance his own agenda in complete contrast to the actual desire of the gentiles who adopted Christianity. Ultimately, for Maimonides, both Christianity and Islam are defective beliefs, but they are preferable to idolatry, for they bring humanity closer to the true religion.[46]

Maimonides perceived Christianity as further from the true religion than Islam. Christianity is only preferable to Islam in that it believes in the divine source of the Torah, which Islam denies. This led Maimonides to his unusual position that one is allowed to teach Torah to Christians (even though "a heathen who studies the Torah deserves death"), because "if they are shown the correct interpretation they may repent."[47] Unlike Islam, which, with all its defects, is a monotheistic faith in all respects, Maimonides considered Christianity to be idolatry: "The Christians are idolaters, and Sunday is their holy day"; and elsewhere, "You should know that this Christian nation, that argues the claim of the Messiah, in all their various sects, are all idolaters."[48]

As the conditions of European Jewry deteriorated between the twelfth and fourteenth centuries, a more extensive body of Jewish anti-Christian polemics developed in western Europe. These anti-Christian polemics, which were written in Hebrew, were intended solely for Jewish readers, to arm them against their spiritual adversaries and help them resist temptations to convert to Christianity.[49] Nevertheless, when public debates were held, Jews were required to state their claims directly before their Christian opponents.

As Christians acquired more sophisticated Jewish, and especially Talmudic, knowledge, the Jews themselves were obliged to expand their own knowledge of Christianity to refute arguments that targeted their core beliefs.[50] Unlike past attitudes toward Christianity, which mostly fed on intra-Jewish traditions, anti-Christian Jewish polemics during this period display a deep familiarity with the Gospels, Christian doctrine, and Christian biblical commentary. Jews developed their own hermeneutical tools to refute Christological biblical hermeneutics and suggested alternative interpretations for the most central verses used by the Christians against them (such as Isaiah 7:14 and Isaiah 53). They adopted Christian arguments and inverted them against the Christians themselves; while Christians attacked the Talmud as an illogical text rife with contradictions, the Jews found contradictions within the Gospels. In opposition to the Christian claim that the Talmud constituted a deviation from the Bible, Jewish polemicists contended that the writing of the church fathers deviated from the Gospels and distorted the "original" Christianity espoused by Jesus and the apostles.[51]

One of the greatest challenges facing the Jews was the Christian contention that the Jews had been doomed to eternal exile as punishment for rejecting Jesus. This claim, based on history rather than Scripture, was particularly problematic since the Jews themselves viewed historical evidence as testimony to the state of their relationship with God. In this context, their dire situation constituted a significant argument against them. In their defense, they argued that their exile was merely temporary. They agreed with the Christians that it was a consequence of their sins but claimed that these sins were less heinous than those attributed to them by Christianity.[52] Some viewed the tribulations of exile as the sacrifice of the righteous, who will merit an even greater reward in heaven, while others argued that the period of exile served a soteriological role in the redemption of humanity as the scattered Jews disseminated the truth.

Christian Talmudic scholars were particularly troubled by some of the harsh anti-Christian expressions within it. In the 1240 Disputation of Paris (which ultimately led to the burning of the Talmud two years later), Nicholas Donin, a Jew who converted to Christianity, attacked the Talmud as a heretical text that contains profanities and blasphemies against Christianity, desecrates its most hallowed beliefs, and instructs Jews to cheat and even murder Christians. Donin emphasized the Talmudic narrative that sentences Jesus to be immersed in boiling excrement and the stories that describe Jesus as the son of a whore. The Tosafist Rabbi Yechiel of Paris, who was obliged to contend with Donin in the 1240 disputation, attempted to clear the Talmud of this accusation by claiming that the Jesus of the Talmud was not the Christian Jesus but another person going by the same name. He also claimed that the gentiles sentenced to death in the Talmud were not the Christians of his time but members of the seven nations of Canaan, the idolaters of the Bible. These claims eventually became extremely widespread and common in Jewish literature. The shift of the church from an attitude of tolerance to one of hostility toward Judaism inevitably motivated Jewish rabbis to work in the opposite direction, even if only for apologetic reasons.[53]

The Modern Era

New patterns began to emerge in the relations between Jews and Christians in the course of the sixteenth century, after the Jews were expelled from Spain and Portugal. One of the characteristics of Judaism in the new age includes the increased introversion of Jewish communities and their relative disengagement from their gentile environment. According to Katz, at this point the Jews more or less lost interest in Christianity and became indifferent toward it.[54] Traces of anti-Christian polemics were still evident in the rabbinical literature, but they were now marginal, appearing in this period in a way that replicated previous polemical compositions, and were not further developed. The center of gravity of Jewish identity shifted from the plane of the bitter struggle with Christianity over matters of faith to the plane of a

natural, ontological, or metaphysical difference between Israel and the nations of the world.

The ontological conception of the difference between Jew and gentile already evident in the Talmud became the prism through which Christian-
Jewish relations were viewed. Christians were now perceived as essentially
different from Jews to the point that even conversion (on either side) would
not be able to eradicate the difference.[55]

These Jewish conceptions, exemplified in the works of Judah Loew ben
Bezalel (the Maharal of Prague) in the sixteenth century, echoed the distinct
difficulties encountered in the Christian world during that period in regard
to the forced converts to Christianity (Anusim), whose Jewishness was perceived to have adhered to them even beyond their baptism. At the same time
that the conception of Christians as metaphysically different from Jews increased in strength, the halakhic conception of Christians as idolaters underwent a certain "tempering." Rabbi Moshe Isserles (the Rama), the foremost
Ashkenazi arbiter in the sixteenth century, used *shittuf* as justification for allowing additional activities beyond the acceptance of an oath.[56] Katz claims
that the use of the concept by the Rama did not exceed that of the Tosafists in
any significant way, since, like them, he only used the principle of *shittuf* in a
formal way, so as to allow already accepted customs.[57] However, Louis Jacobs
considers that the Rama actually made theological use of the idea of *shittuf*.[58]
The meaning ascribed to *shittuf* was subsequently further expanded and perceived as applicable to Christian faith itself (the Trinity was defined as *shittuf*).

Rabbinical literature in the early modern period was subject to censorship,
which omitted passages considered blasphemous or offensive to Christianity.
At the same time, anti-Christian sentiments remained within popular Yiddish literature. Testimonies of Jews who converted to Christianity indicate
that Jewish children in Ashkenaz were educated to abhor Christianity. Anti-
Christian literature was produced for women in Yiddish so as to teach them
how to reject the claims of the rival religion; Ashkenazi Jews compiled historical texts with anti-Christian elements, such as chronicles of the Crusaders'
pogroms, but kept them inside the community to protect them from falling
into Christian hands; *Toledot Yeshu* was translated into Yiddish in many versions, but the Jews themselves forbade it to be reprinted.[59]

Toledot Yeshu was also associated with a collection of practices that had
developed during the early Middle Ages among Jews for Christmas Eve,
which became known in Yiddish as Nittel Nacht. The word *nittel* is derived

from *dies natalis domini,* "the birthday of the Lord" in Latin. But the rabbinical interpreters suggested a different etymology for *nittel,* associating it
with the common moniker for Jesus in Jewish sources as the Hanged Man
(*HaTaluy*)—suggesting that the Nittel Nacht is the Night of the Hanged One.
Many of the customs of Nittel Nacht appeared in the course of the sixteenth
century, even though they were not written down until a much later period
because of the risk. Jews "celebrated" Christmas Eve in a number of specific
ways: they refrained from studying Torah and played cards instead (lest
their Torah study be tallied as merit in favor of Jesus the Jew), refrained
from sex (out of concern that children conceived on that night might convert
to Christianity), and ate garlic (considered to be a potent measure against
demons).[60]

The Talmudic story from the tractate *Gittin,* which describes Jesus as
doomed to pay for his sins in boiling excrement, alongside similar traditions that developed in versions of *Toledot Yeshu,* served as inspiration for a
number of folk customs and stories that focused on excrement and sewage
on Christmas Eve. Jewish children were warned not to defecate on Christmas,
for example, lest the "Hanged One," that is Jesus, should pull them into the
sewer.[61] It was said that on Christmas Eve, Jesus comes back into the world
and crawls through the sewers. The only rest that he can gain is by listening
to Jews studying Torah. For this reason, the Jews on Christmas Eve stop
learning their Torah, so as not to allow Jesus rest from his crawling. Moreover, the Jews feared that when studying, they might repeat passages that
Jesus himself had studied, thereby providing him with merit and animation
and strengthening the forces of evil and impurity in the world.[62] It is still
customary in some Hasidic circles to utilize Christmas Eve as a good time
to cut toilet paper for all the days of Shabbat and holy days (when cutting is
prohibited) throughout the year.

The conditions of European Jewry improved during the seventeenth and
eighteenth centuries, and their relationship with the Christian majority became more complex and extensive. Accordingly, the rabbis, too, developed a
more tolerant attitude toward Christianity, which enabled Jews to establish a
variety of collaborations with Christians. Rabbis demanded that their communities behave with exemplary fairness toward the Christians with whom
they came into contact and were even wont to severely punish Jews who
breached the trust of gentiles or treated them improperly. The criminal behavior of a single Jew could put an entire community at risk, for every Jew

was fully identified with his or her community. The need to behave fairly toward the gentiles was justified not merely by expediency or caution, however, but often also on the basis of ethical virtues and proper conduct.[63]

The distinction between contemporaneous Christians and the idolaters described in the Talmud, which served as a shield against Christian attacks during the Middle Ages and was subsequently entrenched in Jewish literature by censorship (such as replacing the word *goyim* [gentiles] with *akum* [worshippers of the Zodiac]), was now applied as a guiding principle in the rabbinic discussions regarding Christians. The allowances that halakhic arbiters provided for economic ties with Christians during the Middle Ages, which were given only grudgingly on a circumstantial post hoc basis, were expanded by the halakhic arbiters of the seventeenth and eighteenth centuries into comprehensive fundamental positions.

Manifestations of this trend are found in the writings of prominent rabbis from the sixteenth to the nineteenth century. Moses Rivkesh, the seventeenth-century author of *Be'er HaGolah,* explicitly distinguishes between contemporary Christians and the idolaters of the Talmud, deriving from this fundamental position the permit to pray for Christians and the obligation to save them, contrary to the laws related to idolaters in the Talmud. The eighteenth-century rabbi Yechezkel Landau, known as the Noda BeYehudah, embraced a similar position toward Christianity and wrote the following in the apologia that prefaces his *Noda BeYehudah* responsa:

> I explain and exhort in most of my public sermons that one should be very careful in respecting the nations of our times, in whose lands and countries we find shelter. And we are charged with praying for the well-being of kings and ministers and their armies and to pray for the well-being of the country and its residents, and God forbid that we should be ingrates, for they are our benefactors and give us our livelihood and the means to survive. . . . Even more so where the nations of our times are concerned, for these nations within which we reside believe in the main principles of the faith, for they believe in the creation of the world and believe in the prophecy of the prophets and in all the miracles and wonders written in the Torah and the books of the prophets, and it therefore goes without saying that we are required to respect them and esteem them. . . . Wherever we find . . . some disparagement of idolaters or gentiles or Kutim, or some such expressions, do not make the mistake of thinking that they refer to these nations of our times, for

anyone who interprets them in this way is mistaken and deviates from the teaching of the Torah, for such expressions only refer to the ancient nations that believed in the stars and the zodiac.[64]

These passages and similar ones describe Christians as sharing a common religious heritage with Jews.[65] The idea that contemporary gentiles were not idolaters, which had served the sages of the Middle Ages as an excuse to allow certain activities, was thus expanded to distinguish between Christians and idolaters in an absolute and fundamental sense.[66] The idea of *shittuf*, too, which had begun as a pretext for allowing the specific act of accepting an oath from a Christian, was expanded by later arbiters into a principle that expresses leniency toward Christians: "The Sages of Blessed Memory have already determined that the sons of Noah were not prohibited from *shittuf*"; that is, for them, Judaism does not view Christianity as a transgression where gentiles are concerned.[67] This expansion is significant, since it incorporates tolerance toward Christianity itself and not only toward Christians who are not "fanatic" in their adherence to idolatry.[68] A limiting interpretation of the term made it possible to increase halakhic flexibility without changing the attitude toward Christianity; a more expansive interpretation opened the door to religious tolerance.

There is no scholarly consensus regarding the fate of these relatively positive rabbinic positions toward Christianity over the course of the nineteenth century. According to Yosef Salmon, the rabbinic "tolerant" turn toward Christianity, which Katz identified in his book *Exclusiveness and Tolerance*, had ended by the third decade of the nineteenth century. At that point, Salmon argues, central European rabbis began to perceive Christianity as sheer idolatry.[69] Salmon anchors this "hardening" toward Christianity—which he identifies first and foremost in the writings of Moshe (Chatam) Sofer—in the reactionary rabbinic struggle against the emerging Reform movement.[70] Moshe Miller maintains, however, that Chatam Sofer's harsh positions vis-à-vis Christianity are not representative of the rabbinic approach at that time.[71] Central and eastern European rabbis may not have expressed the same degree of openness to Christianity as their German counterparts, but many of them continued to perceive Christianity as *shittuf,* which is allowed to the sons of Noah. According to Miller, the rabbis' resistance to the Reform movement and to the Haskalah (the Jewish Enlightenment) did not have significant implications for their attitude to non-Jews.[72] Moreover, if in czarist Russia the rabbinic attitude to Christianity was characterized by suspicion and hesitation, in central Europe, where the Christian majority culture was relatively tolerant of Jews and where emancipation seemed a feasible option, the rabbis, too, expressed tolerance and gratitude toward the majority society.[73] The later evolution of this history is the focus of the next chapter.

6

Christianity in Contemporary Halakhic Literature

As we have seen, the modern age brought about a positive turn in the Jewish tradition's attitude toward Christianity. As Jacob Katz has argued, while the basic position of halakhists during the Middle Ages was to view Christianity as idolatry, many halakhic scholars of the modern era gradually ameliorated this position, making an effort to broaden more lenient halakhic decisions in a way that would allow Jews to establish ties with the surrounding Christian society.[1] Leading rabbinical figures of the eighteenth and nineteenth centuries did not view Christians as idolaters in the full sense of the word, while those who resided in central Europe (especially in Germany) expressed tolerance, openness, and gratitude toward the Christian majority.

Did this trend of increasing tolerance toward Christianity persist into the twentieth and twenty-first centuries? A number of historical conditions seem to support this possibility. Many important Christian groups have changed their attitude toward Judaism in recent decades and have begun condemning antisemitism. Once the hatred toward Jews abated, it was expected that Jews would reciprocate. The Jews now have a state of their own (which is obligated to uphold Western liberal values) and are no longer dependent on the Christian world. Jews in the Diaspora enjoy substantial religious freedom. The original conditions that gave rise to Jewish hostility toward Christianity have changed, and the ancient enmity, one supposes, would have been made redundant. Thus, the prevalent assumption is that the Judeo-Christian polemic belongs in the past.[2]

Perhaps it is this assumption that has led scholars to disregard the rabbinical Jewish perspective on Christianity in recent decades. Whereas the study of past periods in Jewish-Christian relations is undergoing a renaissance, few studies focus on the current status of these relations, and even fewer on the attitude of contemporary rabbinical Judaism to Christianity. How, then, has the rabbinical position on the issue of Christianity been transformed in the twentieth and twenty-first centuries? How did the process of secularization, the Holocaust, and the founding of the State of Israel affect it? Did Orthodox Judaism continue the tolerant trend highlighted by Jacob Katz?

The only study devoted to the position of Rabbinic Judaism on Christianity in recent decades is Aviad Hacohen's "Modern Rabbinical Conceptions of Christians and Christianity: From Rabbi Kook to Rabbi Ovadiah Yosef," published in 2004.[3] Like Katz, Hacohen equates the modern era with a decrease in religious zeal and an increase in tolerance and sees a tolerant worldview as an essential component of modern identity. According to this conception, the deepening of modernity was supposed to bolster tolerance. Hacohen muses:

> Did the attainment of Jewish political independence and the possibility of true free speech without fear of an "alien government" [*malkhut zarah*] or Christian censorship indeed lead to changes in the halakhic "language" discussing Christianity, both in content and style? Does the latter-day halakhic scholar continue to harbor the memory of Christian persecution in both distant and more proximate historical times, or does he now lift his gaze toward the present and future, wherein interfaith conciliation and tolerance occupy a greater place?[4]

Hacohen ultimately answers these questions in the negative. Christianity, he claims, is still perceived as idolatry "with all its implications" by most contemporary halakhic arbiters "as regards the prohibition against fraternizing with its adherents and the obligation to uproot it from the world."[5] Moreover, this phenomenon is not relegated to a single Orthodox congregation but rather crosses all intra-religious boundaries—Sephardic and Ashkenazi Jews, Zionists and anti-Zionists, conservatives and moderates. Nor is it restricted to a single geographical region; it is prevalent in Israel, in the United States, and even in Europe. Jewish hostility toward Christianity is not a thing of the past; it is present, and it is significant.

Hacohen writes that despite the far-reaching changes that Judaism has undergone in recent decades, Rabbinic Judaism has continued to adhere to a stringent and outmoded perspective in regard to Christianity: "Even the founding of the State of Israel as a regime that upholds democratic values alongside Jewish ones has not brought about any significant change in the attitude of halakhic scholars toward Christianity and its adherents."[6] How is it possible that as far as Christianity is concerned, Rabbinic Judaism refuses to veer right or left from what the ancient halakhic sages commanded, in clear opposition to the zeitgeist? Hacohen implies that instead of lifting its "gaze toward the present and future," which are imprinted with the seal of tolerance, Jewish Orthodoxy chooses to remain mired in the past.

The "mired in the past" hypothesis with regard to Jewish Orthodoxy is held by a number of important scholars, where the impact of Katz's studies can be clearly discerned. According to Katz, traditional society opened up to tolerant perspectives to its very limits in the course of the eighteenth century. In his eyes, only the Jews of the Haskalah, who made the full shift into modernity (though, like Katz himself, without relinquishing their observance of halakha), continued to move tradition forward. With the rise of Orthodoxy, which Katz sees as a reaction to modernity, traditional society retreated from its flirtation with the Enlightenment and seems to have petrified itself in the past while flying the banner of Chatam Sofer's famous maxim, "Anything new is forbidden on the authority of the Torah."[7]

Yosef Salmon's article on the attitude of halakha toward Christianity from the late eighteenth to the middle of the nineteenth century (discussed in Chapter 5) is similarly modeled on Katz's premise. Salmon writes that one can discern a decline in tolerance toward Christianity in the halakhic verdicts of Chatam Sofer and his student and colleague Rabbi Moshe (Maharam) Schick, who are widely considered the founding fathers of Orthodox Judaism.[8] According to Salmon, this withdrawal is related not to changes in relationships with Christians but rather to internal change within the Jewish world itself, having to do with an attempt to defend against the Jewish Reform movement that threatened to turn Jews into pseudo-Christians. Salmon presents the changes in halakha as a reaction to modernity intended to fortify and strengthen traditional Judaism against its detractors, rather than as a change in attitude toward Christianity per se. In this interpretation, Salmon conforms to the classic conception of Orthodoxy as a contra-modernity trend, a view that ascribes the entire ensemble of transformations in Orthodoxy over recent decades to the struggle against the secularization and modernization of Judaism.

This chapter examines the validity of this conception regarding the perception of Christianity in Rabbinic Judaism. It is clear that Christianity is perceived as idolatry by most contemporary arbiters who reject more "tolerant" halakhic traditions—despite the fact that Christian-tolerant positions also have a long history (and are therefore not necessarily signs of "modernization"). However, contrary to the interpretations of this trend provided by such scholars as Hacohen, who are perplexed by the seeming paradox of deeper stringency even as the zeitgeist calls for greater tolerance, it seems that "the attainment of Jewish independent sovereignty and the possibility of true free speech without fear of 'an alien government,'" the very factors that Hacohen perceives as conductive to tolerance, are in fact the underpinnings of contemporary arbiters' withdrawal from more conciliatory halakhic positions and their preference for a more inimical position toward Christianity and its adherents.[9] I will argue here that democracy itself, and the values of free speech and freedom of worship, as well as the secularization of society and the founding of a Jewish state, are factors that are conducive to the liberation of Jews from Christian influence and underline the anti-Christian position within contemporary Rabbinic Judaism.

On the one hand, one may indeed point to a process of hardening in the halakhic perceptions of Christianity, as claimed by Salmon and Hacohen, and this hardening cuts across the entire halakhic spectrum.[10] Moderate positions that expropriate Christianity from the category of idolatry have become marginalized, while positions that strive to distance Christianity from Judaism in the most stringent manner—that is, by defining it as idolatry, with some of the far-reaching consequences of such categorization—have become the mainstream. On the other hand, the halakhic changes toward Christianity cannot be summed up as merely a "heightening of the fence" separating Jews and Christians, for it seems that halakhic arbiters are not content with just reverting to some presumably authentic halakhic tradition that they consider has been distorted out of fear of Christian retaliation. Rather, they utilize their liberation from Christian dominion to express much more assertive anti-Christian positions than one can find in previous generations, even though previous generations were equally—or more—concerned with guarding themselves against the influences of Christian society. In many cases, contemporary halakhic discussions of Christianity do not reflect a trend of segregation from the secular sphere, but, on the contrary, involve the adoption of "secular" and modern norms, perspectives, and values, sometimes as a matter of "politics" but sometimes as a matter of principle, too. Contemporary rabbinical hostility toward Christianity seems to be a by-product of renewed rabbinical thinking on the nature of Jewish identity, which for many generations was determined within the context of a position of inferiority vis-à-vis the Christian world. It is not solely, or even mainly, expressed as a defensive position isolated from the secular world but rather as an assertive movement of expansion, of making one's presence felt and of attempting to "normalize" the Jewish people in their new situation—a situation where Christianity is no longer feared. This trend is prevalent not only in Israeli or Zionist camps within contemporary Jewish Orthodoxy but throughout the spectrum of Jewish Orthodoxy everywhere, including its anti-Zionist branches. This discussion challenges Katz's narrative, which identifies secularization and modernization with interreligious tolerance and interfaith hostility with previous traditions, by demonstrating that modernity is at times connected with forms of hostility, while forms of tolerance are present within tradition.

The Halakhic Status of Christianity within Changing Political Conditions

The founding of the State of Israel gave rise to an acute tension between the unequivocal increase in the power of the Jews and their collective memory as a weak and persecuted minority. From this followed new theological and halakhic uncertainties regarding the policy that should be adopted by the newly established Jewish sovereign government vis-à-vis the Christian minorities under its rule.[11] The position toward Christianity often became a prism through which Jews espousing different flavors of Orthodoxy argued about the theological meaning of the Jewish state.

As we shall see, within these controversies, Orthodox authors often interpreted and paraphrased the following paragraph by Maimonides to formulate their arguments:

Gentile poor are to be supported along with Israelite poor in order to follow "the ways of peace." . . . [Idolaters] are to be greeted, even on their [pagan] holidays, to follow "the ways of peace." . . . All of the above pertains only when Israel is exiled among the nations or when the gentiles overpower. But when Israel overpowers the nations of the world, we are forbidden to tolerate a gentile who worships an alien deity in our midst. Even a temporary resident or a transient merchant should not pass through our land without accepting the seven commandments given to the sons of Noah. For it is said, "They shall not dwell in your land" (Exod. 23:33) even temporarily.[12]

This passage connects a positive, or at least a tolerant, approach to gentiles and idol worshippers ("the ways of peace") with a situation of Jewish political inferiority ("when Israel is exiled among the nations or when the gentiles overpower"). Political superiority ("when Israel overpowers the nations of the world"), conversely, necessitates, for Maimonides, the application of harsh measures against gentiles in the Land of Israel who do not observe the Noahide laws. When considering the scope and meaning of Israeli sovereignty, rabbis often resort to Maimonides's distinctions.

Zionist rabbis, who identified with the state, strove to reconcile the obligations of the Jewish state as a modern democracy with the demands of halakha. The contortionist task of justifying a tolerant policy toward Christianity by the State of Israel therefore fell on their shoulders. Some of these rabbis attempted to formulate an essential religious tolerance in the language of halakha. The second chief rabbi of the State of Israel, Isser Yehuda Unterman, for example, transformed the argument of "for the ways of peace" from a temporary leniency intended to maintain normal relations with gentiles (Christians and Muslims) into a fundamental halakhic position that expressed the Torah's aspiration for peace.[13] Rabbi Hayim David HaLevi, a prominent twentieth-century Sephardic rabbi, adopted Menachem Meiri's vision of Christians as "nations restricted by the ways of religion." He placed the leniencies provided by the sages of Ashkenaz alongside Meiri's lenient opinion, and he relegated Maimonides's perception of Christianity as idolatry to the status of a solitary opinion to diminish the weight accorded him in the halakhic discourse on the issue.[14]

However, the great majority of Orthodox rabbis rejected Unterman's and HaLevi's positions. While careful to maintain a moderate halakhic position toward Christians and Christian sacred sites in Israel as a matter of policy, they refrained from making far-reaching statements about the halakhic status of Christianity.[15] Moreover, many interesting insights regarding contemporary rabbinical perceptions of the balance of power between the Jews and the Christian world may be gained by examining the justifications given by rabbis for their moderate policies.

Moderate halakhic positions toward Christians in Israel are often justified in terms of the Jews' weakness in relation to the Christian world.[16] A
salient example is an article regarding the rights of minorities in the halakha
written by Rabbi Yitzhak (Issac) HaLevi Herzog, Israel's first chief rabbi, in
1947, before the state was established. Herzog defined this issue as "the most
difficult issue associated with the democratic nature of the state," and he attempted to justify the rights of minorities at the halakhic level.[17] Paradoxically, while attempting to reconcile the halakhic tradition with Jewish
political sovereignty, Herzog chose to derive his justification from the de-
pendence of the State of Israel on the nations of the world instead of justifying
minority rights from the position of a sovereign nation. Herzog claimed
that the State of Israel should conduct itself with tolerance toward the Christians living within it because Israel had been given to the Jews "as a gift" by
the nations, and it still needed their support. As long as the Jewish state is
dependent on the nations of the world, Herzog reasoned, it is illogical to
speak of "Israel's overpowering hand" and thereby "put our chances and
our existence at risk from the outset because of severe discrimination
against Christians." To do away with this difficulty, Herzog excluded Christians from the class of idolaters and defined them as resident aliens (*gerim
toshavim*).[18]

In other words, Herzog explained that the Christian minority in Israel was,
in fact, part of a majority group: world Christianity. By thus resurrecting the
traditional Jewish position as a minority within Christianity, Herzog also
made it possible to apply all of the traditional halakhic laws exempting Christianity and Christians. As far as Herzog was concerned, the reason the state
should not "harshly" discriminate "against Christians" was not a matter of
principle but rather of pragmatism. If this weakness were to disappear, so
would the basis for tolerance. The halakhic toolkit that Herzog needed to
rely on made it far more difficult to change the traditional attitude to Judaism and far easier to make circumstantial excuses that would only suspend these laws and not uproot them entirely.

Yet even the hesitant "exemption" from idolatry that Herzog bestowed on
Christians when he classified them as believers in *shittuf* is exceptional in
the halakhic literature of religious Zionism. Most rabbinic arbiters agree on
practical grounds with Herzog's position that it is appropriate to treat Christians in Israel with tolerance, but they are unwilling as a matter of principle
to absolve Christianity of idolatry. Christian "enmity," and the relative weakness of the State of Israel, require Israel to take a more lenient approach to

Christians residing within it, but any formulation that distinguishes Christians from idolaters is not usually made in contemporary halakhic literature. Rabbinic arbiters usually prefer to put off the application of any commandments requiring discrimination against Christians to the messianic future.[19] Even rabbis who view the State of Israel itself as a stage in salvation believe that it is better to postpone implementation of such halakhic laws until the more advanced stages in the progress of redemption, when Israel's hand shall truly "overpower" the nations.

Rabbi Yehuda Gershoni, a student of Rabbi Kook, criticized Herzog's argument in a similar spirit. He claimed that in Israel, the halakhic laws pertaining to idolatry were even more stringent than those applicable overseas, since the protection of trade relations with Christians was based on the Talmud's statement that "the gentiles outside the land [of Israel] are not idolaters."[20] The Land of Israel is particularly sensitive to idolatry, so that even if non-Jews overseas are not considered idolaters, still, in Israel, they are commanded to refrain not only from full idolatry but even from *shittuf* (Gershoni based his argument on the works of the eighteenth-century rabbi Jacob Emden, who expressed positive evaluations of Christianity, too). Tolerance toward Christians, Gershoni wrote, should be justified only circumstantially and not as a matter of principle, "since our hand does not presently overpower and we still need the help of the world's nations."[21]

However, this position, which denies the dominance and power of the State of Israel (and postpones the confrontation with Christianity to a distant future), runs into serious theological problems in view of the state's actual military might. These problems became ever more apparent following the Six-Day War in 1967. After the war, the Satmar Rebbe, Joel Teitelbaum, the greatest critic of the State of Israel in the name of the Torah, pointed to the problem created by the fact that Israel had assumed control of ancient churches. In his essay "Al HaGeulah VeAl HaTemurah" (On salvation and change), he attempted to repudiate the euphoric feeling in Israel that it was the hand of providence that had produced the victory and that the conquests of the war were the "beginning of redemption." The Satmar Rebbe viewed the fact that the State of Israel took control of ancient churches without "uprooting" idolatry from Israel as unequivocal proof that providence was not involved, but rather Satan.[22] Because of the fact that Israel did not "eradicate" Christian idolatry, he considered Israel Defense Forces (IDF) soldiers and the government of Israel to be idolaters themselves. It is worth noting that the Rebbe did not believe that IDF soldiers should have destroyed the churches in the Old City of Jerusalem. He was of the opinion that in the days of the Messiah, the eradication of all idolatrous sites would be an inseparable part of Jewish sovereignty in the Land of Israel, that is, that God himself would cause their destruction. The fact that the State of Israel was power-less to uproot idolatry was to him a proof that its wars were not divinely blessed.

Rabbi Menachem Mendel Kasher, a Gur Hasid who became a Zionist, held the opposite view, according to which the victories of the Six-Day War were seen as obvious miracles. Nevertheless, the salvation process was not yet complete. The fact that the State of Israel left the churches that were cap-tured in the Six-Day War unmolested could therefore be justified as a tem-porary measure. Churches were indeed houses of idolatry, but the State of Israel was not commanded to "eradicate" the sacred sites of Christianity from within it, as long as "Israel's hand does not overpower" to the extent that Is-rael can ensure that the churches shall not be constructed again. In the meantime, Kasher maintained that the State of Israel might incur the wrath of the nations should it fail to respect international laws "prohibiting occu-piers from touching the sacred sites of every nation, and woe betide the nation that transgresses this law. . . . We should not antagonize the nations of the world who have the power to destroy us, God forbid, and all Jews wherever they live."[23] Had the IDF soldiers destroyed the churches in Jeru-salem, Christians would have undoubtedly forced the State of Israel to re-build them, and that would have been a real transgression.[24]

Kasher went a step beyond Herzog's position by suggesting the symbol-ical eradication of Christian sites by assigning them derogatory names:

> It is a good deed to change the name so that it is derogatory in the Land of Israel when they are not conquered, and it may be that this is ap-propriate for our condition in Israel, which is conquered but our hand does not overpower in these places, and we therefore have no obliga-tion to eradicate them, but we do have an obligation to change their names, so that we may observe the commandment of "You shall oblit-erate their name."[25]

Kasher was deliberating on the complexity of the current situation in which the land "is conquered" but the Christian churches "are not con-quered." Even if the conquests of the war expressed God's providence, the churches remained as a testimony that salvation was incomplete. Therefore, Kasher retreated to a compromise—to mock Christianity while tolerating its actual presence. The tension between the redemptive experience of sovereignty and the need to tolerate Christianity was thus transformed into the use of derogatory language, as an expression of a middle way in which freedom could not be translated into actions but was nevertheless manifested in words.

Many other religious Zionist rabbis, particularly those affiliated with the rabbis Abraham Isaac and Zvi Yehudah Kook (to be discussed in Chapter 7), displayed a tension between expressions of hostility toward Christianity and the obligation to treat its believers and sacred sites with respect. I believe this is not because the liberal principles of human rights *forced* them to restrain their urge to observe anti-idolatry halakha in the practical sense (and destroy the churches), but, on the contrary, because they experienced the liberal principles of freedom of speech as *liberating* them to express resentments that had been beneath the surface and declare that Jews no longer needed to constrain themselves for fear of Christianity.

Religious Zionism is not alone in recognizing that the balance of power between Judaism and Christianity has changed. Haredi (ultra-Orthodox) halakhists, who do not have any apparent interest in the political power of the State of Israel, are also contending with the fact that Christianity no longer poses a direct threat to Judaism as it did in the past. One can accordingly identify an ever-increasing tendency to freely express hostility toward Christianity in Haredi circles, too. Despite the expressed Haredi desire to preserve exilic life, subordination toward the Christian world is not a component that halakhic arbiters are particularly keen to retain. Haredi arbiters are often content to define Christianity as idolatry, without considering any practical implications.

Rabbi Moshe Sternbuch, the chief rabbinical judge of the extremist Haredi anti-Zionist congregation (Ha'Edah HaHaredit) in Jerusalem, derives particularly harsh conclusions from his definition of Christianity as idolatry. Sternbuch is a representative of the most radical stream within the Haredi public; he is stringent in matters of halakha, adamantly opposed to the encroachment of modernity into the world of Torah, antagonistic to Zionism and secular Judaism, reclusive, and conservative. Sternbuch has been requested to address the question of whether Christianity should be considered *shittuf,* and his responses have been unequivocal: "Christianity is not mere *shittuf.* Rather, they [Christians] personify our God, blessed be His name, with such descriptors as son, mother, etc., and therefore they are worse; and the same ruling that applies to any idolaters applies to them."[26]

Sternbuch's attitude to Christianity stems in great measure from the traditional desire to maintain a distance between religions. This is the reason, for example, that Sternbuch firmly objects to the innovation one finds in Chabad Hasidism (a different, more "modern" and more prominent, group within world Orthodoxy) and other circles encouraging gentiles to observe the seven Noahide laws.[27] Because he views Christianity as idolatry, Sternbuch forbids this, as it would give the appearance of legitimizing Christians' faith in Christ—as if that faith in itself were not a transgression of the prohibition on idolatry (which is one of the seven Noahide laws). "In this they [who suggest that Christians are observing the seven Noahide laws] mislead them [Christians] to think that their idolatry is allowed and is what His Blessed Name desires, while according to the laws of the Torah and the obligations of the seven Noahide laws, they are still maintaining their idolatry as has been defined by the arbiters." Sternbuch claims that "when one legitimates them as Noahides, they are quick to add a substitute to our religion," that is, to convert Jews to Christianity. Jewish missionary activity may also be perceived as legitimating the Christian mission: Why should gentiles be forbidden an activity allowed by the Jews? Sternbuch raises another concern, that by encouraging Christians to observe the seven Noahide laws, one transgresses the injunction to "give them [idolaters] no quarter" (Deut. 7:2) (in the sense of not giving them free gifts) because the Jews involved in the work of disseminating the laws of Noah to Christians wish to award Christians the merit of observing commandments. Theoretically, it would have been appropriate to *force* Christians to accept the Noahide laws and to kill those who refused to relinquish their idolatry, but such a move might "put the entire house of Israel at risk throughout their places of dispersion," and for this reason, one must forsake the entire matter. One must wait for an age in which "Israel's hand shall overpower the nations," in the language of Maimonides, at which time it will be necessary to "force" the entire gentile world to observe the Seven Laws of Noah rather than convince them to do so.

In other halakhic decisions, Sternbuch goes even further and utilizes the definition of Christians as idolaters as a basis of action rather than inaction. For example, during his incumbency as the rabbi of a Haredi congregation in Johannesburg, South Africa, he gave the Jewish director of a hospital permission to approve the euthanasia of a Christian, something that is forbidden for a Jewish patient. Sternbuch determined that even though killing gentiles is prohibited—"for God made man, including gentiles, in God's image, and it is not permitted to destroy him"—the fact that the patient was a Christian, that is, a gentile who does not observe the seven Noahide laws, opened the door to hastening his death. "For the sick gentile does not observe the seven Noahide laws and thereby violates the prohibition against idolatry when he maintains his faith, for which he deserves death." On this halakhic basis, Sternbuch concluded that the Jewish physician was allowed to provide the Christian patient with assisted euthanasia.

Sternbuch was well aware of the reservation noted by the Tosafists (Tosafot on BT Avoda Zara 64b): killing a gentile idolater is prohibited unless the gentile has been tried by a rabbinical court. Nevertheless, in this case, Sternbuch permitted euthanasia because the gentile idolater himself wished to die: "Although he does not have to die, i.e., one does not have to actually kill him, but when he himself wishes it and he deserves death as an idolater, it is obviously permitted, for he deserves to die under the laws of the Torah and the Jew is not deemed a murderer." Sternbuch's bottom line was that in this era in which idolaters are not tried before a Jewish court and Jews are not supposed to kill them without a trial, the dying man nevertheless "violates the seven Noahide laws, and it goes without saying that those in South Africa do so in their superstitious faith, and we are therefore not obliged to prevent the idolater from carrying out [euthanasia], for they are deemed idolaters, and it is not required to avoid killing them when they so desire when they are suffering."[28]

It seems that it was for two good ends that Sternbuch used the most stringent position toward Christians (one that views them as idolaters who deserve death): to save the gentile from his harsh suffering, and to allow a Jewish doctor to behave according to the conventions of his workplace. Sternbuch subsequently limited the permission for euthanasia and explicitly emphasized that this was totally prohibited in a hospital that also included Jewish patients, to prevent a situation where permission to kill a Jew might be derived from the permission to kill a Christian.[29]

There is no doubt that Sternbuch intended to help the patient by permitting a Jew to alleviate his suffering according to the patient's own worldview. However, the very idea of applying Maimonides's words regarding the killing of gentiles who do not observe the Seven Laws of Noah to a contemporary Christian is a great innovation that requires closer investigation. It would be difficult to imagine the rabbis of previous generations relying on this halakha. Does Sternbuch use this halakhic decision as a contrived halakhic solution—a means to achieve a desired end—or does he view the laws pertaining to idolatry as relevant even in this era in which the Jews do not have the "overpowering" hand? I believe that another halakhic decision by Sternbuch attests to a principled rather than a merely opportunistic position.

Sternbuch was asked if a "maid" (*o'zeret*)—the quotation marks are in the source—employed by a family in Israel could be permitted to go to church on Sundays. Sternbuch replied that it was forbidden. He explained that despite the fact that the Jews' hand does not overpower in this age and cannot coerce the gentiles to observe the seven Noahide laws, when an individual idolater becomes subservient to Jews, it is appropriate to prevent her, even by force, from committing the crime of idolatry:

> In any event, the obligation to force them has not expired if it is in our power, when they are subordinate to us. Even though we do not at present have the power to force everyone, for our hand does not overpower the nations, nevertheless, when one has the power to prevent a violation of the Seven Noahide Laws then we are prima facie commanded to prevent it, and therefore, when they are under our control, we shall not allow Christians to go to church on Sunday when we can prevent it, for they are personifying our blessed God and the greatest arbiters have determined that it is idolatry for all intents and purposes.[30]

Just as in exceptional cases it may be permitted to allow the killing of a Christian, because gentiles who do not observe the seven Noahide laws are deserving of death, so too the obligation to coerce them to observe these commandments is still in force and requires implementation under certain circumstances. When Jews are able to observe this obligation without putting themselves at risk, they must do so. As stated above, while the obligation of religious coercion constitutes a duty, "encouraging" Christians to observe the commandments that bind them is prohibited.

Sternbuch's reservations and his emphasis on the idea that the time has not yet come to apply the most stringent halakhic laws applicable to idolaters does not change the fact that he believes that these laws should be applied even in this day and age, if it can be done without risk. Most of the arbiters of previous generations refrained from all use of such halakhic laws, and many made an effort to neutralize any practical potential that might adhere to them by distinguishing between the Christians of their time and the idolaters described in the Talmud. Sternbuch obviously deviates from this path. His logic indicates, despite his caution, a deep sense of confidence that one can indeed express oneself in this way toward Christianity and that one can freely discuss the practical implications of such commandments. The fact that Sternbuch thus imbues these halakhic laws with contemporary relevance, even if in a limited fashion, is highly significant.

It is important to note that Sternbuch's halakhic verdicts are unusual in Orthodox and ultra-Orthodox circles, in the case of his approach to Christianity as well as in other cases. Sternbuch is an extremist. Nevertheless, Sternbuch's willingness to make use of halakhic tools that had been abandoned for many generations reveals his sensitivity to the transitions in the power relations between Christians and Jews, even in the circles of anti-Zionist ultra-Orthodoxy, which ascribe no sanctity whatsoever to Israeli sovereignty.

Shittuf: Is Christianity Monotheistic?

Rabbi Shalom Mashash was Jerusalem's chief Sephardic rabbi for twenty-five years and was renowned for his original halakhic decisions. Mashash published a halakhic decision in the *Or Torah* monthly at the end of 1997 stating that Christians are not considered idolaters because gentiles have not been warned against *shittuf* (association).[31] Mashash was responding to an American rabbi who asked him if an Orthodox community may contribute money to the restoration of a Christian church that was destroyed by "vandals and religion haters." The rabbi posing the question added that in the event that the Orthodox community should fail to contribute its share (while the Reform and Conservative communities contributed their share), there would be fear of enmity, and he appended a correspondence between three nineteenth-century German rabbis that reflected a similar dispute.[32]

Mashash's response excluded Christians from the category of idolaters on the basis of the Tosafists' determination that it is permitted to accept the oath of a Christian who swears on his God because the Christian faith is categorized as *shittuf,* which is not considered idolatry for gentiles. Rabbi Mashash did not hesitate to permit donations for the restoration of the church, since Christianity is not forbidden to Christians; thus, it is not prohibited to assist them in building their church. Jews are forbidden to physically help in the construction, but a monetary donation does not constitute a problem. Rabbi Mashash compared the issue under consideration to the lending of agricultural tools to gentiles during the Sabbath year (Shemitah, in which agricultural work is prohibited) so that gentiles may work the land. Gentiles are not commanded to let the land lie fallow, so Jews are not prohibited from lending them tools even though they themselves are commanded to keep the Shemitah.[33] Mashash added two additional reasons for permitting the donation for the church: first, the status of present-day gentiles as not being idolaters, and second, concern for the desecration of God's name and for enmity.

However, one prominent figure is conspicuous in his absence from Mashash's scholarly discussion of the halakhic status of Christianity: Maimonides. This omission removes Mashash from the rabbinical mainstream, wherein most rabbis consider Maimonides to be the supreme and even sole authority on everything that concerns the halakhic status of Christianity.

Thus, Rabbi Ovadia Yosef, the most influential and authoritative Sephardic arbiter in Israel in recent decades, firmly based his position on Christianity on Maimonides's opinion. In a number of halakhic verdicts, Yosef explicitly stated that Christians were idolaters and their churches were houses of idolatry for all intents and purposes. When asked if a Jew may visit a church, Yosef wrote that "it is explained in Maimonides (at the end of chapter 11 of the laws of forbidden foods) that Christians are idolaters, and it goes without saying that their churches are true houses of idolatry, so it is very clear that it is forbidden to visit a Christian church."[34] According to Yosef, the Tosafists never intended to exclude Christians from the category of idolaters, and their statements regarding *shittuf* were not intended to ascribe any special status to Christianity. Their intention was only to allow Jews to accept the oath of a gentile, and this too, only on condition that the gentile did not use the words "thou art my God" in reference to anything except God.[35] Yosef repeatedly emphasized that Christians were idolaters: "Based on how Christians behave in church, where they worship their God in bows and genuflections, they are certainly considered to be idolaters, and as stated by Maimonides and other arbiters who have written that Christians are idolaters." Yosef disagreed with the position that distinguished between Christianity and idolatry on the basis of the idea of *shittuf*, and he lauded those arbiters who refused to extend the permission to accept an oath from gentiles into a general principle.[36] According to Yosef, it is strictly forbidden to enter a church, and this prohibition even applies in cases where there is "fear of enmity," that is, even if refraining from entering a church would give rise to enmity against Jews.

Yosef thereby voided two of the strongest arguments on which rabbinical tradition relied in order to permit interactions between Jews and Christians: *shittuf* and fear of enmity. If the extended principle of *shittuf* was intended to remove Christians from the category of idolaters as a matter of principle, the fear of enmity was intended to allow local collaboration with Christians without going into a tangle of definitions and theological conundrums. According to the principle of "fear of enmity," even if Christians were idolaters, it was better not to hurt their feelings in order to avoid putting Jews at risk. Yosef made it clear that he was unwilling to accept any leniency in regard to Christianity based on either principle or other circumstantial pretexts.

This combination of defining Christianity as idolatry and the claim that one should not allow interactions between Jews and Christians on the basis of fear of enmity appeared in an earlier verdict issued by Yosef when he served as a rabbi in Egypt in 1948–1949.[37] In this verdict, Yosef related that he was asked by the chief rabbi of Egypt to represent him at the funeral of a Christian consul held in a church, claiming that one should do so "for the ways of peace." Yosef listed the various arguments that led him to deny the request of the chief rabbi and to refrain from entering a church. After clarifying that contemporary Christians were considered idolaters and that *shittuf* was forbidden to them, Yosef noted that a Jew would be permitted to enter a church only in cases where there was an immediate life threat, that is, if the Jew was subject to a tangible and immediate risk. Yosef claimed that the concept of "fear of enmity" is an obscure and general one that does not provide sufficient grounds for permitting entry into a church.[38] Yosef criticized those arbiters who allowed entering a church and claimed that they did not really have fear of enmity but were instead trying to ingratiate themselves with Christians. This was especially so where "Egypt with its Arab government is concerned, and where foreign consuls do not rule us." Most of the things that arbiters permitted on account of "fear of enmity," continued Yosef, were no longer relevant today, "for it was specifically in their times, when the gentiles would concoct evil calumny, that there was concern that they would make up some libel, but this is not so in our time, since there is freedom and liberty, and 'a person can do nothing to another outside the rule of law.'"[39]

After publishing his verdict permitting contributions for the restoration of a church, Rabbi Mashash was harshly criticized. A rabbi by the name of David Avitan (listed in *Or Torah* as a "rabbi and arbiter in Jerusalem")

reacted with shock to Mashash's responsum in the pages of the period-
ical.[40] Avitan was particularly critical of the absence of Maimonides and
Ovadia Yosef from Mashash's response:

> [Mashash's] statement that Christians are not idolaters, but rather wor-
> shippers of *shittuf,* ignores what Maimonides wrote in his Commen-
> tary on the Mishnah . . . as follows: 'You should know that this Chris-
> tian nation, etc., are all idolaters . . . and they should be treated, regarding
> all matters concerning the Torah, in the same way as idolaters.' (It is
> possible that the rabbis he mentions did not see what Maimonides
> wrote because [Maimonides's words] were censored from the versions
> in their time.)

Avitan continues:

> It is even a greater wonder that [Mashash] seems to have missed what
> the genius Rabbi Ovadia Yosef, may he live a long and good life, wrote
> in his *Yahaveh Daat* responsa (part IV, chapter 45) that Christians are
> idolaters and that it is forbidden to visit a church . . . and he wrote there
> that since it was a Torah prohibition, one should not permit it on the
> basis of the principle of "fear of enmity," for fear that these Christians
> would hate him, and he ends his statements with piercing and moving
> words emphasizing the force of this prohibition. . . . And the conclu-
> sion that may be drawn from this in our regard is that anyone partici-
> pating in the restoration of that building not only aids idolaters but is
> entirely their partner.[41]

Toward the end, Avitan emphasized (following Yosef) that the "fear of enmity" does not justify the permission, because idolatry is a serious transgression. Avitan added the following comment: "Especially since in our
times, there is no 'fear of enmity' at all, because, thank God, few among
[the Christians] are devout, and they are slowly degenerating with God's
help, and this is not similar in any way to the time of the Talmud or the medieval arbiters when [Christians] had cast their fear over the Jews and did
them much evil, as we all know."[42]

It can be seen that Yosef and Avitan perceived the changes in the relations
between Jews and Christians as changes that transformed halakha: secularization ("slowly degenerating with God's help"), freedom of religion ("in our

time, since there is freedom and liberty, and a person can do nothing to another outside the rule of law"), and the fact that Jews are not subject to a
Christian government ("and foreign consuls do not rule us") all serve to severely undermine any justification based on the concept of "fear of enmity."
In short, there is less reason to fear Christianity.

Mashash responded to Avitan's criticism with considerable vehemence,
claiming that Avitan wrote his response on the basis of emotion rather than
reason: "And it seems that [he] even recoiled from hearing this, and this led
him to write what he wrote without reading my words."[43] Mashash disagreed
with Avitan's claim that all the arbiters whom Mashash quoted in his verdict wrote what they did because they were not familiar with the uncensored
Maimonides, specifically where Maimonides defines Christianity as idolatry.
He emphasized once more the distinction made by the arbiters between the
idolaters at the time of the Talmud and contemporary gentiles and claimed
that their opinion that gentiles were not subject to the prohibition of *shittuf*
was well founded. He further made the quite surprising argument that the
reason the *shittuf* arbiters did not address Maimonides's ruling that Christians were idolaters was that this very ruling conflicted with the Talmudic
assertion that gentiles living outside the Land of Israel were not idolaters but
rather merely preserved the behavior of their ancestors.[44] Mashash therefore took his exception as far as it was possible to go by positing that Christians were not idolaters as a matter of principle, even according to the
Talmud. The error, according to Mashash, lay with the more stringent Maimonides rather than with the more lenient Tosafists.

Mashash's criticism of Maimonides's position quickly drew fire. Rabbi Ezra
Batzri, an important arbiter and the chief judge in a Jerusalem rabbinical
court, was asked to write a second opinion on a question directed to Rabbi
Eliezer Hitrik of the Chabad community in Germany: Are Jews allowed to
participate and assist in the founding of a common school for all religions
operated by the Catholic Church? Rabbi Hitrik himself explained to the rabbi
who raised the question that this was prohibited and based his decision on
the halakhic verdict of the American Haredi arbiter Menashe Klein, who
prohibited Jews from attending Catholic institutions of higher education.
However, since he viewed this question as an important one, he also directed
it to Batzri. The latter agreed with Hitrik and made the additional argument
that Christians are considered idolaters according to Maimonides and that
participating in their institutions is tantamount to "benefiting" from
idolatry.

Batzri based his position on that of Maimonides and tried to show that all arbiters, from the Tosafists up to his own time (including Meiri), viewed Christianity as idolatry. Batzri considered that any perception of Christianity as a legitimate religion for gentiles "because *shittuf* is not prohibited to gentiles" was a warped idea (an opinion shared by Ovadia Yosef), arising from a misunderstanding of the Tosafists' position. Batzri found the opinions of Mashash "very dubious," in particular when he had the temerity to criticize Maimonides, purporting that his words contradicted those of the Talmud: "God forbid us from ever even thinking, let alone writing, such things about Maimonides . . . and it is a shame that Rabbi Mashash of blessed memory is deceased, for I am sure that if he were alive, he would erase these responsa were I to show him what I have written."[45]

The positions of Rabbis Yosef, Avitan, and Batzri reflect the mainstream opinion of most contemporary Sephardic arbiters regarding Christianity. One might assume that Sephardic halakhic verdicts would be unique in their preference for Maimonides over Ashkenazi arbiters (with Mashash as an exception to this rule), such that Sephardic arbiters are, in fact, merely preserving a Maimonides-centered tradition. However, nineteenth-century Sephardic arbiters did not rely solely on Maimonides, and their opinions regarding Christianity are more varied. Rabbi Yosef Mashash, who was the chief rabbi of Tlemcen, Algeria, and subsequently of Haifa, Israel, entered a church to discuss articles of faith with a priest and to evaluate his halakhic status, and determined against a classification of idolatry; Rabbi Israel Moshe Hazan, author of the *Krakh Shel Romi* responsa, permitted entering a church and even lauded Christian music at great length; and Rabbi Haim Rahamim Yosef Franko (Harif) excluded Protestants from the category of idolaters.[46] Present-day arbiters reject these positions, sometimes with harsh criticism.[47] Ovadia Yosef, for example, criticized Rabbi Yehuda Assad (Mahari), who wrote that the "idol" of the Christians is not considered idolatry: "It seems, and may his honor the Torah scholar [Assad] forgive me, that his words are very curious in this matter."[48] Christians, according to Yosef, are idolaters who pray to their idol in their church, "and anyone who says 'Thou art my God' to an idol is an idolater."[49] These positions of contemporary Sephardic arbiters constitute not an adherence to a traditional position but rather the formulation of a new position that is less amenable toward Christianity. As indicated by the arguments of these rabbis themselves, this hostility is not an attempt to fortify tradition in the face of historical changes calling for tolerance and a blurring of boundaries, but the contrary; these arbiters are turning their backs on traditions now perceived as having been tainted by fear of the gentiles.

Yet the rejection of the halakhic possibilities opened by the idea of *shittuf* and the criticism directed at moderate opinions expressed by the arbiters of previous generations are not limited to Sephardic rabbis. As we saw in the discussion of Rabbi Sternbuch, Ashkenazi arbiters also prefer to adhere to Maimonides on this issue. Sternbuch is indeed an extreme example. Yet even if Sternbuch stands alone in the implications that he extracts from his halakhic position, his tendency toward Maimonides and away from the more lenient Ashkenazi arbiters is shared by others. The renowned Hasidic arbiter Menashe Klein, for example, also upheld the opinion that *shittuf* is prohibited to gentiles, and since he considered Catholics to be idolaters, Klein forbade attendance at their universities (as well as entering their homes or thanking them).[50] Rabbi Yehuda Herzl Henkin (who is considered a liberal and moderate arbiter affiliated with religious Zionism, discussed below) concurred with Avitan's puzzlement over the fact that Mashash did not mention Maimonides in his responsum.[51] He rejected the overextension of the *shittuf* permit as an error and categorized Christians as idolaters.[52]

Rabbi Eliezer Waldenberg, the author of the *Tsits Eliezer* and one of the most renowned contemporary Ashkenazi Haredi arbiters, also viewed Christians as idolaters.[53] He seemed uncomfortable even with the limited permission to accept an oath on *shittuf*, since a partnership with a Christian would eventually lead to the making of a covenant with Christians, which would give rise to severe divine punishment: "And it is therefore forbidden in my opinion, even in our times . . . , even if the oath is directed at *shittuf*."[54] When asked if "it is permitted to play prayer and supplication segments using church music," Waldenberg expressed deep revulsion toward the author of the *Krakh Shel Romi*, who not only permitted the use of Christian music with prayers in synagogue but extolled it enthusiastically:[55]

And I was quite astounded at the sight, and my heart did not believe what my eyes were reading . . . for the main thrust of that book is to advocate singing in synagogue using the melodies sung by Christians in their churches as part of their worship. . . . How can one sermonize and say that the melodies played by Christians in their worship within their churches are truly melodies of submission that lead to the love of God and to the realization that He is the one true God, when Maimonides and all our great sages have established that their beliefs and rituals are idolatry beliefs and rituals and that they are worse in this than the Ishmaelites? And even as he speaks, [the author] himself mentions their belief in the Trinity? And how does he twist and turn so? . . . Unbelievable! . . . Has he forgotten the words of Rashbi [Rabbi Shimon Bar-Yohai], who stated: It is halakha that the hate of Esau for Yaakov is self-evident?[56]

"Gentiles of Our Times Are Not Idolaters"

One of the halakhic methods to distinguish between Christians and idolaters, which was widely used in the past, was based on the declaration that "gentiles of our times are not idolaters." As shown by Katz, this declaration is a later paraphrased version of the Talmudic declaration that "the gentiles outside the land [of Israel] are not idolaters," which was transformed from a geographic distinction into a temporal one.[57] This declaration served arbiters for both "internal" and "external" use. It made it possible to lift various prohibitions that applied to relations with Christians but also helped contend with accusations of hostility toward Christians that Christians directed at Jews. Distinction between the idolaters mentioned in the Talmud and contemporary Christians became extremely widespread in printed rabbinical literature. To clean rabbinic literature of expressions that might seem to have an anti-Christian significance, certain expressions (such as *goy*) were replaced with expressions that seemed to refer to certain groups in the past (such as *akum*, that is, worshippers of stars and astrology). In many cases, one finds an "apology" at the beginning of rabbinical books—a declaration clarifying that discussions of idolaters only pertain to ancient idolaters and not to contemporary Christians, who are not considered to be idolaters. This, for example, is how Yechezkel Landau opens his *Noda BeYehudah* responsa:

> Wherever we find . . . some disparagement of idolaters or gentiles or Kutim, or some such expressions, do not make the mistake of thinking that they refer to these nations of our times, for anyone who interprets them in this way is mistaken and deviates from the teaching of the Torah, for such expressions only refer to the ancient nations that believed in the stars and the zodiac.[58]

Contemporary halakhic sources that address relations between Jews and Christians sometimes include detailed discussion of the religious status of Christians in our time. Thus, for example, in response to the question, "Is it allowed to rent or sell a building to gentiles if it is known that they will dedicate it to idolatry?" (that is, establish a church), Rabbi Pinchas Avraham Meyers, the chief judge of the rabbinical court in the Hague, attempted to clarify the "opinion of the arbiters as to whether the gentiles of our day fall into the category of idolaters, or they are in fact not well versed in idolatry and are not zealous adherents."[59] Meyers first quotes the more lenient arbiters who at least partially distinguish between the idolaters described in the Talmud, with whom one may not negotiate three days before their holy days, and the gentiles of his own time, "who are not well versed in the nature of idols."[60] He then presents the opposing opinions of Maimonides—who considered Christians to be idolaters for all intents and purposes—and of Menachem Meiri, who opposed the opinion of Maimonides. However, ultimately, Meyers sides with Maimonides and concludes that "even though the gentiles of our time are not zealous in their adherence to idolatry, their worship is idolatry in any case and is therefore forbidden in all cases."[61] According to Meyers, today's Christians, in all their denominations and churches, are all categorized as idolaters:

It is a simple fact . . . that all the various denominations of the religion of Christianity are idolaters just as the gentiles in their times were worshippers of idols, and even those who are not zealous adherents of Christianity and do not believe in their sacred objects and impure forms but only have their own rituals and various traditions, are still categorized as idolaters, even if they are only maintaining the customs of their ancestors. And in our time, there are many sects and churches and various denominations, such as Catholics and Russian-Orthodox and Greeks and Armenians and Mormons and the Church of the Patriarchy and the Coptic Church and the churches of the West and of the East and the various Protestant denominations such as Evangelists and Anglicans and born-again Christians, not to mention various religions and sects from the Far East, such as the people of India, Hindus, and Buddhists and other kinds of impurity, wherein all are equal in that they are all complete idolatry, and the objects of these religions such as their icons and idols and crosses and other shapes and forms and the church rituals, are all true idolatry.[62]

Like Meyers, Rabbi Henkin, too, considered that the extent to which Christians adhere to their religion is irrelevant to the question of whether they are idolaters: "They are idolaters in any case, . . . even when they are not zealous, for what difference does it make if they worship their idols frequently or just go to Mass once a week; they are still worshipping an idol."[63] Rabbi Chaim Binyamin Goldberg recognizes that times have changed but prefers the more restrictive formulation "not zealous in their idolatry" over the more extended statements of "*shittuf* is not prohibited for gentiles" or "gentiles of our time are not idolaters." Even if individual believers are entitled to leniency because of their lack of zealousness, Christianity itself and its rituals retain their status as idolatry or at least as "a vestige of impurity from the evil side [*sitra ahra*]."[64] Any contact of a Jew with a church or a Christian ritual is considered as if the Jew "wants [the church or ritual] to exist," and thus it is prohibited. Goldberg forbids Jews to donate to the building of a church, to issue a building permit for the construction of a church (except on account of "fear of enmity"), or to erect it (even if the Jewish contractor employs only gentiles), and he even forbids a Jewish insurance company from insuring its silver and gold utensils.[65]

In his response to the question regarding the issue of entering a church, Eliezer Waldenberg warned:

> One should imagine that the rule that should be applied here is that all these matters only apply to that [past] time, but in our time, they are not well versed in the nature of idols, etc. . . . It is simple and clear that one should not differentiate in regard to the prohibition on entering a church between ancient times and our time, and in our time too it is forbidden to enter their house of idolatry or even the yard.[66]

Ovadia Yosef made a similar claim that in the matter of entering a church, the words of the *Shulhan Arukh* stating that "in our time they are not idolaters" are not valid, for the cross "in their church is absolute idolatry," and "certainly their house of prayer is termed a house of idolatry."[67]

Beyond the borders of the Haredi community in Israel, the situation is more complex. For example, the chief rabbis of the United Kingdom, the Baron Rabbi Immanuel Jakobovits (who served from 1966 to 1991) and the Lord Rabbi Jonathan Sacks (who succeeded Jakobovits and served until 2013), did allow entry into churches, with some reservations. Jakobovits stated that he did not enter a church during a ritual or a service, and he refused the invitation of Cardinal Willebrands to participate in the interreligious service for peace that Pope John Paul II conducted at Assisi.[68] Interestingly, he reported that he refrained from discussing the issue of whether

Christianity is a monotheistic religion and that he strived to emphasize the common ground between the two faiths rather than their differences. Sacks was paradigmatically inclined to a Jewish perspective that considers the importance of other faith systems, as manifested in his book *The Dignity of Difference*.[69] Like Jakobovits, his involvement in interfaith affairs was done mostly outside of the halakhic realm.

Yet the halakhic controversies on the stature of Christians and the appropriate positioning of Jews vis-à-vis Christianity have not occurred only among Israeli rabbis (though they are more dominant, and expressed more directly, in Israel), or only among ultra-Orthodox circles. When the American rabbi Haskel Lookstein, a Modern Orthodox rabbi who headed the Yeshurun congregation in Manhattan, participated in an ecumenical service that took place in an Episcopal church in honor of the inauguration of US president Barack Obama (in his presence), he was severely reprimanded by the Rabbinical Council of America (RCA).[70] Lookstein claimed that he responded to the invitation to "save Israel," that is, because a close relationship with Obama could turn out to be vital for Jews in both the United States and Israel. The mainstream Orthodox position disagreed. The RCA made it clear that entering churches was unacceptable and was not consistent with its policy. In their public reprimand of Lookstein, the RCA representatives refrained from explicitly stating that Christianity is considered idolatry, contenting themselves with a vague statement that the halakha forbids Jews from entering a church, as well as from participation in interreligious dialogue (based on an article by Rabbi Soloveitchik, which is discussed in Chapter 8). The RCA representatives emphasized that their reservations did not stem from political reasons but only from halakhic considerations, and they sent blessings and wishes for success to the new president.

The Lookstein affair illuminated the fact that even the Modern Orthodox mainstream in the United States no longer considers the political reality as requiring halakhic compromises toward Christianity. As stated by Rabbi Auman in regard to the Lookstein affair, "We are no longer contending here with Rome or Tsarist Russia," and Jews no longer need to protect themselves from the edicts of cruel rulers.[71] Even an invitation from the president of the United States does not justify such an act. The secularization of the public sphere and the freedom of religion have given arbiters free rein to maintain a stringent halakhic attitude to Christianity, without the need to mitigate it for social or political reasons (which was, indeed, a traditional need). As will be further stressed in Chapter 8, the difference between the Israeli context and the American and Continental ones is what takes place beyond the borders of the halakhic discussion; while Orthodoxy in Israel is not engaged with Christianity except in the mostly theoretical halakhic categories (many Orthodox people in Israel have never met a Christian in their lives), Orthodox Jews in the Western Diaspora experience a more diversified encounter with the Christian world and often find ways to circumvent the standing halakhic difficulties and establish good relations with Christians—in other realms.

How Is the Halakhic Status of Christianity Defined?

What is the basis for the widely accepted categorization of Christianity as idolatry among arbiters from diverse Orthodox streams? Is this ruling contingent on such precepts of the Christian faith as the incarnation, or perhaps on Christian rituals, such as Mass? Is any distinction made between the various Christian denominations regarding the intensity of the idolatrous worship ascribed to Christianity?

Rabbi Yehuda Herzl Henkin—an American Israeli liberal religious Zionist—devoted two paragraphs to the precepts of Christian faith to determine if it was considered idolatry and to decide if there were any differences between various Christian denominations and sects with regard to their halakhic status:

> The main point of idolatry is the personification of God, and Christianity is deemed idolatry for a number of reasons: The first is the belief in the Trinity of Father, Son and Holy Spirit that views Jesus as a God, and were it not for this, the split in the unity of the Creator between Father and Holy Spirit would not be considered idolatry for them, so long as they do not personify them, even though it would be heresy [*minut*] for us. Even had they considered Jesus to be the son of God (God forbid) but not God himself and had they not worshipped him, it would have been heresy but not idolatry. And had they considered him the Messiah but not God or the son of God, it would have been an error and a piece of nonsense, but not idolatry. . . . And the second is that they believe their bread becomes the body of Jesus during the Mass ritual, and the third, that they worship images and idols and the form of their worship is by bowing when they make the sign of the cross.[72]

In other words, the belief in Jesus as a supreme God (rather than any minor divinity) incarnated in flesh is the main reason that Henkin viewed Christianity as idolatry. Other reasons are the belief in transubstantiation, where the bread and wine become Christ's flesh and blood in the Eucharist, and the attitude of Christians to the cross and images. These latter reasons are more marginal, according to Henkin, and do not characterize all Christian denominations, which differ from each other in the intensity of their idolatry:

> All this is applicable to Catholic, Orthodox, and Anglican Christianity, but since Luther, the Protestant churches have forsaken the worship of images. And in a church where they do not worship images and only have something as a token reminder, then even the figure of the man on the cross is not idolatry. . . . In any event, most Protestant churches believe in the Trinity and hold the Mass, and since they accept Jesus as a God it is forbidden to enter their houses of prayers. It is only the Unitarians and a few others who do not believe in the divinity of Jesus, and their churches are not houses of idolatry and it is permitted to enter them when they are not holding services, just as it is permitted to enter a mosque, but one should not do so because it may raise suspicion, since most people do not distinguish one church from another.[73]

Henkin thus posits some clear criteria for determining the status of Christianity, and it is on their strength that he makes the determination that Christianity is idolatry. However, it should be noted that Henkin's discussion of Christianity is extremely unusual within rabbinical writings on the subject. It would not be an exaggeration to state that these two brief paragraphs by a single Orthodox arbiter are among the richest sources of knowledge being presently used by halakhic arbiters when they discuss contemporary Christianity.[74]

Most orthodox arbiters never address such questions at all. Their determination regarding the status of Christians is not based on discussions of Christianity but on previous rulings that have assumed canonic status, especially those of Maimonides and the medieval arbiters of Ashkenaz. From time to time, the question of whether Christianity should be reevaluated is raised in passing (more often in discussions among Modern Orthodox circles, as we shall see in Chapter 8), in view of the many changes it has undergone in recent centuries as well as the changes in the attitude of the Christian world toward Judaism. This question rarely leads to any actual attempt to reexamine the Christian world. Orthodox Judaism's lack of familiarity with Christianity is based to a great extent on a circular conception: since the basic assumption is that Christianity is considered idolatry, it is forbidden to study it; since it is forbidden to study it, one cannot change the halakhic position that determines it to be idolatry. Thus, what most arbiters know about Christianity is based on classic polemical literature that goes back to the Middle Ages as collected in *Otsar Vikuhim* (A treasury of debates).

The few attempts to discuss the enormous variety in the Christian world in order to issue halakhic verdicts pertaining to Christianity and its believers have usually been rejected by authoritative Orthodox rabbis out of hand. A case in point is a recent article published by Dror Fixler (a physicist) and advocate Gil Nadal that discusses Maimonides's conception of Christianity and attempts to show that "Maimonides' attitude toward Christians stemmed from the nature of Christianity and its rituals in his day" and is no longer valid in regard to contemporary Christians. Fixler and Nadal claim that present-day Christians have voided either one or both of the elements that made their religion idolatry (that is, the dogma of the Trinity and the worship of images), and as a consequence, "the *sweeping* pronouncement that Christians are idolaters is no longer valid in our time."[75] In view of the many Christian variations and denominations, the authors recommend that each case be individually examined to determine the halakha accordingly.

Fixler and Nadal's attempt was refuted by Rabbi Yaakov Ariel, one of the most prominent rabbis of mainstream religious Zionism in Israel, whose response was published as an appendix to Fixler and Nadal's article.[76] Ariel clarified that so long as Christians adhere to the dogma of the Trinity, their religion is considered idolatry, even if they do not worship any idols, "for this belief includes the belief that a man is 'God' in addition to God himself, and this is idolatry." Ariel adds that even if there are Christian sects that have withdrawn from their belief in the Trinity, as claimed by the authors,

> There is still the issue of the belief of these sects in a single God without any *shittuf.* This requires a deeper theological examination, and one cannot draw any practical conclusions without such investigation of each and every Christian sect. So long as such an in-depth study has

not been conducted, the custom is to rely on the determination of the Tosafists and other Rishonim [medieval rabbis] that Christians are idolaters.[77]

All Christian denominations (barring perhaps the Unitarians, who have rejected the Trinity), then, are considered idolatry until proven otherwise. However, because the prohibitions on approaching idolatry make it very difficult to check if it is indeed idolatry, the halakhic discourse remains forever closed upon itself and continues to feed mainly on the statements of arbiters who lived almost a thousand years ago and whose own familiarity with Christian dogma is also in doubt.

Rabbi Yossi Slotnick of the Ma'ale Gilboa Yeshiva, which is considered the most liberal yeshiva in the religious Zionist world, criticized Ariel's response to Fixler and Nadal in an article titled "The Prohibition on Entering Churches—New Thoughts." In his critique, Slotnick considers how it might be possible to reexamine the halakhic status of Christianity in our times. In this context he criticized the rabbinical discourse on this issue:

> Usually, arbiters who are required to consider this question go back in time, and discuss the definitions of Christianity by the Rishonim. They subsequently settle the issues on the basis of the positions adopted by the Rishonim. They thus discuss the position of Maimonides who states that this belief is idolatry; touch with some sophistry on the word of Rabbenu Tam, a Tosafist who claims in this context (perhaps) that the gentiles are not prohibited from worshipping God along with another (*shittuf*); and then bring the position of Meiri to the table. Of course, hovering in the background are the Jewish saints who preferred death in God's name rather than conversion to Christianity, thereby declaring that Christian faith belongs to the category of idolatry over which one should let oneself be killed rather than transgress.[78]

According to Slotnick, this approach is problematic because historical and sociological reality plays no part in it:

> After asking for your indulgence over my temerity in placing my head between the great arbiters of halakha, I believe that this method is lacking. When coming to determine if certain beliefs and opinions are

contrary to the principles of our religion, we should first ask the believers for their position before we reach our halakhic verdict. Christianity as a religion has undergone many transformations in its two
thousand years of existence. . . . A halakhic arbiter who comes to make
a decision in regard to the belief of another should make an appropriate
effort to understand the terms and language used by the other. . . . It
seems to me unreasonable to content ourselves with no more than evaluations made in the ninth or tenth century, or even at the end of the
Middle Ages. Moreover, we should not even content ourselves with a
general up-to-date status report, but rather it behooves us to examine
in specific detail each and every Christian denomination, for a church
bare of any icon or image of the cross cannot be considered the same
as one that prominently worships the Virgin.[79]

Slotnick criticizes Ariel for classifying all Christians as idolaters "until
proven otherwise": "His words are surprising, for it is quite simple to check
these matters and the information is very accessible. Why then, should our
decision be based on irrelevant information instead of making our determination on the basis of tangible reality?" Slotnick claims that most Christians view themselves as having a monotheistic worldview; that is, they
themselves do not consider their God to be split into a plurality of divinities
but rather as constituting a mysterious unity of the three persons, a concept
that "is beyond all human ken." Why not accept Christians' own testimony
that they believe in the unity of God? Obviously, the idea of the Trinity may
be considered problematic, and one can argue this point with Christians, but
would it not be appropriate to take their own self-concept as monotheists
into consideration when we come to judge them as polytheists? Slotnick emphasizes that he is not attempting to obscure the "deep disagreement that
we have with Christianity as regards the Trinity, salvation, the changing of
the Torah, the election of the Jews, and many other subjects . . . but these
disagreements do not suffice to make them idolaters, neither as gentiles nor
(in my opinion) even as Jews."[80]

A critique has been appended to Slotnik's article in the form of an "editor's comment" on the Ma'ale Gilboa Yeshiva website.[81] The editor was willing
to accept Slotnik's "methodological approach," which views empirical reality
as a datum that should be taken into consideration when coming to determine the halakhic status of contemporary Christians. However, examination of that empirical reality itself leads, in the editor's opinion, to different

conclusions; according to Christian dogma "the Father and the 'Son' are a single entity," and "such a belief, from the point of view of halakha, is idolatry" (the editor did not respond to Slotnick's claim that the self-perception of Christians as monotheists should also be taken into consideration). It is interesting to note that neither Slotnick nor the editor referred to any Christian sources but merely recommended that the issue be considered, while the editor, who agreed with Slotnick's recommendation in principle, referred the readers to the studies of various scholars and arbiters, all of them (modern) Orthodox Jews: the rabbi and historian of medieval Jewish-Christian relations David Berger, the philosopher Michael Wyschogrod (who specializes in Jewish-Christian relations rather than in Christian doctrine), and the two paragraphs provided by Yehuda Herzl Henkin (discussed above).

Thus, most arbiters choose to remain within the internal strictures of halakhic discourse, and refrain from any direct familiarity with Christianity on its own terms. The number of arbiters who quote from the New Testament or any Christian theological writings is negligible. I have found only one contemporary source that discusses the halakhic status of present-day Christians with direct reference to Christian doctrine. This discussion appears in a thick tome titled *Sefer Israel Veha'Amim* (The book of Israel and the nations), which is devoted to changing contemporary Jewish attitudes to gentiles. This book was written in the early 2000s but was not published. This is an exceptional work in the general landscape of the contemporary halakhic oeuvre, which is perhaps one of the reasons that the Hasidic rabbi-scholar who composed it prefers to remain anonymous.[82] At the opening of his book, the author cautions against the severe deterioration that he identifies in the attitude to gentiles in general, a deterioration that he claims is incompatible with the spirit of the Torah.[83] To solve this problem, which he claims "burns and annihilates the soul of Judaism," the author devotes about a thousand pages to clarifying the position of the halakha toward gentiles.

In the chapter he devotes to the attitude of the halakha toward Christians, the author attempts to thoroughly clarify Christian faith and examine it in light of halakhic criteria before deciding the issue. Christians, he claims, conform to the moral standard that Judaism establishes for gentiles.[84] The only issue is their status regarding their religious belief. It is therefore necessary to determine whether belief in the Trinity is considered idolatry.[85] The subsequent philosophical-halakhic investigation conducted by the author leads him to the conclusion that the belief in the Trinity is a false one, but it is not idolatry. He defines it as a "unified *shittuf*," that is, a conception of separate entities as a single entity. And even though this is absurd, it is not idolatry. Like Slotnick, the author takes the fact that Christians view the Trinity as divine unity into consideration, even if the logic underlying such a conception is unclear.

Even when the author of *Sefer Israel Veha'Amim* turns to discuss the halakhic details of the issue and consider the various opinions of the arbiters, he continues to ascribe weight to empirical reality. He attempts to trace the changes in Christian doctrine throughout history and claims that the Trinity is a late doctrinal development in Christianity, which in fact removed its "idolatrous tone." Since he considers Christianity to have undergone a process of change for the better, he presumes to speculate that the Talmudic passages that classify Christians as idolaters refer only to the Christians of the time of the Talmud, who were "the ancient Christians, the students of Saul of Tarsus (Paul the Apostle), who worshipped Jesus alone and did not yet know of the faith of the unified Trinity." The author goes even further and claims that not only should one refrain from making deductions from one period to the next, but it is also possible that the arbiters who classified Christianity as idolatry were wrong because "they were not familiar with the nature of Christianity in their times and thought that they were worshipping Jesus alone, and believing in a non-unified Trinity, which is complete idolatry."[86] He claims that had the arbiters been familiar with the nature of Christianity,

> they would have admitted that Christians are not idolaters, and perhaps this may even be said in regard to the Rishonim, so that had these latter Aharonim [late medieval and modern-era rabbis] known that all of the Christians' worship of Jesus is in fact directed at worshipping God alone, for their erroneous thought is that the entire Trinity is a single God, perhaps these Aharonim would not have deemed them to be idolaters. And perhaps it would even be justified to raise this hypothesis in regard to some of the Rishonim who were stringent in their classification of Christians as idolaters, that they only did so because they were not familiar with the Christian religion in their days, even though they lived among Christians.[87]

A solitary and unique enterprise, *Sefer Israel Veha'Amim* attempts to understand Christian faith as it is understood by its adherents and as it changed throughout history, before it is brought before the judgment of the halakha. Even though it is written on the basis of halakhic tradition and completely adheres to the rules of that genre, the conception of Christianity that arises from this book establishes a dialogue with the real Christian world rather than remaining closeted in the narrow strictures of rabbinical discourse. This is a completely anomalous phenomenon, however, that does not reflect any Orthodox Jewish stream but only the personal worldview of its author.

How should this plethora of examples of a stringent halakhic position toward Christianity, with its persistent struggle against more lenient positions, be understood? Instead of adopting Katz's perspective and perceiving this halakhic hardening as a reactionary response to modernity, liberalism, and secularization, I suggest looking at it exactly the other way around: as an unrestrained embrace of modernity, liberalism, and secularization. In the eyes of many of the halakhic arbiters, it is precisely the process of secularization and the rise of liberal values that released Jews from the need to "come to terms" with Christianity, to censor their literature, to mitigate their halakhic rulings, or to apologetically justify their positions when facing Christians. In other words, Orthodox Jews are not "raising the fences" out of fear of Christianity and "gentile" culture; on the contrary, they part ways from previous, more lenient positions toward Christians precisely because they no longer fear them. The new freedoms brought by the post–World War II liberal ethos gave rise to initiatives of rapprochement and friendships that were previously unimaginable, at the same time that they surfaced old resentments that were repressed under a thick barrier of cultural and political inferiority. To go back to Susannah Heschel's metaphor, the halakhic hardening toward Christianity could be seen as an essential part of the decolonization of Judaism.

7

Christianity in Religious Zionist Thought

A special role is reserved for Christianity in one school of Israeli Orthodox Judaism: the religious Zionist circle composed of the followers of Rabbi Abraham Isaac HaCohen Kook and his son, Rabbi Zvi Yehudah HaCohen Kook. The "Kook school" is considered to be an extremist camp within religious Zionism, a Haredi branch of the more lenient and modernized religious Zionist community (the group is often referred to in Hebrew as "Hardal"—that is, "Haredi-Leumi," National-Haredi). The leaders of this community often infuriate the greater Israeli public with their unrestrained attacks on LGBT and gender equality issues, among other liberal values, as well as their far-right views concerning the Israeli-Palestinian conflict and their vigorous support of the idea of Greater Israel. They tend to be halakhically more stringent than other Orthodox Zionist groups. Yet, as Shlomo Fischer has shown, this is a thoroughly modernized community—in its zealous nationalism, in its struggle for political mobilization, in its determination to take part in all of the state's institutions, and in the philosophical spirit that guides it, which is heavily influenced by German Romanticism, Hegel, and Nietzsche.[1]

The rabbis of this relatively small faction of the Israeli public have published in recent decades a vast and highly polemical literature on Christianity. The roots of this surprising preoccupation with Christianity, which is distinct to this group and does not appear in any other faction of Jewish Orthodoxy, lie in the writings of the community's spiritual ancestor, Abraham Isaac Kook.

Rabbi Abraham Isaac Kook on Christianity

Abraham Isaac Kook's lifetime transcends the historical scope of this book, and I have discussed his attitude to Christianity elsewhere.[2] Yet since his writings set the theological paradigm for much of the contemporary religious Zionist discourse on Christianity, I will briefly describe his views here.

Kook is known for his positive attitude toward secularism, which was uncharacteristic of his ultra-Orthodox milieu. Yet the other side of this view of secularism was a deeply negative attitude toward Christianity. Adopting a Nietzschean style critique, Kook saw the process of secularization as a healthy anti-Christian reaction, as a reaffirmation of this world and a rejection of Christianity's twisted worldview: "The rise of apostasy [*kefirah*] . . . serves no other purpose than saving the world of the filth of Christianity [*minut*]."[3] As Yehuda Mirsky has shown, even World War I (during which Kook was forced to stay in Switzerland and was unable to return to Jerusalem) was to him, notwithstanding its terrible price, an essential revolt of the European nations against the suppressing forces of Christianity, which had burdened them with its life-hating tradition for centuries.[4]

Moreover, Kook regarded modern apostasy and its revolutionary consequences as a necessary step in returning history to its divinely ordered course, a course that had been suspended ever since Christianity emerged out of Judaism. In an interesting variation on Maimonides's philosophy of history (spiced with Hegelianism), Kook depicted a process of maturation of the human spirit, which reaches its peak with the acknowledgment of the God of Israel as the true God.[5] This process begins with idolatry, continues with Christianity and Islam, and ends with humanity's acceptance of the true faith.[6] Yet whereas for Maimonides, Christianity and Islam were instrumental in promoting the divine plan by paving "the way for the king Messiah" and preparing "the entire world to worship God together," Kook considered Christianity not as an *insufficient* stepping stone from idolatry to monotheism, but rather as an attempt to reverse the course of history and turn back the salvation plan.[7] Christianity, which Kook referred to as *minut* (heresy), was for him a demonic spiritual entity seeking to undermine the divine plan in the world and offer an alternative to it. As such, it was worse than the pagan religions it had replaced.

In fact, paganism has a respectful place in Kook's paradigm and a positive evolutionary role to play; its fermenting mental energy and its sensual passion for its gods should have accompanied human faith throughout the stages of its spiritual development.[8] The base "idolatrous inclination" is bound to become purified and refined with the progression of human faith, but the well-developed soul must not renounce it completely.

Christianity, however, disrupted this trajectory in three ways. First, it sought to bestow the faith of Israel on the gentile nations at a time when both Israel and the gentiles were unprepared for this, which led the gentiles to adopt a twisted and heretical version of Judaism and caused a rift between gentiles and Jews. Second, it subverted the singularity and the electedness of Israel. And third, it created a split between matter and spirit, between faith and life. Instead of helping human beings reform and save this world from wrongdoing and materiality, Christianity declared this world devoid of spiritual value.[9]

Yet what is most interesting in Kook's argument is his depiction of the history of Israel in exile, in the Galut, as a history of increasing resemblance to Christianity. According to Kook, the exile did not only testify to Judaism's current inferiority to Christianity; it also gave Judaism a Christian form. Detached from the Land of Israel and the commandments associated with it, Israel was denied the possibility of realizing the potential unity between spirit and matter, body and mind, which is so vital to it. Much like Christianity, Judaism in exile is in a certain sense an "abstract" religious faith, separated from the life of this world with its corporeal elements, and from its national elements in particular.[10] The longer the Jews' exile in the Christian world lasts, the more they despair of redemption, and the more "Christian" they become.[11]

Therefore, for Kook, the process of secularization expressed a healthy departure from the detrimental influence of Christianity, not only for gentiles but for Jews, too. Although Jewish secularization is devastatingly damaging to the tradition of Israel, its initial motivation is right and proper—doing away with the Christian hatred of life. The return of Judaism's vital energies is manifested in the Zionist (secular) movement that revives the national and material aspects of Judaism, repressed at the time of the exile. Ultimately, Zionism is not total apostasy, as it seeks to return the people of Israel to the Land of Israel. Once secularization has completed its mission and cured the Jews and all of humanity of the disease of Christianity, Jewish faith will revert to its original unity. One aspect of this revival, Kook implied, would be the renewal of the direct Jewish influence on the gentile world, without the mediation of Christianity.[12]

Rabbi Zvi Yehudah Kook's Attitude to Christianity

The man who took upon himself the responsibility of implementing Rabbi Kook's legacy and adapting it to the changing conditions of the Jewish community in Palestine, and especially to the nascent State of Israel, was Rabbi Zvi Yehudah Kook, Abraham Isaac Kook's son. Zvi Yehudah Kook was a zealous Zionist who shared his father's sympathy for secular Jews, as well as his father's faith that the Jewish immigration to the Land of Israel and the establishment of a Jewish state on this territory constituted a divinely ordered process and carried a redemptive significance. After the Israeli victory in the Six-Day War in 1967, Kook the son was one of the central figures who interpreted the Israeli conquests as a divine sign meaning that Israelis must strive to extend the borders of the state to include Greater Israel (Eretz Israel HaShlema), in accordance with its biblical geographical depiction, and not settle for a partial territory. Zvi Yehudah Kook thus became the uncontested leader of Gush Emumnim, the movement that encouraged Jewish settlements in the West Bank, Gaza Strip, and Golan Heights.

Zvi Yehuda Kook was the main editor of his father's writings, and his political theology was based on his father's intellectual legacy. Though whether the younger Kook was a loyal interpreter of his father is contested, the father's influence is imprinted in every bit of the son's writing.[13] This is also true with regard to Zvi Yehudah Kook's outlook on Christianity. Nevertheless, the son's preoccupation with Christianity had a different emphasis from the father's; Zvi Zehudah Kook turned his father's theological disdain for the Christian religion into a cultural war against the influence of Christianity on Judaism, and in particular on the Jewish state of Israel. For Zvi Yehudah Kook, the return of the Jews to Zion and their liberation from exile had to be accompanied by their liberation from Christian influence, which he often extended to a liberation from Western influence writ large. He interpreted the Zionist idea of the "normalization" of the Jewish people in terms of de-Christianization rather than secularization. As we shall see, Zvi Yehudah Kook's writings on Christianity are the most virulent pronouncements on the subject one can find, probably throughout the entire Jewish world.

In an early letter (written in 1918, a short time after the Balfour Declaration), Zvi Yehudah Kook reiterated the course of salvation history depicted by his father (in a variation on Maimonides), a course that began with the appearance of Judaism in a climate that was wholly idolatrous, then deviated from the straight path with the appearance of Christianity and Islam that branched out of Judaism, then returned to the path once the Jewish people returned to their land.[14] In this letter, Kook tackled the question put forward by his addressee regarding the contributions of Judaism and Christianity to the general culture. He declared that he was not interested in conducting a historical debate about the values (good and bad) that the religions had bequeathed to general culture but rather wished to focus on a theological discussion of the history of salvation, "from the aspect of the thought of eternal, general and comprehensive history."[15] From this point of view, he claimed, Christianity "was a stumbling block" in the path of the development of the human spirit, and its coming into the world was the result of a "historical mistake."[16] Had matters developed according to their proper order, Kook asserted, reiterating his father's ideas, the lives of the ancient idolaters would have developed naturally, alongside the Jewish people, who should have resided in Zion and expressed themselves and their uniqueness in all areas of life. Out of the natural life of the Jewish people, Kook argued, Israel's spiritual abundance was supposed to gradually seep to the rest of humanity, thereby allowing them to develop their spirituality normally. The Jewish influence on the nations was supposed to take place effortlessly, since all of humanity functions as a single body:

> The blessing that the nations of the world receive from Israel, the living influence that flows [from the people of Israel] into the course of human civilization, does not lie in sermons or the shining example of the lives of the Jewish people and their greats, as paragons of "humanism," ethics, ideals, sanctity, divinity, nor in any abstract, illusional, "Judaism" that wanders about in the world, but rather in Judaism and Jews at one and the same time, for they are within it and never without it and it is within them. . . . In the reality of the *nation itself,* which is the revelation of divine light in the world and in humanity . . . by the mighty torrents that flow and rise . . . from the life of the Jewish nation itself and the power of its might in its prophecy, and priesthood, and wisdom, its temple and its kingdom, in all branches of culture and society, the economy and the politics, and everything they have, and they naturally (von selbst) [*sic*] influence everything.[17]

Christianity, according to Zvi Yehudah Kook, ruptured this divine plan: "The historic spectacle of Christianity led to a disruption in the natural course of this divine historical program, causing a break, a delay, and a re-action." Christianity deviated from the divine plan for history and became what Kook called "the program of non-programmatism." Christianity leads the human race astray and oppresses it, in fine Nietzschean fashion, by disseminating a life-hating worldview. Instead of developing through a connection with living Judaism, Christianity gave the nations the Jewish scriptures that it uprooted from their living context, "based on the teachings of Israel but bereft of its living spirit," thereby leading to the degeneration of life rather than its fulfillment.[18] Mirroring Nietzsche's critique of Christianity as fostering a "slave morality," Kook described Christianity as having created a distorted belief that "bent human stature and deprived it of the force of its creative power, its natural mettle and courage, both material and spiritual."

However, this deviation from the divine plan was also the work of providence:

> Obviously, however, God forgets nothing and there is no forgery or error before him, and from all the degeneration and darkness *in themselves* important aids and lights are always revealed. The twists and turns of history and the distortions of its path, and all the nickels and dimes of usefulness and support for the progress of *human civilization, the distillation of human spirit and the instruction of its morality,* which they gave birth to, and which will most certainly add up to a great global amount, as well as all the assets of the material and spiritual benefits that we will derive from our exile. But God's plan will forever stand, and the program of divine history will not be cancelled, obviously, by human road-twists, even if the latter proliferate and burgeon tens of thousands of times in this way, but will only be stopped and delayed. Throughout these interruptions and delays, it is the ultimate end of the path of history to return, of course, to its essential, natural, and programmatic path.[19]

Zvi Yehudah Kook thus distinguished between the temporal human perspective, which identifies disasters and interruptions in the progress of history, and the eternal divine perspective of God, which foresees and foreordains all action and brings about the delays for the purpose of salvation. Nevertheless, he seemed to struggle with the idea that Christianity indeed profited mankind, since "the twists and turns of history" are but "nickels and dimes of usefulness," obviously of little value when compared to the "great global amount." This, again, echoes the words of Kook the father to the effect that Christianity only slightly "ironed" the moral fabric over the surface of humanity (in regard to idolatry) but did not bring about any substantive change.[20] Zvi Yehudah Kook thus returned to the question of Christianity's contribution to human civilization, which he perfunctorily claimed to wish to evade at the beginning of the letter, and found it to have contributed somewhat to civilization's spirit and morality, but no more than marginally, and no doubt incomparably less than the damage it did.

Alongside the traditional distinction between the divine and the human point of view, Zvi Yehudah Kook clarified that Christianity was an *objective* human deviation from the divine plan (that is, not just from the human point of view), for "the thought of eternal, general, and comprehensive history" was the one that was harmed by the "stumbling block" of Christianity.[21] Christianity might not be able to destroy the divine plan, but it is certainly capable of holding it up.

Zvi Yehudah Kook considered the very attempt to discuss the contribution of Jews to culture as imbued with the spirit of Christianity; any talk about the values or heritage of Judaism that is disengaged from the actual people of Israel and the life of the Jews on their land is a Christian position, because, like Christianity, it disengages the Jewish teachings from the Jewish practice and from the Jews themselves. Thus, Kook took a strident militant position not only against Christianity itself, but also, by association, against its purported influence on the Jewish people, believing that only a return to proud sovereignty would heal the Christian distortions of the Jews themselves.[22] He saw his generation as one on whose shoulders lay the responsibility to return the divine program to its natural course. Like his father, he thought that the mass immigration to the Land of Israel was at the very heart of the process of the "historical redemption," not only of Judaism but of all humankind.[23]

For these reasons, Zvi Yehudah Kook vehemently fought against missionary activities.[24] Yet, perhaps more interestingly, he saw allegedly naïve and secular cultural activities as representing a hidden missionary agenda and as preserving a Christian influence that he believed was unwarranted in the Jewish state. On one occasion, his students crashed a performance of Bach's St. Matthew Passion at the International Convention Center in Jerusalem while proudly singing "David King of Israel Still Lives and Endures," the quintessential song embodying both Jewish messianic hopes for sovereignty and the bone of contention with Christianity.[25] Wishing to cleanse

Jewish culture in Israel of Christian characteristics, Kook went so far as to object to the use of the Gregorian civil calendar in Israel.[26]

One of the prominent manifestations of this approach appears in a political manifesto that Zvi Yehudah Kook authored on the occasion of the first elections to the Israeli Knesset (1949). Titled "Emdatenu Ve'Ekronoteyha" (Our position and its principles), the text was written for the united list of religious parties (the United Religious Front), which eventually gained 16 seats—out of 120—in the first election for the Israeli parliament.[27] The manifesto deals with the "principles of Israel's internal position" and with the way that the Jewish people should exist in their land. A close reading shows that the entire manifesto is an anti-Christian polemic.

It was Zvi Yehudah Kook's contention that the people of Israel were distinguished from the rest of the nations by some of life's most basic elements: the relationship between body and soul, the relationship between humanity and the universe, and the social relationships between people. When the people of Israel are in their normal state, their uniqueness is evident in all these levels of existence. Kook thus wished to place the uniqueness of Jewish existence on the political agenda to ensure that the government of Israel would take steps to provide the conditions that would allow it to flourish. To explain how Jewish uniqueness found expression in these areas of life, Kook turned to Christianity, which he claimed had savaged each and every one of them: "They were harmed by that innovative idolatry that grew at the time through atrophying the grasp of eternity within Israel to the point of the crime of denying it."[28]

First, Christianity disrupted the balance between body and soul by voiding the commandments of kashruth; Zvi Yehudah Kook quoted Matthew 15:11, without explicitly referring to it, and claimed that it was indeed "that which goeth into the mouth" that affected the Israeli soul through the building of the body, rather than those "blasphemous idolatrous utterances" that come out of the mouth that defile a person. Second, Christianity revolted against the uniqueness of Israel as it is expressed in the sanctity of the times, and Shabbat in particular. Here, Kook refers to an event in Mark 2:23–28 (and parallels) where Jesus permitted his hungry disciples to pick stalks of wheat in a field on Shabbat. As part of its renewed habitation of the Holy Land, the Jewish collective was required to maintain the sanctity of Shabbat as a central aspect of its national life in Israel. Finally, Kook called for the founding of Hebrew jurisprudence in Israel and reiterated his father's critique of Christianity, that "the *minut* has abandoned justice" by uprooting the Torah.[29] This manifesto makes clear how central is the polemic with Christianity in any estimation of this leader of the settlement movement's politics.

Similar arguments appeared later throughout Zvi Yehudah Kook's career. Following the visit of Prime Minister Golda Meir to the Vatican in 1973, Kook said the following, which had a decisive influence on his disciples: "When Golda Meir visited the Vatican, the old *galakh* [a medieval derogatory name for Christian priests, referring here to Pope Paul VI] received her, and they hoisted the Israeli flag. How were they not ashamed to do so?! After all, this is their destruction!"[30]

Another characteristic of Zvi Yehudah Kook's anti-Christian rhetoric was the reiteration of classical polemical rabbinic texts in his teaching. He reverted to the most pointed anti-Christian sources in Jewish tradition, from the Curse of the Heretics (Birkat HaMinim) to the Talmudic legends about Jesus and the polemics of the Middle Ages. Kook repeats, for example, the Talmudic story in which Onkelos the Proselyte evokes the spirit of Jesus, "a criminal of Israel" (*poshea Israel*), who was condemned to immersion in boiling excrement:[31]

> In the tractate of Gittin, [Jesus] is called Israel's criminal. All of Christianity is a crime against Israel, a rebellion against us, an insurrection against the eternity of Israel. . . . The Talmud there tells the story of Onkelos the Proselyte . . . , who went and raised "the Criminal of Israel" in a "séance." . . . As their conversation progresses, it becomes evident that "that person" [*oto ha'ish*], Jesus, has been sentenced to boiling excrement. What is the meaning of "boiling excrement"? Fermenting refuse. This description is exactly apt for his personality. . . . Jesus is "excrement" because he has been excreted from the body of the congregation of Israel [*klal Israel*] as waste, though it is "fermenting" because of his myriad impure talents, imaginings, and parables. My father and teacher of blessed memory related that when he was a child, he would smell the stench of a toilet every time he passed by Christian houses of idolatry.[32]

Interestingly, the story, which constitutes one of the most tenacious traditional Jewish attacks on Christianity, served Zvi Yehudah Kook to identify an "organic" connection between Judaism and Christianity. Christianity, he claimed, was once part of the body of Judaism, but it was excreted. The Tal-

mudic idea that Jesus was a "criminal brother," excreted from the congregation of Israel for his crimes—sorcerer, agitator, and provocateur—returned
in Kook's writings. Moreover, Maimonides, Kook reminded his readers,
stated that Jesus had been stoned and hanged in a rabbinical court. Precisely
at a time when Jews in the Diaspora had been advocating for the abolition
of the persistent deicide charge that had been leveled against the Jewish
people throughout the generations, Kook refused to remove the responsibility for the crucifixion of Jesus from the Jews or even to share it with the
Romans. He accused those who wished to do so of sycophancy and apologetic excuses:

> Christians accuse us of being "deiciders." We have murdered idolatry!
> There are Jews who fear the gentiles and attempt to conceal this. For
> example, at Mossad Harav Kook publishing house, they issued a popular
> edition of Maimonides called "Rambam La'Am," and unfortunately,
> those who printed it wanted to keep in the good graces of the gentiles,
> to genuflect before them and cleanse us from blame. They say that we
> did not kill him, but rather the gentiles did. In regard to what Mai-
> monides found (*Laws of Kings,* 11:4, the omissions of Christian Cen-
> sorship), that this person was killed by a rabbinical court, they claim
> that our court delivered him to the Roman court, to their official Pon-
> tius Pilate, and they killed him.[33] . . . But that is a lie. Maimonides did
> not hesitate to explicitly write: "Jesus the Nazarene imagined himself
> to be the Messiah *and was killed by the rabbinical court*."[34] One should
> feel a sense of awe before the sanctity of each and every word of Mai-
> monides. If he wrote it was a rabbinical court, then it was a rabbinical
> court! A Jewish court . . . , not an instance of the gentiles.[35]

This reclaiming of the Gittin story, as well as his bold affirmation of the
deicide charge, served Kook as a strategy in renouncing the victimized "exilic" Jewish identity, by identifying precisely with the central accusations that
the Christian victimizer had made against the Jews throughout the ages. The
contemptuous stories told about Jesus in the Talmud were referred to again
and again in anti-Jewish writings (including, for example, in Luther's *On the
Jews and Their Lies*) and provided, along with the deicide charge, a solid justification for hatred of Jews, and even for outright violence. Instead of rejecting these anti-Jewish accusations, Kook embraced them and internalized them, as if a sovereign, unapologetic Jewish position meant that Jews

must be (almost) as bad as they were in the anti-Jewish, even antisemitic, imagination.

Zvi Yehudah Kook considered the "crime" of Jesus (depicted in the Talmud as "criminal of Israel," *poshea Israel*), and of Christianity in general, to be a crime of heresy against the eternity of Israel. Kook expressed this conception in a polemical article that he wrote in 1957 against the Yiddish author Shalom Asch, who was subjected to Haredi attacks for his 1939 novel on Christianity, *The Man from Nazareth*. In 1957, Asch was recognized by the Israeli establishment, which raised Kook's ire. After calling Asch a "criminal of Israel" who "bows and fawns" before "that man [*oto ha'ish*]," Kook then proceeded to discuss Christianity:

> All the incitement and provocation of "that personality" [*ota ha'ishiut*, from the Jewish name of Jesus, *oto ha'ish*], according to all that idolatry and all of its alien creed and worship, as it arises from it and is based on it, is a *crime against Israel* [*pshi'ah beIsrael*]. This crime against the Almighty is a crime against the very essence of Israel. Its blasphemy is great against the truth of God's name and His revelation in His world, just as it shamefully denies the truth of the Jewish nation's mission and its entire tangible, real and ideal, historical and universal reality. It is expressed in its disgusting loathsomeness, in the raising of "that personality" as if it were divine, as if it were essentially equal-related and obscurely foggily affiliated with the original and real selfhood of the Creator and leader of the universe.[36]

The crime against the Jewish nation, which Zvi Yehudah Kook viewed as Christianity's very quintessence, is the blasphemy of rejecting the divine choosing of the Jewish people and the eternal permanence of that choosing. Kook attacked Christianity for having deified Jesus and "associated" his worship with God, that is, he objected to the Christian belief in association, *shittuf*. However, his main criticism was not directed at the polytheistic tendency reflected in the belief of *shittuf* but rather toward the way in which Christianity purports to replace the Jewish nation with Jesus as God's chosen and true son. "A person who associates [*meshatef*] the name of God with something else [*davar aher*] is uprooted from the world," wrote Kook, "but 'worshipping both God and Israel, his people' is associating (*meshutefet hi*) with the worship of the living god and the sovereign of the world, *for it is not another thing (lefi shehi eynena davar aher)*—'Israel, the Torah and the

Blessed God are all One.'"[37] In other words, it is permissible, according to Kook, to "associate" belief in God and in the Jewish nation, because the nation of Israel is divine. Christianity is idolatry because it blasphemes against the divinity of the people of Israel and deifies a single individual instead: "As compared with the single, criminal and separated personality . . . that purports to seize the place of Israel's eternity, to claim 'I shall rule' in assimilation to divinity—thus becoming idolatry."[38]

Zvi Yehudah Kook presented Christianity as the obverse of Jewish uniqueness and as a heresy against the divine nature of that uniqueness. Like his father, he too believed that Christianity's greatest crime was its attempt to rob the Jewish people of their status as "chosen" and to dispossess them of their eschatological purpose: "The *minut* is the greatest woe of all. It is a war against the eternity of Israel [and against God] from its inception to date."[39] Precisely at the time that Christians were no longer part of the everyday landscape, Zvi Yehudah Kook sought to establish Jewish polity and culture as the antithesis of Christianity. He turned Christianity into a theoretical—even rhetorical—category, serving to differentiate between "authentic" Israeli Judaism and "exilic" Judaism, the latter a Judaism still influenced by its past in Christian lands. He aspired to establish a culture that would be a "purely" Hebrew culture, completely purged of external influences. To protect his flock from Christian influence, Kook reverted to the traditional weapons of Judaism (which had, paradoxically, been developed in the Diaspora). He perceived any attempt to make amends with Christianity as adulation and sycophancy, befitting European Jews, but not Israelis.

The French-Speaking Students of the Kook School

Both father and son Kook believed that the return to the Holy Land and the renewal of national life would cure the Jews of the ills of their exile and would allow them to renew their connection with their unique nature—both spiritual and material. The healing of the nation would ultimately also make it possible to renew the influence of the Jewish people on the nations of the world in an authentic way, rather than through distorted Christian mediation. Once the Jewish people returned to their land, they would fulfill their foreordained role of providing humanity with spiritual guidance and leadership.

While Zvi Yehudah Kook focused entirely on Jews and did not address the spiritual fate of the gentiles at all, some of his students gave considerable thought to the impact of the return to Zion on the relationship between the Jewish nation and other nations. This matter was taken up mainly by Kook's Francophone students: Rabbis Abraham Livni (a proselyte converted from Protestant Christianity), Yehuda Léon Askénazi (known as Manitou), Shlomo Aviner, and Oury Cherki.

Some of these rabbis expanded the ideas of the Rabbis Kook on the need to neutralize not just Christian but Occidental influences on Judaism. Others affiliated with this school focused on the universal message that the Jewish nation residing in Zion is called on to bring to humanity. In contradistinction to the Orthodox Jewish mainstream, most of these rabbis were conversant to one degree or another with the secular and Christian thought that had developed in France, and beginning in 1960s, this group originated a Jewish theology of Christianity. At the heart of this school's literature stand the implications for Christianity of the founding of the Jewish state and the converging of the Jewish people within it. To explore this question, they merged Kook's theology with post-Holocaust Christian perspectives.

According to these rabbis, the Holocaust and the return to Zion brought about a fundamental change in the relationship between the Jewish nation and the Christian nations. Christian self-perception is based on denigration of Judaism, and Jewish success undermines that perception at its very core. The return to Zion forces Christians to define the Jewish people more "genuinely" and the relationships between the two religions are therefore in flux. At the end of this process, Judaism is destined to take its proper place as the ethical and spiritual guide of the human race in its entirety.

Verus Israel: Yehuda Léon Askénazi's Attitude toward Christianity

As post-Holocaust Catholic theologians in France made an effort to rethink their attitude to Judaism and to purge Christianity of its anti-Jewish traits, French Jewish intellectuals also became involved in these efforts. Such were the members of L'école de pensée juive de Paris (the Paris school for Jewish thought), a Jewish intellectual movement that sought to restore French Jewry after the war.[40] The members of the Parisian school held a lively discourse with Catholic theologians, particularly with the "New Theologians" (*les nouveaux théologiens*), who led far-reaching changes in contemporary Catholic thought.[41] The Jewish movement included thinkers such as Jacob Gordin, André Neher, Éliane Amado Levy-Valensi, Emmanuel Levinas, and Yehuda Léon Askénazi. They wrote in French and combined Jewish erudition (the

Bible, Talmud, and Kabbalah) with general philosophy, attracting literate Jews while condemning the West for its moral failure in the Holocaust.[42] Several of their works (especially those of Levinas, which formulate a Jewish moral doctrine in light of the Holocaust) became widely accepted in Catholic circles.

Rabbi Askénazi was a central figure in the Paris school and in post-Holocaust French Jewry. He formulated an encompassing historico-sophic system, radically Zionist, based on biblical and Kabbalistic sources. In the 1950s, he became acquainted with Zvi Yehudah Kook and was greatly influenced by his and his father's thought. After the Six-Day War, Askénazi immigrated to Israel and inspired many of his disciples to follow him. He continued influencing the French Jewish community in Israel and attracted many disciples, including the prominent Zionist rabbis Shlomo Aviner, Avraham Yehoshua Zuckerman, Eliyahu Zeini, and Oury Cherki.

Askénazi knew Christianity better than other thinkers in the circle of Zvi Yehudah Kook and probably better than most Orthodox rabbis of his time. He was aware of the vast intellectual processes taking place within the Christian world after the Second World War and of the aggiornamento (update) in Catholic theology. Askénazi directly witnessed the changes in the attitude of Christian theologians and religious figures toward Judaism following the Holocaust, and he regarded them as a true revolution.[43] The Holocaust, he argued, had profoundly shaken the Christian conscience. After witnessing the Nazis fulfilling what the church had long preached but dared not pursue, Christians made a moral and spiritual decision that such an atrocity should never be repeated.[44] He saw the undertaking of the struggle against antisemitism by church officials as emerging from honest regret and from a sincere wish to repair the Christian doctrine.[45]

However, Askénazi believed that the church was not going far enough. Indeed, the Holocaust had motivated Christians to move closer to Jews and to open a dialogue with them, but Christians did not yet dare to cope with the magnitude of the problem that history posed to them.[46] Although the problem began with the Holocaust—"the murder of Israel on Christian land"—its core was the establishment of the State of Israel—"the resurrection of Israel on Jewish land." The restoration of Jewish sovereignty in the Holy Land, according to Askénazi, added to the moral challenge that Christianity had to face—the challenge of Christian identity:

> Christian consciousness is called on for two complementary questions: on the one hand, it is discovering, through the Holocaust, the Jewish

people as the "suffering Messiah." . . . On the other hand, the revival of
the State of Israel shows them that Jewish identity is becoming Hebrew
once more, and the history of the people of Israel is becoming an actual
history, after two thousand years. All this leads to an embarrassing discovery: "perhaps the Jews are Israel!" . . . And one can further ask: If
the Jews are Israel, who then are the Christians?[47]

The establishment of the State of Israel, according to Askénazi, created
an identity crisis for the church, even if the Christian world had not yet realized it.[48] The identification between contemporary Jews and biblical Israel had pulled the rug out from under the church's self-definition as the
"true Israel" (verus Israel), as proclaimed by the prophets. Events that took
place after the establishment of the state, and especially after the Six-Day
War, further exacerbated this alleged crisis—the visit of Pope Paul VI to Israel (1964), the fourth section in the Second Vatican Council's declaration
Nostra aetate on Jews and Judaism (1965), the visit of Pope John Paul II to
the Great Synagogue of Rome (1986), the diplomatic treaty between Israel
and the Vatican (1993)—all of which, in Askénazi's eyes, had eschatological
significance, testifying that the church was indeed beginning to acknowledge that the Jews were the true inheritors of biblical Israel.[49]

Askénazi viewed the vulnerability of the church regarding its own identity as poetic justice. Throughout the continuous struggle of Esau with Jacob,
Christianity had implanted profound self-doubt in the hearts of the Jews
with regard to their own selfhood, existential doubts that had characterized
Ashkenazi Jewry throughout its diasporic history. The harm that Esau had
caused Jacob (who left the fight limping, according to Gen. 32:32) symbolizes
the self-doubt that Chrisitianty had inflicted on Judaism, to the point that it
forgot its own identity:[50]

As paradoxical as it may seem, the phenomenon of the anusim [forced
converts, usually identified with the history of Spanish Jews] is more
characteristic of the Ashkenazi world, since it is about the Jewish soul
being thrown into the world of Christian resistance—both religious and
secular. In a sense, all diasporic Jews are anusim, sentenced to a humanistic world according to Greco-Roman measures. . . . The life of the
Ashkenazi Jew is more "tragic," in the Greek sense of the word. He [the
Ashkenazi] went through exile while experiencing a grave doubt regarding his own identity, a doubt bearing horrific implications.[51]

To Askénazi, following the restoration of Jewish sovereignty over the Land of Israel, the Jews ceased to be "figures in a Jewish fiction," that is, religious symbols without actual solidity, and returned to the stage of history.[52] The fulfillment of biblical prophecies about the return to Zion testifies to the truthfulness of the literal, Jewish reading of the Bible (a reading "according to the flesh"); thus, the Christian reading of the Bible ("according to the spirit") is wrong.[53]

In a letter to Christian friends, Askénazi argued that the Six-Day War was interpreted by Catholics and Protestants as a messianic event, even if they still hesitated to admit it.[54] With the collapse of the Christian thesis about the prefigurative meaning of the Old Testament, Christianity's entire messianic thesis collapsed as well. Instead of the Jews' testifying to the truthfulness of the Gospel, as argued by Augustine, the Christians had now themselves become witnesses, stupefied by the resurrection of the people of Israel, whose very survival had been a total mystery to them for millennia.[55]

Thus, Askénazi turned the classical Christian perception of Judaism on its head; Christianity existed only to admit its error while facing Jewish redemption. Moreover, the traditional accusation of the Jews as "refusing" to acknowledge the Messiah falls, according to Askénazi, on the shoulders of Christians; the Christians were the ones who refused to acknowledge the Jewish messianic doctrine and rejected the route to salvation that the Jews have offered to all human beings:

> They [Christians] have never succeeded in explaining to us how and why the church had founded its faith, its doctrine, its liturgy and its institutions by rejecting Jewish messianism and its history, while this messianism applies to all of humanity and not solely to the Jews.[56]

Gathering Askénazi's scattered comments reveals that he had made a systematic application of the Christian "teaching of contempt" (to borrow Jules Isaac's term) to the Christians themselves: Christians were the ones who had rejected the good news; they were the ones who misunderstood Scripture; they were the witnesses of the faith; and now, on losing their identity, they are the ones who must justify their existence. Askénazi read Christian anti-Jewish doctrine as a prefiguration of an opposite Jewish perception of Christianity, a perception that became possible only at his time, when the messianic future seemed to be at hand and the hopes of Judaism realized. This role reversal would reach its peak in the *conversio* of the Christians: "The

Christians slowly discover that it is not the Jew that has to be Christianized, but the Christian that has to be Judaized."[57]

Through reversing the traditional Christian doctrine and "Judaizing" it against Christianity, not only did Askénazi attempt to use Christianity's own weapons against it; he also sought to return the Christian doctrine to its Jewish sources (in the spirit of the Catholic principle of *ressourcement*). The Christian doctrine is not a collection of nonsense, Askénazi declared to his Jewish and Christian audience, but a mythological piece that hides a great truth—the truth of Israel, its history and its faith. With this argument, so it seems, Askénazi echoed the Christian idea, present since the thirteenth century, that the Talmud contained important proof of the truthfulness of Christianity.[58] To truly understand Christianity, he maintained, one must return to the Hebrew sources of the Christian myth:

> Behind the Christian myth hides the identity of Israel, which was injected into a fictional figure and literally became an idol and a myth. Thus the Christian myth is not empty of meaning. On the contrary, it is full of meanings—it embodies the identity of Israel posed as a mediator between the Creator and man, and for this it is venerated.[59]

Through the idea that Christianity is a "mythicization" of the Torah, Askénazi managed to create a theological bridge between the Kooks' belief that Christianity was the product of an impure "burst" of paganism into the holiness of Israel and the prevailing discussion in contemporary Christian theological discourse of the need to differentiate between the authentic historical components of the Christian story and its mythical components, imposed by tradition. "The emerging of Christianity," maintained Askénazi, "expressed the penetration of Greek mythical mentality into Jewish identity."[60]

The first Christians, who were themselves Jews, had written the Gospels as parables about the people of Israel—"the meaning of the myths was comprehensible in their time."[61] They were not the ones who sought to idolize the myth, according to Askénazi. But when the Gospel made its way to gentile hands, a pagan dimension was added to the myth.[62] The gentiles confused the parable with its meaning; instead of understanding that Jesus represented the people of Israel and that his passion and resurrection symbolized the covenant of Israel and its redemption, they understood the people of Israel as a symbol for Jesus and the old covenant as representing the new.

The time has come, Askénazi declared, to teach the Christians what their myth really signifies. According to Askénazi, this can be done only by Jews:

> The Gospels, describing the object of Christian faith, have a meaning that needs to be comprehended. This meaning, however, could be deciphered only by the Hebrews, and only if the mythic garb is removed from it. The Christians have argued on many occasions that a veil separates the Jews from the Torah, and that Christians need to explain the Torah to Jews. It is high time to reverse this method. If we want to begin understanding each other, it is necessary, first of all, that Jews explain the Gospel to Christians. . . . Jews must explain to Christians, in the most brotherly way possible, what Christians actually believe. The Jews must clarify that the dignity of the Christians' faith can remain intact on the condition that their religion be purified of its mythical components. In this field, the Jewish-Christian dialogue has not yet begun.[63]

Paul's veil, which absorbed the poisonous essence of Christian-Jewish history for centuries, was applied by Askénazi to the Christians.[64] They, and not the Jews, are the ones who are blindfolded and have hardened hearts, to the point that they can no longer understand the meaning of their own scripture.[65] Paraphrasing Pope John Paul II's famous words that the Jews are the Christians' "elder brothers," Askénazi maintains, "It should be said, without even a shred of irony or humor, that as the Christians' 'elder brothers,' the Jews are obliged to help the Christians in solving their problem of identity."[66]

What will remain of Christianity after the veil is removed from the eyes of Christians? Askénazi maintained that "a Christian may preserve the authenticity of his faith with all dignity as long as he purges from it the mythical reading of the 'passion narrative.'"[67] To him, only if the Christians renounce the myth will a sincere interreligious dialogue be possible. But the "mythical reading" of the passion narrative means the belief in Jesus as the Christ and the Son of God. Could the "authenticity" of the Christian faith be maintained without Jesus's messianism and divinity?

Askénazi was deeply impressed by the aggiornamento of the Catholic Church and had high regard for Christian intellectuals. He participated in interreligious dialogue and encouraged it, spoke well in the theological language of his time, and wrote to Christian as well as Jewish audiences. He often spoke of the need to help Christians and to cooperate with them to produce a "positive theology" of Judaism to substitute the "teaching of contempt" that sees them as perfidious Christ killers.[68] Most importantly, Askénazi believed that the hostility between Christians and Jews was finally coming to an end and that reconciliation was possible. Nevertheless, reading between the lines of Askénazi's work reveals a fierce anti-Christian position. Precisely when the Christian world was repentant about what it had done to the Jews by means of its theology, Askénazi adopted the Catholic teaching of contempt in full. In this sense, by leading Christianity back to its Jewish roots, he did not strive for interreligious reconciliation but sought to once again engulf Christianity in the Jewish womb from which it had originally emerged.

The Return to Zion as a Miracle for Humanity—Abraham Livni

Another thinker who was deeply influenced by the writings of Zvi Yehudah Kook and subsequently influenced the circle of his students was the convert Rabbi Abraham Livni. Livni was deeply shaken by the Holocaust that he witnessed as a Protestant boy in Marseille.[69] He studied theology and philosophy after the war and ultimately decided to convert to Judaism. He went to Israel in 1963 and became acquainted with the Kooks' philosophy. His book *Le retour d'Israël et l'espérance du monde* (The return of Israel and the hope of the world) was first published in French in 1984; a Hebrew translation, by Rabbi Oury Cherki, was published in 1995.[70] The book is still well known in the circles of the Kooks' disciples and is mainly distributed among Jews who return to observance, converts, and Noahides, in the context of Cherki's organization Brit Olam—Noahide World Center (discussed below).

As in the case of most Christian theologians who dealt with the relations between Christians and Jews in the second half of the twentieth century, the point of departure for Livni's discussion is the Holocaust. Like the prominent Christian thinkers of his time, Livni, too, viewed the Holocaust as a call to reexamine God's selection of the Jews as a chosen people and the role of Israel among the nations. If it were not for the endurance of the covenant, it would have been impossible that precisely the Jewish people would experience such inconceivable suffering. Livni conceived of Auschwitz as a "revelation through darkness."[71] The "metaphysical destruction" of the West in the Holocaust, he maintained, was a product of the "Christian lie," that is, the church's claim to be God's chosen people. The physical murder of the Jewish people by the Nazis was "a direct continuation of the moral position of the Christian world, which for two thousand years had already theologically and ethically murdered the Jewish people in its attempt to dispossess it of its self-identity through defamation."[72] This lie led humanity to forget its destiny, until it brought it to a severe identity crisis.[73]

Livni's book deals with the universal destiny of the Jewish people, wherein the return to Zion and the founding of the State of Israel are conditions for the realization of that fate. Like Zvi Yehudah Kook, Livni argues that the main obstacle to the realization of that destiny always was and still remains Christianity.[74] The problem with Christianity arises from replacement theology, which claims that the Jewish people have long since ended their role in the history of salvation. Livni adopted Askénazi's position regarding the "mythicization" of Judaism: Christianity is based on the conversion of the people of Israel into the myth of Jesus. The displacement of the messianic destiny of the Jewish people into the mythical figure of a single person is the root of all evil, because it makes the people of Israel redundant and threatens the very ground under their feet:

> This metaphysical fraud . . . distorts the meaning and the demands of human conscience. . . . The mythic shifting of the Jewish destiny within humanity to the divinized personality of Jesus [takes away] the entire justification for the current existence of the Jewish people. If there is no justification for their existence, they are supposed to cease existing, and if they continue to exist—they should be destroyed. Theologically, it is possible to conceive two covenants—the old and the new—but on an existential level, it is not possible to have two peoples of Israel that were intended to continue simultaneously with the same mission, so it is therefore obvious that one of them is redundant. Theologically, the Jewish people, as the successors of biblical Israel, do not have a right to exist.[75]

Christian theology has turned the tangible existence of the Jewish people into a problem. Like Askénazi, Livni, too, rejected the Maritain-flavored thesis that perceived Jewish history and existence as a "mystery"—a thesis according to which, Livni claimed, "it is impossible for Christianity to relate to the living Jewish reality," since mystery "is something that one flees from as a dangerous thing that belongs to another world."[76] Livni believed that this attempt transformed Western civilization into a culture of forgetfulness. The motivation to deny the existence of the Jewish people shadowed

Western civilization from the very inception of Christianity until modern times, even when it lost its religious context, and even when it wished to treat Jews with tolerance. Livni demonstrated his claim through a discussion of Jean-Paul Sartre's conception of Judaism, since Sartre did not recognize Judaism as having any positive content; he saw it only as something constructed by the antisemitic gaze. For Livni, Western civilization in its entirety, in all its forms, is motivated by the will to forget Israel.[77]

According to Livni, the struggle between forgetfulness and memory is fundamental to an understanding of the conflicted history of the Jewish people and the nations of the world.[78] Following Kook, Livni viewed the Jewish people as the representatives of human teleology who carry the seed of human destiny within them. The Jewish people are the nation of memory because they thread through all of history—from beginning to end—in a chain of promise: "all [of Israel's] history is messianic to a certain extent, a messianic stream that threads throughout it until the project of creation has been brought forth." Other nations, by comparison, "live in forgetfulness and ignorance."[79] They do not remember that history has a purpose and a trend, and they treat it as if it were some meaningless collection of disconnected events. The Christian intentional forgetfulness of Israel lies at the very center of the nations' ignorance:

> Christianity, so it seems, should be set apart, and distinguished from the stream of forgetfulness that is the spirit of contemporary civilization; it believes in a creator God and refers to the Bible, since it declares itself the predestined successor of Judaism. . . . but the truth is that Christianity bears the responsibility for creating the trend of forgetfulness in the world. . . . Indeed, Christian faith bears the seed of forgetfulness within its very root, for it cannot exist unless such forgetting supports in considering itself Israel. In order to be able to read the Bible in this way, it must first forget, and through this forgetting, reject, the Jewish reading. The Christian reading is not a parallel reading to the Jewish one, but a "foreign" reading that reveals a foreign God. And since it will not be able to contend with the Jewish reading, it must eliminate it. Forgetting is the best elimination.[80]

Livni rejected the efforts of the church to describe Christianity and Judaism as two "parallel" readings of Scripture because he viewed the Christian reading as one that undermined the Jewish one.[81] Reconciliation is impossible because the church's enmity toward Israel is fundamental; not only did the church expropriate the Jewish future, it also expropriated the Jewish past—in other words, it completely engulfed Jewish identity. According to the Christian conception, even for the incarnation in the flesh, Jewish history had already manifested the story of the church: "[According to Christianity], the church was not born with Jesus; rather it was always Israel, at least virtually, for Israel of the flesh was in fact the 'figure' of the church, just as the Old Testament was the figure of the New Testament."[82] Christian theology teaches that the people of Israel never existed in the way that the Jews understand it, because the Israelites' metaphysical destiny had always served as a prelude to Christianity, and their existence was a representation of the church as the only true "congregation of Israel."

The declarations of bishops, Christian-Jewish friendship organizations, and the church's official struggle with antisemitism cannot really reconcile the two religions because antisemitism is not the problem but a mere symptom. The problem is the theological crime on which Christianity was built—the church's claim that it, rather than the Jews, is the true Israel, and the substitution of the myth of Jesus for the true faith.[83] As long as the church refuses to recognize the falsity of its own myth, antisemitism will continue to rear its head, and humanity, remaining detached from the people of Israel and their message to the world, will continue to be mired in self-forgetfulness.

In his discussion of the universal destiny of Judaism, Livni entered a discourse, just beginning at the time, that revolved around the Seven Laws of Noah. The Orthodox Jewish discussion of the Noahide religion naturally tends to assume a polemical turn against Christianity, since the latter inscribed on its flag the dissemination of the universal belief of Israel. Judaism was forced to give up disseminating its own universal alternative during its years of exile and emphasized instead its particularity. To transform Judaism into an influential religion (not just through the distorted lens of Christianity), one must first get Christianity out of the way. Livni followed in the footsteps of Elijah Benamozegh, a nineteenth-century Italian rabbi, who is considered the pioneer of the modern discourse on the Noahide religion. In his book *Israël et l'humanité*, Benamozegh discusses the universal message of Judaism for the human race and calls on Christians to accept the seven commandments of the sons of Noah.[84] But where Benamozegh was willing to bestow on Christianity the status of a religion of the sons of Noah, on condition that the Christians institute a few corrections in their religion, Livni was of the opinion that Christianity had been distorted beyond any hope of redemption.[85] He attacked "tolerant" attitudes toward Christianity and accused Benamozegh of "a vaporous tolerant liberal optimism."[86] Like other members of Zvi Yehudah Kook's circle, Livni considered Christianity to be idolatry in all respects and therefore forbidden to all—sons of Noah just as much as Jews.[87] The salvation of the human race would not be able to come about unless Christianity were removed from the stage of history, thus allowing the people of Israel to influence the nations. The rejection of the belief of *shittuf* and the assumption of the seven Noahide laws constituted just the first step.[88] As long as Christianity had a hold on people's hearts, the process could not even begin.

Thus, we return to the formulation of Kook's disciples—Christianity does not "pave the way for the Messiah" but holds him back:

> There is no doubt that Christianity is the most monumental error in the history of mankind. It is a spiritual deviation that corrupts all God's ways of revelation. The myth of incarnation and of redemption by faith laid a huge idolatry stumbling block in the path of mankind's religious consciousness.[89]

Drawing on Abraham Isaac Kook and adapting his theology to the conditions of the post-Holocaust era, the State of Israel, and the evolution in Christian-Jewish relations, Livni and Askénazi both thought that the time was right to renew Israel's place as the light to the nations, this time not by the indirect mediation of Christianity but directly, based on the Jewish universal program of the seven Noahide laws. Their position did not represent a reactionary retreat from contemporary Christian-Jewish dialogue but rather the establishment of an alternative, subversive kind of dialogue between Jews and Christians based on a radical Zionist reading of the signs of the times.

The Polemics of the Year 2000

On the eve of the second millennium CE, Zvi Yehudah Kook's followers published a host of anti-Christian books, articles, and leaflets, including texts composed by Kook himself—"May the Heretics [*minim*] Not Have Hope" (paraphrasing the Jewish benediction of the heretics) and "Judaism and Heresy [*minut*]"—that were included in an anthology titled *Judaism and*

Christianity, edited by Rabbi Shlomo Aviner (whose positions will be discussed below).[90] Also published were the book *The Christian Pitfall,* which consists of a new edition of *The Covenant* by Ya'akov Zurishaday, with comments by Zvi Yehudah Kook;[91] an article by Rabbi Aviner himself, *The Enemy or The Christian Enemy,* which was published in *Judaism and Christianity,* in *The Christian Pitfall,* and as a separate booklet;[92] a booklet by the students of Har Hamor Yeshiva (a central yeshiva of Zvi Yehudah Kook's disciples, which follows a stringent line against combining Torah scholarship with academic education and Western knowledge) regarding the "Christian Friends of Israel," which was distributed among the general public;[93] and articles by Rabbis Oury Cherki and Dan Be'eri, which were published in *Tzohar.*[94] Some of the authors contended with the Christian pilgrimages to the Holy Land at the close of the millennium, and in particular Pope John II's visit to Israel. While the Haredi world almost completely ignored the millennial celebrations, Zvi Yehuda Kook's followers made considerable efforts to raise public awareness of the event and to publicly discuss Christian theological precepts and the relationships of Christianity with Judaism.[95]

The pope's visit in the year 2000 evoked concerns over the Christian mission. In a letter by the Sephardi chief rabbi of Israel, Eliyahu Bakshi-Doron, which was included in a booklet titled *Clarification of Matters Regarding the Christian Friends of Israel,* we read:

> In the proximate period, thousands of Christian pilgrims are scheduled to arrive in Israel, among them missionaries who are liable to trap innocent Jewish souls, whether through direct propaganda or in the context of various institutions of assistance and adoption of settlements and the like. Unfortunately, there are many converts to Christianity who call themselves by various names such as messianic Jews and the like, who entice innocent Jewish souls to alien beliefs, and there are many casualties.[96]

Subsequently, Rabbi Bakshi-Doron warned in a letter against coming closer to pilgrims and cooperating with them and expressed support for Rabbi Aviner for having issued a Torah viewpoint on this matter. The letter of Rabbi Dov Lior, the religious Zionist rabbi of Kiryat Arba, reiterated the warning: "The year two thousand is a great year of extended pilgrimage of Christians to our land, and following this come harsh and bitter consequences. I have heard that they are plotting to come here in their tens of thousands and flood our land and attempt to ensnare poor people in their net by providing support and exerting missionary influence in order to convert them to the Christian faith."[97]

The approach of the millennium was thus a catalyst for an increase in the traditional concern over the Christian mission. Zvi Yehudah Kook himself was a sworn opponent of the mission, maintained ties with the anti-mission organization Yad La'Achim, and was very concerned over the infiltration of Christian culture into the State of Israel. In general, during the first years of the State of Israel's existence, the fear of mission was a great concern within the Jewish public and worried both religious and secular Jews.[98] In 1977, the Israeli government enacted an amendment to the penal code that restricts missionary activity.[99] Over the years, the concern over mission gradually declined, or at least became less prominent in public discourse.

Conciliatory gestures of the Catholic Church and the Christian-Jewish friendships offered by evangelical communities evoked deep suspicions within the circle of Kook's disciples, who perceived all Christian support of Israel, both financial and political, as a missionary strategy. In a booklet discussing the Christian Friends of Israel, the authors explain that evangelical Christians who befriend the Jewish people are only interested in hastening the return of Jesus. Although Christians are not currently attempting to convert Jews to their religion, the authors contend, their actions for the benefit of Israel are missionary in character, since they are interested in bringing the future conversion of Jews in this way. Moreover, because the Christians have realized the depth of Jewish aversion to missionary activity, they mask their missionary intentions and act only with political and economic gestures, "a tactical consideration rather than an expression of a worldview that recognizes the self-worth of the People of Israel."[100]

The anti-Christian ideas of the year 2000 touched on a theological-eschatological struggle regarding the events of the present and their place in the divine plan—or plans—of salvation. Toward the end of the millennium, several rabbis belonging to Zvi Yehudah Kook's circle renewed the ancient Christian-Jewish polemics. The most salient example of this is found in the book *The Christian Pitfall*, which had been published by its original author, Ya'akov Zurishaday, in 1937 under the name *The Covenant*. *The Christian Pitfall* comprises a collection of traditional critiques of the New Testament in which Zurishaday reiterates the classic arguments of the Jewish polemicists of the late Middle Ages: highlighting internal contradictions between the Gospels or within them, mocking the doctrines of Christian faith and showing them to be contrary to logic, and providing historical refutations of the Gospels and alternative hermeneutics to the Christian interpretation of the prophets. Kook added his own commentary to the book while the author was still alive, and as the year 2000 approached, Rabbi Yehoshua Zuckerman (one of the rabbis of the Har Hamor Yeshiva) decided to republish the book with his own comments. "I found it appropriate to republish the book now, close on the arrival of Pope John Paul II in Jerusalem," wrote Zuckerman. "There will probably be much said regarding the Christian religion and the Gospels, and it is appropriate to provide the Jewish people with a theoretical critique of this book."[101]

The combination of the contemporary preface and the archaic genre of the book's body raises questions. Why did Kook's disciples wish to return to the classic polemics with Christianity? Why did they consider the repetition of all those ancient formulas, written by sages in the Middle Ages from a clearly apologetic standpoint, to be beneficial in the year 2000? I believe that they felt that the events of their own period resurrected the old Christian-Jewish polemics from the reverse direction. While medieval Jews were forced to polemicize with Christians to justify their existence before both their Christian hosts and their own communities, which were vulnerable to Christian temptations, now, at the turn of the millennium, it was Christianity that was on trial. In 2000, the thoughts of Kook and Askénazi were enlisted to repulse Christianity with a show of Jewish sovereign power. When the Christian pilgrims came to celebrate their holy history, the Jews would await them in Jerusalem with a historical refutation in the form of the State of Israel. When the Christians arrived in the Holy Land, they would see with their own eyes that the Christian-Jewish polemics had been settled once and for all, and the Christian thesis would collapse.

As we have seen, the inferiority of the Jews in the lands of the Christians was experienced by Jews (and of course by Christians) as a theological inferiority as well, because to a considerable extent, Judaism identified political success as a sign of salvation: "There is no difference between this world and the days of the Messiah except [that in the latter there will be no] bondage of foreign powers."[102] The traditional Jewish strategy to contend with this inferiority was to continue seeing the exile as a temporary phase that would eventually end. Ultimately, for Jews, only history could settle the quarrel. According to Abraham Isaac and Zvi Yehudah Kook and their disciples, that is exactly what occurred. This is how the 2000 version of Zurishaday's book concludes: "The people of Israel are still alive and well despite everything, and the eternity of Israel shall not lie or regret. . . . The lion cub of Judea has been resurrected and has established its state, and this resurrection in its own right undermines the entire foundation of Christian faith."[103]

Christian Mission, Jewish Mission—Rabbi Oury Cherki

Rabbi Oury Cherki did not share his colleagues' sense of vulnerability in the face of the Christian pilgrims of the year 2000. To the contrary, he considered mission to no longer constitute a significant threat for the Jews; they had become inured to it over many centuries of persecution, and the natural revulsion toward Christianity had been deeply inscribed in Jewish hearts thanks to historical memory. In addition, Cherki pointed with sovereign pride to the fact that Israeli law prohibits missionary work.[104] Instead of viewing them as a threat, Cherki viewed the waves of Christian pilgrims arriving in the year 2000 as an educational opportunity. "For the first time in four thousand years," wrote Cherki, "the conditions for realizing our destiny as a nation have finally been established. It is now possible to realize the purpose for which we have been chosen, that is, 'the restoration of the world in the kingdom of God,' 'and all the families of the earth shall bless themselves by you (Gen. 12:3).'"[105]

The many Christians who were about to flood the Land of Israel would therefore be privy to an (almost) unprecedented spectacle: the Jewish people sitting on their own land. Cherki claimed that this would be a transformative spectacle for Christianity, which would ultimately undermine it and bring about the realization of Maimonides's vision in *Laws of Kings*: "They shall immediately revert and realize that their ancestors had inherited lies, and that their prophets and ancestors had led them astray."[106] The Jews should prepare for the meeting with Christians from a position of superiority, secure in their status and deeply familiar with their opponent:

> It is important to establish an official Jewish position—an appeal to the Christian world, not out of any "inter-religious fraternity" or sycophancy, but out of a clear position of superiority—the superiority of a nation whose return to Zion gives it the right and the duty to be "the power that criticizes beliefs" and therefore also demands that they undergo an internal change in light of Israeli guidance.[107]

Rather than Christian mission, Cherki's focus is on the obverse: Jewish mission. Like Zvi Yehuda Kook, Cherki, too, believes that Jewish sovereignty

over the Land of Israel is the ultimate refutation of Christianity, dispelling
such major tenets as the claim that Chrisitans are the "true Israel," the Israel
of the spirit—tenets that were fed mainly by the political weakness of the
Jewish people in the Roman Empire at the beginning of Christianity. The
contrast between the Jewish people's spiritual greatness and their political
weakness confused the gentiles and prevented "the soul of the nations from
seeing the divine value of Jewish nationhood, while the teachings of Moses
attracted hearts as a spiritual creed."[108] Christianity therefore mediated Judaism for the human race while effacing its national aspect, to the point that
that aspect was completely forgotten, so forgotten that people no longer recognized Judaism as a concept with its own content. Cherki claims that
Christian "forgetfulness" is what underlies the ideas of such secular thinkers
as Sartre, who in his anti-antisemitic polemics claimed that the antisemitic
gaze was the one that shaped exilic Jewish identity.[109] However,

> all this changed with the Six-Day War. Since that victory and to this
> very day, Judaism is once more being studied in extensive circles among
> the nations of the world, by some of the most important scholars. . . .
> Our national humiliation is the reason that the nations ignored what
> Judaism had to say: "a poor man's wisdom is scorned, and his words
> are not heeded" (Eccles. 9:16). . . . The events of 1967 signify this return
> even more than the founding of the State of Israel, since in 1948, it was
> still possible to view the state as a mere shelter for hounded refugees,
> rather than an independent entity. The Six-Day War, however, was felt,
> both in Israel and overseas, as a biblical event in the full sense of the
> word, as if the biblical world had burst into the very heart of the twen-
> tieth century.[110]

During the Six-Day War, the Jews conquered large portions of the entire
biblical Land of Israel, and in the circle of Zvi Yehudah Kook, the ultimate
theologian of that war, this was perceived as clear proof of the covenant between the people of Israel and God and a concrete realization of the promises of the Bible. The conquest of the land returned Israel according to the
flesh to the center of the divine plan, while at the same time, Cherki claimed,
it pulled the rug out from underneath Israel of the spirit:

> Indeed, this is something that should concern the West. For if the State
> of Israel indeed belongs to biblical history, for it is possible that the way
> in which the Bible reads history is the correct one; and even more so,

it is possible that the Jewish reading of the Bible is the correct one. This thereby clarifies the status of the people of Israel as the identity successor of the ancient Hebrew nation, and thereby undermines the status of the church.[111]

Cherki thus reiterates the words of his teacher, Askénazi, according to which events will testify to the truth for Christians to the point that they will be awarded a spiritual awakening and the veil will be taken from their eyes. After having explained to the religious-national public what the Christian faith is, he wonders: "How could such an absurd myth have grown, and how could it have spread so throughout civilized humanity?" The key to settling this question, he claims, "depends on understanding the idolatrous psyche."[112] Cherki adopts Askénazi's conception of Christianity as mythologized Judaism and offers a pseudo-psychoanalytic description of Christianity. He claims that authentic Jewish concepts were perceived in a distorted way by the gentile mind, because that psyche is fundamentally different from the Jewish mind. This is Cherki's variation on the idea that Christianity represents an impure union between Judaism and idolatry, already present in the writings of Zvi Yehudah Kook. Now, Judaism has a "great work of sanctity" before it—to purify Jewish concepts of the idolatry that adhered to them and return them to their source.

The Christian idea regarding the death of God is thus a mythical variation of the concept of the departure of the Shekhina (God's dwelling presence, also "Knesset Israel," the eternal congregation of Israel). When the Shekhina resided in Israel, all people felt its presence. The gentiles interpreted this feeling in idolatrous terms and treated the Shekhina as an idol. When the Shekhina left Israel, the gentiles felt that their spiritual world had emptied. Following Abraham Isaac Kook, Cherki relates the spiritual crisis in Israel to the cancellation of idolatrous inclination in humanity: all humans paid the price for the sins of Israel. To cope with their spiritual emptiness, the gentiles developed Greek philosophy and the religions of the East, but these did not dispel their despair. Slowly, the nations began to be drawn to Judaism, "the sole living remnant of God's word in the world." However, because of the idolatrous structure of their psyche, the gentiles could not understand why exactly they were drawn to Israel. They dressed the God of Israel with an idolatrous covering and worshipped him as an idol. This was how the worship of Jesus began. But since "those days were the days when the Shekhina departed," they were obliged to invent the myth of the death of the new god to express the sense of loss. Moreover, they had to blame the Jews for deicide, to express the fact that the Jews were the ones who exiled the Shekhina (and were exiled with it) because of their sins.

In an interview, Cherki presented a different version of the same concept. He mentioned that Askénazi argued before a group of Christian priests that in fact they believed not in a God that made himself "human" to feel the suffering of men and atone for their sins but rather in a God who turned himself into a Jew. In other words, in Cherki's view, Christians believed that spilling the blood of Jews repaired the world. Either way, Cherki believes that underlying Christian doctrine is the recognition of the divine power of the soul of Israel. Now that the congregation (Knesset) of Israel—the Shekhina—has returned to Zion, the gentiles feel that God is alive and well and their faith in Christ is shaken: "The collective psyche of the nations now senses that one can no longer claim that God has been killed, for he has now been resurrected before our very eyes."[113]

Although Zvi Yehuda Kook's disciples refuse to justify Christianity simply on the grounds that as gentiles, Christians' *shittuf* can be excused, they do allow the *shittuf* whereby belief in the soul (the people) of Israel and belief in God coexist, together and simultaneously, in the heart of the believer. They claim that the prohibition of *shittuf* is in associating "the name of God with something else," but that the people of Israel do not constitute "something else."[114] According to Cherki, gentiles should worship Israel rather than Jesus, for Jesus is but a distorted realization of Israel—the soul of humanity in its entirety: "The idea that a Jew is God . . . arises from the power of the soul of Israel in the eyes of the nations—'for the nations of the world are destined to say before [the people of Israel that they are] sacred,' but this great truth regarding the general spirit of the nation was transferred to the image of an individual, and this made their adulation into idolatry."[115]

Cherki sought to renew the message of Israel to humanity through Noahism—that is, through educating the nations to observe the Seven Laws of Noah. Such a project is, of course, revolutionary in its own right and clearly reflects a renewed confidence in the Jews' ability to bring a universal message to the nations and to missionize unapologetically. In his article from 2000, Cherki laid the foundations for the organization that he would establish ten years later: Brit Olam—Noahide World Center.[116] Now, Cherki argues, with the people of Israel having returned to their land, the entire human race is waiting with anticipation for their message. In his eyes, the gentiles realize this state of affairs better than Jews do; while they are looking for ways to come closer to the people of Israel, Jews are hesitant to assume the responsibility: "It is strange for us to imagine that the gentiles are even interested in us. Because of this, we go for cosmopolitan messages of love for every human being, of resistance to violence on behalf of religion, of interreligious encounters, and in the end, what we get is a vegetarian kibbutz. These are pretty values, but they promote nothing."[117]

Cherki considers that to inform the human race of the word of Israel, one should get Christianity out of the way. He claims that he deliberated at great length over the halakhic status that should be accorded Christianity and ultimately determined that legitimating Christianity as a belief in *shittuf* that is permitted to gentiles constitutes "an attempt to vindicate Christianity through the back door" and is therefore "strategically" problematic:

> In reality as I see it, if we want to purely influence the nations of the world we must refrain from going through that conduit. . . . In our time, since the people of Israel have returned to their land and to their strength, why should we lie to people and tell them that they can continue to know God through Jesus, when they have a direct conduit, which is the people of Israel? We are not helping people when we take pity on the beliefs of their fathers and tell them that it is OK to be Christians, when they have an option to achieve a state purified of all remains of paganism through the people of Israel. We must deforest the surface of human faith, and for this reason we do not offer content that makes Christianity acceptable. We offer new content. In our rabbinical court we accept whoever has completely forsaken not only Christian theology, but also all psychological devotion to Jesus.[118]

The Christian Enemy—Rabbi Shlomo Aviner

Shlomo HaCohen Aviner is another prominent Orthodox rabbi operating within the sphere of the Kooks' circle. Although Aviner expressed moderate views vis-à-vis Christianity in the 1980s and did not seem to view Christian theology as a critical issue, his subsequent composition, "The Christian Enemy," and his extensive activity as a publisher around the 2000 events testify that his anxiety over the Christian world had greatly increased.[119]

Instead of the optimistic vision of Rabbis Askénazi and Cherki, which portrays sovereign Judaism as the hope of the entire human race, Rabbi Aviner established a different image: that of a protracted eschatological struggle. In

"The Christian Enemy," Aviner utilizes the ideas of his teachers and peers to confront Christianity while ousting the idea that Jews can exert a positive influence on Christians from his discourse. Aviner reiterates the historical formulation of Abraham Isaac and Zvi Yehudah Kook: human history began with idolaters; the Israeli nation appeared and disseminated morality among the human race; idolaters struggled against God's people but were unable to vanquish them; until ultimately, "in the face of a combined attack by evil men from without and the evil passions from within," the people of Israel collapsed and withdrew into themselves, and their influence over the nations was lost. It was then that Christianity appeared, "out of the collapse of the link to the people of Israel and the trust in the people of Israel."[120] Aviner describes Christianity's heresy against the divine choice of Israel, and in particular the church's declaration that it is the true Israel. He repeats the anti-Christian arguments of his teachers: the theft of identity, the annulment of the Jewish halakhic mitzvoth, the hypocrisy, the neglect of good deeds, and the hybridization of Judaism and idolatry. Christian violence toward Jews receives considerable attention from Aviner:

> "The religion of love" has spilled the most innocent blood throughout human history, the blood of millions, and especially Jewish blood. . . . The Christians did not offer the other cheek to take a slap, but to the contrary, generously disbursed slaps for us throughout history, slaps in the name of the cross. With their cross they smote our bodies and brains, with the cross they stabbed and raped our daughters. They led their crusades through a sea of blood, the blood of innocent Jews, boys and girls. Pogroms, inquisitions, autos-da-fé, humiliations and torture, persecutions and murder, millions of innocent victims for two thousand years were our share. . . . And you oh cruel Jewish father, you who have been forcibly expelled from Spain, do you not see that your baby is crying out from hunger? So out of my love, I will give you bread for it, just in exchange for one little thing, just kiss the cross in my hand. No, we shall not kiss, and we shall not convert to Christianity. What can you give us? We still remember the love of our matrimony with the creator, the true God. . . . You can torment us and make our humiliation into a national sport. You can cry HEP, HEP, in the streets when a Jew passes by, as the signal for a mass attack, beating him and humiliating him, for HEP means Hireosolyma Est Perdita, Jerusalem is lost.[121]

Aviner reconstitutes the Hep-Hep pogroms as a parable for Christianity's theological violence toward the Jewish people, which undermines the Jewish people's faith in their future. "But Jerusalem," continues Aviner, "is not lost. We have an answer to all of your evil! The Jewish people have been resurrected; the Jewish people are awakening after their long exile. . . . And from the negative aspects, you realize the positive: the negative existence of Christianity emphasizes the positive salvation of the Jewish people."[122] Once again, the historical movement of the return to Zion is portrayed as the theological refutation of Christianity by proving the identity of the true people of Israel; redemption is being realized according to the Jewish salvation program, thereby refuting the Christian program. However, in Aviner's version, Christians do not recant, and the veil is not lifted from their eyes; to the contrary: the Christian world is struck with trepidation in the face of the possibility that the people of Israel are being resurrected and struggle to persist with all of their strength. As Maimonides wrote in his *Epistle to Yemen,* the nations of the world do everything in their power to fight Israel, and the triumph of Israel now forced on the nations of the world is not readily accepted by them.

Aviner analyzes historical and contemporary events through this prism; the "Jewish Problem" in Europe was caused by the rise of Zionism only—the Christians wanted to polish off the Jews before it was too late, that is, before they immigrated to Israel.[123] According to this perspective, the Final Solution was a solution to Zionism and was intended to prevent the resurrection of the people of Israel in the land of the fathers. Nevertheless, even the Holocaust did not help the Christians in their plan:

> The State of Israel was founded by divine command. It annuls the main basis of Christian theology, which is founded on the eternal punishment of the people of Israel. In the Jewish people's wanderings and exile, they were considered to have proven the rightness of Christianity, but now they have been resurrected. Reality hits [the Christians] right in the face, and they are helpless to change it. The historical plan is being carried out exactly as the prophets prophesied for the people of Israel, so they must be Verus Israel.

Thus, directly corresponding with Christian theology, Aviner establishes a triumphalist counter-theology: "The entire edifice of Christianity is based on the destruction of the people of Israel, and now the ground is shaking under them with the resurrection of our state. The greatest lie in the history of mankind is gradually evaporating. The last hope of Christianity to destroy us is through mission."[124] Aviner claims that with the last of its strength, Christianity develops new tactics for its struggle with Judaism. The battle tactics of the Catholics include the exertion of political pressure to internationalize Jerusalem, the adoption of a pro-Arab policy, and support for terror organizations "under the guise of justice and humanity." The Protestants use a different tactic: they adopt the Zionist enterprise as a stage in the Christian program of salvation, which culminates in the conversion of all of humanity to Christianity. Either way, "the aspect common to all Christians," writes Aviner, is "the aspiration for the final annihilation of the people of Israel and the State of Israel, at one stage or another."[125]

The Christian-Jewish conflict did not end with the Jews leaving Europe and establishing the State of Israel; it merely changed form. Contrary to what appears on the surface of things, this conflict is still alive and kicking and is far more existentially threatening than the conflict with Islam, because Christianity directs it arrows directly to the heart of Jewish identity. According to Aviner, it is difficult to exaggerate the magnitude of the Christian threat:

> Christianity is the State of Israel's enemy number one. With the Arabs, we have a neighborly dispute that is not fundamental . . . but with Christianity, we have a cosmological battle over essence: Are we the people of Israel or not? Christianity is the greatest calamity that has ever risen against us.[126]

In their intense discourse on Christianity, the small group of Francophone followers of the Rabbis Kook created a new school of thought, which was nourished by the synthesis between a radical version of religious Zionism and an acquaintance with contemporary Christian thought, from biblical criticism to Vatican declarations on Jews and Judaism. This synthesis allowed them to adjust the negative perception of Christianity that is characteristic of the Kooks to the changing political circumstances of Israeli sovereignty, which they theologized through a reverse application of traditional Christian anti-Jewish rhetorical tools against the Christians themselves. Moreover, Christianity served these Francophone rabbis as a rhetorical structure that helped shape the community's ambivalence toward secularism and Western civilization writ large: they argued that secularism is good in that it helps release Jews from Christian influence—as in the case of Abraham Isaac

Kook—yet it is bad in that it continues transmitting Christian values in a secularized guise, through its liberal humanistic outlook.

Though all these rabbis agreed that a new phase in Christian-Jewish relations had been inaugurated as a result of Israeli sovereignty, they differed on how to interpret and respond to the signs of the times. For Askénazi, Livni, and Cherki, Jewish sovereignty pulled the rug out from under Christian doctrine and brought the Jews closer to unmediated Judaism. For Aviner, however, Christianity is still a great threat, even in the Holy Land. The Christians' call for reconciliation is therefore only a pretense; true conciliation between Jacob and Esau is not possible until Esau gives up his share in the father's inheritance once and for all.

8

The Orthodox World and
Christian-Jewish Dialogue

Chapters 6 and 7 focused on the intra-Orthodox discourse on the halakhic and theological stature of Christianity. Christianity within this internal discourse is more an image than a reality; the Orthodox authors discussed in these chapters are less occupied with managing their relationships with actual Christian communities than with imagining (and establishing) a Judaism that exists separately from and independent of Christianity, whether in Israel or in the Diaspora.

This chapter focuses on a different kind of Orthodox literature, which is occupied with the actual encounter between Christians and Jews, and especially with the evolving genre of Christian-Jewish dialogue. Though there is a certain overlap between these literatures in terms of both content and authorship, the Orthodox discourse on Christian-Jewish dialogue usually takes place where everyday encounters between Jews and Christians are prevalent.

These encounters are less of a concern in the State of Israel, where Christians are but a small minority and Christian-Jewish dialogue is seldom perceived as an urgent necessity. Only in specific cases, such as the initiative of the Vatican to establish a formal dialogue with the Chief Rabbinate of Israel or evangelical organizations' projects to support Israeli populations and institutions, do Israeli Orthodox communities turn to consider their attitudes to Christian-Jewish dialogue. Interfaith dialogue is more prevalent in Western Europe, where Christianity is the religion of the majority and Christian communities make extensive efforts to promote interfaith initiatives.

Indeed, in many European states, prominent Orthodox rabbis have been engaged in Christian-Jewish dialogue and cooperation and have been open to Christian-Jewish rapprochement.[1] Yet these interfaith initiatives remain a relatively marginal phenomenon, since in Europe, too, Orthodox communities (which are mostly ultra-Orthodox) tend to separate themselves from other communities—including the greater Jewish community, not to mention the Christian community—since they are of negligent size and the general society is highly secularized. All these factors make Orthodox Jewish dialogue with Christians significant only in relatively small circles in Europe.

The place in which Christian-Jewish dialogue is most significant is the United States, where both Christians and Jews see themselves as partners in the responsibility for the thriving of their common civilization, where religion is far from being a marginal phenomenon, and where the Jewish community consists of a relatively significant minority. The diversity of Christianities and Judaisms in America is also translated into a diversity of relationships between Jews and Christians.

Christian-Jewish coexistence is therefore a crucial aspect of Jewish lives in the United States; it is what makes the question of the Jewish attitude to "real" Christians a pressing matter. Moreover, for many Christians and Jews, this relationship also lays bare significant cultural and political implications, as reflected in the colorful career of the concept of "the Judeo-Christian tradition" in America. The concept gained importance during the 1930s, and it has traveled since then between various political projects: as a liberal strategy against Christian exclusivism, a harbinger of American secularism, a fence against communism, an emphatic insistence on the importance of religion in the shaping of America's public sphere, and a way to exclude Islam and conservatize America's cultural personality.[2] In addition, political pacts such as the evangelical support of the State of Israel are of primary importance to American Jews, while the question of intermarriage penetrates into the most intimate issues of Jewish identity.[3] The Christian-Jewish relationship, therefore, has crucial implications for the Jewish minority in the United States. As a result, Jewish attitudes to the scope, content, and purpose of this relationship are immensely diverse.

Within the diversity of Christian-Jewish encounters in America, a group of Catholic theologians—among them Mary C. Boys, John T. Pawlikowski, Eugene J. Fisher, and Philip A. Cunningham—are leading what is probably the most overarching contemporary effort for constructing Catholic theology vis-à-vis Judaism, in close connections with Jewish scholars and representatives.[4] Professional scholars of Christian-Jewish relations, these theologians have continued to ponder the sensitive issues of this relationship long after the general public interest in the nuances of these theological matters abated and attention turned toward more public and less intellectual instances of Christian-Jewish dialogue. On occasion, they advise the Roman Curia and the national bishops' conference on matters pertaining to Christian-Jewish relations. In their own theological works, their interpretations of authoritative documents are often oriented toward broadening the hermeneutical horizons of these texts in a way that will be both sensitive to Jewish sensibilities and beneficial for Christian-Jewish relations.

The relations between these American Catholic theologians and their Jewish counterparts is taking place not only on the theoretical level but on the institutional level as well, as exemplified in various Catholic academic centers for Christian-Jewish studies and interfaith dialogue, such as the Institute for Jewish-Catholic Relations of Saint Joseph's University in Philadelphia, the Institute of Judaeo-Christian Studies at Seton Hall University in New Jersey, the Center for Christian-Jewish Learning at Boston College, the Catholic-Jewish Studies Program at the Catholic Theological Union in Chicago, and the Center for Catholic-Jewish Studies at Saint Leo University in Florida, among others. Prominent Catholic leaders such as William Cardinal Keeler, Joseph Cardinal Bernardin, and Francis Cardinal George gave strong backing to Catholic-Jewish dialogue in America, which further contributed to the enhancement of Catholic-Jewish relations. For all these reasons, as Rabbi David Rosen, an Orthodox world leader of Christian-Jewish dialogue who lives in Israel, puts it, Christian-Jewish dialogue in America is the "spearhead" of this dialogue in the world.[5]

This diversity of Christian-Jewish encounters in America, as well as the strong dialogical initiatives on behalf of American Catholics, carry specific challenges and symbolic meanings for Orthodox Jews, who approach the Christian-Jewish relationship with the unique set of tools that the rabbinic tradition makes available to them. The Orthodox community must navigate between maintaining solid boundaries between itself and general society and striving to assure its place within that society through cooperation with other religious groups, most prominently with Christian communities.

The need to maintain this delicate equilibrium is similar to the concerns that I have described in the first part of this book, on post–Vatican II Catholicism. As we have seen, rapprochement with the Jews was simultaneously crucial and dangerous for Catholic identity—crucial for the church's ability to adjust to the egalitarian political and ethical sensibilities of the liberal order after World War II, for which the revocation of antisemitism was central, and dangerous to the stability of Catholic doctrine, since Jews and Judaism played (and still play) a central role in the formation of the church's self-perception. John Paul II's main contribution to Christian-Jewish rapprochement was that he solved this tension by transferring the process from the realm of doctrine and theology to the realm of personal and diplomatic relations and public, symbolic-religious gestures. By making this transference, the pope was able to maintain the stability of tradition without exposing it to far-reaching theological experiments while at the same time introducing radical changes to the actual encounter between the Jewish and Christian communities. In other words, Christian-Jewish reconciliation was enabled under John Paul II precisely through the setting of boundaries. This entailed, to a certain extent, a separation, rather than a merging, of the two manifestations of Jews—Jews as an intra-Catholic theological construction versus Jews in their own right as an independent, self-defined people. It was therefore possible for Christians to maintain certain assumptions about mission, future conversion, supersessionism (in a softer version), and the Christological meanings of Jewish suffering, as long as those were not applied directly to the overt dialogue between Jews and Christians. When approaching such dialogue, a friendly conversation based on common convictions was preferred over a focus on doctrinal differences, controversies, and incommensurabilities.

In this chapter, I will explore the Orthodox Jewish parallel to these intra-Catholic controversies and to John Paul II's solution. I will show how the tension between, on the one hand, prioritizing rapprochement even at the price of making profound changes within core Jewish convictions, and, on the other, abstaining from any dialogue in the name of maintaining these convictions, is overcome by a mainstream approach that seeks to limit the scope of Christian-Jewish dialogue and separate it from the realm of doctrine or its Jewish parallel, the halakha.

I focus on intra-Orthodox attitudes toward and controversies about Christian-Jewish dialogue. Since the capital of Christian-Jewish dialogue is the United States, the American scene is at the chapter's center. I will also discuss the Israeli counterparts of these American debates, both where the interfaith initiative is carried to Israel by American Orthodox representatives and where the challenge of Christian-Jewish dialogue comes from elsewhere. I will end the chapter with the somewhat hesitant entrance of the Chief Rabbinate of Israel into Christian-Jewish dialogue.

Between Ultra-Orthodoxy and Modern Orthodoxy in America

The majority of Orthodox Jews in the United States belong to the ultra-Orthodox, or the Haredi, spectrum of Judaism. Ultra-Orthodox communities tend to be largely insular, secluded from the rest of American society, including other Jewish denominations. Ultra-Orthodoxy's relations with other faith communities are seldom negotiated. Nevertheless, two famous letters written by Moshe Feinstein, the leading halakhist and an influential ultra-Orthodox rabbi, in 1967 (less than two years after the publication of Vatican II's *Nostra aetate*) shed light on the mainstream position on Christian-Jewish dialogue within American ultra-Orthodoxy. In his letter to Rabbi Dov Lander, who was planning to participate in an interfaith conference, Rabbi Feinstein wrote the following:

> As regards the fact that His High Torah Honor had promised to come to a place where Catholics and Protestants are gathered with the Sons of Israel, members from the Synagogue Council and also fellow rabbis of the Rabbinical Council . . . it is clear and evident that this is strictly prohibited under the prohibition of becoming an accessory to idolatry, the breaching of which has now spread like the plague in many places following the initiative of the new Poipst [pope], which only intends to convert all Jews from their pure and holy faith to that of the Christian, for it is more convenient to convert people in this manner than through the method of hate and murder utilized by Poipsten before him, and for this reason any negotiations with them, and even talk of mundane matters, and the very act of approaching them is strictly prohibited under the grave prohibition against coming closer to idolatry. . . . It is also forbidden to participate in any such gatherings that I heard they want to convene in Boston and in Rome; anyone who joins with them, whoever they are, are considered inciters who would lead the People of Israel astray, for all the toil that the Catholic missionaries have toiled all those years and only managed to snare so few, here God forbid, through such ignorant rabbis who wish to join them, there is a risk that many more will be converted to Christianity [literally, destroy themselves], and one cannot argue against an inciter that one did not intend

for this to happen, and they are therefore risking their souls, God forbid, in both this world and in the next.[6]

Feinstein couched his reservations about Christian-Jewish dialogue in traditional language. He refused to entertain the idea that there was any real change in the position of the Christian world and interpreted the historical changes as no more than an external pose: instead of the Inquisition and forced baptisms, the Christians had turned to dialogue and sweet persuasion; yet behind its friendly façade, the heart of the church was still filled with the same ancient enmity. Just as they stood before their inquisitors, so Jews were now supposed to stand before the new converters, the architects of "dialogue."

In addition to this letter to Dov Lander, Feinstein wrote another letter on the same subject to Rabbi Joseph Ber Halevi Soloveitchik, the leader of Modern Jewish Orthodoxy in the United States (the largest Orthodox community outside the ultra-Orthodox spectrum).[7] In his letter, Feinstein asked Soloveitchik to join him in his prohibition against participation in such Christian-Jewish meetings. Soloveitchik did not join Feinstein's initiative. Nevertheless, a number of documents that Soloveitchik wrote during the period 1961 to 1967, that is, around the time of Vatican II, stirred an ongoing controversy within Modern Orthodoxy on the question of whether Soloveitchik saw Christian-Jewish dialogue in the same way as his ultra-Orthodox counterpart, or rather, whether he sought to lead Modern Orthodoxy in a different direction, one perhaps more open to Christian-Jewish partnership.

As we shall see, this controversy has roots in Soloveitchik's own writings, whose sophisticated expression points in more than one hermeneutical direction. Yet the controversy is also strongly connected to the greater stake of Modern Orthodoxy, a community that sees the observation of the halakha in its Orthodox interpretation as a binding norm and yet simultaneously engages in general society and is open to the "modern" world, as manifested in the movement's name.[8] Christian-Jewish dialogue, which in recent decades has become a central component of modern culture, naturally belongs to those controversial topics that make the tension between modernity and the Orthodox way of life explicit. Through their polemics on Christian-Jewish dialogue, Modern Orthodox rabbis are also debating about which portions of the Jewish tradition are immune to historical change, the nature of the challenges of the present moment, and whether these challenges should matter for Jewish identity and for the way in which the Jewish community preserves its traditions. In what follows, I will explore the interplay between these questions and the Jewish-Christian encounter in the unique context of Modern Orthodoxy.

Rabbi Joseph Ber Halevi Soloveitchik and His Essay "Confrontation"

Rabbi Joseph Ber Halevi Soloveitchik left a complex legacy concerning Christian-Jewish relations. Apart from his great erudition in rabbinic literature, Soloveitchik was deeply acquainted with both general philosophy and contemporaneous Protestant theology. His work was influenced by such prominent theologians as Paul Tillich, Karl Barth, Rudolf Otto, and Søren Kierkegaard.[9] And yet, notwithstanding the profound dialogue with Christian theology he himself engaged with in his philosophical work, Soloveitchik entertained a deep suspicion of the appropriateness of theological dialogue between Christians and Jews, repeatedly warning his congregation to abstain from it. When the Catholic Church declared its intentions to revise the Catholic theological position vis-à-vis Jews and Judaism, Soloveitchik suspected that a missionary project was lurking behind the transition.[10] "The Catholic Church is coming close to the Protestant approach towards the Jewish people," he wrote, "one of bringing them near through love and praise."[11] Both before and during Vatican II, Soloveitchik repeatedly expressed his objections to Jewish participation in a theological dialogue with Christian representatives.[12] He also objected to the participation of Jews at the council as observers. If the Catholic Church was willing to make a theological "concession" for Jews, he claimed, it would ultimately demand theological concessions from Jews in return.[13] Should any Jews be interested, nevertheless, in helping change the theological positions of the church toward them, Soloveitchik recommended that they converse with "liberal lay Catholics"; they should certainly not "be dealing with the official representatives of the church."[14] To make things as clear as possible, Soloveitchik drew up a long list of specific issues that must not be discussed with Christians (among them, the attitude of Judaism toward Jesus, the idea of the covenant, and ritual in Judaism and Christianity).[15] The theological position of the church toward Jews, he emphasized, is a Christian matter. Any Jewish participation is risky, and it is better to refrain from it.[16] Soloveitchik was therefore opposed to attempts by Jews (such as those of Jules Isaac or Abraham Joshua Heschel) to take part in theological discussions with

Christians.[17] When the second draft of Vatican II's declaration in regard to Judaism was published, he wrote the following statement:

> Instead of complaining bitterly against the Church, they [the Jews who entered a dialogue with the heads of the church] should say "Nostra Maxima Culpa"—in plain Hebrew, Hatanu [we have sinned]—for rushing in where angels fear to tread. The Church is within her rights to interpret our history in her own theological-dogmatic terms. We are the ones who have transcended the bounds of historical responsibility and decency by asking for a theological document on the Jews as "brethren" in faith instead of urging the Church to issue a strong declaration in sociological-human terms affirming the inalienable rights of the Jew as a human being.[18]

Soloveitchik's most well known and controversial utterance on interfaith dialogue was a lecture he gave at the Rabbinical Council of America in 1964, when Vatican II was still convened (before the final version of *Nostra aetate* had been formulated). The lecture was later edited as an essay titled "Confrontation," which was published in the journal *Tradition* in the same year.[19] In this essay, Soloveitchik formulated his approach to interfaith dialogue in philosophical terms.[20] In the first part of the essay, Soloveitchik presents a philosophical argument describing the complex confrontation of humans in and with the world and contemplates the right balance that should be maintained between one's core loneliness and one's ability to position oneself alongside others for the benefit of the world and of humankind.[21] In the second part, Soloveitchik describes the relationships between faith communities as another area of confrontation. The Jewish people thus experience "the problem of a double confrontation. We think of ourselves as human beings, sharing the destiny of Adam in his general encounter with nature, and as members of a covenantal community which has preserved its identity under most unfavorable conditions, confronted by another faith community."[22]

While as a human community, Jews share responsibility for the world with the rest of humanity, as a faith community, they stand alone, incomprehensible and incomparable to any other community. This "difficult task" of a "twofold responsibility" is, for Soloveitchik, at the center of the Jewish vocation: the Jew has always been "a doubly confronted being."[23] Yet modernity posed a threat to this twofold Jewish mission, tempting Jews to rid themselves of the second confrontation, which seemed to contradict the first:

> The emancipated modern Jew, however, has been trying, for a long time, to do away with this twofold responsibility which weighs heavily upon him. The Westernized Jew maintains that it is impossible to engage in both confrontations, the universal and the covenantal, which, in his opinion, are mutually exclusive. It is, he argues, absurd to stand shoulder to shoulder with mankind preoccupied with the cognitive-technological gesture for the welfare of all, implementing the mandate granted to us by the Creator, and to make an about-face the next instant in order to confront our comrades as a distinct and separate community. Hence, the Western Jew concludes, we have to choose between these two encounters. We are either confronted human beings or confronted Jews. A double confrontation contains an inner contradiction.[24]

Modernity, according to Soloveitchik, poses a threat to Jewish particularism and to the Jews' covenantal mission, with the promise of universality and its joint human destiny (which is the first confrontation) dissolving the boundaries between Jews and Christians. Nevertheless, Soloveitchik continues, this modern Jewish imbalance toward reducing the second "confrontation" (between the Jews as a faith community and the rest of humankind)— that is, the compromise of Jewish singularity—came after a long history in which Jews were unable to fulfill their other responsibility, that is, their involvement in the greater human family for the benefit of humankind and creation. This historical imbalance was no fault of their own, since it was gentile society that treated the Jews as if they were "a subhuman objective order separated by an abyss from the human" and prevented them from participating "to the fullest extent in the great universal creative confrontation between man and the cosmic order."[25]

Here, between the lines, Soloveitchik declares not only the detrimental blow of modernity to Jewish identity but also the unprecedented opportunity that it brings for Jews to be finally integrated into the human family in a way that will allow them to take equal part in human civilization—to fulfill their vocation as humans, not only as Jews. It is therefore only in modern times that Jews can truly live the double confrontation to which they are called.

Realizing this opportunity requires a clear distinction between those elements that belong to the one confrontation and those that belong to the other. In what pertains to the faith community's confrontation with another (most pertinently, with Christianity), the incommensurable and separate nature of the covenantal personality of the community must be insisted upon. Soloveitchik depicts three central expressions of the irreducible singularity of a faith community: normativity, axiology, and eschatology. In Soloveitchik's words:

> First, the divine imperatives and commandments to which a faith community is unreservedly committed must not be equated with the ritual and ethos of another community. . . . Particularly when we speak of the Jewish faith community, whose very essence is expressed in the halakhic performance . . . any attempt to equate our identity with another is sheer absurdity. Second, the axiological awareness of each faith community is an exclusive one, for it believes—and this belief is indispensable to the survival of the community—that its system of dogmas, doctrines and values is best fitted for the attainment of the ultimate good. Third, each faith community is unyielding in its eschatological expectations. It . . . expects man . . . to embrace the faith that this community has been preaching throughout the millennia. Standardization of practices, equalization of dogmatic certitudes, and the waiving of eschatological claims spell the end of the vibrant and great faith experience of any religious community.[26]

Insisting on the non-negotiable character of these three elements poses limitations on the nature of the encounter between Christians and Jews. Interestingly, Soloveitchik is willing to accept the idea of a "Judeo-Christian tradition" on the cultural level. It is "when we shift the focus from the dimension of culture to that of faith," to imply a doctrinal and revelational continuum between Judaism and Christianity, that the Judeo-Christian idea becomes "utterly absurd, unless one is ready to acquiesce in the Christian theological claim that Christianity has superseded Judaism [since the Jewish tradition does not concede that Christianity is the authentic continuation of ancient Judaism]."[27] Therefore, "the confrontation [between Christians and Jews] should occur not at a theological, but at a mundane human level."[28]

Moreover, the structure of the power relations between "the community of the many" (that is, Christians) and the "community of the few" (that is,

Jews) turns the theological dialogue from a conversation between equals to one between subjects and objects, even if the Christians are acting from good will and compassion. "We do not revolve as a satellite in any orbit," Soloveitchik states. "As a faith of individuality, the community of the few is endowed with intrinsic worth." Measuring a faith community's worth according to the "service it has rendered to another community, no matter how great and important this service was," Soloveitchik continues, "constitutes an infringement of the sovereignty and dignity of even the smallest of faith communities."[29] In particular, Soloveitchik was appalled by the idea that Jews would be participating in a Christian debate on "whether or not to 'absolve' the community of the few of some mythical guilt," as if this debate were abstracted from the long history of Christian persecution of Jews.[30] Thus, the unbalanced power relation between the communities, the shadow of history that burdens the confrontation, and the Christian appropriation of Jews and Judaism in the service of the Christians' own religious convictions threaten to make any Christian-Jewish theological dialogue undemocratic, nonegalitarian, and irreconcilable with the principle of religious freedom.

Nevertheless, consistent with his double confrontation paradigm, Soloveitchik is careful not to let his critique of Christianity transgress the boundaries of the Christian-Jewish confrontation and intervene in Christian faith, even as this faith cultivates certain convictions regarding Jews and Judaism. The Christian community has the right to address itself to Jews "in its own eschatological terms"; that is, Christians are entitled to believe that Jews must confess Christ, convert to Christianity, or adhere to any other precept that their tradition makes available to them. However, this right should have no practical implications for actual Jews (apparently, Soloveitchik had missionary activity in mind). A "practical program" would be "hardly consonant with religious democracy and liberalism."[31] Nor should Jews advise Christians on how to change their doctrines to become less hostile to Jews and Judaism—this is a process that is, again, confined to the Christian community itself and should not be interfered with from the outside.[32] Even if changes on the Christian side are perceived as welcome by Jews, doctrinal change should not be a part of the interfaith game. Thus, Soloveitchik addresses the Christian-Jewish relationship through a liberal prism, maintaining a strict distinction between the public and private spheres.

Soloveitchik applies the same distinction to the Jewish community itself and warns Jews not to negotiate traditional Jewish views of Christianity with the other faith community:

We certainly have not been authorized by our history, sanctified by the martyrdom of millions, to even hint to another faith community that we are mentally ready to revise historical attitudes, to trade favors pertaining to fundamental matters of faith, and to reconcile "some" differences. Such a suggestion would be nothing but a betrayal of our great tradition and heritage and would, furthermore, produce no practical benefits.[33]

With this statement, Soloveitchik took off the table the idea of an intra-Jewish aggiornamento in response to the doctrinal changes on the Christian side.

By limiting Christian-Jewish dialogue exclusively to the realm of general public human confrontation, Soloveitchik seems to propose that it be secularized. Yet this secularization also entails a call to Jews to cooperate with Christians, on the basis of their joint religious and cultural convictions, against secularizing forces:

As a matter of fact, our common interests lie not in the realm of faith, but in that of the secular orders. There, we all face a powerful antagonist, we all have to contend with a considerable number of matters of great concern. The relationship between two communities must be outer-directed and related to the secular orders with which men of faith come face to face.[34]

These divisions between the first and the second confrontations, between the private and the public, the singular and the universal, are not always readily distinguishable, and, as we shall see, Soloveitchik's theoretical framework received more than one practical translation.

The Reception of "Confrontation" within Modern Orthodoxy

"Confrontation" has become one of Soloveitchik's most controversial works. Its complex reception history began with a short statement published by the Rabbinical Council of America in the same issue of *Tradition,* as an appendix to the essay. The statement repeats the essay's main arguments, turning them into a normative guideline to interreligious relations. The council expresses its content with the new trend of interreligious cooperation and mutual respect and stresses the need for such cooperation in the face of "secularism, materialism, and the modern atheistic negation of religion and religious values."[35] After this justification of cooperation based on the recognition of a joint enemy, the statement quickly retreats to depicting the boundaries of such cooperation, stressing the singularity of the faith community and describing any threat to the intrinsic value of faith as "incongruous with the fundamentals of religious liberty and freedom of conscience."[36] "Confrontation" thus became an authoritative, almost halakhic, standard according to which interreligious cooperation should be measured. However, since the essay was written in equivocal language, which seemed to provoke self-reflection and meditation more than to provide specific instructions, its normative adaptation largely meant the crystallization of an inherent suspicion toward interreligious dialogue in general.[37] As Marc Shapiro noted, instead of cultivating dialogue on a cultural basis, many preferred to retreat from it altogether. In this sense, the Modern Orthodox openness to general civilization seemed to have stopped at the threshold of Christian-Jewish dialogue.[38]

And yet this was not the sole interpretation of the essay. In the decades following the publication of "Confrontation," a diversity of attitudes to Christian-Jewish dialogue emerged among rabbis and thinkers affiliated with Soloveitchik, all of whom anchored their opinions in their teacher's legacy.

Prominent liberal rabbis among Soloveitchik's disciples confronted the prevailing interpretation of "Confrontation" and suggested alternative readings. David Hartman, who orchestrated a pioneering theological discourse between leading theologians and Jewish scholars in the Shalom Hartman Beit Midrash that he had established in Jerusalem (in which Protestant theologian Paul Van Buren was a leading figure), argued that Soloveitchik "does not close the door to Jewish-Christian discussions" but simply "places very careful barriers." In Hartman's view, such dialogue is allowed as long as the Jews remember "that there is a dimension to their faith that permanently condemns them to separateness and isolation," that is, that they manage to maintain their separateness from the other community, resisting the Western tendency to be completely assimilated in civilization to the point of perceiving their Jewish identity as something that conflicts with their membership in the universal community of mankind.[39] It was this kind of Jewish self-positioning that was inappropriate for discourse with Christians on doctrinal matters. At the same time, individuals who took into account the uniqueness of the Jewish faith community were indeed encouraged by Soloveitchik, in Hartman's view, to join the Christian-Jewish dialogue.[40]

Hartman further argued that Soloveitchik's reservations vis-à-vis interfaith dialogue were not a matter of principle but were contingent on circumstances; when he expressed his views, he was cognizant of replacement theology and the forced disputations of the Middle Ages, which did not allow true dialogue between equals. Under appropriate conditions, interfaith dialogue between Jews and Christians might have been acceptable to him.[41]

Rabbi Eugene Korn (former national director of interfaith affairs at the Anti-Defamation League and former academic director of the Center for Christian-Jewish Understanding and Cooperation in Israel) contends that Hartman went too far in treating "Confrontation" as a halakhic ruling. Even without the breach that Hartman found in the essay that permits Jewish experts to dialogue with Christians, "Confrontation" does not correspond to the genre rules of halakhic writings and is therefore void of halakhic authority (and was not intended by Soloveitchik himself to be observed in the halakhic sense). Like Hartman, Korn argues that Soloveitchik's assessment was appropriate for its time but that it is "contingent, since attitudes can change over time—particularly when historical, social and intellectual conditions undergo fundamental shifts." What may have been true in Soloveitchik's day is not necessarily "valid for the twenty-first century or for a different understanding of the dialogical encounter."[42] Soloveitchik, according to Korn, sought to refrain from theological dialogue with Christians because he did not imagine that the church could indeed make such a drastic doctrinal change to the point of retreating from its anti-Jewish teachings and accepting Jews as equal partners; now that such a change has indeed occurred on the Christian side, refraining from dialogue on the part of the Orthodox has lost its justification. This is especially true in a reality that requires Jews and Christians to stand together in confronting the reductionist assumptions of secularists regarding the nature of humankind. Moreover, Korn notes that the essay itself is in dialogue with Christian theology: "Evidently R. Soloveitchik wrote part I with Christian theologians in mind" (a point that is stressed also by Michael Wyschogrod, who sees the first part of the essay as leaning on Kierkegaard, and Alan Brill, who sees the second part as a Barthian analysis). In this sense, "Confrontation" itself is a Christian-Jewish theological dialogue.[43]

Rabbi Irving (Yitz) Greenberg, formerly a professor at Yeshiva University and the rabbi of the liberal Orthodox Riverdale Jewish Center, agrees with Hartman and Korn that Soloveitchik was indeed much more open to Christian-Jewish dialogue than he was often seen as being, and anchors the confusion in Soloveitchik's own identity issues. "Confrontation," Greenberg argues, is an example of "Marrano writing," that is, a text with a hidden subtext that is totally different from the overt message. In Greenberg's eyes, Soloveitchik wished to appease ultra-Orthodoxy, while under the surface, he had opened the door to deep dialogue.[44]

Shlomo Riskin (chief rabbi of the settlement of Efrat and founder of the Ohr Torah Stone Institutions in Israel and the United States) claims that Soloveitchik had indeed permitted Christian-Jewish dialogue under certain conditions, and that were he alive today and aware of the changes that have taken place in the relationships between the church and the Jews, he would change his position. Like his colleagues, Riskin maintains that a close inspection of the Christian world reveals that Christianity has changed its positions on Judaism and is now ready to become a true ally of Jews, a positive moral force in the contemporary world and a counterweight against both secularism and fundamentalist Islam.[45]

Rabbi Alan Brill, professor of Jewish-Christian Studies at the (Catholic) Seton Hall University, New Jersey, agrees with his colleagues that the Catholic Church has moved "from persecutor to greatest friend." However, there is no reason to assume that Soloveitchik, who had witnessed these changes in his lifetime, would have changed his mind on Christian-Jewish dialogue in light of them. Nevertheless, the question about the consistency of Soloveitchik's position does not change the fact that for Brill, the change of times demands that Jews "agree to work to overcome their fear and distrust of the Church":

> Jews need to overcome their sense of minority status and find a new social model for their interactions. We need to move beyond bitterness, both in our relationship with the Church and in our own self-understanding of our place in the world community. And we will need to consider how we have relied on this culture of victimhood even when the other who surrounds us does not wish to destroy us. Since the Jewish theological tradition offers us models ranging from exclusivism to universalism, we should learn to cultivate a self-understanding appropriate for our current confrontations.[46]

In his own grand project of mapping Jewish perceptions of other religions, Brill formulates this criticism in ever stronger words:

> Jews have barely begun to look at their attitudes toward other faiths, albeit this reluctance was forged in an era of persecution. But they do

not look at their own problematic and nasty texts about gentiles; they ignore their own traditional visions of destruction of the other faiths at the end of days. They frequently stigmatize other faiths in a totalizing way and call other faiths idolatry, Amalek, or Molekh based on current political attitudes. They judge other faiths by their worst and cite Judaism at its best. Jews consider Jewish extremists as aberrations and non-Jewish extremists as the norm. They cite modern sanitized Jewish approaches that show how wonderful and tolerant Judaism is toward others, and disown their own anti-gentile texts written over the millennia. At the same time, however, they assume that other faiths are shackled to their prior texts as understood in prior ages, and do not allow the possibility that other religions have modern understandings of themselves.[47]

Many of the pro-dialogue Modern Orthodox rabbis see changing political and cultural transitions as requiring a softening of Orthodox suspicion toward Christians and a new openness to Christian-Jewish dialogue— whether formulated in bold words, such as Brill's, or in milder form, such as Korn's or Riskin's. History, then, matters, both in the sense that the historic change in Christianity's attitude to Judaism is perceived as real and in the sense that this change places a demand on Jews to reevaluate their own attitudes to Christians and to adapt them to the present reality.

Modern Orthodox rabbis who are less keen on the argument of historical change, perhaps perceived as a slippery slope, extract Soloveitchik's support of dialogue from the superficiality of the distinction between the "secular" and the "religious," which does not correspond to Soloveitchik's encompassing perception of the religious experience. For religious people, they often argue, the separation between theological (intimate) content and secular (universal) content is artificial.[48] Rabbi Shalom Carmy (who regularly authors a column in the neoconservative Catholic magazine *First Things*), Meir Soloveitchik (rabbi of Congregation Shearith Israel in Manhattan, director of the Straus Center for Torah and Western Thought at Yeshiva University, and Joseph Ber Soloveitchik's great-nephew), and the philosopher Michael Wyschogrod (who wrote many theological works on Christian-Jewish relations) challenge the idea that the "theological" can indeed be differentiated from the "cultural" in a way that allows refraining from one of these discourses while approving engagement with the other. "The line between discussion of social and ethical matters and 'theology' is not always easily drawn," Carmy argues. Or, in Meir Soloveitchik's words, "Jewish and Christian ethicists, the Rav tells us, cannot speak without referencing religious, biblical categories."[49]

For Wyschogrod, reading "Confrontation" as a call to secularize Christian-Jewish dialogue does not cohere with Joseph Soloveitchik's perception, even as formulated in the essay itself. When Soloveitchik states that "our common interests lie not in the realm of faith, but in that of the secular orders," Wyschogrod reminds us, he adds "a most revealing footnote," according to which for the person of faith, there is no "secular," since "God claims the whole, not a part of man, and whatever He established as an order within the scheme of creation is sacred."[50] Wyschogrod argues that it is therefore

> simply not possible to split a Jew into two, demanding of him to keep what is most important about his very identity out of the dialogue. All Jewish values are ultimately rooted in revelation and to pretend otherwise is to play a charade which will convince no one. The option is whether to talk with Christians or not to talk with them. If we refuse to talk with them, we can keep theology and everything else out of the dialogue. If we do not refuse to talk with them, we cannot keep what is most precious to us out of the discussion.[51]

In the end, Wyschogrod concludes, Soloveitchik's essay did not close Orthodoxy to Christian-Jewish dialogue, but rather did the opposite:

> "Confrontation" ended the era of Orthodox withdrawal from Jewish-Christian dialogue. If experience and logic have shown that it is not possible to separate the secular from the religious, the dialogue must continue in accordance with its inner dynamics. Such a dialogue will not hurt Judaism. My experience has been that Jews who meet religious Christians emerge strengthened in their faith and grateful for the righteous gentiles who, through Christianity, have approached the God of Israel.[52]

The Case of Rabbi Irving Greenberg

These strong statements on the part of Soloveitchik's followers, both liberals and conservatives, do not mean that their perceptions of the scope, intentions, and price that should be paid to engage in Christian-Jewish dialogue are agreed upon. Each of these rabbis and scholars draws the line differently. Whenever one of these figures transcends the boundaries that are accepted in the community, he faces a critical resistance on behalf of his colleagues. It is precisely the debate regarding the status of Christianity within the Jewish halakhic and doctrinal tradition that is carefully avoided and that creates an immediate stir whenever it is raised in the agenda of Christian-Jewish dialogue.

One of the most prominent examples of such a stir was the public debate surrounding Irving Greenberg's theological work. The liberal Rabbi Greenberg articulated a positive Jewish theology of Christianity for decades, breaking the Modern Orthodox status quo by proposing intra-Jewish revisions of traditional perceptions, and, moreover, by doing this in the context of Christian-Jewish dialogue. In 1984, responding to an invitation by the American Protestant theologian Roy Eckardt, Greenberg published "The Relationship of Judaism and Christianity: Toward a New Organic Model," in which he sought to depict Christianity as an organic and legitimate evolution out of Judaism: "Judaism and Christianity were jointly and severally intended to play a part in an infinite creator's plan to perfect the world."[53]

The boldest and certainly most controversial argument that Greenberg made in his 1984 article was that Jesus was a "failed," rather than a "false," messiah. Jesus, according to Greenberg, did not hold to the wrong values, and therefore should not be regarded as "false." Like other central biblical heroes such as Abraham, Moses, and Jeremiah, he held to the right values and upheld the covenant, "but . . . did not attain the final goal" and therefore failed.[54] Greenberg not only placed Jesus in the dignified company of Abraham, Moses, and Jeremiah, who were all failed messiahs because they were unable to complete their redemptive tasks (a statement that offends Orthodox sensibilities for downgrading the biblical heroes and not least for uplifting Jesus); he also hinted at the possibility that Jesus's messianic vocation could indeed be completed in the future.[55] Moreover, Greenberg did not negate the possibility that the incarnation actually took place:

> Obviously, many Jews will argue that closing the biblically portrayed gap between the human and the divine, between the real and the ideal, by Incarnation, is idolatrous. . . . But even if Incarnation is contradictory to some biblical principles, the model itself is operating out of classic biblical modes—the need to achieve redemption, the desire to close the gap between the human and divine. . . . One can argue that

the Incarnation is improbable and violative of other given biblical principles. . . . But one can hardly rule out the option totally, particularly if it was intended for gentiles and not intended for Jews.[56]

Greenberg's depiction of Jesus was strongly contested by the Modern Orthodox community, which already had troubles with Greenberg's openness to liberal Jewish streams. Rabbi Herschel Schachter, a leading *rosh yeshiva* (dean) at the Rabbi Isaac Elchanan Theological Seminary at Yeshiva University, one of the most prominent arbiters of Modern Orthodoxy in the United States and a direct disciple of Soloveitchik, saw Greenberg's claims about Christianity as heretical, and he appealed to the Rabbinical Council of America (RCA) to remove Greenberg's rabbinical credentials.[57] The RCA opened an investigation of Greenberg's writings, accusing him of "a blatant equating of Judaism and Christianity."[58] After a long struggle, the charges were dropped for fear that the debate would become public and "generate a negative picture of an intolerant Orthodoxy that would cause public relations damage to the community."[59] However, as Greenberg notes, "The entire affair left a permanent residue of mistrust" toward him and weakened his standing within the Orthodox community.[60]

Greenberg continued to develop his theology of Christianity long after that gloomy affair had passed. Instead of an exclusive divine election of the people of Israel, Greenberg put forward a plurality of covenantal trajectories ("covenantal pluralism"), even viewing Christianity as a "covenantal partner" that complements Judaism in its task of Tikkun Olam and saves it from the lurking chauvinistic temptation that accompanies it whenever it holds to the idea of an exclusive election.[61]

Upon the publication of *For the Sake of Heaven and Earth,* a collection of Greenberg's previous essays along with some new works, Rabbi David Berger of Yeshiva University (a disciple of Soloveitchik who is also a renowned scholar of medieval Christian-Jewish relations and arguably the most prominent policymaker in the area of Christian-Jewish relations within Modern Orthodoxy) reminded the Orthodox community of the reasons why Greenberg's reflections on Christianity transgressed—and still transgress—the boundaries of a proper Orthodox approach. Besides emphasizing the places where Greenberg crosses traditional lines in departing from the positions of previous generations, from Maimonides to Jacob Emden, and compromises the idea of Israel's unique election, Berger recognized an additional problem in Greenberg's work. This difficulty pertained not to Greenberg's unorthodox doctrines but to the fact that he elegantly avoided transmitting his theological musings through halakhic categories or clear doctrinal state-ments.[62] This tendency is epitomized, according to Berger, in Greenberg's famous eschatological parable. "After entering the dialogue," writes Green-berg, "I wrote a short story in which the Messiah comes at the end of days. Jews and Christians march out to greet him and establish his reign. Finally they ask if this is his first coming or his second coming—to which the Mes-siah smiles and replies, 'No comment.' . . . Perhaps we will then truly realize that it was worth it all along for the kind of life we lived along the way."[63] Berger criticizes this parable in the following manner:

> Aside from the cavalier attitude toward a fundamental point of con-tention in the historic Jewish-Christian debate, this story ends too early. What if the Jews and Christians in this narrative would go on to ask the Messiah, "Are you the second person of the triune God?" "Is the New Testament sacred scripture on a par with the Torah?" One hopes—but unfortunately one cannot be sure—that Greenberg's Mes-siah would not say, "No comment." . . . Greenberg is well aware that the question missing from his eschatological tale, namely, the divinity of Jesus, presents an especially intractable obstacle to the sort of rap-prochement that he advocates, and it is not surprising that his discus-sions of the incarnation reflect considerable unease. He makes matters easier for himself by providing definitions of idolatry that do not evoke technical halakhic parameters. Thus, idolatry is the affirmation of "all human absolutes." . . . Greenberg's theological definitions . . . help dis-tract the reader from the need to apply traditional categories in evalu-ating Christian doctrine.[64]

In Greenberg's tale, the Messiah himself sees fit to avoid halakhic and doc-trinal questions. In fact, Greenberg provokes the eschatological imagina-tion precisely to educate Jews and Christians that when all is said and done, doctrines and truth claims do not *really* matter. Since such a position does not put so much weight on Orthodox truth claims and is open to living with alternative truths, it is fundamentally unorthodox. On the other hand, by marginalizing doctrinal and halakhic questions, Greenberg is able to remain within the confines of Soloveitchik's paradigm: not negotiating what is non-negotiable.

Rabbi David Berger versus "Dabru Emet"

Berger's intervention in Greenberg's case was anything but coincidental. As we saw in Chapter 4 with the debate on "Reflections on Covenant and Mission," in which Berger orchestrated the Orthodox criticism of the United States Conference of Catholic Bishops' clarification note, Berger does not miss an opportunity to rebuke both Christians and Jews whenever they cross the lines that confine the dialogue to each party's affirmation of its own identity, inspired by a conservative reading of Soloveitchik's "Confrontation."[65] Another such transgression, according to Berger, characterized an interdenominational Jewish statement on Christianity published as an advertisement in September 2000 in the *New York Times,* titled "Dabru Emet: A Jewish Statement on Christians and Christianity."[66] "Dabru Emet" ("speak truth") was composed by four Jewish scholars in response to the hand that the church had extended in *Nostra aetate* and in other declarations that followed. It was the first time that an organized, cross-denominational attempt had been made on the Jewish side to formulate a response to more than three decades of Christian deliberations and declarations on Jews and Judaism. The changes on the Christian side, the authors argued, "merit a thoughtful Jewish response. Speaking only for ourselves . . . we believe it is time for Jews to learn about the efforts of Christians to honor Judaism. We believe it is time for Jews to reflect on what Judaism may now say about Christianity." The statement then provides a list of eight brief statements about Christianity from a Jewish perspective. To an eye unversed in the complexities of the Christian-Jewish relationship, these eight points, including "Jews and Christians worship the same God" and "Jews and Christians seek authority from the same book—the Bible," may seem like a benign attempt to delineate the most obvious common denominators between the two religions for the sake of creating a peaceful reciprocity.[67] Yet the Orthodox response to the statement did not see it that way.

Four days after "Dabru Emet" appeared, the Orthodox Union issued a short critical response, written by Berger. Berger's criticism was directed at the raison d'être of the statement, which was the reassessment of the Jewish "view of Christianity in light of Christian reassessments of Judaism." Berger saw "this inclination toward theological reciprocity" as "fraught with danger," as had already been warned against in "Confrontation."[68] "Rabbi Soloveitchik worried that theological dialogue would create pressure to 'trade favors pertaining to fundamental matters of faith, to reconcile "some" differences,'" Berger later stated in an essay explicating his critique of "Dabru Emet."[69]

The paradigmatic problem that Berger identified in "Dabru Emet" was embodied especially in the first statement of the document, that "Jews and Christians worship the same God":

> Although it is proper to emphasize that Christians "worship the God of Abraham, Isaac, and Jacob, creator of heaven and earth," it is essential to add that worship of Jesus of Nazareth as a manifestation or component of that God constitutes what Jewish law and theology call *avodah zarah*, or foreign worship—at least if done by a Jew. Many Jews died to underscore this point, and the bland assertion that "Christian worship is not a viable choice for Jews" is thoroughly inadequate.[70]

Stressing this point would have been inappropriate—if not entirely offensive—in the context of a dialogical statement such as "Dabru Emet." Getting into the nuanced and idiosyncratic halakhic debate regarding the status of Christianity could not but be distasteful and counterproductive. Berger himself described how when he brought the halakhic issue to the table in trying to explain why Jews should refrain from an interfaith service in St. Patrick's Cathedral in New York, "an important official in the New York Archdiocese . . . complained about my expressing such an assessment of Christianity after all that Catholics had done to reassess their negative image of Judaism."[71] Even as Berger made it clear that he did not regard Christianity as idolatry for (gentile) Christians but merely for Jews (according to the *shittuf* principle) and made a further effort to explain why *avodah zarah* should be translated not as "idolatry" but as "foreign worship" ("not suggesting that Christians attribute divinity to icons"), the very discourse could easily become a disaster in public relations and a massive obstacle for Christian-Jewish dialogue. From Berger's perspective, since it is impossible to enter a theological dialogue without touching these sensitive points, which are essential for the Jewish tradition, it is preferable to avoid such dialogue in the first place.

Berger's criticism of "Dabru Emet" was accepted as a guideline within the Orthodox world (the RCA adopted his statement, too). In the end, among about two hundred Jewish leaders and rabbis who signed "Dabru Emet," there were only fourteen Orthodox signatories (Greenberg among them, as well as David Rosen and Yechiel Eckstein, to be discussed below). "Dabru

Emet" may have signified a new Jewish discourse on Christianity, but the absence of Orthodox support has significantly curtailed its authority.

Yet again, Modern Orthodox participants in Christian-Jewish dialogue kept providing Berger and other concerned Modern Orthodox leaders with materials for critique, while showing an eagerness to dive into the theological traditions and retrieve sources and strategies that could provide for good dialogical strategies. A few of these advocates for dialogue reside in Israel. In Israel, the question of dialogue with the Christian world is discussed mostly in connection with the evangelical friends of Israel, or "Christian Zionists." In a number of cases, it is Orthodox Jewish contact people who mediate the relationships between evangelical donors and Jews who receive the donations, thus "rendering them Kosher" in the eyes of the Jewish public.[72] Three prominent figures who studied with Soloveitchik and have fostered the Christian-Jewish dialogue in Israel are Rabbi Yechiel Eckstein (who died suddenly in 2019), former head of the charity organization International Fellowship of Christians and Jews, and Rabbis Korn and Riskin.

Rabbi Yechiel Eckstein and the International Fellowship of Christians and Jews

Since the beginning of the 2000s, the Orthodox community in Israel has been in deep disagreement over the legitimacy of accepting contributions from evangelical Christians. The disagreement erupted in full force when a prominent Christian-Jewish organization, the International Fellowship of Christians and Jews, burst onto the Israeli scene. The founder of the fellowship, Rabbi Yechiel Eckstein, a graduate of Yeshiva University who had founded the organization in Chicago in 1983 and immigrated to Israel in 2002, drew scathing Orthodox criticism until the end of his life. Eckstein devoted himself, according to his own self-description, to "building bridges" between Jews and Christians, and he collected huge sums of money from evangelical donors (by some accounts, more than $1.5 billion by the time of his death in 2019) for investment in the welfare of Israeli society.[73]

Eckstein was thoroughly familiar with the evangelical worldview and spoke its language with great facility. In his book *The Journey Home*, Eckstein formulated a kind of evangelical Christian-Jewish theology through a joint literary journey with a Christian friend to the Holy Land.[74] In the book, a Baptist Christian and an Orthodox rabbi help each other "find their faith," each in his own religion. Through the spiritual support that Eckstein provides his Christian friend, he turns his heart to "the love of Israel" in evangelical style. Eckstein himself finds that even though Jesus is not the Messiah of the Jews, he did bring salvation to the nations by grafting the wild branches on the good olive tree—to paraphrase Romans 11. Eckstein's book is full of symbolic symmetry between the two religions: the crucifixion of Jesus for Christians is compared with the Shoah of the Jews, while the resurrection of Jesus is paired with the return to Zion and the founding of the State of Israel. While his Christian friend in the book, Jamey, discovers the depth of Jesus's Jewishness through Eckstein, Eckstein himself aspires to reconnect Jesus to his Jewish brethren after almost two thousand years of alienation.[75] At the end of the book, Eckstein himself undergoes a kind of conversion to Zionism and decides to leave Chicago for Israel. The book was published a short time before Eckstein's actual immigration to Israel, in parallel with the opening of the offices of the International Fellowship of Christians and Jews and the flare-up of the controversy that surrounds it to this day.

Eckstein often reiterated his objection to missionary activities among Jews (an activity that has been largely abandoned by the Catholic Church but is still broadly considered as obligatory by evangelical Christians). On the other hand, he succeeded in igniting the religious imagination of Christians in fundraising events in ways that could easily have been interpreted as encouraging missionary activities. Thus in a clip uploaded to the internet by his opponents (in the context of a controversy surrounding summer camps funded by his organization in 2014) we see Eckstein facing a group of donors and explaining to them that the best way to fulfill their religious mission among the Jewish people is through support and charity that will open the hearts of Jews to the hand outstretched to them. Here are some of the things that Eckstein says in the clip:

> Let me tell you something as a rabbi. . . . Your job is not to bring Jews or anyone else to Christ. That's not your great commission. Your job and your commission is to be a witness of God's love through Christ, in your life, and to make that available to the whole world. *But you don't convert anyone.* That is God and the Holy Spirit that bring about a change and a conversion. That's not your doing, right? Amen! And rather, your job is to live the life that others would say, "Well, that's what's called lifestyle evangelism!" Don't you think that when a Jew runs to the bomb shelter, as missiles are coming down, and sees a sign saying,

"Given by Christians with love to Israel and the Jewish people," don't you think that is a far greater witness than passing out tracts in the middle of Times Square or whatever? I believe that Christians can fulfil their great commission vis-à-vis the Jewish people, with whom they had this terrible relationship for two thousand years; *today Christians can fulfil it and probably be more effective,* by blessing Israel and the Jewish people. That's how you say it: through your deeds of love, you are saying more about your caring and loving the Jewish people than all the tracts that you could give out.[76]

Eckstein thus recommends that Christians replace their traditional distribution of leaflets with donations to the State of Israel. Is he thereby asking them to cease their activities for the conversion of Jews, or to increase their efficiency? This obfuscation shows Eckstein's talent for staying in touch with both worlds. However, despite his caution and his ability to raise funds, and despite the great sympathy for him on the part of the secular heads of Israel's institutions, Eckstein paid a heavy price for his daring positions.[77] The price was harsh criticism, bordering on excommunication and threats from the Orthodox Israeli public.[78]

Many rabbis and prominent rabbinical institutions in Israel have issued halakhic decisions that forbid receiving any help from the International Fellowship of Christians and Jews, claiming that it is a missionary fund. These include Rabbi Avraham Shapira, the chief Ashkenazi rabbi; Rabbi Mordechai Eliyahu, the chief Sephardi rabbi, who at first permitted receiving help from the fellowship but later recanted and added his signature to Rabbi Shapira's halakhic decision; Rabbi Shmuel Auerbach, one of the most important Ashkenazi arbiters, who led a radical ultra-Orthodox flank and issued a halackic decision on the subject in which he castigated any reliance on the fellowship fund as a terrible "blasphemy" that introduced "the force of impurity into the sacred places"; Rabbi Nissim Karelitz, cousin of the ultra-Orthodox leader Hazon Ish and a prominent Haredi arbiter, who wrote that this was a disgrace and a great shame and forbade it as "blasphemy"; Rabbi Moshe David Tendler, an important halakhist of the Modern Orthodox community in Monsey, New York (and a relative of Rabbi Moshe Feinstein), who called upon the rabbis of Israel to excommunicate Eckstein as an inciter and provocateur and more; and Rabbi Ovadia Yosef, chief Sephardi rabbi from 1973 to 1983, who denounced the fellowship and its founder ("the Christian Convert"), Rabbi Eckstein.[79] The Rabbinical Court of the Haredi community issued a halakhic decision forbidding receiving any assistance from the fund out of concern for future missionary activity, itself based on the prohibition against "things associated with idolatry, for the name of their god is thereby elevated"; that is, it is forbidden to use things that help idolatry, and for this reason, it is forbidden to receive donations from a gentile in public.

Among the more conservative religious Zionist rabbis (the Hardalim, or the rabbis affiliated with the *kav* [hard-line] yeshivot), the opposition to the International Fellowship of Christians and Jews was the harshest.[80] Within these circles, Eckstein's activity was perceived as a national humiliation. This clearly shows that even where the interest in establishing friendly relations with Christians was great, Orthodoxy was not quick to extend its hand.

Eugene Korn, Shlomo Riskin, and the Jewish Evangelization Project

The liberal rabbis Eugene Korn and Shlomo Riskin sought to apply the policies of their teacher, Joseph Soloveitchik, more leniently than most of their Modern Orthodox counterparts. Although they might not "trade favors" with Christians or "reconcile some differences" in the most austere Soloveitchikean sense, their way of extracting positive attitudes toward Christians from traditional Jewish sources, sometimes while ignoring other traditions, often more dominant, was certainly more experimental than a mainstream reading of "Confrontation" allows.

In several of his works, Korn argued that Judaism always "taught that the Jewish covenant was not the only valid religion or the sole way to salvation." It should therefore be regarded as having a "natural theological openness" toward other religions.[81] Following Moses Mendelssohn, Korn, too, believes that Maimonides's statement that the just among the nations "will have a portion in the world to come" is evidence that Judaism is not a fanatical faith and that it exceeds Christianity in its tolerance, since the latter always claimed that "there is no salvation outside the Church" (and this despite the fact that this utterance in Jewish tradition was almost never directed at actual flesh-and-blood gentiles and was arguably rather a later apologetic development).[82] According to Korn, Judaism also preceded Christianity in its conception of a "double covenant" (a principle that Korn adopted from Protestant theology), for the seven Noahide laws testify to the fact that God had offered humanity two ways to salvation: 613 commandments (mitzvoth) for the Jews and seven laws for the sons of Noah. Because of this, Korn finds a rich tradition of religious tolerance within Judaism.

Unlike Greenberg, Korn does delve into halakhic categories, if only to re-interpret them in line with his tolerant positions. He identifies with the ha-lakhic position of Menachem Meiri, to which he ascribes far greater weight than it had in the course of history, and certainly far greater than it has in today's rabbinical discourse.[83] Moreover, according to Korn, apart from Mai-monides, who viewed Christians as idolaters ("to many moderns this may sound strange"), most of the Ashkenazi arbiters held a "positive belief" re-garding Christians and did not consider Christians to be idolaters, certainly with regard to the halakhic laws governing daily life.[84] Maimonides, claims Korn, wrote what he did because he did not know Christians and only relied on "books" for his knowledge, while Meiri lived in Christian society in an era of relatively good Christian-Jewish relations in the latter part of his life: "Me'iri encountered believing Christians as living human beings, discussed religion with Christian priests, and understood that Christians could be moral and religiously sophisticated people. It made no sense to him to categorize them as idolaters, identical to the pagans to which the Bible and the Talmud refer."[85] Korn, then, paints a picture completely inverted from that which arises in most of the Orthodox Jewish world, according to which it was the severe pres-sure exerted by Christians during that period, especially in the area where Meiri lived and during his time, that led Meiri to "falsify" Judaism's arguably "authentic" approach to Christianity—an approach fully preserved by Mai-monides alone, because he did not labor under the threat of Christians.[86]

Korn's ideas were adopted and developed by Shlomo Riskin, a prominent figure active in the education of Zionist Christians on Jews and Judaism.[87] Riskin maintains close ties with the evangelical preacher John Hagee, one of the most prominent leaders of the evangelical world. (Hagee established and heads the Cornerstone Church in Texas and manages the evangelical radio and television channel John Hagee Ministries, which is broadcast across the United States and beyond. Hagee also founded the Christian-Zionist organization Christians United for Israel.)[88] In 2008, Riskin founded the Center for Jewish-Christian Understanding and Cooperation, a school for teaching Judaism to Christians.

Riskin is not a systematic theologian, and he has published mainly in the field of Torah exegesis, which makes it difficult to extract a cohesive theolog-ical view from his diverse discussions on the issue. In analyzing Riskin's posi-tions, I noticed two distinct projects that he wishes to promote: the first is to further a cultural-ethical Jewish and Christian mission for the liberalization of the world; the second is to disseminate Judaism among Christians with the aim of promoting the Maimonidean plan of redemption (according to

Riskin's interpretation), which predicts the conversion of the entire human race to Judaism.

Riskin objects to the widespread argument that Judaism is not a missionary religion. Just like the Christians, Jews, too, have a duty to spread the tidings of their God. It was only because of their weakness over their many years of exile that the Jews were prevented from observing this commandment, to the point that they ultimately forgot it.[89] Riskin claims that in addition to the covenants that God made with the Jews through Abraham and subsequently through Moses, he also made a third covenant—a moment before they entered the Promised Land (Deut. 27). This covenant comprises twelve universal moral commandments (among them prohibitions against incest, murder, and idolatry). It was supposed to have been inscribed on the stones of the Jordan River, and according to the sages, it was translated into seventy languages. According to Riskin, "This is the covenant of Universal Redemption, which can only come about if the nations of the world accept fundamental biblical morality. It is the covenant that squarely places upon the Jewish people the responsibility of teaching the moral truths of the bible to the world."[90] The universal covenant of salvation requires the people of Israel to announce God's tidings to everyone rather than keep them to themselves. The reason that God chose to make the covenant at that particular time, according to Riskin, was because of the challenge of sovereignty that the people of Israel were about to accept on their entry into the Promised Land.[91] Now that the Jews have had the good fortune to return to the Land of Israel and renew their sovereignty within it, the time has also come to resume the fulfillment of the universal charge imposed on them by God and distribute the gospel of Jewish morality among the gentiles.

What is the gospel that should be disseminated among the nations, according to Riskin? Does it comprise the seven Noahide laws and the twelve commandments included in Deuteronomy 27, or does it comprise the 613 commandments of the Torah? In other words, are Jews commanded to teach humanity basic ethical rules, or are they supposed to convert all of humanity to Judaism? Riskin's ethical project focuses on global dissemination of an ethical doctrine based on the seven Noahide laws (while his other project, discussed below, focuses on exposing the gentiles to the Jewish faith). Maimonides stated that when Israel's hand shall overpower, the people of Israel should not be content with preaching the seven Noahide laws to the gentiles but rather were obliged to force the gentiles to accept them (and kill whoever refused to do so, a fact that Riskin omits).[92] The justification for this, according to Riskin, is that the principles of monotheist ethics are so vital to the existence of human society ("in our global village, where one extreme madman can set off a nuclear war and destroy the world") that "we have the right to coerce, if necessary, people to accept these universal laws of morality."[93] In this way, Riskin transforms the religious coercion proposed by Maimonides from an idea with fundamentalist overtones (to say the least) to a concept more resonant to a liberal-humanist ear, one that serves the "Jewish-Christian" struggle against a more immediately threatening fundamentalism, that of radical Islam.

Riskin (following Korn) perceives Maimonides as a pluralist proponent who allowed all humans freedom of religion, as long as they observed the seven Noahide laws (in the spirit of Meiri, who treated gentiles with tolerance if their religion required them to maintain certain moral standards). According to Riskin, Judaism upholds two routes to salvation, one for Jews and one for gentiles. This option that Judaism offers the gentiles, to be saved via the seven Noahide laws without converting to Judaism, makes it a tolerant religion that does not force itself on others (and is thereby superior to Christianity). At this point, Riskin aligns with the Protestant tradition of the double covenant theory, according to which the Jews will be saved in their Jewishness and the Christians in their Christianness.[94] To utilize Maimonides as a model of pluralistic liberalism, Riskin is obliged to mask the Maimonidean fanaticism; he makes no mention of the fact that Maimonides had forbidden the gentiles from creating a new religion and had only allowed the sons of Noah the binary option of either basing their entire religious existence on the seven laws of Noah or converting to Judaism.[95]

Riskin thus utilizes the seven Noahide laws and the commandments of Deuteronomy 27 as a universal ethical paradigm that is the only one that allows normal social existence. He does not impose the burden of disseminating this gospel in the modern world on the shoulders of the Jewish people alone but rather views it as a Christian-Jewish mission, and even as a political-religious-cultural partnership of the entire enlightened world, especially when facing fundamentalist Islam.[96] In this, Riskin draws on the words of Maimonides that endow Christianity and Islam with the positive role of disseminating monotheism: "Even though he considered Christianity to be idolatry (contrary to most medieval arbiters), [Maimonides] greatly esteemed the success of Christianity in disseminating the positive principles and central values of the Judeo-Christian tradition throughout the world."[97] Now, Christians, Jews, moderate Muslims, and humanist secular people are supposed to work shoulder to shoulder to testify to the universal truth (whose origins lie in Judaism) for the salvation of the world.[98]

Yet Riskin takes Maimonides a step further, to what seems to be quite a different project. As we have seen, Riskin justifies coercion where the seven Noahide laws are concerned, because these are vital to normal social existence (and their observance also entitles gentiles to a portion in the world to come). But what about Maimonides's messianic vision that in the future, all of humankind is destined to return to the "true religion"?[99] In a number of places, Riskin reiterates that in his reading, Maimonides had foreseen that all of humanity would one day convert to Judaism. The pluralism that Riskin based on Maimonides's conception of the seven Noahide laws, which allows the gentiles to remain in their gentility as long as they comply with the ethical criteria embedded in these laws, is thus no more than an interim compromise; in the messianic future, such pluralism will disappear, for all of humanity will eventually convert.

Riskin seems to also extract from this eschatological vision of the conversion of humankind to Judaism a permit to act for its implementation in the immediate present. In this, he relies on a responsum (exceptional in halakhic tradition) of Maimonides that permits teaching Christians Torah (though not Muslims, who deny that the Torah was divinely revealed) so that they can recant their erroneous interpretations and as a means to "draw them closer to our truth."[100] He concludes that Maimonides was of the opinion that it is permitted and even desirable to proselytize Judaism among Christians and draw them to Torah and the mitzvoth:

> It is therefore clear beyond all doubt that we must teach the gentiles Torah; it is our duty to teach them the seven Noahide commandments, and beyond that more, as much as possible, according to their desire. And this is exactly what we do at the Center for Jewish-Christian Understanding and Cooperation: We teach the Jewish roots of Christianity, the foundations of the Written and Oral Law that Jesus himself had studied and observed. In 2011, 6,650 Christians came to study these lessons.[101]

Thus, underlying the curriculum offered Christians at the Center for Jewish-Christian Understanding and Cooperation in Efrat is a missionary program that is not completely disclosed (even though Riskin claims that he does openly explain this to Christians). The Christians come to learn about Jesus and are thereby exposed by teachers to the fundamentals of Judaism. Instead of fearing a hidden evangelical mission, as his rabbinical colleagues do, Riskin adopts a Christian strategy toward the Christians themselves; under the gestures of friendship, one finds a striving—though quite refined—for religious conversion.

Riskin's activity within the evangelical community has drawn scathing criticism from the religious Zionist and Modern Orthodox public. The positive regard for Jesus, the close proximity to Christians, and above all, his support for a theological dialogue with Christians, have all required Riskin to justify his position to the disciples of Soloveitchik.[102] In an article that he published in the Israeli religious-national newspaper *Makor Rishon*, Riskin discussed the essay "Confrontation" at length and justified dialogue with Christians on the basis of the arguments described above, that is, the claim that Soloveitchik's essay opened a path for Christian-Jewish dialogue so long as a number of basic rules are maintained, and that had Soloveitchik witnessed the far-reaching changes that have taken place in the Christian world with regard to the Jewish people since he wrote his essay, then he would certainly have agreed that theological dialogue is important and would perhaps have changed his position.[103]

Riskin's ethical-universal project may be reconciled with Soloveitchik's position. It is, however, harder to justify Riskin's Torah for Christians project. Berger published a critical response in *Makor Rishon*, rejecting Riskin's interpretation of "Confrontation" (with arguments similar to those he used in a debate with Korn a few years earlier).[104] Berger also directed harsh criticism at Riskin's missionary activities, claiming that action taken by Jews to convert Christians may be interpreted as legitimating similar actions on the part of Christians. Berger was particularly bothered by the unusual way Riskin interpreted Maimonides's responsum, in which the license to teach Torah to Christians was primarily based on the chance of converting them to Judaism:

> Whoever relies on an interpretation of said Maimonidean methods to justify theological dialogue with Christians pushes us into an extremely dangerous arena. Jews unconditionally demand that Christians involved in dialogue with us should not do so with an intention to convert us to Christianity. Obviously, Rabbi Riskin also subscribes to this position, and he therefore stipulates that the Christians participating in his enterprise and the Catholics are not interested in converting us

to their religion. And yet, he now tells us, as well as any Christian becoming aware of his article, that our purpose is to convert Christians. . . .
In the way that Rabbi Riskin quotes Maimonides, "it is permitted to
teach Christians the commandments and draw them to our religion . . .
If they are shown the correct interpretation they may repent."[105]

Indeed, in the article that he had published in *Makor Rishon,* Riskin had
emphasized his strict opposition to Christian mission, to the point that he
burned Bibles incorporating the New Testament that had been sent by Christian missionaries to new Jewish immigrants in Efrat. Following Berger's response in the press, I asked Riskin how he reconciled the demand that
Christians refrain from any attempt to convert Jews with the call to Jews to
convert their Christian interlocutors. Riskin explained that the difference between Jewish mission and Christian mission—a difference on which he
relies to distinguish between permitted (Jewish) missionary activity and
forbidden (Christian) missionary activity—lies in the salvatory nature of
the seven Noahide laws and the fact that Judaism provides the gentiles with
a portion in the world to come. As far as Riskin is concerned, since Jews
believe that Christians may also be saved *extra synagogam,* any religious
preaching directed at them does not have the same coercive nature that characterizes Christian evangelism (though, it must be remembered, the seven
Noahide laws are supposed to be *forced* on the gentiles).[106] Even though there
is a similarity between Christian eschatology (in which all Jews are destined
to convert to Christianity) and Jewish eschatology (in which all Christians
are destined to convert to Judaism), Judaism is in fact more pluralistic in
that it believes that the gentiles can be saved without converting to Judaism,
while (most) Christians do not believe in such an option.

A few months after the Riskin-Berger controversy, Riskin's enterprise was
attacked by another representative of the Modern Orthodox congregation
in America, Rabbi Herschel Schachter. Schachter already had a history of interventions in Christian-Jewish dialogue. As mentioned previously in this
chapter, Schachter unleashed a campaign against Greenberg when he published his Jewish theology of Christianity. Following the discourse in *Makor
Rishon,* Schachter posted a scathing critique of Riskin without actually
naming him.[107] Schachter, who views himself as a faithful disciple of Soloveitchik (based on a close and personal acquaintance), criticizes Riskin
on a theological-political basis and objects to Riskin's legitimization of the
Christian affinity with Jerusalem and the Holy Land. Schachter reminds

readers that Christians have claimed that the covenant between the Jewish people and God was void. For this reason, as far as he is concerned, when Christians talk of their spiritual ties with the Holy City, they are striving to undermine the status of the Jewish people as the chosen. Jewish sovereignty over Jerusalem expressly contradicts the Christian claim of a lapsed covenant between God and the Jewish people, but Christians have a vested theological interest in voiding the covenant, whether through the internationalization of Jerusalem or through conversion of the Jews residing within it.[108]

Schachter rejects Riskin's and Korn's interpretation of Soloveitchik's words, putting forward his own interpretation as more authoritative. He mentions that he had heard directly from Soloveitchik, his rabbi (who was quoting his own grandfather, Rabbi Chaim Soloveitchik of Brisk), that Christians are idolaters (whereas Riskin believes that they are worshippers of *shittuf*) and that it is forbidden to teach Torah to Christians. A Jew who teaches idolaters Torah only encourages them to deepen their idolatry, because everything they learn will serve them in their worship of "that man" (*oto ha'ish*).

Soloveitchik, claims Schachter, warned against such relations with Christians, whether in dialogue or in writing, both in his essay "Confrontation" and elsewhere. Schachter protests that despite Soloveitchik's warnings, various rabbis who call themselves "his disciples" have taken a totally opposite position and have attempted to base their distorted views on the words of the "Rav" (as Soloveitchik is often called). Schachter concludes his article with a warning to the rabbis operating in the Holy Land to curb their messianic fervor, lest in the throes of the enthusiasm that it fosters, it may aid and abet both idolatry and conversion (*shemad*).[109]

Christian-Jewish Dialogue in Conservative Style

It should be noted that this was not the first time Schachter had identified Christian worship as idolatry. Just before John Paul II's funeral in 2005, Schachter referred the Modern Orthodox community to his book of halakhic responsa, in which he recalled that Soloveitchik, at the time of John F. Kennedy's funeral, forbade not only participation in a religious Christian ritual but even watching such a ceremony on television: "And what's the difference if he enters a church, which is forbidden, or brings the church into his home"?[110]

This comment offended Christians who stood in good relationship with the Orthodox community. It was once again Rabbi Yehiel Poupko, who represents the Chicago Jewish community in its relationship with the

Catholic Church, the mainline Protestant denominations, and the evangelical community, who had to lower the flames in a personal conversation with a high-ranking Catholic official who called him on the way to the funeral, puzzled by Schachter's comments.[111]

Interestingly, Yehiel Poupko perceives his close ties with Christian communities as going hand in hand with a strictly conservative interpretation of Soloveitchik's approach. To him, it is precisely an adamant Orthodox position that facilitates a significant Christian-Jewish dialogue in which neither side compromises the core contents of their faith. When a relationship is truly significant, Poupko explained to me in one of our conversations, one does not need to speak about the relationship so much as to live it. According to Poupko, his Christian interlocutors are well aware that he is willing to die in order not to transgress the boundaries of his faith, and that he would have never agreed, for example, to enter a church for the sake of Christian-Jewish fraternity. Yet this is not perceived as an insult to his Christian counterparts, but rather as an unwavering affirmation of his own faith. This is true also for the Christian side: "If you ever meet a Christian that does not believe you need Christ, don't trust him," Poupko says, quoting what he had once heard from a prominent rabbi, "because if he does not respect his own faith, he won't respect yours either."[112] Together with several other prominent Orthodox figures (Meir Soloveitchik, Carmy, and Wyschogrod among them), Poupko challenges the dichotomy between an eager liberal community and a reluctant conservative community, introducing a third Modern Orthodox alternative to Christian-Jewish relations.

The obvious difficulty that conservative Orthodox communities experience vis-à-vis Christianity emerges from halakha; as in the case of Feinstein and many of the other rabbis discussed in this book, a conservative halakhic approach defines Christianity as *shittuf*; that is, in the lenient case, it is idolatry if professed by Jews but not gentiles, and in the austere view, it is idolatry for both Jews and gentiles. Halakha poses strict boundaries on the interaction between Jews and idolaters, boundaries that severely limit the space for Christian-Jewish exchange both emotionally and practically. The conservative unwillingness to introduce changes into halakha means, from the outset, refraining from dialogue with Christians.

Yet along with the liberal phenomenon of Christian-Jewish dialogue, a current of dialogue between Orthodox Jews and conservative Christians has emerged in the circles of Modern Orthodoxy. The justification for this dialogue is that even if Christians were indeed idolaters—or, preferably, "foreign worshippers," a literal translation of the Hebrew term *ovdey avoda zarah*, since these Orthodox thinkers emphasize that there is indeed a difference between paganism and Christianity—they are still believers, and in this sense, they are closer to Orthodox Jews than to atheists.[113] Even if the theological differences between Jews and Christians are as deep as they always were, a greater chasm separates believers from non-believers and binds Jews and Christians to a common destiny.

This affinity between Christians and Jews, recognized by conservative Modern Orthodox authors who engage in Christian-Jewish dialogue, is naturally read back into Soloveitchik's works. It is a misunderstanding of Soloveitchik, argues Carmy, to assume that he preferred that his community cooperate with "neutral" secular society rather than with believing Christians:

> When RCA officers balked at organizational participation in a Catholic-initiated conference on "Man as the Image of God," on the grounds that this was "theology," the Rav remarked sarcastically that a conclave on "Man as a Purely Naturalistic Being" would not have set off the same alarms.[114]

Meir Soloveitchik similarly laments that "many readers of R. Soloveitchik's essay conclude that he banned Jewish-Christian communication that is even loosely linked to religious beliefs."[115] And later: "Orthodox Jews have long adhered to the Rav's restrictions in engaging in interfaith dialogue of a theological nature, but little dialogue has taken place between religious Jews and Christians on the distinctly biblical morality that we share."[116] Even the strictest adherence to Soloveitchik's restrictions does not exclude a religiously motivated dialogue between Christians and Jews against the great forces of secularism:

> Now the Rav's reference to the "threat of secularism" can be understood. The Rav referred to the attempt to strip moral discourse of its religious nature and render our ethical language into a tongue wholly foreign to Christians and Jews. Combating the "threat of secularism" is, for the Rav, part and parcel of man's moral stewardship of the world; it is an endeavor in which religious Jews and Christians are natural allies.[117]

This does not imply that Christians are assigned to a "better" halakhic category than *shittuf,* and the authors are even careful not to absolve

Christians so quickly from the blame of transgressing the Noahide laws. In Meir Soloveitchik's words:

> Even if one views *shittuf* as no violation of the first of the sheva mizvot benei [sons of] Noah, tremendous differences between Jews and Christians exist; this is a difference for which Jews have been willing to die. While Christians believe in God, they also assume that a human being that once lived on this earth is that God, and they worship God, as well as that human being, with that assumption in mind. At the same time, even if one assumes that *shittuf* is impermissible for benei Noah, certain conceptions of who God is will always be shared by Jews and Christians. In that sense, both Jews and Christians can invoke the Creator of Heaven and Earth and, *to some extent,* mean the same thing. . . . That they share this moral language makes both Jews and Christians "men of God," and gives them a common way of speaking about morality.[118]

Meir Soloveitchik, at times, makes even bolder statements, as in his criticism of Jacob Neusner's reverence for Jesus as a "great teacher": "Jesus is not someone with whom we can have this sort of 'dialogue.' If we deny his divinity, then we can respond with nothing short of shock and dismay when we read the words of a man who puts himself in place of God."[119] The doctrinal rift between Jews and Christians cannot be overcome, nor should Christian-Jewish dialogue try to reconcile it. Yet "even if Christians and Jews profoundly disagree about the truth, they are united in the belief that there *is* a truth to be sought."[120]

And again, in Berger's words:

> R. Walter Wurzburger reported that R. Soloveitchik once persuaded a wavering Catholic doctor who was treating him not to leave the Church, even as R. Hershel Schachter testifies that the Rav rejected the view that Christian-style *shittuf* is permissible to Noahides. Apparently, this sort of forbidden *shittuf,* with its adherence to moral codes and recognition of the Creator of heaven and earth, is preferable to atheism and moral bankruptcy. Moreover, I can affirm from experience that when this nuanced position is presented sensitively to Christians of good will, it does not undermine cordial inter-faith relations; indeed, it sometimes even enhances them.[121]

It is thus secular liberalism—the cultural paradigm that enabled post–World War II Christian-Jewish dialogue in the first place—that is currently seen by conservative Modern Orthodox Jews as a joint enemy that unites them with their Christian counterparts. Yet the affirmation of their respective traditions against the secularist (and often relativist) blurring of religious truth claims requires them to emphasize the incommensurability of their traditions and to surface precisely the elements of Judaism that are often marginalized from Christian-Jewish dialogue for the sake of good relations. Against the secularism that, seeing all religions as equally nonsensical, melts them together in an undifferentiated mass, Judaism and Christianity must struggle to stress the differences between their respective truth claims.[122]

This "third path" of Orthodoxy vis-à-vis Christian-Jewish dialogue sheds light on an interesting tension within Orthodoxy with regard to modernity. As we have seen in previous chapters, secularism is an ever present, silent partner in the Christian-Jewish relationship. It was the liberal post–World War II order that facilitated Christian-Jewish dialogue, but the same order also endowed Jews with the right to distance themselves from dialogue and at times even to express overt disdain for Christianity. For the conservative branch of Modern Orthodoxy discussed in this chapter, secularism again unites Christians and Jews, but this time not as an enabling space but as a common rival. Either way, the attitude toward the secularity of the public sphere is very often a primary catalyst for the formulation of Orthodox Jewish attitudes to Christianity.

The Dialogue between the Vatican and the Chief Rabbinate of Israel

Joseph Soloveitchik's restrictions transcended the boundaries of American Modern Orthodoxy to provide a paradigmatic policy within larger circles of Orthodoxy with regard to Christian-Jewish dialogue. A final example of Soloveitchik's influence concerns the Israeli Chief Rabbinate's engagement in dialogue with representatives of the Vatican. In the year 2000, in the context of his historic visit to Jerusalem, Pope John Paul II suggested that a joint committee be set up by the Holy See and the Chief Rabbinate of Israel, and the Chief Rabbinate accepted this invitation. Since that time, a group of Catholic officials (including not a few cardinals) and Orthodox rabbis has convened once every year, alternating between Rome and Jerusalem.

It must be stated from the very outset that the following discussion of the relations between the Chief Rabbinate and the Vatican is based on relatively

sparse sources, of which the most important are interviews conducted with
three rabbis who have participated in these meetings: David Rosen, the late
She'ar Yashuv Cohen, and the late David Brodman. The conclusions drawn
from these interviews are my own and are not necessarily entirely consistent with what these rabbis have stated. Moreover, in many cases, the discussion is based on my experience in searching for relevant information, no
less than on the actual sources obtained.

It seems that John Paul II considered the relationship with the Chief Rabbinate of Israel important because he viewed it as a kind of parallel institution to the Holy See within the Catholic world—a central religious authority
for the Jewish people. It should be noted, however, that the Chief Rabbinate
is perceived differently within the Israeli context; though it enjoys a formal
authority as the organ of the state in charge of religious services, it is not
necessarily held as the highest spiritual authority, especially not by Orthodox
communities, which usually affiliate themselves with specific rabbinic figures
as their authoritative teachers (as in the case of Joseph Soloveitchik for Modern
Orthodoxy, Ovadyah Yosef for Sephardi Orthodoxy, and Zvi Yehudah Kook
for Gush Emunim, for example). In most cases, the Chief Rabbinate's role is
more administrative and representational than spiritual, even if some chief
rabbis are highly esteemed by their respective communities.

Nevertheless, the encounter with the Chief Rabbinate, as a central Jewish
religious authority, holds a theological significance from the Catholic perspective. It may be argued that Orthodox Jewry is the church's preferable
partner (or as described by the CEO of the Chief Rabbinate, Oded Wiener:
"The Catholics view their relations with the Rabbinate as a major achievement because they view Orthodox Judaism as the authentic Judaism").[123]
As a result, this formal Orthodox institution was perceived as an important
counterpart for interfaith dialogue.

Those changes that did take place within Orthodoxy after World War II
often led to a more forceful insistence on what separates Jews from Christians rather than to a search for commonalities and rapprochement. The
Chief Rabbinate of Israel was therefore not particularly eager to enter into
an interfaith dialogue with the Catholic Church. Pope John Paul II's invitation came as a surprise.

On accepting the challenge of a dialogue with the Vatican, the rabbis had
to formulate their own interpretation of the relationship. Soloveitchik's approach provided them with the tools to do so. They chose not to give the
dialogue a deep religious significance but to see it as a matter of diplomacy,

that is, to regard it as a formal service to the State of Israel, or at the most as a process to right a historical wrong, which could have implications for the welfare of Jews everywhere.[124] They felt that the dialogue gave them the right to protest when they considered the church to have retreated to its old anti-Jewish positions, such as when Joseph Ratzinger (as Benedict XVI) published his new version of the Good Friday prayer for the Jews or when he rescinded the excommunication of the Holocaust-denying bishop Richard Williamson.

Whatever the forces that drove the Chief Rabbinate of Israel into an interfaith dialogue with the Vatican, it is quite obvious that the Chief Rabbinate attaches far less importance to this relationship than the church does, and invests far fewer resources in it—intellectually, spiritually, and practically. Obviously, friendly formal relations between a prominent rabbinical body and high church officials constitute a significant historical precedent in the relations of the church and the Jewish people. The very existence of a bilateral conference indicates renewed thinking of the relationships in view of the changed times, regardless of the content of the meetings. However, apart from the formal aspect, which signals that rabbis and cardinals can convene without hostility, it is difficult to estimate the achievements or purposes of the committee, at least from the Jewish side of the fence.

Right from the outset, the Chief Rabbinate rabbis announced that they intended to adopt Soloveitchik's approach to interfaith dialogue with the Vatican, that is, to refrain from any discussion of "controversial subjects" and to focus instead on common denominators—general social subjects such as preventing bloodshed, working for peace, preventing promiscuity, and maintaining the sanctity of the family.[125] Over the years, rabbis who were more acquainted with the academic world, such as Daniel Sperber, professor of Talmud at Bar-Ilan University, and Abraham Steinberg, an expert on medical ethics from the Hebrew University of Jerusalem, were chosen to accompany the Chief Rabbinate's delegation in this interreligious endeavor.

The rabbis were aware of the theological transformations that have taken place in the perception of Judaism in the Catholic Church, but they were not interested in discussing any of the details of this matter. It was enough to know that the Catholic Church had renounced antisemitism, replacement theology, and missionary activities among Jews. Rabbi She'ar Yashuv Cohen, who led the first Chief Rabbinate delegations, summed up his perspective of the basic assumptions of the Catholic Church that made the dialogue possible:

The Jewish people remain the chosen people, because God does not take back the gifts he gives. . . . It is as if the Church is also chosen, and we are partners. We were both chosen by God according to the [Catholic] theory. We did not argue the point. That's *their* theory. It is important for the Jews who live in Christian countries, in South America and in Europe too, that the relations be of this nature, rather than relations of persecution and danger or risk to Jews. For this reason we did not find it appropriate to reject the hand that was extended towards us for peace, with all the necessary precautions that have to be taken in order to avoid making this into a forum for missionary activity. Christianity believes in "giving" salvation. We agreed that we do not need salvation, because we were chosen by God from the outset. . . . So missionary work is therefore unnecessary in any case. We were promised that they would stop missionary work among Jews, . . . the theory is that Jews do not require missionary work. We don't need the salvation that idolaters require.[126]

The Chief Rabbinate's representatives are thus aware of the deep transformation in the Catholic Church's attitude to Judaism, but any discussion of the nature and implications of that transformation remains beyond the pale of discourse. The rabbis are not interested in analyzing the finer theological points of the change and in fact derive all theological information that they may require from specialists, or rather from a single specialist who was nominated to this role at the very outset of the bilateral committee's activities—Rabbi David Rosen.

Rabbi Rosen, who was born in South Africa in 1951, began his career as the rabbi of South Africa's largest Jewish community before becoming chief rabbi of Ireland. Familiar with the Christian world and its many nuances and thoroughly versed in contemporary Catholic theology and its attitude to Judaism, Rosen quickly became the most prominent Orthodox Jewish figure in interfaith dialogue. Rosen enjoys great honor in the Christian world. In 2005, for example, he received a knighthood from the pope for his contribution to the reconciliation of Catholics and Jews. Like the Modern Orthodox protagonists of Christian-Jewish dialogue in the United States, Rosen is perceived as being representative of Orthodoxy by Christians far more than he represents Orthodoxy in the eyes of his fellow Jews. It is Rosen who analyzes Christian texts and decides which material should be brought before the Chief Rabbinate for its perusal. Rosen describes his role (referring to himself in the third person) as follows:

The Chief Rabbinate requires a rabbi who has Orthodox credentials, who they can rely on in this regard, but also has a bit of experience and can explain, who is familiar with the material. . . . Most of the rabbis believe that there is change [in the Catholic world] and someone has to represent us in these contacts [with the church]. We don't really want to do this, so it's good that there is someone like David Rosen who will do these things. . . . The prevalent attitude was . . . that someone has to get the job done.[127]

Rosen is far more deeply engaged with interfaith dialogue than any of his colleagues at the Chief Rabbinate, and he works to promote halakhic and theological positions that are more moderate than what is usually accepted within Orthodoxy.[128] Like Korn and Greenberg, he too deliberates over the question of the covenant, exploring how it may be possible for Christians to share it without Jews acknowledging Christ's divinity or obliterating the boundaries separating the two communities.[129] Rosen wishes to view the relations of Christians and Jews with God as part of the divine plan and as two affinities to God that may differ but are also complementary. When I asked him if he discusses these subjects with his colleagues on the bilateral committee, he responded in the negative.[130]

Just as controversial theological issues are not discussed at the bilateral committee, so too are halakhic issues avoided. The representatives of the Chief Rabbinate on the committee justify their activity mostly "for fear of enmity" and to preserve "the ways of peace"; they do not place their heads between the rock of Maimonides and the hard place of the Tosafists. Since Maimonides himself considered Christianity, despite its idolatry, to be paving the way for the Messiah, the Rabbinate rabbis consider that even according to Maimonides, Christianity has a certain positive role. At the same time, concerning the definition of Christianity (at least Catholic Christianity) at the halakhic level, they tend to assume, according the rabbis She'ar Yashuv Cohen and David Brodman, a more stringent position (even though they "feel" that they attend to the conception of the Tosafists and Meiri).[131] At the funeral of Pope John Paul II, for example, the rabbinical delegation took a detour so as to avoid entering a church: "It goes without saying that we encounter this problem from time to time. We try, without emphasizing the negative aspects [to explain] that according to our religion, it is forbidden to enter the place of worship of another religion."[132]

This testimony reveals the depth of the discomfiture that the rabbis have to contend with when they attempt to mask (sometimes to the point of juggling) the halakhic discontent that they feel at every meeting, and in particular those meetings that take place in Rome.[133] Are the cardinals aware of these Jewish halakhic difficulties? When I asked David Brodman, the ultra-Orthodox rabbi of the town of Savion, about the position of the Christian complement of the bilateral committee regarding the halakhic status of Christianity, Brodman related that the German cardinal Walter Kasper had asked him and his colleagues when the committee first began its activities if their opinion sided with Maimonides or with Meiri. This indicates that church officials are aware of the issue, at least in general outline. It would be unreasonable to assume that they do not understand why the rabbis refuse to enter their churches or why they are asked to conceal their crosses when they visit synagogues. It seems that the church's representatives operate out of the sense that having been the party that had wronged the other, they are now obligated to display a greater measure of sensitivity. In the long accounting with the Jews, such small slights on the part of the Jews pale to insignificance when compared with the humiliation and degradation of the Jews in the past.

Thus, the halakhic discussion, just like the theological discussion, is also gently circumvented. At the annual meetings of the bilateral committee, neither of the communities speaks its natural language. The areas forbidden for speech are far deeper and wider than the permitted zone. It is perhaps for this reason that the joint declarations of the committee are usually mere exchanges of diplomatic formulations rather than any products of joint thinking. The Chief Rabbinate of Israel, in its role as representative of the State of Israel, thus treats the Catholic Church with diplomatic courtesy, but it makes every effort to minimize the importance of these encounters within the Jewish world itself. The committee has very few publications in Hebrew, and its activity is almost unknown in Israel.

The Orthodox Jewish preoccupation with Christian-Jewish dialogue is fundamentally a response more to a Christian initiative than to an intra-Jewish need. In this sense, contemporary Christian-Jewish dialogue continues a centuries'-old tradition in which the church unilaterally dictated the terms of Christian-Jewish relations.

However, the firm and consistent stance of Modern Orthodoxy on the issue of interfaith dialogue has, to a certain extent, turned the original tables. Jewish Orthodoxy has pressed the Catholic Church to forgo discussions of the issues that most interest it, such as doctrine, theology, and ritual. The

Rabbinical Council of America publicly eschewed an ecumenical prayer service during Obama's inauguration because it took place in a church, and leading rabbis publicly proclaim on the pages of prominent Christian venues that Christianity is regarded by halakha as *avoda zara*. When an Orthodox rabbi disseminated a letter criticizing the missionary intimations of the United States Conference of Catholic Bishops, the problematic sentences were subsequently removed from the conference's agenda. This is a reverse situation to that which prevailed in Christian-Jewish disputations in the past, in which Christians decided on the content, form, and parameters of the matters to be discussed so as to ensure "victory." These new behaviors are firmly embedded in the secular American milieu; by adopting the tolerant-liberal principles of "general" American culture, Orthodoxy now remonstrates publicly and distances itself unapologetically from engaging in theological dialogue with Christians.

Yet beneath the persistent asymmetries that characterize the contemporary setting, similar patterns within both communities can also be discerned. Just as in the Catholic world, the Orthodox discourse is diverse and polyphonic (for both communities, this is especially true in the United States). Yet in the Orthodox community as in the Catholic, the preferred strategy is to transfer the dialogue to non-doctrinal realms in order to prevent it from threatening established traditions. In both communities, two distinct conversations take place—an internal conversation in which Jewish and Christian truth claims largely remain mutually exclusive, and a public-facing discourse based on gestures and symbols, sometimes even friendships, within which a lot of smoke is spread to veil core doctrinal differences and discrepancies, and which focus, in their stead, on common religious grounds. Authoritative figures in both communities put their weight into maintaining the separation between these two discourses, restraining overly radical theological efforts, and preventing rapprochement from penetrating so deeply into their established traditions that the borders between them would blur. The dialogue is heavily dependent on an agreement on what to be silent about.

Epilogue

During the course of the fourth century CE, Christianity became tolerated in the Roman Empire, and it was subsequently made the official religion of the empire. This historical turn forced the church to contend with a tremendous identity challenge. Up to that point, the church had seen itself as a small and persecuted community, alienated from the world and ever ready to sacrifice itself on the altar of its faith. Now it had to adapt that self-conception to a wholly different reality, one in which church membership became profitable even in the course of earthly existence and the church itself held incomparable political capital, power, and status. The surprising reconciliation between the church and the Roman Empire demanded a significant theological effort on the part of the Christian leadership to allow the church to reshape itself without undermining the essential principles of the Christian faith. This process played a significant role in the development of Christian theology and its approach to the world, power, politics, and history.

The church had to choose between two theological visions of history. One of these was articulated by Eusebius of Caesarea, a friend of Emperor Constantine and his biographer. According to Eusebius, the Christianization of the Roman Empire was the realization (though only partial) of the prophecies of the Old Testament. The Christian Empire was an expression of the divine plan of redemption and a tool for its promotion. Augustine of Hippo, one of the greatest theologians of the West, however, developed a different

conception following the deterioration of the empire in the West, and especially after the sacking of Rome at the hands of the Visigoths in the year
410—a conception based on a clear distinction between political history and
the program of salvation. In response to the accusation by pagans that it was
the Christianization of Rome that had led to its political decline and to the
defeats on the battleground, Augustine retorted in his *City of God* that the
plan of salvation was progressing as it should, regardless of the rise and fall
of kingdoms. "Sacred history" is a process focused on safely bringing the
community of the elect to its goal—the kingdom of heaven. This process fully
manifests the divine will, and its final result is assured. The other process is
that of human history. This latter process is subject to the laws of this
world and has no impact whatsoever on the final accounting. The rise and
fall of empires, be they Christian or not, were, according to Augustine,
expressions of the power systems operating in a world that God left to its
own devices to act as it would. In this world, it may happen that evil parties have the upper hand while good parties have the lower. However,
whatever Christian defeats may be suffered in this world will not prevent
Christianity from winning the war; the triumphs of non-Christians do
not indicate anything of God's grace and do not testify to the righteousness of
the church's enemies.

These two historical conceptions continued to coexist in Catholic tradition. When Christians had the upper hand, they turned to Eusebian ideas,
and when they suffered defeats, Augustine was celebrated.

This double Catholic conception of history was also connected to the
church's attitude toward the Jews. Christianity viewed the exile of the Jews
and the destruction of Jerusalem as evidence that the Jewish interpretation
of Scripture was erroneous, for the prophecies of the prophets of Israel had
not come true for "Israel of the flesh." The church attacked Judaism for its
tendency to interpret God's edicts as if they applied in this world, as if the
observance of the practical commandments—rather than heartfelt faith in
God's grace—would promise them salvation. God had become disaffected
with the Jews and expressed his discontent by destroying the temple in Jerusalem and scattering the Jews in their lands of exile, enslaving them to
the seventy nations. Their miserable historical fate was perceived as a proper
punishment for their excessive adherence to the historical world, for their
refusal to accept as their Messiah the one whose kingdom was not of this
world, because he did not live up to their expectations as a worldly king.

The success of Christianity, "Israel of the spirit," was perceived within the polemic with Judaism as a reflection of God's grace and as proof that the church was the chosen people in whom the prophecies were fulfilled. Christianity thus criticized the "Eusebian" messianism of Judaism, or, rather, its carnal adherence to the literal sense of the Old Testament, which identified earthly success with spiritual triumph, while at the same time, it used the same Eusebian perception of history to validate Christian belief against Judaism. Historical events served as witnesses to the truthfulness of a theology that sought to negate history as a site from which one could learn about God's plan. The Christian-Jewish polemic was therefore a polemic about "right" political theology, whereas concrete political transitions were used as witnesses in the theological debate.

The Catholic Church enjoyed tremendous power between the twelfth and sixteenth centuries (until the rift between Catholics and Protestants) and up to the eighteenth century in Catholic countries, until the ideas of the Enlightenment began to undermine the ecclesiastical monopoly on matters of the spirit. Subsequently, the church began to lose its power in the West. The secularization processes that grew strong in the West after World War II forced the church to relearn how to exist in a position of weakness. The shaky status of the church in a multicultural postmodern world gave rise to a deep reflective process in the context of which the church refrained, once more, from identifying historical processes as having messianic significance.

Once the church's historical triumphalism (the idea that the church was leading a firm spiritual war in which it was destined to triumph) was taken off the table, the idea that Jewish inferiority evinced the annulment of the choosing of the Jewish people was also removed. The possibility that the Final Solution might be evidence of God's wrath toward the Jews made intolerable the traditional Christian perception of Jewish suffering as evidence of God's will. The obverse idea, that Jewish suffering indicated a special divine fondness for the Jews, became more plausible, but in the absence of any possibility of actually deciphering the mysteries of history and for fear of making utterances that would be perceived as being in bad taste, the church carefully retreated from such an interpretation. Within a European civilization that had become quite alienated from the politically involved and imperious church that had led it in the past, the Jews were suddenly perceived, in Catholic eyes, as incorporating Augustine's vision of *ecclesia peregrina* in their own flesh; they were pilgrims who had traversed their exile without

identifying themselves with worldly power. The Jews became a source of ec-
clesiastic inspiration for a church that now found itself in "exile," within the
very territory that had once been its home.

The church's hermeneutical project of returning to its rejected Jewish roots
is another aspect of this dramatic turn in the church's perception of history.
The tremendous importance that the church ascribes to its Jewish past raises
the suspicion that it is attempting to identify itself as an intra-Jewish denomination. The warmth with which the church has embraced the idea of Jesus's
and Paul's uncritical Jewishness does not arise solely from the historical logic
of this position, but mainly from the consequent existential position that perceives Judaism and Christianity as two versions, in equally good standing,
of the Jewish past—as two interpretations that have developed organically
from a common soil, without superiority or dispossession. The previous conception of Christianity as a revolutionary religion that had made the old
world utterly obsolete and brought salvation to humanity is now considered
to be an abusive anachronism. Such convictions may also fuel a perception
that secular modernity has made Christianity obsolete, not unlike the logic
of Christian replacement theology.

It seems that the contemporary church not only denies the religious significance of political power as a manifestation of God's love, as Augustine
did, but also finds it difficult to continue insisting that the church itself is
the cause of history. Its eschatological and soteriological concepts have become increasingly diffuse, as has its identity as the bearer of the keys to the
kingdom of heaven. The church no longer threatens anyone with eternal
damnation and rarely speaks of the Last Judgment. Its mission to humanity
is no longer contingent on declaring the Gospel before heathens or on encouraging political forces to conduct crusades for the glory of God, but rather
on good deeds and charity. The church now offers a sense of belonging and
an anchor of identity in this world more than salvation in the next. Even its
claim for exclusivity has become quite porous. It is possible to maintain relations with God without being a member of the church; a person can be
saved as a Christian without being baptized into the church or even being
aware of their Christianity. Even the once adamant claim that the church
was the true Israel has disappeared. The covenant with the Jews is no longer
considered to have been annulled, and Jewish primogeniture is no longer
considered to have been transferred to Christians, so that in some mysterious way, one of the main claims of the Christian project has dissipated.
What is the overall theological meaning of these changes in the Christian
worldview? The church has not specified.

This theological unclarity is not a byproduct of the change that the church is undergoing but rather one of its key elements. The church was not content to merely dampen the thrust of triumphalist doctrines to adjust to the spirit of the times. Rather, it initiated a fundamental change in the very status of doctrine qua doctrine, assimilating the prevalent Western distaste toward any truth claims or purportedly comprehensive theories. Catholic theology fell into disfavor, and the church sought other means to express itself and to communicate with the world.

It was John Paul II who put an end to the theological flourishing that had characterized Vatican II. John Paul II was a man of doctrine who sought to guard the core pillars of tradition from the threats posed by the spirit of the time. Nevertheless, he was deeply responsive to that very spirit and sought to fit church life to the greater context of the twentieth century. He carefully separated doctrine from other realms that, in his eyes, were more appropriate for reform and even for revolution. In this sense, he was not a conservative pope but rather a great innovator. Yet his inventiveness was quite dissimilar to that of Vatican II, and the language in which it was couched was utterly different. John Paul II adopted a pastoral turn of phrase suffused with religious symbolism. He developed an idiom that fostered emotional identification and an atmosphere of openness while intentionally blurring the more glaring contradictions between Catholic tradition and the prevalent lifestyle in the latter half of the twentieth century (it is better to stick a note into the cracks of the Western Wall than to poke around the unpleasant question of whether the Jews can be saved without converting to Christianity). The church under John Paul II changed not only the message itself, as the reformers of Vatican II had attempted to do via meticulous theological study of doctrine, but also the medium; doctrine itself was now perceived as an obstacle to the church's mission in the world.

The incumbency of Pope Francis, which exceeds the bounds of this book, has also been nourished by the consequences of this reform: "The church's pastoral ministry cannot be obsessed with the transmission of a disjointed multitude of doctrines to be imposed insistently," declared Pope Francis in 2013, a few months after his election.[1] As radical as such an utterance may sound from the mouth of a pope, it has actually been quite a long while since the church has been obsessive in matters of doctrine. Notwithstanding the great differences between them, John Paul II and Francis are not opposites but partners in the conviction that even the greatest reforms should be done without resorting to far-reaching theological and doctrinal deliberations.

It seems that only Joseph Cardinal Ratzinger failed to understand this deep shift in church sensibilities. As John Paul II's right hand in his battle with theologians within the liberal camp, Ratzinger aspired to cleanse theology of outside influences, not so that it would become a cultivated yet carefully confined nature preserve, but rather to retain theology as a central instrument in the church's relations with the faithful and with the rest of the world. Ratzinger was obsessed with matters of doctrine; he wished to steer "the small boat of thought," as he called it in his sermon before the college of cardinals that had elected him pope, as it is "carried about by every wind of doctrine" that toss it to and fro on the tempestuous seas of opinion.[2]

Nevertheless, despite his intention to hold onto theology as the eldest daughter of the church, Ratzinger in fact served the general trend initiated by John Paul II, which corresponded with postmodern abhorrence for grand theories and rational schemes—the very trend that was pushing theology to the margins of Catholic life. By the time Ratzinger became Pope Benedict XVI, the church no longer knew what to do with an intellectual at its head. The Catholic public was no longer in need of books on Jesus of Nazareth penned by a German professor but was rather in need of a photogenic presenter, attentive to current trends and having mass appeal; a person who pursued a new ethics that would take the new liberal aspirations into account—compassion for fragile populations, sensitivity to excluded persons and to the environment, an understated and nonjudgmental attitude toward the LGBT community.

Ratzinger, as Pope Benedict XVI, had not been fit to fulfill such a role. His sermons were always overly complex and somewhat impenetrable, and he seemed to be insufficiently cognizant of political correctness, as evidenced by some of his embarrassing remarks, especially an anti-Muhammad quotation from the Byzantine emperor Manuel II, which Benedict saw fit to include in a lecture at the University of Regensburg. He seemed to be out of touch and to ignore the internet as a source of information (as evidenced by his blunder in the matter of the Holocaust denier Richard Williamson). Benedict XVI was considered a distant, highbrow, and dour pope who was more comfortable with books than with people. Even the audacious act of withdrawing from the Holy See did not change the public image of him as a hidebound conservative.

Ratzinger's interventions in the church's discourse on Jews and Judaism, as both cardinal and pope, demonstrated this continuously and powerfully. Yet even after his retirement from the papacy, Benedict XVI was unable to maintain a low profile and burst into Christian-Jewish dialogue with theological reproof. In the summer of 2018, the emeritus pope published an article on Christian-Jewish relations in the theological journal *Communio,* probably at the request of Cardinal Koch (the head of the Commission for Religious Relations with the Jews).

As was his wont, taking cover in the idea of necessary theological clarification, Benedict entered head-on into the most sensitive areas in the Christian-Jewish relationship, polemicizing with both Jews and fellow Catholics at the same time. A number of theological matters, Benedict wrote, had been discussed in a way that he found misleading in a prior document issued by the Commission for Religious Relations with the Jews in 2015 ("The Gifts and the Calling of God Are Irrevocable") on the occasion of *Nostra aetate*'s fiftieth anniversary.[3] These "matters" included such doctrinal conundrums as the claim that "Israel was not replaced by the Church," and "the covenant was never revoked," a statement that, as we have seen, was uttered without further comment by John Paul II in 1980. These claims, Benedict now expounded, "are basically correct, but are in many respects imprecise and must be given further consideration."[4] This was Benedict's polite way to confront John Paul II's equivocal statements about the Jews' theological stature.

After this preamble, Benedict reverted to forming his regular argument, which included a scholarly enumeration of the horizons of Catholic hermeneutics and what lies beyond them (as if he were still leading the Congregation for the Doctrine of the Faith). Little in the article went beyond what Benedict had already asserted in the past, namely that in certain respects, one can still talk of an expiration of the original divine covenant with the Jews, even of replacement. Though "a static view of substitution or nonsubstitution" fails to capture the Christian-Jewish relationship, which is better understood as a "salvation history, which finds its recapitulation in Christ," substitution does take place in certain instances. Temple worship, for example, has been definitively replaced with the sacrifice of God's lamb—that is, Christ—even if this replacement does not entail annulment but is rather framed in terms of transformation and realization.[5]

Moreover, Benedict did not leave the minefield of Christian-Jewish relations after intervening "only" with the volatile concepts of replacement and revocation; he also declared that ascribing any messianic portent to the Jews' return to their land did not accord with Christian theology—a contention that most proponents were very careful not to explicitly state, even if they tended to agree with it.[6] Benedict also brought back to the table the Jewish refusal to acknowledge Christ and the price Jews had to pay for their decision (like all other humans who refuse God's call): "The love of God cannot simply ignore man's no," he wrote. "It wounds God himself and thus necessarily man too."[7] Finally, Benedict encouraged Christians to return to Jesus's conversation with the two Jewish disciples on the way to Emmaus, in which Jesus "reads the Old Testament anew with them," thus showing them the Christological meanings hidden in their scriptures, as a paradigmatic conversation for contemporary Christian-Jewish dialogue.[8]

Even before the article had been translated into English, it had already astounded and stupefied the advocates of Christian-Jewish dialogue, not only because a pope emeritus broke the silence that was expected of him after he had withdrawn from his position, but also because he had (once again) disrupted the balance between Jews and Christians by conducting theological investigations of areas that had been declared better left in silence. The critics could only console themselves with the fact that Benedict was no longer a figure of authority.

Once again, Benedict—the very symbol of theology—appeared as a threat to Christian-Jewish reconciliation, an obsolete traditionalist, even an antisemite. Even though Benedict's article mostly reiterated his past positions (and is full of references to his previous works), the bare fact of the pope emeritus's theological interference in the discourse was perceived as offensive, as a move that sowed confusion and fostered tensions rather than restoring order, as Benedict probably hoped it would. It seemed then that the former pope had refused to accommodate the fact that Christian-Jewish reconciliation had organized itself around an intentional theological ambiguity. Even after he had admitted his limitation and released the reins, it was the relationship between Jews and Christians that tempted him to reopen old wounds.

It is possible that if Jews had been more enthusiastic about Christian-Jewish dialogue, the church might have chosen to deepen its theological disputations rather than avoid them, as it ultimately did. However, it was very clear that the Jewish world was largely uninterested in theological discourse with Christians, both because it found it unimportant and because it resisted such discourse as a matter of principle, as expressed by Rabbi Joseph Soloveitchik in his article "Confrontation."

Nevertheless, even though the reluctance of large portions of the Jewish world to engage in any significant intellectual effort to rehabilitate their relations with the church may have played a part in the diminution of the theological space that the church accorded to the Catholic discussion of Judaism, it is certainly not the only factor impacting this process. No less significant was the sense that gradually spread throughout the church that theology qua theology had become oppressive and antiquated. Rather, Kosher meals at the Vatican, friendly chats, and shared photo-ops came into favor as the way to build a common culture and to convey messages of friendship in a far more efficient manner. Ceremony, symbolic gesture, custom, and practice are now perceived as far more important than any reiterated unequivocal proclamation of doctrinal principles. In this regard, it is certainly possible that the spirit of Schillebeeckx was ultimately accepted by the Catholic world, notwithstanding the ire of the Congregation for the Doctrine of the Faith. The church has been shedding its Greek tradition in favor of a more "Jewish" language (as imagined by the church), a language of action, legend, and gesture that prefers ad hoc solutions to concrete conflicts over a burdensome sack full of principles.

Just as the church has backtracked and reinvented itself as the imagined Jewish community that it had left behind, Orthodox Jews, too, are bent on restoration; but their restoration is very different from the Catholic one, and rather than melancholic self-doubt, it is full of renewed energy and confidence. Throughout history, Jews have experienced themselves as a persecuted minority willing to sacrifice themselves to sanctify the name of heaven. To the extent that they identified with any political regime, they did so only in a very limited sense. Just as in Christianity, within the Jewish tradition, too, there were different conceptions of messianic times, which coexisted in parallel, some more historical and political and some less so. However, a central stream of Jewish thought identified the future release from exile, the return to the Land of Israel, and the building of the Third Temple—clearly historical and political events—with the vision of salvation. The Jews continued to expect the coming of the day when God would bring them historical salvation (and often received ridicule for this expectation from their Christian hosts, and subsequently their secular hosts as well). Because of their insistence on a future earthly salvation, the Jews were forced to contend theologically with the Christian claim regarding the realization of Hebrew prophecies in Christians rather than in Jews. At least on the surface, history appeared to be against them. The main theological thrust of the Jews was invested in justifying their exile in Christian lands. Their plight as a persecuted and derided minority was conceived as part of their unique relationship with God, a relationship in which the punishment (the state of Jews in the world) expressed God's unique interest rather than his forsaking. Christians (and to a lesser extent Muslims) were considered to be the tool used by God to punish the chosen people. However, the inferior status of the Jews, prolonged and painful as it may have been, was only temporary, a necessary intensifier for the final triumph of Judaism, which, when the time came, would turn the tables: the kingdom of Edom (Christendom) would collapse, and the kingdom of Judea would be rebuilt on its ruins, this time in full synchronization between the will of God and the twists and turns of history.

In the second half of the twentieth century, Jews found themselves suddenly not only as wielders of political power but also as the lords of the Holy Land. In many respects, the challenge that the founding of the State of Israel has presented to Judaism is similar to that presented to Christianity by the Christianization of the Roman Empire: it is a revolution that demands that Judaism reestablish its relationship with history, politics, and the Other. It demands that spiritual leaders return to the Jewish sources and reinterpret them according to the changing conditions. Every group in the Jewish world (not only in Israel) faces this challenge in its own way: by partially or fully rejecting temporal power, by secularizing it, or by vesting it with theological meaning.

The establishment of a sovereign Jewish state in the Land of Israel in the twentieth century does not realize all of the traditional eschatological expectations of the Jews. It is, however, closer to the realization of such expectations than at any other stage in history (at least since the Bar Kokhba revolt). The partial similarity between eschatological-historical visions embedded in the Jewish tradition and contemporary Jewish reality evokes a drive to provide explanations and interpretations.

Because of their historical importance, the relations between Israel and the church have also been reinterpreted. Since in the preceding centuries most Jews lived in Christian countries, it was Christianity that signified the ultimate Other for them, an Other that not only differed from them but also constituted the direct cause of their suffering and humiliation. The harsh tribulations of exile are strongly associated in Jewish consciousness with the church. The fact that the church has lost its political assets in the world (and to a certain extent has also lost its power as a foundation of Western civilization) while Jews have gained political power has given rise to theological questions—and halakhic questions as well—regarding the proper relations between the former master and the former slave.

As we have seen, Christianity often serves as a hermeneutical tool in the hands of Orthodox rabbis to shape their perceptions of the current historical moment—to evaluate the pros and cons of secularization, to measure the extent of Jewish sovereignty, to fathom what it means to no longer be a persecuted and exiled minority, and to contextualize the twentieth-century rollercoaster within the Jewish take on the history of salvation. The extensive debates on Christian-Jewish theological dialogue, on the churches in Old Jerusalem, or on entering churches for the reason of fear of enmity are part and parcel of the awesome deliberation on how to adapt Jewish history and tradition to the unprecedented upheavals of the times.

In many cases, Jewish independence and political empowerment have entailed a retreat from expressions of tolerance toward Christianity that had once been quite common in European rabbinical literature of the modern era, as they are now construed as mere products of Christian oppression. Because the toleration of Christian otherness was imprinted within Jewish consciousness as intertwined with Jewish inferiority, and often with Christian oppression, the resolution of this oppression and inferiority has also involved a retreat from toleration, which seems to have lost its justification. The end of Christian pressure has released an old and deep resentment against Christianity, which was forcibly suppressed by various means throughout the centuries. The formerly oppressed often use the very weapons of the former oppressor against that oppressor, revealing a conflictual subjectivity that understands its own freedom as a mirror image of the oppressor.

Nevertheless, Orthodox Jews are conscious of the contradictory trajectories of history, and they are not indifferent to the demands laid on them to amend terms with Christianity, demands generated by the threat of secularization, new types of antisemitism, tension with Islam, and the general requirements and obligations of sovereignty and citizenship within liberal and post-liberal orders. Those streams of Orthodoxy that are overtly open to modernity especially acknowledge the new covenant between Jews and Christians as the edict of the hour. Yet even among these circles, the charged history of Christian-Jewish relations, which is imprinted in large swaths of the Jewish tradition, stirs far-reaching controversies. If in ultra-Orthodox and religious Zionist circles Christianity is often all but a hermeneutical category through which to debate the meaning and extent of Jewish power and sovereignty, or the place of the recent political upheavals in the history of salvation, in Modern Orthodox circles, the dialogue with actual Christians provides an impetus to reposition the Jewish tradition vis-à-vis history—to define the specific historical challenges of the time, to determine whether historical change of such gravity as Christian-Jewish rapprochement is at all possible, and to decide if and to what extent historical change should be a factor in how Modern Orthodox Jews approach and observe their tradition.

The heated debate over how Jews should position themselves vis-à-vis a friendly Christian community—which was, until recently, often perceived in Orthodox Jewish consciousness as a *contradictio in adiecto*—is glaringly apparent in a tension between two recent Orthodox statements on Christianity, both written on the jubilee of *Nostra aetate*. The first statement, titled "To Do the Will of Our Father in Heaven: Toward a Partnership between Jews and Christians," was released at the end of 2015 by some of the veteran fighters in the interfaith dialogue trenches (some of the more prominent among them, such as Shlomo Riskin, Eugene Korn, Irving Greenberg, and David Rosen are discussed in Chapter 8) under the umbrella of the Center for Jewish-Christian Understanding and Cooperation (founded by Rabbi Riskin). The authors of this declaration attempted to breathe life into some of the now spurned pro-Christian rabbinic sources of the modern age, quoting such luminaries as Jacob Emden, Samson Raphael Hirsch, Naftali Zvi Berliner, Moses Rivkes, and even the more positive reflections of Maimonides, to retrieve a positive attitude to Christianity from established Jewish traditions.

In opposition to the mainstream Orthodox attitude to Christian-Jewish dialogue, the statement makes strong theological arguments. Christianity, it argues, is willed by God, who "employs many messengers to reveal His truth." Accepting the extended hand of Christians is indeed "the will of Our Father in Heaven." Christianity, therefore, is "neither an accident nor an error, but the willed divine outcome and gift to the nations"; as "Christians are congregations that work for the sake of heaven who are destined to endure, whose intent is for the sake of heaven and whose reward will not be denied." The statement evokes the prevalent modern distinction between contemporaneous Christians and ancient idolaters, quoting Rivkes that "the Sages made reference only to the idolater of their day who did not believe in the creation of the world, the Exodus, G-d's miraculous deeds and the divinely given law. In contrast, the people among whom we are scattered believe in all these essentials of religion."

Most distinctly, the statement defines Christianity as a covenantal partner (Greenberg's imprint is strongly felt here), as "both Jews and Christians have a common covenantal mission to perfect the world under the sovereignty of the Almighty." Thus, striving to seize the historic opportunity that is laid before them, the authors of the statement call their community "to over-come . . . fears in order to establish a relationship of trust and respect" with the Christian community.

This bold statement, however, was written by a small group of Modern Orthodox rabbis who represent only the extreme liberal approach to the question at hand, an approach that is highly debated even among the rela-tively open Modern Orthodox circles, not to mention other parts of the Orthodox (and ultra-Orthodox) community. It is therefore not surprising that major rabbinical authorities of the Orthodox world would not allow a handful of dialogue-favoring rabbis to have the last word on this sub-ject. Thus it happened that after many decades of complete disregard on the part of the Orthodox community, a second rabbinical statement on Chris-tianity abruptly appeared within a short time after the release of "To Do the Will of Our Father in Heaven." This latter statement, titled "Between Jeru-salem and Rome," was signed by three prominent Orthodox organizations: the Chief Rabbinate of Israel, the Conference of European Rabbis, and the Rabbinical Council of America.[9] Like the former statement, this one, too, expressed a positive attitude toward the reconciliatory tone adopted by the church and recognized the importance of the friendship that has devel-oped between Christians and Jews since *Nostra aetate*: "We applaud the work of popes, church leaders, and scholars who passionately contributed to these developments, including the strong-willed proponents of Catholic-Jewish dialogue at the end of World War II, whose collective work was a leading impetus for *Nostra aetate*." It, too, attends to the Orthodox hesita-tion around the process of reconciliation, stating that while "initially, many Jewish leaders were skeptical of the sincerity of the Church's overtures to the Jewish community, due to the long history of Christian anti-Judaism," "over time, it has become clear that the transformations in the Church's attitudes and teachings are not only sincere but also increasingly profound, and that we are entering an era of growing tolerance, mutual respect, and solidarity between members of our respective faiths."

However, contrary to the first statement, which is saturated with the spirit of Soloveitchik's liberal disciples, this second statement is filled with the spirit of their conservative critics, who are less amenable to celebrating Christianity as a "covenantal" partner in the world's salvation, or even to unequivocally endow it with the status of a fellow monotheist faith:

> The core beliefs of Christianity that center on the person of "Jesus as the Messiah" and the embodiment of the "second person of a triune God" create an irreconcilable separation from Judaism. The history of Jewish martyrdom in Christian Europe serves as tragic testimony to the devotion and tenacity with which Jews resisted beliefs incompatible with their ancient and eternal faith, which requires absolute fidelity to both the Written and Oral Torah.

Hinting at the principle of *shittuf,* the statement declares:

> Despite those profound differences, some of Judaism's highest authorities have asserted that Christians maintain a special status because they worship the Creator of Heaven and Earth Who liberated the people of Israel from Egyptian bondage and Who exercises providence over all creation.

The focal point of this second rabbinical statement, which carried far greater authority within the Orthodox world, was the veteran Soloveitchikean contention that the doctrinal disagreements between Judaism and Christianity were incommensurable and that it was therefore pointless to discuss them. The statement includes a positive mention of the representatives of the Chief Rabbinate of Israel who had been involved in a dialogue with the Vatican and had made a conscious effort to "carefully avoid matters pertaining to fundamentals of faith," out of respect for "the differences between the two religious traditions." The authors, however, were not content with this acknowledgment, and they added, "We, both Catholics and Jews, acknowledge that this fraternity cannot sweep away our doctrinal differences." "The theological differences between Judaism and Christianity," they reiterated, "are profound." Reconciliation and dialogue are possible, they wrote, "despite those profound differences," adding that "the doctrinal differences are essential and cannot be debated or negotiated; their meaning and importance belong to the internal deliberations of the respective faith communities. Judaism . . . will forever remain loyal to its principles, laws and eternal teachings." Moreover, "doctrinal differences and our inability to truly understand the meaning and mysteries of each other's faiths do not and may not stand in the way of our peaceful collaboration for the betterment of our shared world and the lives of the children of Noah." The proliferation of these expressions of acquiescence continues throughout the declaration. Nevertheless, and again in Soloveitchik's spirit, the statement identifies the joint challenges of radical secularism and radical Islam as justifying a Christian-Jewish cooperation.

Why did the authors of the second statement place such emphasis on the doctrinal differences between Christianity and Judaism? Reading the two declarations side by side evokes the feeling that the more tolerant sources of the modern era, which are frequently quoted throughout the first rabbinical statement, are perceived by the authors of the second statement as masking "profound theological differences" and perhaps succumbing to theological compromises, so that the three rabbinical councils chose to reject them. In other words, while both statements stand as conciliatory gestures toward the Catholic Church, their differences in many ways form the poles of internal Modern Orthodox debate on the appropriate attitude to Christian-Jewish dialogue.

Is the latter statement, which emphasizes the deep doctrinal rift between the two religions, more faithful to the spirit of Jewish tradition than the former? Are the authors of the second rabbinical statement right in perceiving the first statement's *ressourcement* to the positive evaluations of previous generations as adapting eternal truth claims to the vicissitudes of the times, and particularly to the demands of the Christian majority? Are their rejection of the modern "positive" sources and their opposition to theological dialogue with Christians not in themselves a consequence of changing political circumstances, in particular to the increasing power of Israel's hand, just as the grip of the Catholic Church grows softer? In fact, the Orthodox ability to stand firm in determining the borders of Christian-Jewish dialogue not only for Jews but also for Christians is in itself an innovation, unprecedented in the history of Christian-Jewish encounters.

Yet even the second statement, though signed by these three representative Orthodox institutions, does not capture the entire scope of contemporary Orthodox attitudes to Christianity. Out of a sense that the necessity to tread cautiously around Christian might has lessened or even disappeared, many rabbis and Torah scholars revert to the anti-Christian exegesis found in traditional texts and even to anti-Christian sources that had been excluded from written discourse for hundreds of years (and, as I have shown here, when

one deviates from the toned-down discourse of Modern Orthodoxy, one encounters fiercer manifestations of this tendency). This literary activity
clearly testifies to a prevalent feeling among Orthodox Jewish scholars that
the present age allows Judaism free and independent expression, which had
not been possible for hundreds of years, including the most aggressive and
offensive aspects of its tradition.

Just as the church is searching its past for sources of inspiration for a
peaceful life alongside others, sources that will help it rehabilitate its image
after serving as a party that aided and abetted Western imperialism and inspired Western oppression, Orthodox Judaism wishes to rid itself of the
sanctification of weakness that characterized it during the preceding two
thousand years. It has now harnessed itself to the impossible project of
cleansing from its sources all traces of relations with Christianity in a search
for a pure and primordial form of Judaism that is not subsumed within the
world of the Other, as it has been for such a long time. Judaism now seeks
to establish a different past for itself, an appropriate past, a past that would
have transpired had not Christianity "set pitfalls in the order of history and
in the progress and development of the human spirit," to use Zvi Yehudah
Kook's phrase.[10] Many Orthodox Jews reject the hand extended to them by
Christians, refuse to amend their own hostility toward Christianity, and even
retreat, from time to time, to those volatile anti-Christian Talmudic traditions that insulted the Christians so much that they were used to justify hatred of Judaism and violence toward Jews throughout history. In this new
process of Jewish emancipation, the old resentments against Christianity are
released. Paradoxically, these very same resentments not infrequently bear
a reverse semblance to classical Christian anti-Judaism, internalized into
Jewish subjectivity and reactivated against the Christians—not regardless of,
but precisely *because* of the Christians' extended hand.

Looking at these two stories—of Catholics and Orthodox Jews—together
shows how familiar this tension between the Christian extended hand and
the Jewish refusal to accept it actually is; once again, Jews are invited to a
"great supper," to use Luke's words (14:15–25), and they decline, with varying
degrees of politeness. This is the same fundamental structure in which the
Jews are seen as stubbornly adhering to the past, refusing to accept the edict
of the hour, refusing to go in the direction in which Western civilization is
marching. Each party is persistent in its traditional role, this time within the
context of the post–World War II liberal vision of interfaith reconciliation.

This dynamic of a Christian embrace met by a Jewish pushback, however, hardly implies a stagnation of Judaism or of Christianity or the adherence of either one to the past. Each of the religious communities depicted in this book is updating its tradition and extracting new principles from its sources that befit its reading of the signs of the times. The body of both traditions is constantly moving and transforming, working itself out within the changing cultural and political context of our time. Today, too, Jews and Christians serve as symbols for each other, perhaps more than as flesh and blood counterparts. While Catholic officials befriend the Jews to reestablish the church's position within a secularized Western civilization, Orthodox rabbis distance themselves from Christianity to achieve the same goals. Jewish diaspora and political inferiority serve Catholics as inspiration for their post-sovereign, diasporic state in the West, just as Christian weakness serves as a mirror for Jewish self-sovereignty, its image assisting Orthodox Jews in establishing their independence and practicing their new liberties in the same liberal global context.

Thus, reconciliation cannot be seen only as a break from tradition; it finds its language within tradition, and as a result, it has to take into account the entire body of contradictory perceptions, of ebbs and flows that have characterized it through the ages. In fact, the very thought of an age of reconciliation that brings an end to the old relationship, with all its problems, is in itself supersessionst, suffused with anti-Jewish elements. Perhaps, notwithstanding the deepening friendship between Christian and Jewish communities, a reconciliation with the inherent tensions between the Jewish and the Christian traditions is also in place.

Notes

Introduction

1. Pope Paul VI, "Declaration on the Relation of the Church to Non-Christian Religions (Nostra Aetate) (October 28, 1965)," Vatican, http://www.vatican.va/archive/hist_councils/ii_vatican_council/documents/vat-ii_decl_19651028_nostra-aetate_en.html.

2. Susannah Heschel, *The Aryan Jesus: Christian Theologians and the Bible in Nazi Germany* (Princeton, NJ: Princeton University Press, 2008), 27; Heschel, "Revolt of the Colonized: Abraham Geiger's *Wissenschaft des Judentums* as a Challenge to Christian Hegemony in the Academy," *New German Critique* 77, no. 2 (1999), 61–62.

3. See Jean-Paul Sartre's introduction to Frantz Fanon, *The Wretched of the Earth,* trans. Richard Philcox (New York: Grove, 2004).

Chapter 1: Historical and Theological Transitions

1. The literature dealing with the Jewishness of Jesus is vast. Some of the more prominent studies include the groundbreaking books of Geza Vermes (*Jesus the Jew: A Historian's Reading of the Gospels* [London: Collins, 1973]) and E. P. Sanders (*Jesus and Judaism* [Philadelphia: Fortress Press, 1985], as well as Sanders's other works). For newer studies, see Amy-Jill Levine, *The Misunderstood Jew: The Church and the Scandal of the Jewish Jesus* (New York: HarperCollins, 2006); Daniel Boyarin, *The Jewish Gospels: The Story of the Jewish Christ* (New York: New Press, 2012); Peter Schäfer, *The Jewish Jesus: How Judaism and Christianity Shaped Each Other* (Princeton, NJ: Princeton University Press, 2012); Paula Fredriksen, *When Christians Were Jews: The First Generation* (New Haven, CT: Yale University Press, 2018). On the "Jewishness" of the New Testament as a

whole, see Marc Zvi Brettler and Amy-Jill Levine, eds., *The New Jewish Annotated New Testament: New Revised Standard Version* (Oxford: Oxford University Press, 2011).

2. See in particular Krister Stendahl, "The Apostle Paul and the Introspective Conscience of the West," *Harvard Theological Review* 56, no. 3 (1963): 199–215, as well as his *Paul among Jews and Gentiles, and Other Essays* (Philadelphia: Fortress Press, 1976). See also the works of E. P. Sanders, Lloyd Gaston, James D. G. Dunn, Haikki Räisänen, and John G. Gager. The study on Paul and Judaism continues to evolve with work by Paula Fredriksen, Pamela Eisenbaum, Mark Nanos, Kathy Ehrensberger, and Bill Campbell, among others.

3. See, for example, the various articles collected in Adam H. Becker and Annette Yoshiko Reed, eds., *The Ways That Never Parted: Jews and Christians in Late Antiquity and the Early Middle Ages* (Tübingen: Mohr Siebeck, 2003).

4. On the scholarly freedom that was enabled by Vatican II and the process of rapprochement between Judaism and Christianity, see Israel Jacob Yuval, *Two Nations in Your Womb: Perceptions of Jews and Christians in Late Antiquity and the Middle Ages,* trans. Barbara Harshav and Jonathan Chipman (Berkeley: University of California Press, 2006), 21.

5. John G. Gager, *The Origins of Anti-Semitism: Attitudes toward Judaism in Pagan and Christian Antiquity* (Oxford: Oxford University Press, 1985), 10.

6. Stendahl, "The Apostle Paul." See also John Gager, *Reinventing Paul* (Oxford: Oxford University Press, 2000), 42–74.

7. See, for example, Menahem Kister's illuminating article that sees Paul's opposition between grace and works as a clear innovation to what one finds in previous rabbinic literature: "Deeds, Reward, and Divine Mercy: Jewish Views and Pauline Passages," *Journal for the Study of Judaism* 52 (2021): 1–44. On Paul as the inventor of the goy (gentile) / Jew division, see Adi Ophir and Ishay Rosen-Zvi, *Goy: Israel's Multiple Others and the Birth of the Gentile* (Oxford: Oxford University Press), 140–178.

8. On Marcion's perception of Paul, see John W. Marshall, "Misunderstanding the New Paul: Marcion's Transformation of the *Sonderzeit* Paul," *Journal of Early Christian Studies* 20, no. 1 (2012): 1–29.

9. See Heinz Schreckenberg, *Die christlichen Adversus-Judaeos-Texte und ihr literarisches und historisches Umfeld (1–11 Jh)* (Frankfurt a.M.: Peter Lang, 1982).

10. Becker and Reed, *The Ways That Never Parted,* 1–16.

11. Daniel Boyarin, *Border Lines: The Partition of Judaeo-Christianity* (Philadelphia: University of Pennsylvania Press, 2007).

12. See, for example, Paula Fredriksen, "What 'Parting of the Ways'? Jews, Gentiles, and the Ancient Mediterranean City," in Becker and Reed, *The Ways That Never Parted,* 61–63; Daniel Boyarin, "Semantic Differences; or, 'Judaism' / 'Christianity,'" in Becker and Reed, *The Ways That Never Parted,* 65–85.

13. Paula Fredriksen, *Augustine and the Jews: A Christian Defence of Jews and Judaism* (New York: Doubleday, 2008). On the applications of the Augustinian paradigm on me-

dieval Christianity's attitude to Jews and Judaism, see Jeremy Cohen, *Living Letters of the Law: Ideas of the Jew in Medieval Christianity* (Berkeley: University of California Press, 1999), 67–145.

14. Cohen criticized Frederiksen for overly stressing the positive side of Augustine's account of Jews and Judaism and emphasized the darker side of Augustine's approach as well as its historical consequences: "Review Article: Revisiting Augustine's Doctrine of Jewish Witness," *Journal of Religion* 89, no. 4 (2009), 77–78. See Augustinus, *De Civitate Dei* 18:4; Cohen, *Living Letters,* 22–31; Fredriksen, *Augustine and the Jews,* 304–52.

15. On Gregory the Great's attitude to the Jews, see Cohen, *Living Letters,* 73–94; Anna Abulafia, *Christian-Jewish Relations 1000–1300: Jews in the Service of Medieval Christendom* (London: Routledge, 2014), 19–33.

16. See Robert Moore's controversial book *The Formation of a Persecuting Society: Authority and Deviance in Western Europe 950–1250* (Oxford: Blackwell, 1987).

17. See Jeremy Cohen, *The Friars and the Jews: The Evolution of Medieval Anti-Judaism* (Ithaca, NY: Cornell University Press, 1986), 51–76.

18. Abulafia, *Jewish-Christian Relations,* 210–212.

19. Cohen, *Christ Killers: The Jews and the Passion from the Bible to the Big Screen* (Oxford: Oxford University Press, 2007), 125–135.

20. Cohen, *Christ Killers,* 93–112.

21. On the vagueness of this decision, see John Tolan, "The First Imposition of a Badge on European Jews: The English Royal Mandate of 1218," in *The Character of Christian-Muslim Encounter: Essays in Honour of David Thomas,* ed. Douglas Pratt et al. (Leiden: Brill, 2015), 145–166.

22. David Nirenberg, *Communities of Violence: Persecution of Minorities in the Middle Ages* (Princeton, NJ: Princeton University Press, 1996), 53.

23. Norman Roth, *Conversos, Inquisition and the Expulsion of the Jews from Spain* (Madison: University of Wisconsin Press, 1995), 34.

24. David Nirenberg, "Conversion, Sex, and Segregation: Jews and Christians in Medieval Spain," *American Historical Review* 107, no. (2002): 1072–1078.

25. Michael Alpert, *Crypto-Judaism and the Spanish Inquisition* (New York: Palgrave, 2001), 11–13 .

26. My use of *doctrine* draws on Jaroslav Pelikan's broad definition of what is believed, taught, and confessed in the church rather than the limited meaning of content authoritatively and officially articulated by the magisterium. See Pelikan, *The Christian Tradition: A History of the Development of Doctrine,* vol. 1: *The Emergence of the Catholic Tradition (100–600)* (Chicago: University of Chicago Press, 1971), 3–7.

27. Elisheva Carlebach, *Divided Souls: Converts from Judaism in Germany, 1500–1750* (New Haven, CT: Yale University Press, 2001), 33.

28. On Luther, see Thomas Kaufmann, *Luther's Jews: A Journey into Anti-Semitism,* trans. Jeremy Noakes and Lesley Sharpe (Oxford: Oxford University Press, 2017). On the

Reformation and antisemitism, see David Nirenberg, *Anti-Judaism: The Western Tradition* (New York: Norton, 2013), chap. 7.

29. Stephen G. Burnett, *Christian Hebraism in the Reformation Era (1500–1660): Authors, Books, and the Transmission of Jewish Learning* (Leiden: Brill, 2012), 271–278.

30. John W. O'Malley, *Vatican I: The Council and the Making of the Ultramontane Church* (Cambridge, MA: Belknap Press of Harvard University Press, 2018).

31. Pius IX, "Dogmatic Constitution Pastor Aeternus (18 July 1870)," Vatican, http://www.vatican.va/content/pius-ix/la/documents/constitutio-dogmatica-pastor -aeternus-18-iulii-1870.html.

32. John W. O'Malley, *What Happened at Vatican II* (Cambridge, MA: Harvard University Press, 2008), 63–64.

33. See the encyclical of Pius X, *Pascendi dominici gregis,* in *Enchiridion symbolorum definitionum et declarationem de rebus fidei et morum,* ed. Heinrich Denzinger, Editio XLV (Freiburg: Herder, 2017), 871–886.

34. See the manifesto produced by the French theologian Jean Daniélou, one of the founders of *La nouvelle théologie* (who pioneered post-Holocaust Christian-Jewish dialogue): Jean Daniélou, "Les orientations présentes de la pensée religieuse," *Études* 249 (1946): 5–21.

35. The most prominent figures within the *nouvelle théologie* school were Jean Daniélou, Yves Congar, Karl Rahner, Henri de Lubac, Marie-Dominique Chenu, Pierre Teilhard de Chardin, Hans Küng, Hans Urs von Balthasar, Edward Schillebeeckx, and Joseph Ratzinger.

36. I do not enter here into the controversy of whether the council had intended to update the church's message or merely its medium, that is, whether it was more concerned with self-reflection and inner reform than with refining its relationship to the external world. For this debate, see Gavin D'Costa, *Vatican II Catholic Doctrines on Jews and Muslims* (Oxford: Oxford University Press, 2014), 10–58; O'Malley, *What Happened at Vatican II;* Peter Hünermann, Alberto Melloni, and Giuseppe Ruggieri, eds., *Chi ha paura del Vaticano II?* (Roma: Carocci, 2009).

37. David Kertzer, *The Popes against the Jews: The Vatican's Role in the Rise of Modern Anti-Semitism* (New York: Knopf, 2011), 86–105, 152–165.

38. The literature commonly distinguishes between the traditional anti-Judaism prevalent in the premodern Christian world and based on religious hatred, and the modern and often racial hatred called antisemitism that is more characteristic of secular, modern society. The latter is considered more deterministic. Despite some controversy, most researchers accept that distinction, which is also the official position of the Catholic Church. It is criticized, however, by such historians as David Kertzer and Alberto Melloni, who argue that the church insists on this artificial distinction to avoid responsibility for the Holocaust. See Kertzer, *The Popes,* 7; Melloni, "'Noi ricordiamo': Aspects et problèmes d'un document du Vatican sur la Shoah," *Recherches de Science Religieuse* 87, no. 1 (1999): 59–68. Another critic, John Connelly, argues that historically, there has

never been such a clear-cut distinction in Catholics' minds between their religious and racial hostility toward Jews. See Connelly, *From Enemy to Brother: The Revolution in Catholic Teaching on the Jews, 1933–1965* (Cambridge, MA: Harvard University Press, 2012), 6. The church's position is laid out in the highly controversial 1998 publication "We Remember: A Reflection on the Shoah" (further discussed in Chapter 3). Fr. Giovanni Sala defended the church's stand on antisemitism in "Antigiudaismo o antisemitismo? Le accuse contro la Chiesa e la 'Civiltà Cattolica,'" *Civiltà Cattolica* 3647 (2002): 419–431.

39. Connelly, *From Enemy to Brother*, 174–175.

40. Connelly, *From Enemy to Brother*, 97.

41. Oesterreicher subsequently served as an expert advisor of Cardinal Augustin Bea in formulating the Second Vatican Council's "Declaration on the Relationship of the Church to Non-Christian Religions."

42. Connelly, *From Enemy to Brother*, 174–209.

43. The most prominent example was Pius XII's Christmas Message in 1942. See John Cornwell, *Hitler's Pope: The Secret History of Pius XII* (New York: Penguin, 2000), 291–293.

44. Grazia Loparco, "L'assistenza prestata dalle religiose di Roma agli ebrei durante la seconda guerra Mondiale," *Le donne nella Chiesa e in Italia*, ed. Luigi Mezzadri and Maurizio Tagliaferri (Cinisello Balsamo: San Paolo, 2007), 245–285.

45. See Jane Clements, "Reading New Testament Texts," in *The Holocaust and the Christian World: Reflections on the Past, Challenges for the Future*, ed. Carol Rittner, Stephen D. Smith, and Irena Steinfeldt (London: Beth Shalom Holocaust Memorial Centre and Yad Vashem International School for Holocaust Studies, 2000), 214–216.

46. The first to attribute the now-famous "silence" to the pope was playwright Rolf Hochhut in the controversial 1963 play *Der Stellvertreter: Ein christliches Trauerspiel* (*The Deputy*, trans. Richard and Clara Winston [Baltimore: Johns Hopkins University Press, 1997]). In the research literature, historian Saul Friedländer discussed Pius XII's half-hearted response to the Holocaust as early as in 1964: Friedländer, *Pie XII et le IIIe Reich; documents* (Paris: Seuil, 1964). On the theological reasons for Pius XII's "silence," see Gershon Greenberg, "Crucifixion and Holocaust: The Views of Pope Pius XII and the Jews," in *Pope Pius XII and the Holocaust*, ed. Carol Rittner and Joseph K. Roth (London: Bloomsbury, 2002), 137–153. For a positive evaluation of Pius's activity for the Jews at the time of the Holocaust, see David G. Dallin, *The Myth of Hitler's Pope: How Pope Pius XII Rescued Jews from the Nazis* (Washington, DC: Regnery, 2005). It should be noted that according to Mark Riebling, Pius was involved in plotting the assassination of Hitler; *Church of Spies: The Pope's Secret War against Hitler* (San Francisco: Ignatius, 2016).

47. See Jacques Maritain, "Le mystère d'Israël," in *Le mystère d'Israël et autres essais* (Paris: Desclée, De Brouwer, 1965), 19–62. See also Thérèse-Martine Andrevon, "Le mystère d'Israël dans l'œuvre de Jacques Maritain," *Recherches de science religieuse* 101, no. 2 (2013), 211–231.

48. "So that you may not claim to be wiser than you are, brothers and sisters, I want you to understand this mystery: a hardening has come upon part of Israel, until the full number of the Gentiles has come in" (Rom. 11:25).

49. Connelly, *From Enemy to Brother*, 182.

50. See Norman Tobias, *Jewish Conscience of the Church: Jules Isaac and the Second Vatican Council* (Cham: Palgrave Macmillan, 2017).

51. Connelly, *From Enemy to Brother*, 240.

52. Connelly, *From Enemy to Brother*, 5.

53. Isaac published a book with this title in 1962: *L'enseignement du mépris: vérité historique et mythes* (Paris: Fasquelle, [1962]) (published in English as *The Teaching of Contempt: Christian Roots of Anti-Semitism*, trans. Helen Weaver [New York: Holt, Rinehart and Winston, 1964]). He had tried to persuade Pius XII to revise the doctrine, but the pope showed little willingness to do so. Isaac's contacts with John XXIII proved more fruitful. Tobias, *Jewish Conscience*, 163–182, 185–186.

54. Alberto Melloni, *Fra Istanbul, atene e la guerra. La missione di A. G. Roncalli (1935–1944)* (Genoa: Marietti, 1992). For Roncalli's efforts to save Jews while in Turkey, see Dina Porat, "A Triangle of Time, War and Holocaust," in *Roncalli and the Jews during the Holocaust: Concern and Efforts to Help*, ed. Dina Porat and David Bankier, vol. 20, *Search and Research: Lectures and Papers* (Jerusalem: International Institute for Holocaust Research, 2014), 11–32 (Hebrew).

55. On the various historical versions of this prayer, see Hubert Wolf, *Pope and Devil: The Vatican's Archives and the Third Reich*, trans. Kenneth Kronenberg (Cambridge, MA: Belknap Press of Harvard University Press, 2010), 81–125.

56. Alberto Melloni, "The Generation of 'Nostra Aetate,'" in *In Our Times: Documents and Studies about the Catholic Church and the Jews in the Shadow and Aftermath of the Holocaust*, ed. Dina Porat, Karma Ben Johanan, and Ruth Braudee (Tel Aviv: University of Tel Aviv Press, 2016), 252–268 (Hebrew).

57. During Pius XII's term in office, the Vatican banned one of Congar's most important books, *Vraie et fausse réforme dans l'église* (Paris: Cerf, 1950), arguing that reforms had played an essential role in church history, and forbade him to teach and publish. John XXIII, however, invited him to take part in the preparatory discussions in 1960. The diary Congar wrote during the council is a detailed documentation of the processes undergone by the church during those critical years; see Yves Congar, *Mon journal du concile* (Paris: Cerf, 2002).

58. D'Costa, *Vatican II*, 128.

59. Connelly, *From Enemy to Brother*, 242.

60. There is a clear tension between the strong hold of the deicide charge within the Catholic tradition and the idea that the guilt for the crucifixion is spread over the entire human race. This latter perception is expressed in the Tridentine Catechism; see the English translation by John A. McHugh and Charles J. Callan (1923) at http://www.angelfire.com/art/cactussong/TridentineCatechism.htm.

61. Connelly, *From Enemy to Brother,* 247. Connelly (p. 269) argues that even after *Nostra aetate* was published, both Bea and Paul VI made comments in line with the deicide charge.

62. Giovanni Miccoli, "Two Sensitive Issues: Religious Freedom and the Jews," in *History of Vatican II: Church as Communion: Third Period and Intersession, September 1964–September 1965,* ed. Giuseppe Albergio and Joseph A. Komonchak, vol. 4 (Maryknoll, NY: Orbis / Leuven: Peeters, 2003), 152.

63. Connelly, *From Enemy to Brother,* 250.

64. Giovanni Miccoli, "Two Sensitive Issues," 152.

65. *Nostra aetate,* Article 4, Vatican, https://www.vatican.va/archive/hist_councils/ii _vatican_council/documents/vat-ii_decl_19651028_nostra-aetate_en.html.

66. D'Costa, *Vatican II,* 133–134.

67. *Nostra aetate,* Article 4.

68. Connelly, *From Enemy to Brother,* 266.

69. See Joseph Sievers, "'God's Gifts and Call Are Irrevocable': The Reception of Romans 11:29 through the Centuries and Christian-Jewish Relations," in *Reading Israel in Romans: Legitimacy and Plausibility of Divergent Interpretations,* ed. Cristina Grenholm and Daniel Patte (Harrisburg, PA: Trinity Press International, 2000), 129. Sievers agrees with Connelly that the turning point in interpreting Romans 11:29 hinges on works by Léon Bloy and his students Jacques and Raïssa Maritain but attributes decisive influence on the council also to the Protestant theologian Karl Barth's interpretation of this verse. See "'God's Gifts,'" 149–150.

70. *Nostra aetate,* Article 4.

71. Connelly, *From Enemy to Brother,* 266; Sievers, "'God's Gifts,'" 153.

72. The declaration merely deplores antisemitism practiced "at any time and by anyone."

73. See D'Costa, *Vatican II,* 119–120.

74. *Nostra aetate,* Article 4. The council fathers were also mindful of the intense controversy triggered by the contemporary play *The Deputy,* which, as mentioned, had critically damaged Pius XII's reputation. They feared that explicit reference to the Holocaust would play into the hands of his detractors by being interpreted as condemning his alleged silence. Eastern Catholic patriarchs responsible for Christian communities in Arab countries also vehemently opposed the declaration and almost succeeded in removing the document from the council's agenda. It was published nevertheless, but the opposition led to a softening of the wording against antisemitism, with the word *condemns* in the first draft eventually replaced by *decries* (*deplorat*). See Mauro Valeti, "Completing the Conciliar Agenda," in *History of Vatican II: The Council and the Transition: The Fourth Period and the End of the Council, September 1965–December 1965,* ed. Giuseppe Albergio and Joseph. A Komonchak, vol. 5, (Maryknoll, NY: Orbis / Leuven: Peeters, 2006), 212, 220; Connelly, *From Enemy to Brother,* 265.

75. D'Costa, *Vatican II,* 133. In a recent work, D'Costa engages within this question in an attempt to establish a coherent theological approach to contemporary Jewry by

bridging the doctrinal lacunae that exist throughout the Vatican's postconciliar statements on the issue. See D'Costa, *Catholic Doctrines on the Jewish People after Vatican II* (Oxford: Oxford University Press, 2019).

76. Philip A. Cunningham, Norbert J. Hofmann, and Joseph Sievers, eds., "Appendix I: Drafts Leading to the Conciliar Declaration *Nostra Aetate*—A. Decretum de Iudaeid (November, 1961)," in *The Catholic Church and the Jewish People: Recent Reflections from Rome* (New York: Fordham University Press, 2007), 191.

77. Cunningham, Hofmann, and Sievers, "Appendix I," 195.

78. Heschel's dictum appeared first in the *Herald Tribune,* September 3, 1964, and then in *Time* magazine, September 11, 1964.

79. Connelly, *From Enemy to Brother,* 253.

80. Maimonides, *Laws of Kings,* 11:10–11. On the Jewish reliance on this source, see later chapters on Judaism's relation to Christianity. Connelly argues that Oesterreicher had received the idea of relying on Zephaniah from his colleague Karl Thieme; see *From Enemy to Brother,* 254.

81. *Nostra aetate,* Article 4.

82. Connelly, *From Enemy to Brother,* 274–275.

Chapter 2: After Vatican II

1. See Giuseppe Alberigo, "The Christian Situation after Vatican II," in *Vatican II: The Unfinished Agenda: A Look to the Future,* ed. Lucien Richard, Daniel J. Harrington, and John W. O'Malley (New York: Paulist Press, 1987), 18–19.

2. The founders included Hans Küng, Edward Schillebeeckx, Yves Congar, Gregory Baum, Karl Rahner, Joseph Ratzinger, Henri de Lubac, and Johann Baptist Metz, as well as Hans Urs von Balthasar, who did not take part in the council but became one of the most influential twentieth-century Catholic theologians. Lieven Boeve and Gerard Manion, eds., *The Ratzinger Reader: Mapping a Theological Journey* (London: T & T Clark, 2010), 3; Massimo Faggioli, *Vatican II: The Battle for Meaning* (New York: Paulist Press, 2012), 50–53.

3. Hans Urs von Balthasar, *Martin Buber on Christianity: A Dialogue between Israel and the Church,* trans. Alexander Dru (London: Harvil Press, 1961), 21–22. First published in German in 1958.

4. *Nostra aetate,* Article 4.

5. See, for example, the works of Jean Daniélou, published around the time of the council: *The Theology of Jewish Christianity,* trans. John A. Baker (Chicago: Henry Regnery, 1964); *The Dead Sea Scrolls and Primitive Christianity,* trans. Salvator Attanasio (Baltimore: Helicon Press, 1958). See also Clemens Thoma, *A Christian Theology of Judaism,* trans. Helga B. Croner (New York: Paulist Press, 1980), 37–83; Balthasar, *Martin Buber,* 21–22.

6. Thoma, *A Christian Theology,* 67–71. See also Thoma, "Points of Departure," in *Brothers in Hope,* ed. John M. Oesterreicher, vol. 5, *The Bridge: Judaeo-Christian Studies* (New York: Herder and Herder, 1970), 164–165.

7. Thoma, *A Christian Theology,* 112.

8. Gregory Baum, *Is the New Testament Anti-Semitic? A Re-examination of the New Testament,* rev. ed. (Glen Rock, NJ: Deus Books and Paulist Press, 1965), 153. The first edition was published in 1961.

9. Commission for Religious Relations with the Jews (CRRJ), "Notes on the Correct Way to Present the Jews and Judaism in Preaching and Catechesis in the Roman Catholic Church," http://www.christianunity.va/content/unitacristiani/en/commissione-per-i-rapporti-religiosi-con-l-ebraismo/commissione-per-i-rapporti-religiosi-con-l-ebraismo-crre/documenti-della-commissione/en2.html.

10. Baum, *Is the New Testament Anti-Semitic?* 293.

11. Franz Mußner, *Tractate on the Jews: The Significance of Judaism for Christian Faith,* trans. Leonard Swidler (Philadelphia: Fortress, 1984), 150–152.

12. Baum, *Is the New Testament Anti-Semitic?* 252.

13. Agostino Bea, *La chiesa e il popolo ebraico* (Brescia: Morcelliana, 1966), 13–14. Bea refers to 1 Thessalonians 2:15, et seq.

14. Baum, *Is the New Testament Anti-Semitic?,* 290; Bea, *La chiesa,* 82.

15. Bernard Depuy, "What Meaning Has the Fact That Jesus Was Jewish for a Christian?" in *Christians and Jews (Concilium),* ed. Hans Küng and Walter Kasper (New York: Seabury Press, 1975), 74. Interestingly, Karl Rahner presented a more conservative approach to Jesus's Judaism even in the 1980s: "I have the right to say that whether Jesus had black or blond hair, wore a beard or not, is inconsequential for me in the final analysis. . . . From there one can naturally ask whether the Jewishness of Jesus belongs above all to the aforementioned contingent characteristics of Jesus or whether as such it has a specific religious significance for us Christians." See Karl Rahner and Pinchas Lapide, *Encountering Jesus—Encountering Judaism: A Dialogue,* trans. David Perkins (New York: Crossroad, 1987), 50. First published in German in 1984.

16. Bea, *La chiesa,* 45.

17. Hans Küng, "Introduction: From Anti-Semitism to Theological Dialogue," in Küng and Kasper, *Christians and Jews,* 9.

18. Küng, "Introduction," 4; Aduard Schillebeeckx, *Jesus: An Experiment in Christology,* trans. Hubert Huskins, vol. 6 of *The Collected Works of Edward Schillebeeckx* (London: Collins, 1979), 229–256.

19. Thoma, *A Christian Theology,* 113; CRRJ, "Notes." The commission refers to BT Sotah 22b.

20. Thoma, *A Christian Theology,* 115; see also Mußner, *Tractate on the Jews,* 109.

21. For example, Mußner, *Tractate on the Jews,* 114.

22. Schillebeeckx, *Jesus,* 256–271.

23. Thoma's book, for example, includes an introduction by Flusser. Klausner is also quoted often in these writings, as in Thoma, *A Christian Theology*, 106; Mußner, *Tractate on the Jews*, 109–110.

24. This idea is already present in Henri de Lubac, *Exégèse médiévale: Les quatre sens de l'écriture* I (Paris: Aubier, 1959), 314.

25. Hans Küng, *On Being a Christian*, trans. Edward Quinn (Garden City, NY: Doubleday, 1976); italics in the original.

26. Rosemary Radford Ruether, *Faith and Fratricide: The Theological Roots of Anti-Semitism* (New York: Seabury Press, 1974), 23–31.

27. Ruether, *Faith and Fratricide*, 64–71.

28. Rosemary Radford Ruether, "Anti-Semitism in Christian Theology," *Theology Today* (1974): 365.

29. Ruether, *Faith and Fratricide*, 117–226.

30. Milder theological moves in the same direction are also evident in more authoritative texts written in the following decades. See, for example, the Pontifical Biblical Commission, "Instruction on Scripture and Christology" (1984): "But one may not simplify this question excessively, as if any historian, making use only of scientific investigation, could prove it [the Resurrection] with certainty as a fact accessible to any observer whatsoever. In this matter there is also needed 'the decision of faith,' or better 'an open heart,' so that the mind may be moved to assent." This is an unofficial translation by Joseph A. Fitzmyer, S.J. (1985), published on the website of the Center for Christian-Jewish Learning at Boston College, https://www.bc.edu/content/dam/files/research_sites/cjl/texts /cjrelations/resources/documents/catholic/pbc_christology.htm.

31. Ruether, *Faith and Fratricide*, 248–249.

32. Gregory Baum, introduction to Ruether, *Faith and Fratricide*, 6.

33. Schillebeeckx, *Jesus*, 436, 570.

34. Schillebeeckx, *Jesus*, 564.

35. Schillebeeckx, *Jesus*, 559.

36. Schillebeeckx, *Jesus*, 576–581.

37. Schillebeeckx, *Jesus*, 591.

38. Hans Küng, "Letter of Professor Küng to Cardinal Höffner (February 21, 1977)," in *The Küng Dialogue: Facts and Documents* (Washington, DC: Publications Office United States Catholic Conference, 1980), 114.

39. Küng devoted a thick tome to Judaism at a later stage in his career. See Hans Küng, *Judaism*, trans. John Bowden (London: SCM Press, 1995).

40. Küng, *On Being a Christian*, 173–174; italics in the original.

41. John Pawlikowski, *What Are They Saying about Christian-Jewish Relations?* (New York: Paulist Press, 1980), 56.

42. Johann Baptist Metz, *Jenseits bürgerlicher Religion: Reden über die Zukunft des Christentums* (Munich: Kaiser & Grünewald, 1980), 29–50.

43. Metz, *Jenseits*, 35.

44. Johann Baptist Metz, "Facing the Jews: Christian Theology after Auschwitz," in *The Holocaust as Interruption*, ed. Elisabeth Schüssler Fiorenza and David Tracy, *Concilium* 175 (Edinburgh: T. & T. Clark, 1984), 27; my italics.

45. Metz, *Jenseits*, 29. Metz refers to the theology of his teacher, Karl Rahner.

46. Metz, "Facing the Jews," 32.

47. Eva Fleischner, *Judaism in German Christian Theology since 1945: Christianity and Israel Considered in Terms of Mission* (Metuchen, NJ: Scarecrow Press, 1975), 135.

48. Jean Daniélou and André Chouraqui, *The Jews: Views and Counterviews* (Glen Rock, NJ: Newman Press, 1967), 69.

49. The English translation is taken from Bea, *The Church and the Jewish People*, trans. Philip Loretz (New York: Harper and Row, 1966), 91–93, with minor changes. For the Italian see Bea, *La chiesa*, 82–84.

50. Bea, *La chiesa*, 85.

51. Bea, *The Church and the Jewish People*, 96 (*La chiesa*, 86). Emphasis in the original.

52. Bea, *The Church and the Jewish People*, 96 (*La chiesa*, 86–87).

53. Jacques Maritain wrote in 1941: "Jesus Christ suffers in the passion of Israel. In striking Israel, the anti-Semites strike Him, insult Him and spit on Him." And subsequently: "To persecute the house of Israel is to persecute Christ, . . . in His fleshy lineage and in His forgetful people whom He ceaselessly loves and calls. . . . If there are any in the world today—but where are they?—who give heed to the meaning of the great racist persecutions and who try to understand that meaning, they will see Israel as drawn along the road to Calvary, by reason of [its] vocation. . . . Despite itself Israel is climbing Calvary, side by side with Christians—whose vocation concerns the kingdom of God more than the temporal history of the world; and these strange companions are at times surprised to find each other mounting the same path. As in Marc Chagall's beautiful painting, the poor Jews, without understanding it, are swept along in the great tempest of the Crucifixion." Maritain, *Ransoming the Time*, trans. Harry Lorin Binsse (New York: Gordian Press, 1972), 177. Hans Urs von Balthasar wrote in a similar vein twenty years later: "Anyone who strikes Israel strikes the Messiah, who, as God's suffering servant, gathers up in himself all the afflictions of God's servant, Israel." *Explorations in Theology II: Spouse of the Word*, trans. A. V. Littledale and Alexander Dru (San Francisco: Ignatius Press, 1991), 293.

54. Maritain, *Ransoming*, 154–155.

55. Quoted in Alan T. Davies, *Anti-Semitism and the Christian Mind: The Crisis of Conscience after Auschwitz* (New York: Herder and Herder, 1969), 85.

56. Balthasar, *Explorations*, 295.

57. According to Balthasar, just as the argument about God's *rejection* of the Jewish people is valid only historically and not eschatologically, the claim regarding the continuity of their chosenness ("For the gifts and the calling of God are irrevocable," Rom. 11:29) is eschatologically but not historically valid. "This distortion," he argues, "is indeed the one remaining chance open to Jewish ideology, with whose Communist

or liberal stamp we are familiar." On the whole, it would seem that Balthasar identifies quite a few common denominators between Marcionism, with its total rejection of the Old Testament, and Judaism, with its total rejection of the New Testament. Only the church, he believes, can maintain the right tension between the historical and eschatological. See also Anthony C. Sciglitano, *Marcion and Prometheus: Balthasar against the Expulsion of Jewish Origins in Modern Religious Thought* (New York: Crossroad, 2014), 101.

58. Balthasar, *Explorations,* 292.

59. Jacques Maritain, *On the Church of Christ: The Person of the Church and Her Personnel,* trans. Joseph W. Evans (Notre Dame, IN: University of Notre Dame Press, 1973), 173; emphasis in the original.

60. Hans Urs von Balthasar, *Theo-Drama—Theological Dramatic Theory, III. Dramatis Personae: Persons in Christ,* trans. Graham Harrison (San Francisco: Ignatius Press, 1992), 391.

61. Katherine Sonderegger, *That Jesus Christ Was Born a Jew: Karl Barth's "Doctrine of Israel"* (University Park: Pennsylvania State University Press, 1993).

62. Balthasar, *Theo-Drama,* 398.

63. Balthasar, *Theo-Drama,* 393–394.

64. In this spirit, theologians repeatedly explained that the passage in Matthew (27:25) "His blood be on us, and on our children!" does not constitute self-condemnation but rather a prophetic reading, according to which Jesus's sacrificial blood is destined to expiate the sins of the Jews in the future, like the Passover sacrifice. See Maritain, *On the Church of Christ,* 172; Mußner, *Tractate on the Jews,* 309–310; Johannes Willebrands, "Are the New Testament and Christianity Antisemitic (Oxford, 1985, and Rome, 1986)," in *Church and Jewish People* (New York: Paulist Press, 1992), 86.

65. Mußner, *Tractate on the Jews,* 130.

66. Mußner, *Tractate on the Jews,* 51.

67. Marcel Jacques Dubois, "Christian Reflection on the Holocaust," *Sidic: Journal of the Service international de documentation judéo chrétienne* 7, no. 2 (1974), 15.

68. Thoma, *A Christian Theology,* 159.

69. Dubois, "Christian Reflection," 15.

70. Jean-Marie Lustiger, *The Promise,* trans. Rebecca Howell Balinski (Grand Rapids, MI: Eerdmans, 2007), 50. Lustiger wrote this in 1979, a short time before he was nominated to the position of bishop of Orléans.

71. John T. Pawlikowski, *Christ in Light of the Christian-Jewish Dialogue* (New York: Paulist Press, 1982), 142. Emphasis in the original.

72. Eva Fleischner, "The Christian and the Holocaust," *Journal of Ecumenical Studies* 7 (1970), 333.

73. Dubois, "Christian Reflection," 12.

74. Dubois, "Christian Reflection," 12–13.

75. Metz, *Jenseits bürgerlicher Religion,* 32.

76. Anthony J. Kenny, *Catholics, Jews, and the State of Israel* (New York: Paulist Press, 1993), 45–46.

77. Paul E. Sigmund, "The Catholic Tradition and Modern Democracy," *Review of Politics* 49, no. 4 (1987), 530–548.

78. See for example Ruether, *Faith and Fratricide*, 248; Mußner, *Tractate on the Jews*, 50. See also the statement issued by the German bishops in 1980 that "a Christian must understand when Jews point to this still-outstanding 'balance of promise' and do not want to see Jesus of Nazareth as the promised one." See "The Church and the Jews: German Bishops' Conference, Bonn 1980," Boston College, https://www.bc.edu/content/dam/files/research_sites/cjl/texts/cjrelations/resources/documents/catholic/german_church_jews.html.

79. Amnon Raz-Krakotzkin, "Exile within Sovereignty: Critique of 'The Negation of Exile' in Israeli Culture," in *The Scaffolding of Sovereignty: Global and Aesthetic Perspectives on the History of a Concept,* ed. Zvi Ben-Dor Benite, Stefanos Geroulanos, and Nicole Jerr (New York: Columbia University Press, 2017), 393–420.

80. See for example Ruther, *Faith and Fratricide,* 217–226.

81. Quoted in Riccardo Calimani, *Storia del pregiudizio contro gli ebrei: Antigiudaismo, antisemitismo, antisionismo* (Milano: Oscar Mondadori, 2007), 400.

82. Edward H. Flannery, "Theological Aspects of the State of Israel," in *The Bridge: A Yearbook of Judeo-Christian Studies,* vol. 3, ed. John M. Osterreicher (New York: Pantheon, 1958), 302.

83. Yves Congar, "The State of Israel in Biblical Perspective," *Blackfriars* 38, no. 447 (1957), 247–248.

84. Congar, "The State of Israel," 248; my emphasis.

85. Congar, "The State of Israel," 248–249.

86. Flannery, "Theological Aspects of the State of Israel."

87. Jacques Maritain, "Post-Scriptum (1964)," in *Le mystère d'Israël et autres essais* (Paris: Desclée de Brouwer, 1965), 243. On Maritain's attitude to the State of Israel, see Richard Francis Carane, *Passion of Israel: Jacques Maritain, Catholic Conscience, and the Holocaust* (Scranton, NJ: University of Scranton Press, 2010), 124–126.

88. Maritain, "Post-Scriptum (1964)," 250.

89. Crane, *Passion of Israel,* 244–245. Charles Journet vehemently objected to this.

90. Charlotte Klein noted this affinity in her article "The Theological Dimensions of the State of Israel," *Journal of Ecumenical Studies* 10, no. 4 (1973), 706.

91. Alain Marchadour, David Neuhaus, and Carlo Maria Martini, *The Land, the Bible, and History: Toward the Land That I Will Show You* (New York: Fordham University Press, 2007), 162.

92. Commission for Religious Relations with the Jews (CRRJ), "Guidelines and Suggestions for Implementing the Conciliar Declaration 'Nostra Aetate' (no. 4)," http://www.christianunity.va/content/unitacristiani/en/commissione-per-i-rapporti-religiosi-con-l-ebraismo/commissione-per-i-rapporti-religiosi-con-l-ebraismo-crre/documenti-della-commissione/en3.html.

93. French Bishops' Committee for Relations with Jews, "Statement by the French Bishops' Committee for Relations with Jews (April 16, 1973)," Council of Centers on Jewish-Christian Relations, https://www.ccjr.us/dialogika-resources/documents-and -statements/roman-catholic/other-conferences-of-catholic-bishops/cefr1973.

94. United States Conference of Catholic Bishops, "Statement on Catholic-Jewish Relations, National Conference of Catholic Bishops, November 20, 1975," in *Bridges: Documents of the Christian-Jewish Dialogue,* ed. Franklin Sherman, vol. 1, *The Road to Reconciliation (1945–1985)* (New York: Paulist Press, 2011), 221. See also the amendment to this declaration, as issued by the US Conference of Catholic Bishops in 1985: Bishops' Committee for Ecumenical and Interreligious Affairs, "Guidelines for Catholic-Jewish Relations (1985 Revision)," United States conference of Catholic Bishops, http://www .usccb.org/prayer-and-worship/liturgical-year/lent/guidelines-for-catholic-jewish -relations.cfm.

95. CRRJ, "Notes." For an analysis of the position of this statement vis-à-vis the question of the promised land, see Adam Gregerman, "Is the Biblical Land Promise Irrevocable?: Post–*Nostra Aetate* Catholic Theologies of the Jewish Covenant and the Land of Israel," *Modern Theology* 34 (2018): 138–139. See also Philip A. Cunningham's concise summary of the difficulties that Catholic theology faces with regard to the Land of Israel in the context of Christian-Jewish relations, "Emerging Principles of a Theology of Shalom," *Horizons* 44 (2017): 292–295.

96. French Bishops' Committee for Relations with Jews, "Statement by the French Bishops." See also the discussion of this declaration by Marchadour and Neuhaus, *The Land,* 164–165.

97. Thoma, *A Christian Theology,* 176.

98. CRRJ, "Notes."

99. Conférence épiscopale française, "Orientations."

100. Ignace de la Potterie and Bernard Dupuy, "People, Nation, Land: The Christian View," in *Fifteen Years of Catholic-Jewish Dialogue 1970–1985: Selected Papers,* International Catholic-Jewish Liaison Committee (Vatican City: Libreria Editrice Vaticana, 1988), 13.

101. Ruether, *Faith and Fratricide,* 228.

102. Jakob J. Petuchowski, "The Dialectics of Salvation History," in Oesterreicher, *Brothers in Hope,* 76.

103. Mußner, *Tractate on the Jews,* 47.

104. John M. Oesterreicher, "The Theologian and the Land of Israel," in Oesterreicher, *Brothers in Hope,* 241–242.

105. The question of the Land of Israel in Catholic theology and Christian-Jewish relations is being currently revisited by Catholic theologians who seek to extract a clearer position on the issue from magisterial texts. See Gavin D'Costa, *Catholic Doctrines on the Jewish People after Vatican II* (Oxford: Oxford University Press, 2019), 105–140. D'Costa argues that it is possible to trace within these texts a theological move toward a

position that he calls "minimalist Catholic Zionism." I disagree with him on this point and see the official texts that he relates to as much less unequivocal. For a collection of articles from Catholic, Protestant, and Jewish authors, see Philip A. Cunningham, Ruth Langer, and Jesper Svartvik's recent volume *Enabling Dialogue about the Land: A Resource Book for Jews and Christians* (New York: Paulist Press, 2020).

106. "The religious interpretation of Israel," as stated by Ruether, "as a promised land given by God and as a land whose restoration was regarded as a messianic event, impedes the search for that pluralism. . . . Stuck between a religious orthodoxy forged in the Diaspora and secular nationalism, Israel awaits the rebirth of that prophetic tradition that can transform Zionism into a language of self-criticism in the light of the ultimate Zion of justice and peace which is still to be achieved." Ruether, *Faith and Fratricide*, 227. Ruether subsequently became one of the foremost theologians providing a critique of the Israeli-Palestinian conflict and Christian Zionism. See, for example, "Christian Zionism and Main Line Western Christian Churches," in *Challenging Christian Zionism: Theology, Politics and the Israel-Palestine Conflict,* ed. Naim Ateek, Cedar Duaybis, and Maurine Tobin (Jerusalem: Sabeel Liberation Theology Center, 2005), 154–162.

107. *Nostra aetate,* Article 4.

108. For the history of this dogma, see Francis A. Sullivan, *Salvation outside the Church? Tracing the History of the Catholic Response* (New York: Paulist Press, 1992); Bernard Sesboüé, *Hors de l'église pas de salut: Histoire d'une formule et problèms d'interprétation* (Paris: Desclée de Brouwer, 2004). The magisterium's deliberation on the correct interpretation of the dogmatic formula "Extra Ecclesiam Nulla Salus" began well before Vatican II, most notably in the United States in the 1940s and 1950s.

109. *Unitatis redintegratio,* Vatican, https://www.vatican.va/archive/hist_councils/ii _vatican_council/documents/vat-ii_decree_19641121_unitatis-redintegratio_en.html, see section 3. See also Sullivan, *Salvation,* 141–151; Sesboüé, *Hors de l'église,* 231.

110. As explicated by Sullivan, *Salvation,* this was not a complete innovation of the council, but was greatly expanded by it.

111. The disregard for hell as a possible destiny for those outside the church is the main concern expressed in Ralph Martin's *Will Many Be Saved? What Vatican II Actually Teaches and Its Implications for the New Evangelization* (Grand Rapids, MI: Eerdmans, 2012). Parting ways with Sullivan's reading of *Lumen gentium,* Martin argues against what he calls the "salvation optimism" of Sullivan and others (55–56), that *Lumen gentium* does not assume that all will be saved and leaves the option of hell open. This option, for Martin, is essential for the justification of the church's mission.

112. Pope Paul VI, *Lumen gentium,* section 16, Vatican, https://www.vatican.va/archive /hist_councils/ii_vatican_council/documents/vat-ii_const_19641121_lumen-gentium_en .html. See also "ad Genes," section 3, Vatican, https://www.vatican.va/archive/hist_councils /ii_vatican_council/documents/vat-ii_decree_19651207_ad-gentes_en.html. See also Pelikan, *The Emergence,* 14–27.

113. *Nostra aetate,* Article 2.

114. Pope Paul VI, "Gaudium et Spes (December 7, 1965)," section 22. Vatican, https://www.vatican.va/archive/hist_councils/ii_vatican_council/documents/vat-ii_const_19651207_gaudium-et-spes_en.html . See also Sesboüé, *Hors de l'Église,* 237–239.

115. *Lumen gentium,* section 48.

116. *Lumen gentium,* section 9.

117. *Lumen gentium,* section 16; my emphasis.

118. *Lumen gentium,* section 16.

119. Sesboüé, *Hors de l'Église,* 231–234.

120. Sullivan, *Salvation,* 161.

121. Apostolic Exhortation of His Holiness Pope Paul VI, "Evangelii Nintiandi," Vatican, http://www.vatican.va/content/paul-vi/en/apost_exhortations/documents/hf_p-vi_exh_19751208_evangelii-nuntiandi.html

122. *Evangelii nuntiandi,* section 80.

123. See Sullivan, *Salvation,* 182–189.

124. *Evangelii nuntiandi,* section 53.

125. Franz Mußner, "'Ganz Israel wird gerettet werden' (Röm 11,26): Versuch einer Auslegung," *Kairos* 18, no. 4 (1976), 251.

126. Ronan Hoffman, "Conversion and the Mission of the Church," *Journal of Ecumenical Studies* 5, no. 1 (1968), 16.

127. See the translation, and the discussion regarding other translations, in Hubert Wolf, *Pope and Devil: The Vatican's Archives and the Third Reich,* trans. Kenneth Kronenberg (Cambridge, MA: Belknap Press of Harvard University Press, 2010), 84.

128. See Wolf, *Pope and Devil,* 124.

129. Lustiger, *The Promise,* 101.

130. Lustiger, *The Promise,* 124.

131. CRRJ, "Guidelines and Suggestions."

132. Tomasso Federici, "Mission and Witness of the Church," in *Fifteen Years of Catholic-Jewish Dialogue 1970–1985: Selected Papers,* International Catholic-Jewish Liaison Committee (Vatican City: Libreria Editrice Vaticana, 1988), 57–58.

133. Federici, "Mission and Witness," 58.

134. Federici, "Mission and Witness," 58.

135. Federici quotes from Paul VI in his inaugural speech before the synod of bishops in September 1974. See, Federici, "Mission and Witness," 61.

136. Federici, "Mission and Witness," 61.

137. CRRJ, "Notes."

138. CRRJ, "Guidelines and Suggestions."

139. See especially "The Church's Mandate to Evangelize in Relation to Judaism" in Commission for Religious Relations with the Jews (CRRJ), "'The Gifts and the Calling of God are Irrevocable' (Rom. 11:29): A Reflection on Theological Questions Pertaining to Catholic-Jewish Relations on the Occasion of the 50th Anniversary of 'Nostra

Aetate' (no. 4)," Vatican, http://www.vatican.va/roman_curia/pontifical_councils/chrstuni /relations-jews-docs/rc_pc_chrstuni_doc_20151210_ebraismo-nostra-aetate_en.html.

Chapter 3: John Paul II and Christian-Jewish Reconciliation

1. A number of American Catholic experts on Christian-Jewish relations have succeeded in maintaining an alert and vibrant theological discourse on the Christian-Jewish connection, while continuing, mildly but persistently, to discuss the questions that John Paul II sought to set aside. See especially the numerous studies of John Pawlikowski, Mary Boys, Eugen Fisher, and Philip Cunningham. Along with their (mostly liberal) Jewish counterparts, this group still holds the theological torch in Christian-Jewish relations. Nevertheless, this is a discourse that remains confined to the limits of Christian-Jewish dialogue and rarely applies to other fields of Catholic theology. In this sense, it is less of a threat to the stability of Catholic doctrine than were the works of the 1970s and early 1980s.

2. Eamon Duffy, *Saints and Sinners: A History of the Popes* (New Haven, CT: Yale University Press, 2014), 379–380; Peter Hebblethwaite, *The New Inquisition? The Case of Edward Schillebeeckx and Hans Küng* (San Francisco: Harper & Row, 1980), 104.

3. See the encyclical by John Paul II, "Redemptor Hominis (4 March 1979)," Vatican, http://www.vatican.va/content/john-paul-ii/en/encyclicals/documents/hf_jp-ii _enc_04031979_redemptor-hominis.html.

4. Hebblethwaite, *The New Inquisition?*, 13.

5. Hebblethwaite, *The New Inquisition?*, 77.

6. John Kirk, "John Paul II and the Exorcism of Liberation Theology: A Retrospective Look at the Pope in Nicaragua," *Bulletin of Latin American Research* 4, no. 1 (1985): 33–47; Duffy, *Saints and Sinners*, 372–373.

7. Jeffrey L. Klaiber, "Prophets and Populists: Liberation Theology, 1968–1988," *Americas* 46, no. 1 (1989): 10–15; Duffy, *Saints and Sinners*, 373.

8. David Gibson, *The Rule of Benedict: Pope Benedict XVI and His Battle with the Modern World* (San Francisco: HarperCollins, 2006), 185.

9. Gibson, *The Rule of Benedict*, 197–201.

10. The pope confronted these criticisms in his Christmas address to the Roman Curia, where he offered to interpret the day of prayer in the spirit of Vatican II's Christocentric focus. See *L'Osservatore Romano*, weekly edition in English, January 5, 1987, 6.

11. On the tension between official and popular, implicit, theology (*teologia implicita*) in the Medieval veneration of the saints, see Aviad Kleinberg, *Flesh Made Word: Saints' Stories and the Western Imagination* (Cambridge, MA: Belknap Press of Harvard University Press, 2008). In the case discussed here, the pope himself held this duplicity; he acted in the popular realm as he allowed no one to act in the theological realm.

12. Darcy O'Brien, *The Hidden Pope: The Untold Story of a Lifelong Friendship That Is Changing the Relationship between Catholics and Jews: The Personal Journey of John Paul II and Jerzy Kluger* (New York: Daybreak, 1998).

13. Tad Szulc, *Pope John Paul II: The Biography* (New York: Scribner, 1995), 41, 68–70; David G. Dalin, "John Paul II and the Jews," in *John Paul II and the Jewish People: A Jewish-Christian Dialogue*, ed. David G. Dalin and Matthew Levering (Lanham, MD: Rowman and Littlefield, 2008), 16–17.

14. Jonathan Huener, *Auschwitz, Poland, and the Politics of Commemoration, 1945–1979* (Athens: Ohio University Press, 2003).

15. Huener, *Auschwitz*, 198–199.

16. See "Apostilic Piligrimage to Poland—Holy Mass at the Concentration Camp, Homily of His Holiness John Paul II (Auschwitz-Bierkenau, 7 June 1979)," Vatican, https://www.vatican.va/content/john-paul-ii/en/homilies/1979/documents/hf_jp-ii _hom_19790607_polonia-brzezinka.html.

17. Referring to Auschwitz as Golgotha paraphrases Jacques Maritain's 1944 letter to Charles Journet. See Richard Francis Crane, "Jacques Maritain, the Mystery of Israel, and the Holocaust," *Catholic Historical Review* 95, no. 1 (2009): 25–56.

18. "Homily of His Holiness John Paul II (Auschwitz-Bierkenau, 7 June 1979)." For the reasons for choosing these specific languages, see Huener, *Auschwitz*, 217.

19. See also the news coverage of the mass: John Vinocur, "Pope Prays at Auschwitz: 'Only Peace!'" *New York Times*, June 8, 1979.

20. See also Adam Gregerman, "Interpreting the Pain of Others: John Paul II and Benedict XVI on Jewish Suffering in the Shoah," *Journal of Ecumenical Studies* 48, no. 4 (2013): 443–456.

21. John Paul II, "Address to Jewish Leaders in Warsaw (June 14, 1987)," Center for Dialogue and Prayer in Oświęcim, https://cdim.pl/1987-06-14-john-paul-ii-address-to -jewish-leaders-in-warsaw,1769; Aposteliche Reise in die Bundesrepublik Deutschaldn, "Ansprache von Johannes Paul II. an die Midglieder des Zentralrates des Juden (Erz-bischöfliche Residenz in Köln - Freitag, 1. Mai 1987)," Vatican, https://w2.vatican.va /content/john-paul-ii/de/speeches/1987/may/documents/hf_jp-ii_spe_19870501_cons -centrale-ebrei.html.

22. John Paul II, "Address of Pope John Paul II to the International Leaders of the 'Anti-Defamation League of B'nai B'rith' (Thursday, 2 March 1984)," Vatican, http://www .vatican.va/content/john-paul-ii/en/speeches/1984/march/documents/hf_jp-ii_spe _19840322_anti-defamation-league.html.

23. Pope John Paul II, "Address to Representatives of the West German Jewish Com-munity, Mainz, West Germany (November 17, 1980)," Council of Centers on Jewish-Christian Dialogue (CCJR), https://www.ccjr.us/dialogika-resources/documents-and -statements/roman-catholic/pope-john-paul-ii/jp2-80nov17.

24. John Paul II, *Redemptoris missio*, December 1990, Vatican, https://www.vatican .va/content/john-paul-ii/en/encyclicals/documents/hf_jp-ii_enc_07121990_redemptoris

-missio.html. Another prominent example is *Crossing the Threshold of Hope,* trans. Vitorio Messori (New York: Random House, 2005).

25. John Paul II, "Address to Jewish Leaders in Warsaw."

26. Pastoralbesuch in Österreich, "Ansprache von Johannes Paul II. an die Vertreter der jüdischen Gemeinde (Wien, Freitag 24. Juni 1988)," Vatican, https://w2.vatican.va /content/john-paul-ii/de/speeches/1988/june/documents/hf_jp-ii_spe_19880624 _comunita-ebraica.html.

27. John Paul II, "Message of His Holiness John Paul II on the Occasion of the 50th Anniversary of the Beginning of the Second World War," Vatican, https://www .vatican.va/content/john-paul-ii/en/messages/pont_messages/1989/documents/hf_jp-ii _mes_19890827_anniv-ii-guerra-mondiale.html.

28. John Paul II, "Address to the Viennese Jewish Community (Vienna, June 24, 1988)," Council of Centers of Jewish-Christian Relations, https://www.ccjr.us/dialogika -resources/documents-and-statements/roman-catholic/pope-john-paul-ii/jp2 -88june24.

29. "Ansprache von Johannes Paul II. an die Midglieder des Zentralrates des Juden." For a critique from a Jewish perspective on Stein's beatification, see Sergio I. Minerbi, "Pope John Paul II and the Jews: An Evaluation," *Jewish Political Studies Review* 18, no. 1–2 (2006): 15–36.

30. Shalom Goldman, *Jewish-Christian Difference and Jewish Identity: Seven Twentieth-Century Converts* (Lanham, MD: Lexington Books, 2015), 45–72.

31. Jean-Marie Lustiger, *Le choix de Dieu: Entretiens avec Jean-Louis Missika et Dominique Wolton* (Paris: Éditions de Fallois, 1987), 19–70.

32. Jean-Marie Lustiger, *Dare to Believe: Addresses, Sermons, Interviews 1981–1984,* trans. Nelly Marans and Maurice Couve de Murville (New York: Crossroad, 1986), 41. See also Lustiger, *Le choix,* 44–45.

33. Jean-Marie Lustiger, *La promesse* (Paris: Parole et Silence, 2002), 168–169. For this reason, Lustiger saw the Hebrew-speaking Catholic community in Israel as carrying a special promise.

34. Lustiger, *La promesse,* 50–52, 58–59, 99–102; *Le choix,* 71–76.

35. The discussion of Marcion as the father of antisemitism often appears in ecclesiastical documents on the Christian-Jewish bond from the 1950s onward, and especially after Vatican II. See for example [West] German Bishops' Conference, "The Church and the Jews, Bonn, April 28, 1980," in *Bridges: Documents of the Christian-Jewish Dialogue,* ed. Franklin Sherman, vol. 1, *The Road to Reconciliation (1945–1985)* (New York: Paulist Press, 2011), 240. This will be discussed further in the next chapter; also Lustiger, *Le choix,* 79.

36. See Jean-Marie Lustiger, *Cardinal Jean-Marie Lustiger on Christians and Jews,* ed. Jean Duchesne (New York: Paulist Press, 2010), 81–88; Lustiger, *Le choix,* 80–82. See also Amos Funkenstein's criticism of this claim, "Lustiger Pashut To'e," *Haaretz,* April 29, 1995 (Hebrew).

37. Bernard Suchecky, "The Carmelite Convent at Auschwitz: The Nature and Scope of a Failure," *Yale French Studies* 85, Discourses of Jewish Identity in Twentieth-Century France (1994): 162.

38. Judith Hershcopf Banki, "Historical Memories in Conflict," in *Memory Offended: The Auschwitz Convent Controversy*, ed. Carol Rittner and John K. Roth (New York: Praeger, 1991), 158.

39. Suchecky, "The Carmelite Convent," 161.

40. Avraham Weiss described the events in "Let the Nuns Pray Elsewhere (October 15, 1989)," in Rittner and Roth, *Memory Offended*, 255–257.

41. Banki, "Historical Memories," 161.

42. Waldemar Chrostowski, "Controversy around the Auschwitz Convent," *Occasional Papers on Religion in Eastern Europe* 10, no. 3 (1990), 26.

43. Suchecky, "The Carmelite Convent," 167; Cited in John Pawlikowski, "The Auschwitz Convent Controversy: Mutual Misperceptions," in Rittner and Roth, *Memory Offended*, 65.

44. See Yehuda Bauer, "Auschwitz: The Dangers of Distortion (September 30, 1989)," and Elie Wiesel and Carol Rittner, "An Interview," in Rittner and Roth, *Memory Offended*, 251–253 and 113–115.

45. Shilansky raised the issue in the Knesset in May 1986. See "HaYeshiva HaMataiyim VeSheh Shel HaKnesset HaAhat Esre: HaKamat Minzar HaKharmelistim BeAuschwitz [The 207th meeting of the 11th Knesset: The Establishment of the Carmelite Convent in Auschwitz] (28.5.1986)," Knesset, https://fs.knesset.gov.il/11/Plenum/11_ptm_530650 .PDF.

46. Zev Garber and Bruce Zuckerman, "Why Do We Call the Holocaust 'The Holocaust?' An Inquiry into the Psychology of Labels," *Modern Judaism* 9, no. 2 (1989): 197–211.

47. See, for example, Minerbi, "Pope John Paul II and the Jews"; Donald J. Dietrich, *God and Humanity in Auschwitz: Jewish-Christian Relations and Sanctioned Murder* (New Brunswick, NJ: Transaction, 1995), 86.

48. Anthony J. Kenny, *Catholics, Jews, and the State of Israel* (New York: Paulist Press, 1993), 10–21.

49. UPI, "The Text of Pope's Speech at Rome Synagogue: 'You Are Our Elder Brothers,'" *New York Times*, April 14, 1986.

50. I thank Alberto Melloni for sharing earlier drafts of the speech with me. For Melloni's analysis of the speech, see *Le cinque perle di Giovanni Paolo II: I gesti di Wojtyła che hanno cambiato la storia* (Milano: Mondadori, 2011), 29–50.

51. "The Text of Pope's Speech at Rome Synagogue: 'You Are Our Elder Brothers.'" Alberto Melloni argues that the repetition of the words *by anyone* implies the responsibility of Pius XII. See Melloni, *Le cinque perle*, 29–50.

52. The Hebrew reads: "The beginning of the growth of our salvation." This saying is part of the religious Zionist mainstream Jewish prayer for the sake of the State of Israel.

53. Cited in Giovanni Caprile, "Vita della chiesa: Il papa al tempio ebraico di Rome," *La Civiltà Cattolica* 3261, vol. 2 (1986), 270.

54. Melloni, *Le cinque perle,* 47.

55. "The Text of Pope's Speech at Rome Synagogue: 'You Are Our Elder Brothers.'"

56. Besides the biblical allusion, the pope's expression also echoed Adam Mickiewcz's allusion to the Jews as the Christians' older brothers, worthy of respect and dignity. For Mickiewcz's approach to the Jews, see Abraham G. Duker, "The Mystery of the Jews in Mickiewicz' Towianist Lectures on Slav Literature," *Polish Review* 7, no. 3 (1962): 40–66.

57. On the double meaning embedded in this phrase, see Melloni, *Le cinque perle,* 45–46.

58. Carol Rittner and John K. Roth, Introduction to *Memory Offended,* 1.

59. Edward Idris Cassidy, *Ecumenism and Interreligious Dialogue: Unitatis Reintegratio, Nostra Aetate* (New York: Paulist Press, 2005), 194.

60. Frank J. Coppa, *The Papacy, the Jews, and the Holocaust* (Washington, DC: Catholic University of America Press, 2006), 52–54.

61. Coppa, *The Papacy,* 275.

62. See John Paul II's introduction to Commission for Religious Relations with the Jews (CRRJ), "We Remember: A Reflection on the Shoah," March 16, 1998, Council of Centers on Jewish-Christian Relations, https://www.ccjr.us/dialogika-resources/documents-and-statements/roman-catholic/vatican-curia/we-remember.

63. CRRJ, "We Remember," section 2.

64. CRRJ, "We Remember," section 3.

65. CRRJ, "We Remember," section 3.

66. CRRJ, "We Remember," section 4.

67. CRRJ, "We Remember," section 4.

68. David Kertzer, *The Popes against the Jews: The Vatican's Role in the Rise of Modern Anti-Semitism* (New York: Knopf, 2011), 3–4.

69. Coppa, *The Papacy,* 209–210; Susan Zuccotti, *Under His Very Windows: The Vatican and the Holocaust in Italy* (New Haven, CT: Yale University Press, 2000), 324–325.

70. Coppa, *The Papacy,* 280.

71. Philip Cunningham mentioned to me that the Vatican deliberately never asked the Jews for forgiveness but addressed the plea for forgiveness to God alone.

72. International Theological Commission, "Universal Prayer: Confession of Sins and Asking for Forgiveness (Day of Pardon–12 March 2000)," Vatican, http://www.vatican.va/news_services/liturgy/documents/ns_lit_doc_20000312_prayer-day-pardon_en.html. Apart from asking for forgiveness of the Jews, the church asked forgiveness for sins in general, sins committed in the service of truth, sins against the unity of the church, sins committed in actions against love, peace, the rights of peoples and respect for cultures and religions, sins against the dignity of women and the unity of the human race, and sins in relation to fundamental human rights.

73. International Theological Commission, "Universal Prayer."

74. "Devarav Shel Ha'Afifyor Yohanan Paulos HaSheni BeYad Vashem, 23.3.2000," Yad Vashem, https://www.yadvashem.org/he/pope-visits/john-paul/speech.html.

75. "Devarav Shel Ha'Afifyor Yohanan Paulos HaSheni BeYad Vashem." My italics.

76. Pope John Paul II, "Address to Representatives of the West German Jewish Community, Mainz"; "The Text of Pope's Speech at Rome Synagogue: 'You Are Our Elder Brothers.'"

Chapter 4: Joseph Ratzinger and the Jews

1. See Joseph Ratzinger, *Many Religions—One Covenant: Israel, the Church and the World,* trans. Graham Harrison (San Francisco: Ignatius Press, 1999), 17.

2. Two examples of this genre are the book coauthored by Gilles Bernheim, then chief rabbi of France, and Philippe Barbarin, the archbishop of Lyon, *Le rabbin et le cardinal: Un dialogue judéo-chrétien d'aujourd'hui* (Paris: Stock, 2008); and the one coauthored by Jorge Borgoglio, the archbishop of Buenos Aires (and future Pope Francis), and his friend Abraham Skorka, a Conservative rabbi, *Sobre el cielo y la tierra* (Buenos Aires: Editorial Sudamericana, 2010).

3. Pontifical Biblical Commission (PBC), *The Jewish People and Their Sacred Scriptures,* Vatican, http://www.vatican.va/roman_curia/congregations/cfaith/pcb_documents /rc_con_cfaith_doc_20020212_popolo-ebraico_en.html. The document's authors were biblical scholars and not high-ranking church officials. For this reason, notwithstanding that it is an important document that was overseen and approved by the hierarchy, it does not enjoy a great official authority.

4. In fact, this argument was already made by de Lubac; see Henri de Lubac, *Exégèse médiévale: Les quatre sens de l'écriture I* (Paris: Aubier, 1959), 313–314.

5. PBC, *The Jewish People,* section 2.

6. PBC, *The Jewish People,* section 2.

7. According to Philip Cunningham, this indication of Jesus's "traits" in the Messiah that will come opens an eschatological horizon for both Jews and Christians, who will both recognize the Messiah according to their own different but legitimate standards. It is not that one perception would be proved wrong and the other right, but "each community, by seeing each other's recognition, would fully understand for the first time the 'rightness' of not only its own point of view, but of the other's as well." See Philip Cunningham, "Emerging Principles of a Theology of Shalom," *Horizons* 44 (2017): 299. It is also possible, however, to read this paragraph as pointing to the universal acknowledgment of Jesus as Christ.

8. PBC, *The Jewish People,* section 2; my italics.

9. This argument appears already in Balthasar. See Anthony C. Sciglitano, *Marcion and Prometheus: Balthasar against the Expulsion of Jewish Origins in Modern Religious Thought* (New York: Crossroad, 2014). The connection between Nazi antisemitism and the

renunciation of the Old Testament is exemplified in Susannah Heschel's study of the Institute for the Study and Elimination of Jewish Influence on German Church Life. See Heschel, *The Aryan Jesus: Christian Theologians and the Bible in Nazi Germany* (Princeton, NJ: Princeton University Press, 2008).

10. Joseph Ratzinger, "Preface," in PBC, *The Jewish People*.

11. Augustinus, *Confessiones*, 3.4. The Jewish scholar Michael Wyschogrod protested against Ratzinger's reference to the Hebrew Bible as containing brutal narratives and saw it as evidence of old anti-Jewish residues. Ratzinger dialogued consciously with replacement theology and was well aware of its implications, and he did not make an effort to avoid such implications only because they could have drawn such criticism. See Michael Wyschogrod, "The Jewish People and Their Sacred Scriptures in the Christian Bible, by the Pontifical Commission (Rome, 2001)," in *New Perspectives on Jewish-Christian Relations in Honor of David Berger,* ed. Elisheva Carlebach and Jacob J. Schacter (Leiden: Brill, 2012), 522.

12. Ratzinger, "Preface." In reading this paragraph, it is hard not to notice the criticism Ratzinger directed at the legacy of the Enlightenment.

13. See Ratzinger, *Many Religions,* 19, 28.

14. Concilium Vaticanum Secundum, *Constitutio dogmatica de divina revelatione: Dei verbum,* November 18, 1965, section 4:16, Vatican, https://www.vatican.va/archive/hist_councils/ii_vatican_council/documents/vat-ii_const_19651118_dei-verbum_en .html. See *Catechism of the Catholic Church* IV, 129 (Vatican City: Libreria Editrice Vaticana 1993); Augustinus, *Quaestiones in heptateuchum* 2.73.

15. David Nirenberg, *Anti-Judaism: The Western Tradition* (New York: Norton, 2014), 97–106.

16. Joseph Ratzinger, "The Heritage of Abraham: The Gift of Christmas (December 29, 2000)," Boston College, https://www.bc.edu/content/dam/files/research_sites /cjl/texts/cjrelations/resources/articles/ratzinger.htm.

17. Benedict XVI, "Address by the Holy Father, Visit to the Auschwitz-Birkenau Camp (May 28, 2006)," Vatican, http://www.vatican.va/content/benedict-xvi/en/speeches /2006/may/documents/hf_ben-xvi_spe_20060528_auschwitz-birkenau.html.

18. Hans Hermann Henrix believes that this is one of the key points in Ratzinger's theology of Judaism, as it ties the contemporary Jews in a Gordian knot with God, thereby unequivocally affirming their importance in the history of salvation. See Henrix, "Pope Benedict XVI and the Jews: A Relationship under Suspicion?," *Israel Affairs* 16, no. 4 (2010): 537–538.

19. Jacob Neusner, *A Rabbi Talks with Jesus* (Montreal: McGill-Queen's University Press, 2000). The dialogue around the book had begun before Ratzinger was elected pope. Several years later, he chose to include the references to Neusner's book in his own.

20. From the back cover of the book.

21. Pope Benedict XVI, *Jesus of Nazareth,* vol. 1, *From the Baptism in the Jordan to the Transfiguration,* trans. A. J. Walker (New York: Doubleday, 2007), 105.

22. Benedict XVI, *Jesus of Nazareth*, vol. 1, 102, 106.

23. Roland Deines, "Can the 'Real' Jesus Be Identified with the Historical Jesus? A Review of the Pope's Challenge to Biblical Scholarship and the Ongoing Debate," in *The Pope and Jesus of Nazareth: Christ, Scripture and the Church*, ed. A. Pabst and A. Paddison (London: Veritas Series, SCM Press, 2009) 199–232.

24. Benedict XVI, *Jesus of Nazareth*, vol. 1, 106–107.

25. Benedict XVI, *Jesus of Nazareth*, vol. 1, 109–110.

26. Ratzinger, "The Heritage of Abraham."

27. Benedict XVI, *Jesus of Nazareth*, vol. 1, 114–116.

28. Benedict XVI, *Jesus of Nazareth*, vol. 1, 118.

29. Ratzinger, *Many Religions*, 40.

30. Ratzinger, *Many Religions*, 101.

31. Pope John Paul II, "Address to Representatives of the West German Jewish Community, Mainz." This is criticized in David Berger, "*Nostra Aetate* after Fifty Years: Covenant and the Election of Israel," in *A Jubilee for All Time: The Copernican Revolution in Jewish-Christian Relations*, ed. Gilbert S. Rosenthal (Eugene, OR: Pickwick, 2014), 233–247; see also Henrix, "Pope Benedict XVI and the Jews," 555.

32. Benedict XVI, "Address by the Holy Father."

33. Ratzinger, *Many Religions*, 69.

34. Ratzinger, *Many Religions*, 41.

35. Ratzinger, *Many Religions*, 55–56.

36. Ratzinger, *Many Religions*, 68.

37. Ratzinger, *Many Religions*, 71.

38. Benedict XVI, *Jesus of Nazareth*, vol. 1, 118.

39. This is mentioned by Christoph Schmidt in another context: "Rethinking the Modern Canon of Judaism—Christianity—Modernity in Light of the Post-Secular Relation," in *Is There a Judeo-Christian Tradition?: A European Perspective*, ed. Nathan Emmanuel and Topolski Anya (Berlin: De Gruyter, 2016), 165–184.

40. Benedict XVI, *Jesus of Nazareth*, vol. 1, 122.

41. Congregation of the Doctrine of Faith (CDF), "Declaration '*Dominus Iesus*' on the Unicity and Salvific Universality of Jesus Christ and the Church," Vatican, https://www.vatican.va/roman_curia/congregations/cfaith/documents/rc_con_cfaith_doc_20000806_dominus-iesus_en.html.

42. Pope Paul VI, *Lumen gentium*, Vatican, https://www.vatican.va/archive/hist_councils/ii_vatican_council/documents/vat-ii_const_19641121_lumen-gentium_en.html.

43. See Ratzinger, "The Ecclesiology of the Constitution on the Church, Vatican II, 'Lumen Gentium,'" *L'Osservatore Romano: Weekly Edition in English*, September 19, 2001, 5.

44. The immediate impetus for the dissemination of *Dominus Iesus* was the publication of Jesuit theologian Jacques Dupuis's *Toward a Christian Theology of Religious Plu-*

ralism (Maryknoll, NY: Orbis, 1997), and his following interrogation by the CDF. CDF, *Dominus Iesus*, 16; italics in the original.

45. CDF, *Dominus Iesus*, 21.

46. This quote is taken from John Paul II's encyclical *Redemptoris Missio: On the Permanent Validity of the Church's Missionary Mandate* (December 7, 1990), Vatican, http://w2 .vatican.va/content/john-paul-ii/en/encyclicals/documents/hf_jp-ii_enc_07121990 _redemptoris-missio.html. See section 36.

47. CDF, *Dominus Iesus*, 22.

48. CDF, *Dominus Iesus*, 23.

49. See John T. Pawlikowski's "Moderator's Remarks" in "*Dominus Iesus*: A Panel Discussion," *CTSA Proceedings* 56 (2001), 98.

50. Boys spoke on the same panel with Pawlikowski. See Mary C. Boys, "Comments of Mary Boys," in "*Dominus Iesus*: A Panel Discussion," 116.

51. See Edward Kessler and Eugene Fisher, "A Dialogue of Head and Heart," *Tablet: The International Catholic News Weekly* 254, November 18, 2000, 1556–1559.

52. David Berger, "On *Dominus Iesus* and the Jews" in *Persecution, Polemic, and Dialogue: Essays in Jewish-Christian Relations* (Boston: Academic Studies Press, 2010), 378–384.

53. Nevertheless, apart from the impression of this significant event, these two authors were not so far from each other in their positions about Judaism. On the complexity (even ambivalence) of Kasper toward the "old covenant," see "Superiority without Supersessionism: Walter Kasper, *The Gifts and the Calling of God Are Irrevocable,* and God's Covenant with the Jews," *Theological Studies* 79, no. 1 (2018), 36–59.

54. Walter Kasper, "*Dominus Iesus*," delivered at the 17th Meeting of the International Catholic-Jewish Liaison Committee, New York, May 1, 2001, Boston College, https://www .bc.edu/content/dam/files/research_sites/cjl/texts/cjrelations/resources/articles/kasper _dominus_iesus.htm.

55. "It is evident that, as Christians, our dialogue with the Jews is situated on a different level than that in which we engage with other religions. The faith witnessed to by the Jewish Bible [the Old Testament for Christians] is not merely another religion to us, but is the foundation of our own faith." Ratzinger, "The Heritage of Abraham."

56. Kasper, "*Dominus Iesus*."

57. Kasper, "*Dominus Iesus*."

58. Pawlikowski believed that Ratzinger indeed considered the Jews a separate category and that he would have excluded them from the rule established by *Dominus Iesus*. See John T. Pawlikowski, "Reflections on Covenant and Mission Forty Years after *Nostra Aetate*," *Crosscurrents* 56, no. 4 (2007), 87.

59. CDF, *Dominus Iesus*, 13.

60. Joseph Ratzinger, *God and the World: Believing and Living in Our Time. A Conversation with Peter Seewald,* trans. Henry Taylor (San Francisco: Ignatius Press, 2002). Originally published in German in 2000.

61. Ratzinger, *God and the World,* 148–150.

62. Ratzinger, *God and the World,* 148–150.

63. See Ratzinger, *Many Religions,* 104–105.

64. Ratzinger, *Many Religions,* 104–105.

65. Benedict XVI, "Visit to the Synagogue of Romer: Address of His Holiness Benedict XVI (Sunday, January 17, 2010)," Vatican, https://w2.vatican.va/content/benedict-xvi/en/speeches/2010/january/documents/hf_ben-xvi_spe_20100117_sinagoga.html.

66. Consultation of the National Council of Synagogues (NCS) and delegates of the Bishops Committee for Ecumenical and Interreligious Affairs (BCEIA), "Reflections on Covenant and Mission," August 12, 2002, USCCB, http://www.usccb.org/beliefs-and-teachings/ecumenical-and-interreligious/jewish/upload/Reflections-on-Covenant-and-Mission.pdf.

67. NCS and BCEIA, "Reflections," 7.

68. NCS and BCEIA, "Reflections," 5.

69. Avery Dulles, "Covenant and Mission," *America* 187, no. 12, October 21, 2002, 8–11.

70. Dulles, "Covenant and Mission," 8–11.

71. Avery Dulles, "The Covenant with Israel," *First Things,* November 2005, 16–21.

72. Dulles, "Covenant and Mission."

73. Similarly, Gregerman claims that Kasper avoids exhausting his theological arguments and purposely preserves a certain ambiguity in order to avoid offending Jewish sensibilities. See Adam Gregerman, "Superiority without Supersessionism: Walter Kasper, *The Gifts and the Calling of God Are Irrevocable,* and God's Covenant with the Jews," *Theological Studies* 79, no. 1 (2018): 43–44.

74. United States Conference of Catholic Bishops, Committee on Doctrine and Committee on Ecumenical and Interreligious Affairs, "A Note on Ambiguities Contained in *Reflections on Covenant and Mission,*" June 18, 2009, rev. October 13, 2009, USCCB, http://www.usccb.org/about/doctrine/publications/upload/note-on-ambiguities-contained-in-reflections-on-covenant-and-mission.pdf.

75. This passage, which was later omitted from the "Note," appears in a letter to the press by David Berger and Fabian Schonfeld, "Response to Statement of the United States Conference of Catholic Bishops on Covenant, Mission, and Dialogue," July 8, 2009, CCJR, https://www.ccjr.us/dialogika-resources/themes-in-today-s-dialogue/conversion/berger09june29.

76. Berger and Schonfeld, "Response to Statement." For Berger's interventions in similar matters, see Michael Wyschogrod, *Jews and "Jewish Christianity": A Jewish Response to the Missionary Challenge* (Toronto: Jews for Judaism, 2002). For more on Berger, see Chapter 6.

77. I am grateful to Rabbi Poupko for sharing his unpublished speech with me. The quotations from this undated document are reproduced here with his permission.

78. Pope Benedict XVI, "Summorum Pontificum: On the Use of the Roman Liturgy Prior to the Reform of 1970," Vatican, http://w2.vatican.va/content/benedict-xvi/en

/motu_proprio/documents/hf_ben-xvi_motu-proprio_20070707_summorum
-pontificum.html.

79. For this prayer, see Hubert Wolf, *Pope and Devil: The Vatican's Archives and the Third Reich,* trans. Kenneth Kronenberg (Cambridge, MA: Belknap Press of Harvard University Press, 2010), 124.

80. For the Anti-Defamation League's criticism of Benedict XVI's move, see Anti-Defamation League press release, "ADL Calls Vatican Prayer for Conversion of Jews 'A Theological Setback' and 'A Body Blow to Catholic-Jewish Relations,'" July 6, 2007, Boston College, https://www.bc.edu/content/dam/files/research_sites/cjl/texts/cjrelations/topics/1962_missal.htm.

81. For the translation see Wolf, *Pope and Devil,* 125.

82. For a review of the various criticisms sounded in Europe against Benedict XVI's prayer, see Hans Hermann Henrix, "The Controversy Surrounding the 2008 Good Friday Prayer in Europe: The Discussion and Its Theological Implications," *Studies in Christian-Jewish Relations* 3 (2008): 1–19.

83. The chief rabbi of Rome, Riccardo Di Segni, for example, feared that this meant a severe regression in the Holy See's relations with the Jews. See Luigi Accattoli, "Nuova preghiera per gli ebrei I rabbini: Il problema resta," *Corriere della Sera,* February 6, 2008, 25. See also Cardinal Lehmann's response to the criticisms against Benedict XVI: Karl Cardinal Lehmann, "Nicht grenzenlos belastbar: Zur Diskussion um die Karfreitagsfürbitte im jüdisch-christlichen Dialog, Gastkommentar," *Glaube und Leben: Kirchenzeitung für das BistumMainz* 64, no. 14 (April 6, 2008), 9.

84. For the responses of Jews in Germany, see Henrix, "The Controversy," 9. The Chief Rabbinate in Israel also threatened to suspend its dialogue with the Vatican.

85. See, for example, Edward Kessler, "More Than Mere Satchel Bearers," *Tablet: The International Catholic News Weekly,* February 16, 2008, 11.

86. See the declaration by the Christian-Jewish Discussion Group of the Central Committee of German Catholics, "Störung der christlich-jüdischen Beziehungen—Zur Wiedereinführung des tridentinischen Ritus (April 4, 2007)," Zentralkomitee der Deutschen Katholiken, https://www.zdk.de/veroeffentlichungen/pressemeldungen/detail/Stoerung-der-christlich-juedischen-Beziehungen-Zur-Wiedereinfuehrung-des-tridentinischen-Ritus-402a.

87. Henrix, "The Controversy," 12.

88. Cardinal Walter Kasper, "Das Wann und Wie entscheidet Gott," *Frankfurter Allgemeine Zeitung,* March 20, 2008, http://www.faz.net/aktuell/feuilleton/debatten/karfreitagsfuerbitte-das-wann-und-wie-entscheidet-gott-1512132.html.

89. Kasper, "Das Wann und Wie entscheidet Gott."

90. Later in the controversy over the prayer, Kasper clarified that even if it were possible to be saved without explicitly acknowledging Christ, this certainly did not mean that it was possible to be saved without Christ at all. The interpretation of the statement "*extra ecclesiam nulla salus*" could not be stretched so far as to claim that salvation was

possible *"extra Christum."* See Walter Kasper and Hanspeter Heinz, "Theologische Schwerpunkte im christlich-jüdischen Gespräch," *Freiburger Rundbrief* 14 (2007): 21, quoted by Henrix, "The Controversy," 18.

91. Lehmann, "Nicht grenzenlos belastbar," 9.

92. Christoph Schönborn, "Judaism's Way to Salvation," *Tablet: The International Catholic News Weekly* 262, March 29, 2008, 8–9.

93. Schönborn, "Judaism's Way to Salvation," 8–9.

94. Benedict XVI, *Jesus of Nazareth,* vol. 2, *Holy Week: From the Entrance into Jerusalem to the Resurrection,* trans. Philip J. Whitmore (San Francisco: Ignatius Press, 2011), 41–47.

95. Benedict XVI, *Jesus of Nazareth,* vol. 2, 45. The pope quotes from Bernard de Clairvaux, *De Consideratione* 2.3.

96. See "Visit to Yad Vashem Memorial—Address of His Holiness Benedict XVI, Jerusalem (May 11, 2009)," Vatican, http://w2.vatican.va/content/benedict-xvi/en/speeches /2009/may/documents/hf_ben-xvi_spe_20090511_yad-vashem.html.

97. For an example of the harsh criticism of the pope during his visit to Israel, see Aviad Glickman, "Yad VaShem: Akhzava MeHa'afifyor—'Efo HaBa'at HaZa'ar?'" *Ynet,* May 11, 2009 (Hebrew), http://www.ynet.co.il/articles/0,7340,L-3714270,00.html; see also Boaz Bismuth, "Yad VaShem: 'Me'ukhzavim'" *Israel Hayom,* May 12, 2009 (Hebrew).

Chapter 5: Christianity in the Jewish Tradition

1. Michael Meerson and Peter Schäfer et al., eds., *Toledot Yeshu: The Life Story of Jesus: Two Volumes and Database* (Tübingen: Moher Siebeck, 2014). See also Peter Schäfer, "Agobard's and Amulo's *Toledot Yeshu,"* in *Toledot Yeshu ("The Life Story of Jesus") Revisited: A Princeton Conference,* ed. Peter Schäfer, Michael Meerson, and Yaacov Deutsch (Tübingen: Mohr Siebeck, 2011), 27–48. The first to systematically study this work were Samuel Krauss, *Das Leben Jesu nach Jüdischen Quellen* (Berlin: S. Cavalry, 1902), and the chief rabbi of Rome, Ricardo Di Segni, "La tradizione testuale delle Toledòth Jéshu: Manoscritti, edizioni a stampa, classificazione," *La Rassegna Mensile di Israel* 50, no. 1 (1984): 83–100, and *Il vangelo del ghetto* (Rome: Newton Compton editori, 1985).

2. David Berger, *Persecution, Polemic, and Dialogue: Essays in Jewish-Christian Relations* (Boston: Academic Studies Press, 2010), 79. See also Robert Chazan, *Fashioning Jewish Identity in Medieval Western Christendom* (Cambridge, UK: Cambridge University Press, 2004), 7.

3. Jacob Katz, *Exclusiveness and Tolerance: Studies in Jewish-Gentile Relations in Medieval and Modern Times* (Oxford: Oxford University Press, 1961), 15–16.

4. Chazan, *Fashioning Jewish Identity,* 72.

5. Israel Jacob Yuval, *Two Nations in Your Womb: Perceptions of Jews and Christians in Late Antiquity and the Middle Ages,* trans. Barbara Harshav and Jonathan Chipman (Berkeley: University of California Press, 2006), 68–87.

6. Peter Schäfer, *Jesus in the Talmud* (Princeton, NJ: Princeton University Press, 2007).

7. Robert Travers Herford, *Christianity in Talmud and Midrash* (London: Williams & Norgate, 1903), 359–360; Schäfer, *Jesus in the Talmud*, 95–96.

8. See Yuval's critique of the "mother and daughter" image in *Two Nations in Your Womb*, 26–30, as well as Anna Sapir Abulafia, *Christians and Jews in the Twelfth-Century Renaissance* (London: Routledge, 1995), 63.

9. Daniel Boyarin, *Border Lines: The Partition of Judaeo-Christianity* (Philadelphia: University of Pennsylvania Press, 2004), 5.

10. Yuval, *Two Nations in Your Womb*, 22.

11. Eli Yassif, "'Toledot Yeshu': Folk-Narrative as Polemics and Self Criticism," in Schäfer et al., *Toledot Yeshu Revisited*, 101–135.

12. See David Biale, "Counter-history and Jewish Polemics against Christianity: The *Sefer toldot yeshu* and the *Sefer zerubavel*," *Jewish Social Studies* 6, no. 1 (1999): 130–145.

13. Anna Sapir Abulafia, *Christian Jewish Relations 1000–1300: Jews in the Service of Medieval Christendom* (London: Routledge, 2014), 145. This alternative terminology is also connected with the Talmudic tradition of distorting the names of various forms of idolatry in a derogatory fashion.

14. See also David Berger, "Al Tadmitam VeGoralam Shel HaGoyim BeSafrut Ha-Pulmus HaAshkenazit," in *Jews Facing the Cross: The Persecutions of 1096 in History and Historiography*, ed. Yom Tov Assis, Jeremy Cohen, Ahron Keidar, Ora Limor, and Michael Toch (Jerusalem, Magnes, 2000), 91 (Hebrew).

15. See Yuval, *Two Nations*, 113–114, 117–118.

16. See Haym Soloveitchik, "Halakhah, Hermeneutics, and Martyrdom in Medieval Ashkenaz (Part I of II)," *Jewish Quarterly Review* 94, no. 1 (2004): 77–108. Even haggadic sources often required radical reinterpretation to enlist them for justifications of the behavior of the Ashkenazi community as martyrdom.

17. Haym Soloveitchik, "Religious Law and Change: The Medieval Ashkenazic Example," *AJS Review* 12, no. 2 (1987), 205–221; Katz, *Exclusiveness and Tolerance*, 83–84.

18. Katz, *Exclusiveness and Tolerance*, 153–154. See also Jeremy Cohen, *Sanctifying the Name of God: Jewish Martyrs and Jewish Memories of the First Crusade* (Philadelphia: University of Pennsylvania Press, 2004), 91–105; Elliot R. Wolfson, "Martyrdom, Eroticism, and Asceticism in Twelfth-Century Ashkenazi Piety," in *Jews and Christians in Twelfth-Century Europe*, ed. Michael Signer and John Van Engen (Notre Dame, IN: University of Notre Dame Press, 2001), 171–220.

19. Israel Jacob Yuval, "HaSafah VeHasmalim Shel HaKhronikot Ha'Ivriot BiYeme Masa'ey HaTslav," in Assis et al., *Jews Facing the Cross*, 116–117.

20. See Katz, *Exclusiveness and Tolerance*, 34–36.

21. BT Chulin 13b.

22. Gershom ben Yehudah, *Teshuvot Rabenu Gershom Meor HaGolah*, ed. Shlomo Eidelberg (New York: Yeshiva University, 1957), section 21, 75.

23. Shlomo Yitzchaki, *Teshuvot Rashi BiShlosha Halakim,* ed. Israel S. Alfenbein (New York: Schlezinger Brothers, 1943), section 327, 337 (Hebrew).

24. See also Jacob Katz, "The Vicissitude of Three Apologetic Passages," *Zion* 23–24, no. 3–4 (1958–1959): 186–187 (Hebrew).

25. See Israel Ta-Shma, "Judeo-Christian Commerce on Sundays in Medieval Germany and Provence," *Tarbiz* 47, no. 3–4 (1978): 199–205 (Hebrew).

26. BT Sanhedrin 63b.

27. Tosafists on BT Sanhendrin 63b. Compare also to Tosaffot BT Bechorot 2b.

28. See the translation and the discussion in Katz, *Exclusiveness and Tolerance,* 35.

29. BT Sanhedrin 63a.

30. Katz, "The Vicissitude," 9–10; Katz, *Exclusiveness and Tolerance,* 34–36. For a concise discussion of the association principle, see also David Berger, *The Rebbe, the Messiah and the Scandal of Orthodox Indifference* (London: Littman Library of Jewish Civilization, 2001), 175–177.

31. Katz, *Exclusiveness and Tolerance,* 34.

32. Gershom ben Yehuda, *Teshuvot Rabenu Gershom,* 75; italics mine. Jacob Katz's translation in *Exclusiveness and Tolerance,* 34. David Berger agrees with Katz on this matter: Berger, *Persecution, Polemic, and Dialogue,* 71–72.

33. Menachem Meiri, *Beit HaBehirah Al Masekhet Avoda Zara,* ed. Avraham Soffer (Jerusalem: Kedem, 1971), 46 (Hebrew).

34. See Meiri, *Beit HaBehirah,* 56, 59. As regards Meiri, see Moshe Halbertal, *Between Torah and Wisdom: Rabbi Menachem Ha-Meiri and the Maimonidean Halakhists in Provence* (Jerusalem: Magnes Press, 2000), 80–108 (Hebrew).

35. Haym Soloveitchik, "Rupture and Reconstruction: The Transformation of Contemporary Orthodoxy," *Tradition* 28, no. 4 (1994), 121–122.

36. Daniel J. Lasker, "The Jewish Critique of Christianity under Islam in the Middle Ages," *Proceedings of the American Academy for Jewish Research* 57 (1990–1991): 121–153; Chazan, *Fashioning Jewish Identity,* 76–80.

37. Daniel J. Lasker, "Rashi and Maimonides on Christianity," in *Between Rashi and Maimonides: Themes in Medieval Jewish Thought, Literature and Exegesis,* ed. Ephraim Kanarfogel and Moshe Sokolow (New York: Ktav, 2010), 3–21.

38. Lasker, "Rashi and Maimonides," 60.

39. Moshe ben Maimon, *Igeret Teyman LeRabbenu Moshe Ben Maimon: Hamakor Ha'Aravi VeShloshet HaTargumim Ha'Ivryim,* ed. Avraham Shlomo Halkin (New York: American Academy of Jewish Studies 1952), 13. Contrary to other sources, Maimonides clarified that Jesus was not a bastard, because even though Jesus was born outside wedlock, his father was a gentile, and the category of bastardy does not apply to gentiles: "Jesus the Nazarene, who was from Israel, even though his father was a gentile and his mother was an Israelite, we hold firm by the principle that should 'a gentile or a slave impregnate a Jewess, the progeny is kosher' [BT Yevamot 45a], but

they called him 'bastard' to emphasis his disrepute." This emphasis is important for the theological dimension of Maimonides's perception of Christianity as a hybrid of Judaism and idolatry.

40. Moshe ben Maimon, *Igeret Teyman;* and see also Maimonides, *Laws of Kings,* 11:4.

41. BT Sanhedrin 43a.

42. Moshe ben Maimon, *Igeret Teyman,* 18.

43. See Amos Funkenstein, *Maimonides: Nature, History, and Messianic Beliefs,* trans. Shmuel Himelstein (Tel-Aviv: MOD books, 1997), 51–52.

44. Maimonides, *Laws of Kings,* 11:4.

45. A similar role is ascribed to Christianity by Rabbi Judah Halevi, *The Kuzari (Kitab Al Khazari): An Argument for the Faith of Israel,* trans. Hartwig Hirschfeld (New York: Schocken, 1964), 226–227: "God has a secret and wise design concerning us, which should be compared to the wisdom hidden in the seed which falls into the ground, where it undergoes an external transformation into earth, water and dirt, without leaving a trace for him who looks down upon it. It is, however, the seed itself which transforms earth and water into its own substance, carries it from one stage to another, until it refines the elements and transfers them into something like itself, casting off husks, leaves, etc., and allowing the pure core to appear, capable of bearing the Divine Influence. The original seed produced the tree bearing fruit resembling that from which it had been produced." See also Daniel Lasker, "Proselyte Judaism, Christianity, and Islam in the Thought of Judah Halevi," *Jewish Quarterly Review* 81, no. 1–2 (1990): 75–91.

46. Funkenstein, *Maimonides,* 62–63.

47. BT Sanhedrin 59a; Moshe ben Maimon, *Teshuvot HaRambam,* trans. and ed. Yehoshua Blau (Jerusalem: Mekitsei Nirdamim, 1959), 284 (Hebrew and Arabic).

48. Maimonides, *Laws of Idolatry,* 9:4; Commentary on the Mishnah, Avoda Zara 1:3. See *Mishnah Im Perush Rabenu Moshe Ben Maymon: Seder Nezikin,* trans. and ed. Yosef Kafih (Jerusalem: Mosad Harav Kook, 1965), 225 (Hebrew). The term used to describe the "holy days" of idolaters, which is also used to describe the holy days of Christians, is the biblical term *id,* which connotes failure, trouble, or calamity and is used to mock idolatry and its rituals.

49. Chazan, *Fashioning Jewish Identity,* 14.

50. Berger, *Persecution, Polemic, and Dialogue,* 80–88.

51. See Ram Ben-Shalom, *Facing Christian Culture: Historical Consciousness and Images of the Past among the Jews of Spain and Southern France during the Middle Ages* (Jerusalem: Ben Zvi, 2007), 154 (Hebrew).

52. This argument has characterized rabbinic literature since the conversion of the Roman Empire to Christianity in the fourth century CE. See Yuval, *Two Nations,* 32.

53. Katz, *Exclusiveness and Tolerance,* 112–113.

54. Katz, *Exclusiveness and Tolerance.* For a different approach, see Haim Hillel Ben-Sasson, "Concepts and Reality in Late Medieval Jewish History," *Tarbitz* 29 (1960): 297–312.

55. Katz, *Exclusiveness and Tolerance,* 138–142. See also David Berger, "Jews, Gentiles, and the Modern Egalitarian Ethos: Some Tentative Thoughts," in *Formulating Responses in an Egalitarian Age,* ed. Marc Stern (Lanham, MD: Rowman & Littlefield, 2005), 87–88; Elliot R. Wolfson, *Venturing Beyond: Law and Morality in Kabbalistic Mysticism* (New York: Oxford University Press, 2006), 70–80.

56. Moshe Isserles, *Darkhei Moshe MiTur Orah Hayim* (Fiorda: Hayiam Ben Zvi Hircsh, 1760), 25 (153).

57. Katz, "The Vicissitude," 183–185.

58. Louis Jacobs, "Attitudes toward Christianity in the Halakhah," in *Gevurot HaRomah,* ed. Ze'ev W. Falk (Jerusalem: Mesharim, 1987), xxiv–xxv.

59. Elisheva Carlebach, "The Anti-Christian Element in Early-Modern Yiddish Culture," in *Braun Lecture in the History of the Jews in Prussia,* no. 10 (Ramat Gan: Bar-Ilan University, 2002), 11. At the same time, Christians in the new age were aware of this text and even published it themselves.

60. Marc Shapiro, "Torah Study on Christmas Eve," *Journal of Jewish Thought and Philosophy* 8, no. 2 (1999): 327–328.

61. BT Gittin 57a.

62. Shapiro, "Torah Study on Christmas Eve," 348–350.

63. Katz, *Exclusiveness and Tolerance,* 157–160.

64. Yechezkel Landau, "Hitnatslut," in *Noda BeYehudah: Mahadura Kama* (Prague: unknown publisher, n.d.), 8 (Hebrew).

65. See Katz, *Exclusiveness and Tolerance,* 167; Azriel Shochat, "The German Jews' Integration within their Non-Jewish Environment in the First Half of the 18th Century," *Zion* 21, no. 3–4 (1957): 207–235 (Hebrew).

66. See also Katz, "The Vicissitude," 186–193.

67. This statement is taken from Jacob Emden, the Jewish scholar and polemicist of the eighteenth century, cited in Katz, "The Vicissitude," 181.

68. Louis Jacobs, *Judaism and Theology: Essays on the Jewish Religion* (London: Vallentine Mitchell, 2005), 108–109.

69. Yosef Salmon, "Christians and Christianity in Halakhic Literature from the End of the Eighteenth Century to the Middle of the Nineteenth Century," *Modern Judaism* 33, no. 2 (2013): 125–147.

70. Salmon, "Christians and Christianity," 139–140.

71. Moshe Miller, "Rabbi Samson Raphael Hirsch and Nineteenth-Century German Orthodoxy on Judaism's Attitude toward Non-Jews" (PhD diss., Yeshiva University, 2014), 47–52.

72. Miller, "Rabbi Samson Raphael Hirsch," 55–60, 69–72.

73. Miller, "Rabbi Samson Raphael Hirsch," 66–73.

Chapter 6: Christianity in Contemporary Halakhic Literature

1. Jacob Katz, *Exclusiveness and Tolerance: Studies in Jewish-Gentile Relations in Medieval and Modern Times* (Oxford: Oxford University Press, 1961).

2. A salient example may be found in Israel Jacob Yuval, *Two Nations in Your Womb: Perceptions of Jews and Christians in Late Antiquity and the Middle Ages,* trans. Barbara Harshav and Jonathan Chipman (Berkeley: University of California Press, 2006), 20: "The Christian-Jewish debate that started nineteen hundred years ago, in our day came to a conciliatory close."

3. Aviad Hacohen, "Natsrut VeNotsrim Be'ynaiym Rabaniyot Ba'Et HaHadasha: MeHarav Kook Ve'Ad Harav Ovadia Yosef," *Mahanaim: A Review for Studies in Jewish Thought and Culture* 15 (2004): 89–124 (Hebrew).

4. Hacohen, "Natsrut VeNotsrim," 90.

5. Hacohen, "Natsrut VeNotsrim," 123.

6. Hacohen, "Natsrut VeNotsrim," 123.

7. See Moshe Samet, "The Beginnings of Orthodoxy," *Modern Judaism* 8, no. 3 (1988): 249–269.

8. Yosef Salmon, "Christians and Christianity in Halakhic Literature from the End of the Eighteenth Century to the Middle of the Nineteenth Century," *Modern Judaism* 33, no. 2 (2013): 125–147.

9. Hacohen, "Natsrut VeNotsrim," 90.

10. The movement of halakha toward stringency in the Orthodox world has been discussed in many forums; see Haym Soloveitchik, "Rupture and Reconstruction: The Transformation of Contemporary Orthodoxy," *Tradition* 28, no. 4 (1994): 64–130; Benjamin Brown, "Stringency: Five Modern-Era Types," *Diné Israel* 20–21 (2001): 123–237 (Hebrew).

11. See Ariel Picard, "Ma'amad HaNokhri BeMedinat Israel BePsikat Rabaney HaTsiyonut HaDatit," *Reshit* 1 (2009): 187–208 (Hebrew).

12. Maimonides, *Laws of Idolatry,* 10:5–6.

13. Mishnah Gittin 5:9; Isser Yehuda Unterman, "Darkhei Shalom VeHagdaratam," *Morasha* 1 (1971): 5–10 (Hebrew).

14. In 1987, HaLevi gave his famous lecture on the status of non-Jews according to halakha, "Darkhei Shalom BaYehasim Ben Yehudim LeShe'eynam Yehudim," *Tehumin* 9 (1988): 71–81 (Hebrew). As noted by Aviezer Ravitsky, in this lecture, HaLevi withdrew from his previous position, according to which Christianity is absolute idolatry as perceived by Maimonides. See Ravitsky, "Ways of Peace and the Status of Gentiles according to the Rambam: An Exchange of Letters with Rabbi Hayym David Halevi," in *Living Judaism: Essays on the Halakhic Thought of Rabbi Hayyim David Halevi,* ed. Zvi Zohar and Avi Sagi (Jerusalem & Ramat Gan: Shalom-Hartman Institute and Bar-Ilan University, 2007), 271–274 (Hebrew).

15. Hacohen, "Natsrut VeNotsrim "; Picard, "Ma'amad HaNokhri."

16. Regarding non-Jews in general, Rabbi Shaul Israeli, one of the most prominent arbiters of religious Zionism, made it clear that as long as "the hand of Israel does not overpower," there is no obligation to realize Maimonides's recommendations that "they shall not dwell in your land" (Exod. 23:33) and expel non-Jews. According to Israeli, Israel's hand will overpower in the sense intended by Maimonides only when the majority of world Jewry shall return to Israel and the commandments of the Jubilee that depend on this shall once more be observed. It will then be possible to exile all non-Jews who refuse to accept the Seven Laws of Noah before a Jewish rabbinical court. In other words, Israeli chose to put off the actualization of Maimonides's edicts in favor of maintaining the status quo. Shaul Israeli, "Ma'amad HaNokhri BaMedina haYisraelit," in *Amud Hayemini,* (Jerusalem: Erets Lamdah, 2000), section 12, 114–138 (Hebrew).

17. Yitzhak HaLevi Herzog, "Zekhuyot HaMi'utim Al Pi HaHalkha," *Tehumin* 2 (1981): 169 (Hebrew). For an extensive study of Herzog's overall project, see Alexander Key, *The Invention of Jewish Theocracy: The Struggle for Legal Authority in Modern Israel* (Oxford: Oxford University Press, 2020).

18. Herzog, "Zekhuyot HaMi'utim," 174–175. Herzog's halakhic argument comprises two stages: first, exclusion of Christians from the class of idolaters, and second, defining Christians as resident aliens (*gerim toshavim*) who have a right to reside in the Land of Israel. To absolve Christians from the crime of idolatry, Herzog defined Christianity as a faith of *shittuf* rather than a polytheistic faith. To define Christians as resident aliens, Herzog had to circumvent the fact that they did not accept the seven Noahide laws before a Jewish rabbinical court, a procedure that Maimonides established as a precondition to accept a gentile as a resident alien. In this regard, Herzog relied on an exemption provided by R. Abraham Isaac Kook in regard to the sale of real estate to Muslims, in which Kook defined Muslims (who according to halakha are not considered idolaters) as resident aliens despite the fact that they had not accepted the seven Noahide laws before a rabbinical court. See Abraham Isaac Kook, *Mishpat Cohen* (Jerusalem: Mossad Harav Kook, 1993), "Hilkhot Shemitah VeYovel," section 58, 122 (Hebrew). See also Yitzhak HaLevi Herzog, *Psakim UKtavim,* vol. 1 (Jerusalem: Mossad Harav Kook, 1989), "Teshuvot Orah Hayim," section 27, 124–125 (Hebrew).

19. There are a number of counter examples, such as Rabbi Yehuda Herzl Henkin's discussion of Christianity. Henkin stresses that Christianity is idolatry but believes that in the future, Christians will repent their ways, so that the Jews will not be required to coerce them to keep the seven Noahide laws. See his discussion in *Bnei Banim,* vol. 3 (Jerusalem: Tsur-Ot, 1998), section 36, 132.

20. BT Chulin 13b.

21. Yehudah Gershoni, "HaMi'utim VeZekhuyotehem BeMedinat Israel Le'Or HaHalakha," *Tehumin* 2 (1981): 189.

22. Yoel Teitelbaum, *Kuntres Al HaGeulah VeAl HaTemurah* (Brooklyn, NY: Hotzaat Yerushalayim, 1985), 6: "And especially the conquest of the Old City and the location of the Temple are now filled, in our many sins, with idolatry."

23. Menachem Kasher, *HaTkufah HaGdolah* (Jerusalem: Tora Shlemah, 2001), 304.

24. Kasher quotes the Jewish sage of the Second Temple period, Yohanan ben Zakai (Mekhilta Devarim, 12:2): "Do not hasten to destroy the idolatry altars of the gentiles lest you be obliged to build them with your own hands; do not destroy an altar of bricks, lest they command you to erect one of stone in its stead; do not destroy an altar of stone, lest they command you to erect one of wood in its stead" (Kasher, 305).

25. Kasher, *HaTkufah HaGdolah,* 307, based on BT Avoda Zara 35b and Sifrei Devarim 61.

26. Moshe Sternbuch, *Teshuvot VeHanhagot,* vol. 3 (Jerusalem: unknown publisher, 1997), "Yoreh De'ah," section 365, 420.

27. Sternbuch, *Teshuvot VeHanhagot,* "Yoreh De'ah," section 365, 420. See the statements of the Lubavitcher Rebbe (Menachem Mendel Schneerson), "The Seven Noahide Commandments," *Hapardes* 9, section 52, 7.

28. Sternbuch, *Teshuvot VeHanhagot,* 420.

29. Sternbuch, *Teshuvot VeHanhagot,* 421–422.

30. Sternbuch, *Teshuvot VeHanhagot,* section 164, 191.

31. Shalom Mashash, "Im Efshar La'azor LeNotsrim BeVinyan HaKnesyia Shelahem," *Or Torah* 346 (1997): 842–845 (Hebrew). This response was subsequently published in Rabbi Mashash's book *Shemesh VeMagen,* vol. 3 (Jerusalem: unknown publisher, 2000), "Orah Hayim," section 30, 61 (Hebrew).

32. Rabbi Mordechai HaLevi Horowitz (the Frankfurt rabbinical court chief judge), *Shu"t Mateh Levi,* vol. 2 (Frankfurt am Main: Yaakov Halevi Horowitz, 1933), "Yoreh De'ah," section 2, 80–85 (Hebrew); Yitzchak Una (the Manheim rabbinical court chief judge), *Shoalin VeDorshin* (Tel Aviv: Mispahat HaMehaber, 1964), section 35, 56 (Hebrew); David Zvi Hoffman (head of the Rabbinical Seminary in Berlin), *Sefer Melamed LeHo'il,* vol. 3 (Frankfurt am Main: Hermon, 1926), section 148, 149 (Hebrew). These rabbis agreed that *shittuf* is not prohibited to gentiles, (that is, that Christians are not considered idolaters), but they disagreed on the question of whether Jews are allowed to donate money for the construction of Christian places of worship.

33. Mashash, *Shemesh VeMagen,* 62.

34. Ovadia Yosef, *Yahaveh Da'at,* vol. 4 (Jerusalem: Or Hamizrach and the Hazon Ovadia Yeshiva, 1981), section 45, 235 (Hebrew).

35. Yosef bases his determination on the *Sefer Noda BeYehuda* (Jerusalem: A. Blum, 1988), "Yoreh De'ah," section 148, 212 (Hebrew), where it is claimed that the words of Isserles (see in the introduction) have misled people to believe that *shittuf* is not forbidden for gentiles.

36. In this Yosef relies on the writings of Rabbi David Leib Zilberstein, author of the *Shviley David* responsa; Rabbi Eliezer Deitch, author of the *Pri HaSadeh* responsa; and Rabbi Ovadia Hadaya, author of the *Yaskil Avdi* responsa.

37. Ovadia Yosef, *Yabi'a Omer,* vol. 2 (Jersualem: Porat Yossef, 1956), "Yoreh De'ah," section 11, 146–149 (Hebrew).

38. Rabbi Shaul Israeli relies on this verdict of Yossef in a responsum prohibiting participation in ceremonies conducted by adherents of other religions. See BeMar'eh HaBazak, vol. 6 (Jerusalem: Kollel Eretz Hemed, 2008), section 61, 164 (Hebrew). Nevertheless, Israeli is of the opinion that *shittuf* is not prohibited to Christians, that is, that they are not considered idolaters.

39. Yosef raised these arguments against the position of the nineteenth-century rabbi Eliyahu Saliman Mani, one of the great rabbis of Iraq and the chief rabbi of Hebron. Mani, *Zikhronot Eliyauh,* vol. 1 (Ramat Gan: Nir David, 1998) "Muktzeh," section 8, 149 (Hebrew).

40. David Avitan, "Be'Inyan Ezra LeNotsrim BeVinyan Haknesiya Shelahem," *Or Torah* 357 (1997): 932–933 (Hebrew).

41. Avitan, "Be'Inyan Ezra," 932.

42. Avitan, "Be'Inyan Ezra," 933.

43. Mashash, *Shemesh VeMagen,* "Orah Hayim," section 31, 62.

44. BT Chulin 13b.

45. Ezra Batzri, *Sha'arei Ezra* (Jerusalem: Machon Haktav, 2014), "Yoreh De'ah," section 8, 49.

46. Yosef Mashash, *Maim Hayaim,* vol. 2 (Jerusalem: unknown publisher, 1985), "Yoreh De'ah," section 108, 198; Rahamim Yosef Franko, *Sha'arei Rahamim,* vol. 1 (Jerusalem: Machon Haktav, 2010) section 5, 55.

47. Israel Moshe Hazan, *Krakh Shel Romi* (Livorno: Moshe Yeshuah Tobina, 1872), section 1, 4a. See also Ovadia Yosef, *Yabi'a Omer,* 148–149. Quoted by Rabbi Batzri, *Sha'arei Ezra,* 50.

48. Yehudah Assod, *Teshuvot Mahari* (Lemberg: unknown publisher, 1873), "Yoreh De'ah," section 170, 55.

49. Yosef, *Yabi'a Omer,* 148.

50. Menashe Klein, *Mishneh Halakhot,* vol. 16 (New York: Machon Mishneh Halakhot Gdolot, 1989), section 96, 200–208.

51. Henkin, *Bnei Banim,* section 31, 128.

52. Henkin, *Bnei Banim,* section 31, 128–135.

53. Eliezer Waldenberg, *Tsits Eliezer,* vol. 14 (Jerusalem: E. Y. Waldenberg, 1981), section 91, 167.

54. Eliezer Waldenberg, *Tsits Eliezer,* vol. 15 (Jerusalem: E. Y. Waldenberg, 1983), section 48, 128.

55. Rabbi Israel Moshe Hazan, *Krach Shel Romi,* chapter 1, 4 (Livorno: Moshe Yeshua Tobina Press, may his soul rest in paradise, 1872).

56. Waldenberg, *Tsits Eliezer,* vol. 13, chapter 12 (Jerusalem, EI Waldenberg, 1978), 30. Rabbi Waldenberg quotes Sifri on the Book of Numbers, 69.

57. BT Chulin 13b; Katz, *Exclusiveness and Tolerance,* 33–35.

58. Yechezkel Landau, "Hitnatslut," in *Noda BeYehudah: Mahadura Kama* (Prague: unknown publisher, n.d.), 8.

59. Pinchas Avraham Meyers, *Divrei Pinhas* (Jerusalem: unknown publisher, 1989), section 52, 403–408. Like most arbiters, Meyers uses the word *tiflah* (frivolity) in this context, a traditional Jewish play on the word *tfilah* (prayer). The declaration "gentiles of our times are not idolaters" is often coupled with declarations originating in medieval Ashkenazi Judaism that "gentiles of our times are not idolaters but are merely emulating the customs of their ancestors," or "gentiles of our times are not well versed in the nature of idols" or "are not zealous in their adherence to idolatry" (403).

60. Meyers, *Divrei Pinhas,* 403.

61. Meyers, *Divrei Pinhas,* 306.

62. Meyers, *Divrei Pinhas,* 407.

63. Henkin, *Bnei Banim,* section 35, 23.

64. Hayim Binyamin Goldberg, *Ben Yehudi LeNokhri: Inyaney Yoreh De'ah* (Jerusalem: self-published, 1994), "Yoreh De'ah," section 27, 375.

65. This is also the position of Rabbi Tzvi Pesach Frank. See *Har Tzvi* (Jerusalem: Makhon Harav Frank, 1976), "Yoreh De'ah," section 117, 105–106.

66. Waldenberg, *Tsits Eliezer* 14, section 91, 167.

67. According to the *Shulhan Arukh: Yoreh De'ah,* "Hilkhot Avoda Zara," section 148, section 12; Ovadia Yosef, *Yabi'a Omer,* 148.

68. Immanuel Jakobovits relates that he consulted a rabbinical court on this matter of entering a church during a ritual or a service; see his *HaRav HaLord: Sihot Im Michael Shashar* (Jerusalem: Shashar Publications, 1996–1997), 120–122 (Hebrew). Jakobovits refused the invitation of Cardinal Willebrands to participate in the interreligious service for peace that Pope John Paul II conducted at Assisi, because he did not allow participation in interreligious rituals. See Jeffery M. Cohen, ed., *Dear Chief Rabbi: From the Correspondence of Chief Rabbi Immanuel Jakobovits on Matters of Jewish Law, Ethics and Contemporary Issues 1980–1990* (Hoboken, NJ: Ktav, 1995), 39.

69. Jonathan Sacks, *The Dignity of Difference: How to Avoid the Clash of Civilizations,* rev. ed. (London: Continuum, 2002).

70. See Jacob Berkman, "Orthodox Group: Rabbi Violated Rules by Joining National Prayer Service," *Jewish Telegraphic Agency,* January 21, 2009, http://www.jta.org/2009/01/21/news-opinion/politics/orthodox-group-rabbi-violated-rules-by-joining-national-prayer-service. For Lookstein's response to the RCA's critique, see "New York—Rabbi Lookstein in Letter Defends His Participation in Interfaith Services in a Church," *Voz Iz Neias? The Voice of the Orthodox Jewish Community,* January 25, 2009, http://www.vosizneias.com/26285/2009/01/25/new-york-rabbi-lookstein-in-letter-defends-participating-interfaith-services-in-a-church/. For a halakhic discussion of this affair, see Michael J. Broyde and Kenneth Auman, "Entering a Sanctuary for Hatzalat Yisrael: An Exchange," *Hakirah: The Flatbush Journal of Jewish Law and Thought* 8 (2009): 53–68.

71. Broyde and Auman, "Entering a Sanctuary," 64.

72. Henkin, *Bnei Banim,* section 35, 116.

73. Henkin, *Bnei Banim,* section 35, 116–117.

74. Aviad Hacohen expresses wonder over the erudition displayed by Henkin's responsum regarding the various facets of Christian faith. See Hacohen, "Natsrut VeNotsrim," 115.

75. Dror Fixler and Gil Nadal, "Ha'im HaNotsrim BeYamenu Ovdey Avoda Zara Hem?" *Tehumin* 22 (2002): 68–77 (Hebrew). Emphasis in the original.

76. Yaakov Ariel, "Nispah Bet: He'arot LeMa'amram Shel Dror Fixler and Gil Nadal, "Ha'im HaNotsrim BeYamenu Ovdey Avoda Zara Hem?" *Tehumin* 22 (2002): 77–78 (Hebrew).

77. Ariel, "Nispah Bet."

78. Yossi Slotnick, "Isur Kenisa LeKnesiyot—Hirhurim Hadashim," Yeshivat Ma'aleh Gilboa, January 11, 2017, http://www.maalegilboa.org//article/ל-כניסה-איסור.

79. Slotnick, "Isur Kenisa LeKnesiyot."

80. Slotnick, "Isur Kenisa LeKnesiyot."

81. The editors of the publication are Rabbi Yehuda Gilad and Dr. Kalman Neuman. See Kalman Neuman, "He'arat Ha'Orekh," Yeshivat Ma'aleh Gilboa, http://www.maalegilboa .org/article/ל-כניסה-איסור.

82. Anonymous, *Sefer Israel VeHa'Amim,* unpublished manuscript (Jerusalem: Israel and the Nations Institute, 2012). The quotations are presented here with the consent of the author.

83. Anonymous, *Sefer Israel VeHa'Amim,* 21.

84. Anonymous, *Sefer Israel VeHa'Amim,* 613.

85. Anonymous, *Sefer Israel VeHa'Amim,* 532.

86. Anonymous, *Sefer Israel VeHa'Amim,* 602.

87. Anonymous, *Sefer Israel VeHa'Amim,* 605. The author clarifies that the ignorance of the halakhic arbiters regarding Christianity was unavoidable because of the charged relationship between the Jewish community and its Christian neighbors.

Chapter 7: Christianity in Religious Zionist Thought

1. See Shlomo Fischer, "Self-Expression and Democracy in Radical Religious Zionist Ideology" (PhD diss., Hebrew University of Jerusalem, 2007).

2. Karma Ben Johanan, "Wreaking Judgment on Mount Esau: Christianity in R. Kook's Thought," *Jewish Quarterly Review* 106, no. 1 (2016): 76–100.

3. Abraham Isaac Kook, *Shemonah Kevatsim,* vol. 2 (Jerusalem: Mossad Harav Kook, 2004) Kovets 6:207, 257 (Hebrew).

4. Yehuda Mirsky, *Rav Kook: Mystic in a Time of Revolution* (New Haven, CT: Yale University Press, 2014), 126.

5. See, for example, Kook, *Shemonah Kevatsim* 2, Kovets 7:92, 302; Kovets 5:147, 121 (Hebrew).

6. For instance, Kook, *Shemonah Kevatsim* 2, Kovets 7:120, 356.

7. Maimonides, *Laws of Kings,* 11:4.

8. See also Kook, *Shemonah Kevatsim* 2, Kovets 5:254, 179.

9. Kook, *Shemonah Kevatsim* 2, Kovets 5:47, 74; Abraham Isaac Kook, *Eder HaYakar Ve'Ikvey HaTson* (Jerusalem: Mossad Harav Kook, 5745 / 1985), 31 (Hebrew).

10. See Abraham Isaac Kook, "LeMahalakh Ha'Ideot BeIsrael," in *Orot* (Jerusalem: Mossad Harav Kook, 2005), 110 (Hebrew).

11. In his "Letter 4475," *Igrot HaRa'aya,* vol. 3 (Jerusalem: Mossad Harav Kook, 1965), 164, Kook criticized the ultra-Orthodox movement Agudat Israel for its objection to the Balfour Declaration using surprisingly similar terms to the ones he uses against Christianity: "a sect well-known for its venomous self-righteousness, which cannot stand any development of national life, particularly when it comes to the people of Israel in the Land of Israel. . . . And the consequences, which they prefer, are the deepening of exile, the patient gathering of crumbs under the table of Ashkenaz, and on the basis of such false fear of heavens, *minut* and the conversion that defiles [*HaHamara HaMego'ala*] its nest, and such venomous eggs are only too quick to hatch." The Jewish refusal to acknowledge the workings of the redemption is thus considered by Kook to be heresy, because this is the precise essence of *minut*—challenging the divine plan and making the people of Israel forget their destiny.

12. Kook, *Eder HaYakar,* 33.

13. See Dov Schwartz, *Challenge and Crisis in Rabbi Kook's Circle* (Tel Aviv: Am Oved, 2001) (Hebrew).

14. Zvi Yehudah Kook, "Igeret 71," in *Tsemah Zvi* (Jerusalem: unknown publisher: 1991), 179.

15. Kook, "Igeret 71," 179.

16. This echoes Maimonides's expression regarding Jesus as a stumbling block in *Laws of Kings,* 11:4: "Has there been ever a greater stumbling block than this?"; Kook, "Igeret 71," 179.

17. Kook, "Igeret 71," 170; emphasis in the original.

18. Kook, "Igeret 71," 180.

19. Kook, "Igeret 71," 181; emphases in the original.

20. Abraham Isaac Kook, *Sehmona Kevatsim* 2, Kovets 7:45, 314: "Its outside demeanor may have been slightly straightened out, but the purpose [of Christianity] is but one, not to sanctify the will, life, the coarse world and the essential nature in accordance with the order prepared for it by God's great plan, founded in the Jewish nation, in a sacred nation, and from its bifurcations many nations could have drawn sustenance, each nation according to its content, its morality and its natural, historical and racial readiness, its education and geographic and economic status, with all the social and personal contents that accrue to that—not this was the direction of the *minut*'s propensity."

21. Kook, "Igeret 71," 179, 180: "This set the path of the 'historical error,' the 'nonprogrammatic program': the influence of a spirit and morality and a general-universal calling in the name of God, outside the divine program, not from within the general

course of life's creativity, but out of mortal thoughts, aspirations and illusions regarding God's name."

22. Kook, "Igeret 71," 182–184.

23. Kook, "Igeret 71," 182–183.

24. Zvi Yehudah Kook maintained close ties with the ultra-Orthodox anti-missionary organization Yad La'Achim. He protested the founding of the Christian village Nes Ammim, and more. See, for example, Zvi Yehudah Kook, "Al Kefar HaMisyonerim," in *LeNetivot Israel,* vol. 2 (Kiryat HaYeshiva Beit El: MeAvney HaMakom 2007), 584 (originally published in the religious Zionist daily newspaper *HaTzofe,* September 11, 1962).

25. For a short discussion of the attitude of Zvi Yehudah Kook toward Christianity in general and missionary activity in particular, see Gideon Aran, *Kookism: The Roots of Gush Emunim, Settler Culture, Zionist Theology, and Contemporary Messianism* (Jerusalem: Carmel, 2013), 187–191 (Hebrew).

26. Two articles on this subject were collected in Zvi Yehudah Kook's book *LeNetivot Israel 2:* "HaMinyan Sheanu Monim Kan," 567 (originally published in *Hed HaMoatsa Hadatit, Jerusalem* 3, Av 1956); and the "HaShana Ha'Ezrahit Ha'Hadasha?" (originally published in *HaTzofe,* January 9, 1958), 568.

27. Zvi Yehudah Kook, "Emdatenu Ve'Ekronoteyha," in *LeNetivot Israel,* vol. 1 (Jerusalem: Agudat Zahav Ha'Arets, 1990), 191.

28. Kook, "Emdatenu Ve'Ekronoteyha," 189.

29. Kook, *Shemonah Kevatsim 2,* Kovets 5:95, 96.

30. Zvi Yehudah Kook, *Yahadut VeNatsrut,* ed. Shlomo Aviner (Beit El: Sifriyat Hava, 2001), 44.

31. See BT Gittin 57a. See also Zvi Yehudah Kook, "HaPesha BeIsrael," in *Lenetivot Israel 2,* 544; "Emdatenu Ve'Ekrnoteya," 191.

32. Zvi Yehudah Kook, *Yahadut VeNatsrut,* 36–37. Kook refers to his father's words in *Shemonah Kevatsim 1,* Kovets 2:58, 268.

33. Indeed, in a footnote, the editor of *Mishneh Torah* in the "Rambam La'Am" series (*Mishneh Torah: Mahadura Menukedet Im Perush La'Am,* vol. 17 [Jerusalem: Mossad Harav Kook, 1965], 416 [Hebrew]) wrote as follows: "And they delivered him to the Roman authorities, and they tried him for treason for having declared himself the Messiah king of Israel."

34. Maimonides, *Laws of Kings,* 11:4.

35. Kook, *Yahadut VeNatsrut,* 28–29.

36. Kook, "HaPesha BeIsrael," 535.

37. Based on BT Sukkah 45b; based on 2 Chronicles 35:3; paraphrasing the Zohar 3:73a.

38. Kook, "HaPesha BeIsrael," 536.

39. Kook, *Yahadut VeNatsrut,* 23.

40. See Armand Abecssis, "L'école de pensée Juive de Paris," *Pardès* 23 (1997), 229–231.

41. See Jürgen Mettepenningen, *Nouvelle théologie—New Theology: Inheritor of Modernism, Precursor of Vatican II* (London: T. & T. Clark, 2010); Hans Boersma, *Nouvelle Théologie and Sacramental Ontology: A Return to Mystery* (Oxford: Oxford University Press, 2009). See also Gabriel Flynn and D. Murray, *Ressourcement: A Movement for Renewal in Twentieth-Century Catholic Theology* (Oxford: Oxford University Press, 2012).

42. See Yosef Charvit, "Identity and History—The Cultural Heritage of R. Yehouda Leon Askénazi (Manitou)," *Pe'amim: Studies in Oriental Jewry* 91 (2002), 109 (Hebrew).

43. Léon Askénazi, "Préface," in Jean Vassal, *Les églises, diaspora d'Israël?* (Paris: Albin Michel, 1993), 9. See also Askénazi, "Lettre à quelques amis chrétiens," in *La parole et l'écrit: Textes réunis et présentés par Marcel Goldmann*, vol. 1 (Paris: Albin Michel, 1999), 438; *The Secret of the Midrash: A Hebraic Moral Identity* (Tel Aviv: Miskal, 2009), 135 (Hebrew).

44. Léon Askénazi, "Il était une foi," in *La parole et l'écrit: Textes réunis et présentés par Marcel Goldmann,* vol. 2 (Paris: Albin Michel, 2004), 602.

45. Yehuda Léon Askénazi, *HaMa'amin VeHaPhilosoph: Shiurey HaRav Yehuda Léon Askénazi,* ed. Shlomo Aviner, (Beit El: Sifriyat Hava, 2013), 175; Askénazi, "Tant que dure la nuit," in *La parole* 1, 422.

46. Askénazi, "Préface," 9; *The Secret of the Midrash,* 149.

47. Askénazi, "Préface," 9.

48. Askénazi, "Il était une foi," 602; Askénazi, "Quand l'âme chrétienne redécouvre Israël . . . ," in *La parole* 1, 470

49. Askénazi, "L'Église recconaît que les Juifs sont Israël," in *La parole* 1, 497–498.

50. Abraham Isaac Kook, *Shemonah Kevatsim* 2, Kovets 7:92, 341.

51. Askénazi, "Israel BeGalut HaIslam VeHanatsrut," *Shevet Ve'Am: Bamah LeBerur Be'ayot Hevra VeTarbut Shel Yehadut Sfarad VeHanizrah Ba'Arets VeBagolah,* second series 1 (1971), 89–90 (Hebrew).

52. Askénazi, *The Secret of the Midrash,* 157–158.

53. Askénazi, "Tant que dure la nuit," 423.

54. Askénazi, "Lettre à quelques amis," 438; see also Yosef Charvit, "Christianity and Islam in the Philosophy of Rabbi Yehuda Leon Ashkenazi (Manitou)—Chronicles and 'the End of Days,'" in *On Repentance and Redemption: Presented to Binyamin Gross,* ed. Dov Schwartz and Ariel Gross (Ramat-Gan: Bar-Ilan University Press, 2008), 270–271 (Hebrew).

55. Askénazi, "Il était une foi," 602. Askénazi had called on Christians to renounce the idea of the "mystery of Israel" (according to Rom. 11:25–26). Seeing Jewish existence as a divinely ordered "mystery" was a dominant idea in the Catholic French discourse at the time, largely the result of a famous article of that name authored by the influential Catholic philosopher Jacques Maritain. See Maritain, *Le mystère d'Israël et autres essais* (Paris: Desclée de Brouwer, 1965). Maritain saw the Holocaust as evidence of the mysterious providence of God over his chosen people. Askénazi challenged this idea: "It is not enough to point to the 'mystery of Israel.' After all, it is the same mystery that has led

directly to the mystery of the Inquisition butchers, and, less directly, in our time, to the mystery of the gas chambers of the Holocaust." See Askénazi, "Quand l'âme chrétienne redécouvre Israël," 470–471.

56. Askénazi, "Tant que dure la nuit," 424.

57. Askénazi, *HaMa'amin VeHaPhilosoph*, 173.

58. See Jeremy Cohen, *The Friars and the Jews* (Ithaca, NY: Cornell University Press, 1983).

59. Askénazi, *The Secret of the Midrash*, 135; see also Askénazi, *HaMa'amin VeHaPhilosoph*, 173–178.

60. Askénazi, *HaMa'amin VeHaPhilosoph*, 150.

61. Askénazi, *HaMa'amin VeHaPhilosoph*, 157.

62. Askénazi held Paul responsible for this transformation, as he was both a Torah scholar and a Greek philosopher and falsified the Hebrew meaning of the Torah. See Askénazi, *HaMa'amin VeHaPhilosoph*, 191–198.

63. Askénazi, *The Secret of the Midrash*, 158.

64. 2 Corinthians 3:13–16: "Not like Moses, who put a veil over his face to keep the people of Israel from gazing at the end of the glory that was being set aside. But their minds were hardened. Indeed, to this very day, when they hear the reading of the old covenant, that same veil is still there, since only in Christ is it set aside. Indeed, to this very day whenever Moses is read, a veil lies over their minds; but when one turns to the Lord, the veil is removed."

65. At this point, Askénazi follows Maimonides's account of Christianity as a phase in the divine plan of salvation, unwillingly preparing the hearts of gentiles for the true Messiah (see Maimonides, *Laws of Kings*, 11:4). For Askénazi, too, precisely from their own scriptures will the Christians come to discover the truth behind them and acknowledge the true Messiah. Though Christian religion had "familiarized" their hearts with the religious ideas of Judaism, it gave them an erroneous version of Judaism. Now the time had come to renounce the fake version and return to the original.

66. Askénazi, *The Secret of the Midrash*, 149–150, 159.

67. Askénazi, *HaMa'amin VeHaPhilosoph*, 176–177.

68. This idea was further developed by Askénazi's non-Jewish disciple, Jean Vassal, in his book *Les églises, diaspora d'Israël?* (Paris: Albin Michel, 1993).

69. Livni's family took part in saving thousands of Jews at the village of Le Chambon-sur-Lignon in central France.

70. Abraham Livni, *Le retour d'Israël et l'espérance du monde* (Monaco: Collection Hatsour & Editions du Rocher, 1984); Abraham Livni, *Shivat Zion Nes La'Amim*, trans. Oury Cherki (Jerusalem: El Artsi, 1995) (Hebrew).

71. Livni, *Le retour d'Israël*, 24.

72. Livni, *Le retour d'Israël*, 28.

73. Livni, *Le retour d'Israël*, 35

74. Livni, *Le retour d'Israël*, 261. Livni subsequently became convinced that Islam, too, was holding up salvation.

75. Livni, *Le retour d'Israël*, 38.

76. Livni, *Le retour d'Israël*, 206.

77. Livni, *Le retour d'Israël*, 206–208.

78. Livni, *Le retour d'Israël*, 208–212.

79. Livni, *Le retour d'Israël*, 209.

80. Livni, *Le retour d'Israël*, 211.

81. See the discussion of the conception of the Jewish Bible in Christian scripture in Chapter 3.

82. Livni, *Le retour d'Israël*, 212.

83. Livni, *Le retour d'Israël*, 213.

84. Élie Benamozegh, *Israël et l'humanité* (Paris: Albin Michel, 1977). Benamozegh encouraged his most devoted student, the Christian Aimé Pallière (who had edited *Israël et l'humanité* and published it after the death of Benamozegh), not to convert to Judaism but rather to disseminate the Noahide religion. It should be noted that the Jewish mission (which, though it does not involve conversion, does comprise recognition of the religious superiority of Judaism) in nineteenth-century Europe was an extremely unusual phenomenon. As regards Aimé Pallière, see Raniero Fontana, *Aimé Pallière: Un "cristiano" a servizio di Israele* (Milano: Ancora, 2001).

85. There are internal contradictions in the writings of Benamozegh concerning the nature and scope of these corrections. See Raniero Fontana, "A Noachide Profile," *European Judaism* 44, no. 2 (2011): 106–115.

86. Livni, *Le retour d'Israël*, 299.

87. Livni conducts a detailed discussion of the idea of *shittuf* and the various halakhic approaches regarding it. Livni, *Le retour d'Israël*, 301–304.

88. Livni, *Le retour d'Israël*, 301–304.

89. Livni, *Le retour d'Israël*, 255.

90. Zvi Yehudah Kook, *Yahadut VeNatsrut*.

91. Ya'akov Zurishaday, *Habrit: Divrey Bikoret Al "HaBrit HaHadasha" HaNimtsaim BeSifrut Israel Ha'Atika*, 4th ed. (Jerusalem: publisher unkown, 1970) (Hebrew); Ya'akov Zurishaday, *HaMokesh HaNotsri* (Tel Aviv: Miskal, 2000) (Hebrew).

92. See, for example, Shlomo Aviner, "Ha'Oyev HaNotsri," in Kook, *Yahadut VeNatsrut*, 71–83 (Hebrew).

93. Avner Shalev, ed., *Berurey Devarim Be'Inyan Notsrim Yedidey Israel* (Jerusalem: HaTenuah LeToda'ah Yehudit, 2000) (Hebrew). The booklet does not include any indication as to its authors.

94. Oury Cherki, "Anahnu VeHaNatsrut—Iyun BeAktualya," *Tzohar: Ktav Et Torani* 2 (2000): 95–106 (Hebrew); Dan Be'eri, "HaNotsrim, Shear HaAdam Ve'Anahnu," *Tzohar: Ktav Et Torani* 2 (2000): 107–112 (Hebrew). Tzohar is an Orthodox Zionist

organization acting to bridge gaps between the secular and the religious, considered lenient and open.

95. A noteworthy exception in this context is the booklet *HaZiyuf HaGadol: Kol Ha'Emet Al HaZiyuf HaNotsri* (The great hoax: The entire truth about the Christian hoax), edited by Z. Katz-Shur (Bnei Brak: no publisher, 1999) (Hebrew), which seems to have originated in Haredi society and was distributed in very large quantities on the eve of the millennium. The booklet contains quotations from the disputation literature, from the Talmud, and from *Toledot Yeshu,* as well as illustrations of torture instruments used by inquisitors in the Middle Ages. My thanks to Dr. Orit Ramon for bringing this booklet to my attention.

96. *Berurey Devarim BeYachas LaNotsrim Ohavey Israel* (Jerusalem: HaTenuah leToda'ah Yehudit [the movement for Jewish consciousness], 2000), 6. The booklet does not indicate the names of its authors. I received it, gratefully, from Mina Fenton, formerly a member of the Mafdal religious Zionist party and a member of the Jerusalem City Council. Fenton has led the campaign against accepting funds from Christian Evangelicals and has worked closely with R. Aviner on this subject. She explained that the booklet was disseminated by the Har Hamor students of R. Zvi Tau.

97. *Berurey Devarim,* 7.

98. Amnon Ramon, *Christians and Christianity in Jerusalem and the State of Israel* (Jerusalem: Jerusalem Institute for Policy Research, 2002), 42–51 (Hebrew).

99. Ramon, *Christians and Christianity,* 96.

100. *Berurey Devarim,* 21.

101. Yehoshua Zuckerman, "Mavo," in Zurishaday, *HaMokesh HaNotsri,* 7.

102. BT Berachot 34b; Maimonides, *Laws of Kings,* 12:2.

103. Zurishaday, *HaMokesh HaNotsri,* 287. It would be plausible to assume that this is Zvi Yehudah Kook's comment on the text, which was embedded in it by the editors (it does not appear in the original version of the book). See also Aviner, "Ha'Oyev HaNotsri": "But the tables have been turned! The Jewish People is no longer a downtrodden people, but rather an important and respected people, with a state and army of its own, with power and an economy, the lion cub of Judea is treading the stages of the earth" (71).

104. Cherki, "Anahnu VeHaNatsrut," 95–96.

105. Cherki, "Anahnu VeHaNatsrut," 96.

106. Maimonides, *Laws of Kings,* 11:4.

107. Cherki, "Anahnu VeHaNatsrut," 96.

108. Cherki, "Anahnu VeHaNatsrut," 98.

109. Cherki, "Anahnu VeHaNatsrut," 98–99.

110. Cherki, "Anahnu VeHaNatsrut," 99.

111. Cherki, "Anahnu VeHaNatsrut," 99.

112. Cherki, "Anahnu VeHaNatsrut," 102.

113. Cherki, "Anahnu VeHaNatsrut," 103.

114. According to BT Sukah 45b; Sanhedrin 63a; Cherki follows Zvi Yehudah Kook, "HaPesha BeIsrael," 536.

115. Cherki, "Anahnu VeHaNazrut," 103.

116. See the Noahide World Center's website: https://noahideworldcenter.org/wp_en/.

117. Ariel Horwitz, "HaRamkol Shelanu Klapey Ha'Enoshut Nidlak MeHadash," *Makor Rishon—Musaf Shabbat,* November 30, 2012, at the Musaf Shabbat website, https://musaf -shabbat.com.

118. Horwitz, "HaRamkol."

119. Shlomo Aviner, "Yahas HaYahadut El HaOlam HaNotsri," *Tehumin* 8 (1987): 368–370 (Hebrew).

120. Aviner, "Ha'Oyev HaNotsri," 74.

121. Aviner, "Ha'Oyev HaNotsri," 75–76.

122. Aviner, "Ha'Oyev HaNotsri," 76.

123. Cherki makes a similar argument, that Europe's secularization is intended to allow Christians to destroy the Jewish people without any theological obstacles. See Cherki, "Anahnu VeHaNatsrut," 102.

124. Aviner, "Ha'Oyev HaNotsri," 82.

125. Aviner, "Ha'Oyev HaNotsri," 79–80.

126. Aviner, "Ha'Oyev HaNotsri," 79–80.

Chapter 8: The Orthodox World and Christian-Jewish Dialogue

1. See, for example, Gilles Bernheim and Philippe Barbarin, *Le rabbin et le cardinal: Un dialogue judéo-chrétien d'aujourd'hui* (Paris: Stock, 2008); Jonathan Sacks, The *Dignity of Difference: How to Avoid the Clash of Civilizations,* rev. ed. (London: Continuum, 2002).

2. For the complexities of the term "Judeo-Christian," see K. Healan Gaston, *Imagining Judeo-Christian America: Religion, Secularism, and the Redefinition of Democracy* (Chicago: University of Chicago Press, 2019). Jewish authors have not often resisted this symbolic depiction of their contribution to American civilization, precisely because of a certain tension they experienced between the "Judeo-Christian" image and their own self-perception. See also Warren Zev Harvey, "The Judeo-Christian Tradition's Five Others," in *Is There a Judeo-Christian Tradition?,* ed. Emmanuel Nathan and Anya Topolski (Berlin: De Gruyter, 2016), 211–224.

3. See Shaul Magid's groundbreaking *American Post-Judaism: Identity and Renewal in a Postethnic Society* (Bloomington: Indiana University Press, 2013).

4. See, among others, Philip A. Cunningham, *A Story of Shalom: The Calling of Christians and Jews by a Covenanting God* (New York: Paulist Press, 2001); Philip A. Cunningham and Arthur F. Starr, eds., *Sharing Shalom: A Process for Local Interfaith Dialogue between Christians and Jews* (Mahwah, NJ: Paulist Press, 1998); Mary C. Boys, *Has God Only One Blessing? Judaism as a Source of Christian Self-Understanding* (Mahwah,

NJ: Paulist Press, 2005); Mary C. Boys, ed., *Seeing Judaism Anew: Christianity's Sacred Obligation* (Lanham, MD: Rowman and Littlefield, 2005); John T. Pawlikowski, *Christ in the Light of the Christian-Jewish Dialogue* (New York: Paulist Press, 1982); Pawlikowski, *The Challenge of the Holocaust for Christian Theology* (New York: Center for Studies on the Holocaust, 1994); Eugene J. Fisher, *A Life in Dialogue: Building Bridges between Catholics and Jews* (St. Petersburg, FL: Media Books, 2017).

5. David Rosen, "The Jewish-Christian Dialogue in the US: The Spearhead," *Mahanaim: A Review for Studies in Jewish Thought and Culture* 15 (2004): 61–67.

6. Moshe Feinstein, *Igrot Moshe,* vol. 6 (Brooklyn: R. Moshe Feinstein, 1982), Yoreh De'ah 3:43, 378.

7. Feinstein, *Igrot Moshe,* 378–379.

8. For a thorough discussion of the various positions within the Modern Orthodox community regarding Soloveitchik's stand on the relationship between tradition and modernity, see Lawrence Kaplan, "Revisionism and the Rav: The Struggle for the Soul of Modern Orthodoxy," *Judaism: A Quarterly Journal of Jewish Life and Thought* 48, no. 3 (1999): 290–311.

9. David Hartman, *Love and Terror in the God Encounter: The Theological Legacy of Rabbi Joseph B. Soloveitchik* (Woodstock, VT: Jewish Lights, 2004), 133–136. See also Christian M. Rutishauser, *The Human Condition and the Thought of Rabbi Joseph B. Soloveitchik,* trans. Katherine Wolfe (Jersey City, NJ: Ktav, 2013), 107–134.

10. Soloveitchik objected to overt mission work as well, as indicated by his letter discussing the missionary school in Israel. Joseph B. Soloveitchik, "On the Cable to Prime Minister Eshkol," in *Community, Covenant, and Commitment: Selected Letters and Communications,* ed. Nathaniel Helfgot (Brooklyn, NY: Ktav, 2005), 212.

11. Joseph B. Soloveitchik, "On Jewish Participation in the Vatican II Ecumenical Council of 1962 (a)," in Helfgot, *Community, Covenant, and Commitment,* 247.

12. Joseph B. Soloveitchik, "On Interfaith Relationships (a)," in Helfgot, *Community, Covenant, and Commitment,* 259–262; "On Interfaith Relationships (b)," in Helfgot, *Community, Covenant, and Commitment,* 263–265.

13. Soloveitchik, "On Jewish Participation in the Vatican II Ecumenical Council of 1962 (a)," 248. See also "On Jewish Participation in the Vatican II Ecumenical Council of 1962 (b)," 249–252; and "On Relations with the Catholic Hierarchy," in Helfgot, *Community, Covenant, and Commitment,* 257–258.

14. Soloveitchik, "On Jewish Participation in the Vatican II Ecumenical Council of 1962 (a)," 248.

15. Soloveitchik, "On Interfaith Relationships (a)," 260.

16. Soloveitchik, "On Relations with the Catholic Hierarchy," 258.

17. For an eye-opening comparison of the positions of Soloveitchik and Heschel as regards dialogue with the Christian world, see Reuven Kimelman, "Rabbis Joseph B. Soloveitchik and Abraham Joshua Heschel on Jewish-Christian Relations," *Modern Judaism* 24, no. 3 (2004): 251–271.

18. Soloveitchik, "On Interfaith Relationships (b)," 264.

19. Joseph B. Soloveitchik, "Confrontation," *Tradition* 6, no. 2 (1964): 5–29.

20. There is disagreement among Rabbi Soloveitchik's researchers as to the nature of his objection to interreligious dialogue. Some view his reservations as a retreat from his openness to the modern world and concern over "what they will say in Brisk" (now Brest, located in Belarus); see David Singer and Moshe Sokol, "Joseph Soloveitchik: Lonely Man of Faith," *Modern Judaism* 2, no. 3 (1982): 255. Others claim that Soloveitchik's reservations are grounded in the modern philosophical ideas that he embedded in his philosophy; see Daniel Rynhold, "The Philosophical Foundations of Soloveitchik's Critique of Interfaith Dialogue," *Harvard Theological Review* 96, no. 1 (2003): 101–120. For a discussion of "Confrontation" in the dialectical philosophy of Rabbi Soloveitchik, see Alan Brill, "Triumph without Battle: The Dialectic Approach to Culture in the Thought of Harav Soloveitchik," in *Rabbi in the New World: The Influence of Rabbi J. B. Soloveitchik on Culture, Education and Jewish Thought*, ed. Avinoam Roznak and Naftaly Rotenberg (Jerusalem: Van Leer Institute and Magness Press, 2010), 118–144 (Hebrew); see also Hartman, *Love and Terror*, 131–165.

21. Soloveitchik, "Confrontation," 5–17.

22. Soloveitchik, "Confrontation," 17.

23. Soloveitchik, "Confrontation," 17.

24. Soloveitchik, "Confrontation," 18.

25. Soloveitchik, "Confrontation," 28.

26. Soloveitchik, "Confrontation," 28.

27. Soloveitchik, Confrontation," 22–23.

28. Soloveitchik, Confrontation," 24.

29. Soloveitchik, Confrontation," 23.

30. Soloveitchik, Confrontation," 21.

31. Soloveitchik, Confrontation," 21.

32. Soloveitchik, Confrontation," 25.

33. Soloveitchik, Confrontation," 25.

34. Soloveitchik, Confrontation," 24.

35. "Statement Adopted by the Rabbinical Council of America at the Mid-Winter Conference, February 3–5, 1964," in *Tradition* 6, no. 2 (1964): 28.

36. "Statement Adopted by the Rabbinical Council of America."

37. Hartman, *Love and Terror*, 132–133; Angela West, "Soloveitchik's 'No' to Interfaith Dialogue," *European Judaism* 47, no. 2 (2014): 96.

38. Marc Shapiro, "Confrontation: A Mixed Legacy," Boston College, https://www.bc.edu/content/dam/files/research_sites/cjl/texts/center/conferences/soloveitchik/Sol_shapiro.htm.

39. Hartman, *Love and Terror*, 150.

40. Hartman, *Love and Terror*, 150. Several rabbis have testified that Rabbi Soloveitchik himself participated in a number of Christian-Jewish dialogue events and that he

permitted several of his students to do so. See David Rosen, "Orthodox Judaism and Jewish-Christian Dialogue," paper presented at the conference "Revisiting 'Confrontation' after Forty Years," November 2003, Boston College, https://www.bc.edu/content /dam/files/research_sites/cjl/texts/center/conferences/soloveitchik/sol_rosen.htm.

41. Hartman, *Love and Terror*, 154–155. David Rosen claims that had Soloveitchik witnessed the changes that the church implemented in regard to Judaism in the years subsequent to the publication of "Confrontation," it is possible that we would have changed our mind. See Rosen, "Orthodox Judaism."

42. Eugene Korn, "The Man of Faith and Religious Dialogue: Revisiting 'Confrontation,'" *Modern Judaism* 25, no. 3 (2005): 294.

43. Korn, "Man of Faith," 308.

44. Irving Greenberg, *For the Sake of Heaven and Earth: The New Encounter between Judaism and Christianity* (Philadelphia: Jewish Publication Society, 2004), 11.

45. Shlomo Riskin, "Covenant and Conversion: The United Mission to Redeem the World," in *Covenant and Hope: Christian and Jewish Reflections: Essays in Constructive Theology from the Institute for Theological Inquiry*, ed. Robert W. Jenson and Eugene Korn (Grand Rapids, MI: William B. Eerdmans, 2012), 99–128. See also Greenberg, *For the Sake of Heaven and Earth*, 43.

46. Alan Brill, *Judaism and Other Religions: Models of Understanding* (New York: Palgrave Macmillan, 2010), 236–237.

47. Alan Brill, *Judaism and World Religions: Encountering Christianity, Islam, and Eastern Traditions* (New York: Palgrave Macmillan, 2012), xiii.

48. Soloveitchik addressed this point himself in another document that he devoted to interreligious dialogue. As far as he was concerned, even if the world with all its spaces were to be experienced as religious, one should still differentiate between "the universal and the public" aspect of religion and "private world of faith." See Soloveitchik, "On Interfaith Relationships (a)," 261–262. Kaplan complains of the extension of this argument made by liberal circles to justify participation in theological dialogue. Kaplan, "Revisionism and the Rav," 304–305.

49. Meir Soloveitchik, "A Nation under God: Jews, Christians, and the American Public Square," *Torah U-Madda Journal* 14 (2006–2007), 70.

50. Soloveitchik, "Confrontation," 24.

51. Michael Wyschogrod, "Orthodox Judaism and Jewish-Christian Dialogue," Boston College, January 28, 1986, https://www.bc.edu/content/dam/files/research_sites/cjl/texts /center/conferences/soloveitchik/sol_wyscho.htm.

52. Wyschogrod, "Orthodox Judaism and Jewish-Christian Dialogue."

53. Reprinted in Greenberg, *For the Sake of Heaven and Earth*, 49.

54. Irving Greenberg, "The Relationship of Judaism and Christianity: Toward a New Organic Model," *Quarterly Review* 4 (Winter 1984): 14.

55. Greenberg, "The Relationship of Judaism and Christianity," 14–15; Greenberg, *For the Sake of Heaven and Earth*, 231.

56. Greenberg, "The Relationship of Judaism and Christianity," 14–15; Greenberg, *For the Sake of Heaven and Earth,* 232–233.

57. Zev Eleff and Seth Farber, "Antimodernism and Orthodox Judaism's Heretical Imperative: An American Religious Counterpoint," *Religion and American Culture: A Journal of Interpretation* 30, no. 2 (2020), 237–272.

58. As Greenberg puts it in his own account of the episode in *For the Sake of Heaven and Earth,* 34.

59. Greenberg, *For the Sake of Heaven and Earth,* 35.

60. Greenberg, *For the Sake of Heaven and Earth,* 35.

61. See the chapter on "covenantal pluralism" in Greenberg, *For the Sake of Heaven and Earth,* 185.

62. Berger, "Review Essay: Covenants, Messiahs and Religious Boundaries," *Tradition* 39, no. 2 (2005), 71.

63. Greenberg, *For the Sake of Heaven and Earth,* 122.

64. Berger, "Review Essay," 71.

65. See David Berger, "Revisiting 'Confrontation' after Forty Years: A Response to Rabbi Eugene Korn," In *Persecution, Polemic, and Dialogue* (Boston: Academic Studies Press, 2010), 385–391.

66. National Jewish Scholars Project, "Dabru Emet: A Jewish Statement on Christians and Christianity," *New York Times,* September 10, 2000. The full document with signatures is available at https://icjs.org/wp-content/uploads/2020/06/Dabru-Emet.pdf.

67. In the witty words of Jon Levenson, "In *Dabru Emet,* this imperative to find common ground is perhaps most evident in the earnest and anodyne platitude with which the document concludes. 'Jews and Christians,' we are told, 'must work together for justice and peace'—a stand that has no doubt provoked dismay among those bent on working apart in the service of injustice and war." See "How Not to Conduct Jewish-Christian Dialogue," *Commentary,* December 2001, 5.

68. "Statement by Dr. David Berger Regarding the New York Times Ad by Dabru Emet," Orthodox Union Advocacy Center, September 14, 2000, https://advocacy.ou .org/statement_by_dr_david_berger_regarding_the_new_york_times_ad_by_dabru _emet/.

69. David Berger, "Dabru Emet: Some Reservations about a Jewish Statement on Christians and Christianity," in *Persecution, Polemic, and Dialogue,* 392–398.

70. "Statement by Dr. David Berger Regarding the New York Times Ad by Dabru Emet."

71. Berger, "Revisiting 'Confrontation,'" 389.

72. There are several organizations that promote such relations, such as Christian Friends of Israeli Communities Heartland; the Israeli branch of the organization is managed by Israeli American Orthodox Jew Sandra Baras. The organization Center for Jewish-Christian Understanding and Cooperation is managed by Rabbi Shlomo Riskin. The organization Israel Allies is managed by Rabbi Binyamin Elon.

73. See Isabel Kershner, "Rabbi Yechiel Eckstein Dies at 67; Fostered Israeli-Evangelical Ties," *New York Times,* February 7, 2019.

74. Yechiel Eckstein, *The Journey Home: A Novel* (Chicago: Shavti House, 2001).

75. As shown by Neta Stahl, this was an accepted theme in Hebrew-Zionist literature. Neta Stahl, *Other and Brother: Jesus in the 20th-Century Jewish Literary Landscape* (Oxford: Oxford University Press, 2012).

76. The video is available at https://jewishisrael.com/video/the-ifcj-s-yechiel -eckstein-tells-christians-a-better-way-to-carr. The emphasis is mine.

77. In an interview, for example, Eckstein related that he is not called to the Torah in synagogue. See Zvika Klein, "Hu Megayes Shney Miliard Sha'ch BeAsor. Az Lama Lo Ohavim Oto?" *NRG,* May 16, 2014, http://www.nrg.co.il/online/11/ART2/579/542.html (Hebrew).

78. See, for example, Yair Sheleg, "Vikuah Hilkhati Soer: Ha'im Mutar LeKabel Trumot MeHanotsrim Ha'Evengalistim," *Haaretz,* October, 14, 2002, http://www.haaretz.co.il/misc /1.831932 (Hebrew); Shimon Cohen, "Fenton Neged 'Masa Tslav HaKesef' HaNotsri," *INN,* September 26, 2011, http://www.inn.co.il/News/News.aspx/226535; Yair Etinger, "Krav Ben RaBanim Shamranim LeMetunim Mesaken Et Proyekt HaDegel Shel Piron," *Haaretz,* June 20, 2014, http://www.haaretz.co.il/news/education/.premium-1.2354492 (Hebrew). See also Mina Fenton, "Sakanah: 'Kayts Shel Yedidut'—Begidah Le'umit Ye-hudit," *Srugim,* May 15, 2014, at the Srugim website http://www.srugim.co.il (Hebrew); Daniel Bashach, "Kakh Metakhnenim Anshey HaKeren LeYedidut Le'Hashpi'a Al Ha-Yeladim Shelakhem," *Kipa,* June 29, 2014, http://www.kipa.co.il/now/57560.html (Hebrew); Benny Toker, "Mina Fenton: Mitbayeshet BeTenu'at Emunah," *INN,* September 18, 2014, http://www.inn.co.il/News/News.aspx/284158 (Hebrew).

79. Yosef's denunciation was published in the official Shas newsletter *Maayan Ha-Shavua* (issue no. 804, the Shlach Lecha weekly portion, 2006), which documented a meeting between Rabbis Yosef, Shlomo Amar, and Simcha Karelitz—this despite the fact that in an earlier halakhic decision, Rabbi Yosef stated that it *was* permitted to take donations from Christian missionaries if there was no direct connection between the donor and the recipient. See Ovadia Yosef, *Maayan Omer,* vol. 6 (Jeruslaem: Naki Family, 2010), section 67, 102 (Hebrew).

80. See for example Uri Polack, "Harav Lior: Issur Hilkhati BeKabalt Kesafim Mi-Notsrim," *Kipa,* October 11, 2011, http://www.kipa.co.il/now/46473.html (Hebrew). Nev-ertheless, it has been claimed that despite his halakhic position on this matter, Rabbi Lior's yeshiva received a donation from an American church. See Yehoshua Breiner, "MiHi HaToremet HaMafti'a LeYeshivato Shel Harav Lior?," *Walla,* July 22, 2011, http://news .walla.co.il/item/1843172 (Hebrew). See also Rabbi Eliezer Melamed, a relatively strict reli-gious Zionist rabbi, who expresses a nuanced position on that matter: "Hanotsrim ShMekaymin Et Nevu'at Yeshayhu," *Yeshiva,* November 2013, https://www.yeshiva.org.il /midrash/22817 (Hebrew). See also Shlomo Aviner, "Masa Tslav HaKesef," *Sifriat Hava,* September 2, 2012, http://www.havabooks.co.il/article_ID.asp?id=1295 (Hebrew).

81. Eugene Korn, "Rethinking Christianity: Rabbinic Positions and Possibilities," in *Jewish Theology and World Religions,* ed. Alon Goshen-Gottstein and Eugene Korn (Oxford: Littman Library of Jewish Civilization, 2012), 194.

82. Maimonides, *Laws of Kings,* 8:11; Jacob Katz, "The Vicissitude of Three Apologetic Passages," *Zion* 23–24, no. 3–4 (1958–59): 174–181.

83. The Talmud, according to Rabbi Korn, does not deal with the question of the theological status of Christians (he does not directly quote the clear Talmudic statement in the tractate of *Avoda Zara* that a Christian "should always be forbidden" [BT Avoda Zara 7b] and only makes brief mention of a disagreement, which he immediately masks with the words of Meiri that what is intended is not Christianity but the Persian religion).

84. Korn, "Rethinking Christianity," 195, 198.

85. Korn, "Rethinking Christianity," 196.

86. See the previous chapters in this regard for rabbis who held these views. See especially the third part of Eliyahu Zeini, *Hesed Le'umim Hatat* (Haifa: Or VeYeshu'ah, 2017), which explains Meiri's lenient position on Christianity as an attempt to appease Christians for fear of Christian violence.

87. See Alan Brill's discussion of Riskin in *Judaism and World Religions,* 105–109.

88. Victoria Clark, *Allies for Armageddon: The Rise of Christian Zionism* (New Haven, CT: Yale University Press, 2007), 256–284.

89. Riskin, "Covenant and Conversion," 100.

90. Riskin, "Covenant and Conversion," 106.

91. Riskin, "Covenant and Conversion," 106, based on BT Sota 37b.

92. According to Maimonides, *Laws of Kings,* 8:10.

93. Riskin, "Covenant and Conversion," 112; 113.

94. For the inspiration that Riskin draws from Christian theologians, see Brill, *Judaism and World Religions,* 105–109.

95. Maimonides, *Laws of Kings,* 10:9.

96. Moreover, at the time that the Jews were focused on their ethnic survival and could not disseminate the universal morality among the nations, the Christians were doing so, and for this, according to Riskin, the Jews should thank them (Riskin, "Covenant and Conversion," 127). At this point, Riskin inverts Maimonides's position; he defines Christianity as a religion that conforms to the seven Noahide laws (in certain places *shittuf* according to the Tosafists and in other places "nations restricted by the ways of religion" according to the opinion of Meiri), while claiming that fundamentalist Islam has become idolatry (he derives this from Meiri by associating the definition of idolatry with moral corruption), because it does not obey universal ethical directives; "Islamic fundamentalism has turned Allah into Moloch (Satan), and made every mosque that preaches the doctrine of suicide bombing a hell-haven of idolatry." See Shlomo Riskin, "Nadav and Avihu's 'Strange Fire,'" *Dallas Jewish Week Menu,* March 27, 2003, https://www.dallasjewishweek.com/dallas-jewish-week-8832.html. See also Brill, *Judaism and World Religions,* 106.

97. Shlomo Riskin, "Dialog Yehudi-Notsri: Hashiva Mekhudeshet," *Makor Rishon—Musaf Shabat,* May 17, 2012, at the Musaf Shabbat website, https://musaf-shabbat.com.

98. Riskin, "Dialog Yehudi-Notsri."

99. Riskin clarifies that researchers disagree as to what Maimonides meant by "the true religion," that is, whether he thought that the entire human race would eventually convert to Judaism and observe the 613 commandments or that he designated Judaism as such to maintain the difference between Israel and the nations, even in the days of the Messiah. Riskin, "Covenant and Conversion," 118–119. See also Menachem Kellner, *They Too Are Called Human: Gentiles in the Eyes of Maimonides* (Ramat-Gan: Bar-Ilan University, 2016) (Hebrew).

100. Riskin, "Covenant and Conversion," 119. See his reference to Maimonides, especially to Moshe ben Maimon, *Teshuvot HaRambam,* 284.

101. Riskin, "Dialog Yehudi-Notsri."

102. Raphael Ahren, "Efrat Rabbi Retracts Praise for 'Rabbi Jesus' over Orthodox Ire," *Haaretz,* January 1, 2010, http://www.haaretz.com/jewish-world/2.209/efrat-rabbi-retracts -praise-for-rabbi-jesus-over-orthodox-ire-1.260643. See also Hillel Fendel, "Rabbi Riskin Explains 'Resurrection' Remarks," *Arutz Sheva,* September 26, 2009, http://www.israel nationalnews.com/News/News.aspx/132109#.VIgIoDGUf-s.

103. Riskin, "Dialog Yehudi-Notsri."

104. The conference took place on November 23, 2003. See Berger, "Revisiting Confrontation."

105. David Berger, "Emunah BeRashut HaYahid," *Makor Rishon—Mussaf Shabat,* November 16, 2012, at the Musaf Shabbat website, https://musaf-shabbat.com.

106. Quoted from an interview that I conducted with Rabbi Riskin at Efrat, May 30, 2013. See also Eugene Korn, "Extra Synagogam Sallus Est? Judaism and the Religious Other," in *Religious Perspectives on Religious Diversity,* ed. Robert McKim (Leiden: Brill, 2017), 37–62.

107. Hershel Schachter, "Experimental Judaism: Playing with Fire (2012)," *TorahWeb,* https://www.torahweb.org/torah/2012/parsha/rsch_reeh.html.

108. Very similar claims were written by the Haredi rabbi Yoel Schwartz in his polemical book *HaYahadut Mul Benoteya HaSorerot* (Jerusalem: no publisher, 2003), 14–16 (Hebrew).

109. The controversy between the two rabbinical groups subsequently continued in the press in both Israel and the United States. Both Riskin himself and Sondra Baras, the director of "Christian Friends of Israeli Communities," wrote responses to Berger's response to Riskin's articles. See Sondra Baras, "Notsri Shel HaYom Eyno Notsri Shel Pa'am [Today's Christian is not the Christian of old times]" and Shlomo Riskin "HaZmanim Hishtanu [Times have changed]," *Markor Rishon—Musaf Shabat,* December 7, 2012, at the Musaf Shabbat website https://musaf-shabbat.com. Schachter's sharp article drew scathing criticism that was published in *Jewish Week* by activists of the Committee of Christian Jewish Relations, including Eugene Korn and Alan Brill. See Gary Rosenblatt,

"YU's Schachter Accused of Obsolete Views on Church," *Jewish Week,* August 28, 2012, https://jewishweek.timesofisrael.com/yus-schachter-accused-of-obsolete-views-on -church/.

110. Hershel Schachter, *Nefesh HaRav: LiMlot Shanah LePtirat Maran HaRav Joseph Dov HaLevi Soloveitchik Zts"l* (Brooklyn: Flatbush Beth Hamedrosh, 1999), 130 (Hebrew). See Schachter's joint announcement with several other colleagues in *Torah Musings* on April 5, 2005, three days before the pope's funeral, https://www.torahmusings.com/2005 /04/papal-funeral/.

111. Poupko recently (2021) inaugurated an educational program, under the auspices of the Jewish United Fund of Metropolitan Chicago and the Catholic Theological Union, for rabbis to become acquainted with Christianity.

112. Quoted from interview I conducted with Rabbi Poupko online, January 17, 2021.

113. David Berger, "On *Dominus Iesus* and the Jews," in *Persecution, Polemic, and Dialogue,* 381; "Dabru Emet: Some Reservations about a Jewish Statement on Christians and Christianity," 391–392 (also quoted in Meir Soloveitchik, "A Nation under God," 67).

114. Shalom Carmy, "'Orthodoxy Is Reticence'—Taking Theology Seriously," Boston College, https://www.bc.edu/content/dam/files/research_sites/cjl/texts/center/conferences /soloveitchik/sol_carmy.htm.

115. Soloveitchik, "A Nation under God," 64.

116. Soloveitchik, "A Nation under God," 81.

117. Soloveitchik, "A Nation under God," 74.

118. Soloveitchik, "A Nation under God," 68.

119. Meir Soloveitchik, "No Friend in Jesus," *First Things* 179, January 2008, 31.

120. Soloveitchik, "No Friend in Jesus."

121. Berger, "Review Essay," 75.

122. In Arthur A. Cohen's words, "European intellectuals came to regard Judaism and Christianity as essentially similar—similar not with respect to truth, but rather with respect to the untruth which they share." See *The Myth of the Judeo-Christian Tradition* (New York: Schocken, 1971), xvii–xviii. See also Meir Soloveitchik's "The Virtue of Hate," *First Things* 130, February 2003, as well as his other essays.

123. This is how Weiner phrased it in a conference conducted at the Jerusalem Institute of Israel Research on October 22, 2013. See also Weiner's words as presented in Yair Sheleg, "Berit Hadasha," *Makor Rishon—Musaf Shabat,* April 11, 2016, at the Musaf Shabbat website, https://musaf-shabbat.com.

124. This, for example, was the conclusion of an interview that I conducted with Rabbi David Brodman in Kiryat Ono, June 13, 2014. This also echoes the reason behind "for fear of enmity."

125. This is what Rabbi She'ar Yashuv Cohen explained to me in an interview I conducted with him in Haifa on February 21, 2012. Oded Wiener repeated this principle in Sheleg's article "Habrit HaHadasha." One may become acquainted with the selected subjects in the declarations of the bilateral committee that are published on the Vatican

website: http://www.vatican.va/roman_curia/pontifical_councils/chrstuni/sub-index /index_relations-jews.htm. The documents in Hebrew appeared in the booklet *From Plight to Well-Being: A New Age in the Relation of Jews and Christians* as published by the Konrad Adenaaur Fund and the Jewish American Committee in 2014.

126. Interview with Rabbi She'ar Yeshuv Cohen, Haifa, February 21, 2012.

127. Interview with Rabbi David Rosen, Jerusalem, February 13, 2012.

128. Rosen has been among the signatories of an Orthodox rabbinical statement on Christianity, in honor of the fiftieth anniversary of *Nostra aetate*. See "Orthodox Rabbinic Statement on Christianity," *CJCUC,* December 5, 2015, https://www.cjcuc.org/2015 /12/03/orthodox-rabbinic-statement-on-christianity/. The new statement testifies to an effort to recruit the Orthodox world to support the change. I discuss this further in the Epilogue.

129. See for example, the joint book published by Rabbi Rosen and the Protestant preacher R. T. Kendall, *The Christian and the Pharisee: Two Outspoken Religious Leaders Debate the Road to Heaven* (London: Hodder and Stoughton, 2006). See also Rosen's "Learning from Each Other—Reflections of a Jew Address at Fordham University, October 28, 2003," available on his website, https://www.rabbidavidrosen.net/wp-content /uploads/2016/02/Learning-From-Each-Other-Reflections-of-a-Jew.pdf.

130. David Rosen is responsible not only for bringing Catholic content to the writing of the bilateral committee members but also for procuring Jewish sources that can be used by them to formulate a tolerant position toward Christians. He claims, for example, that he was the one who showed them the words of Jacob Emden that "Christians and Muslims are a congregation that is convened for God—and it will endure," or the words of the Rabbi Moses Rivkes, the author of *Be'er HaGola,* that Christians are monotheists and Jews are obligated to pray for their well-being. See Rosen's article, "Ach Esau LeYa'akov: Ha'Olam HaNotsri Meshane Gisha Klapey HaYahadut [Esau is Jacob's brother: The Christian world is changing its attitude to Judaism]," *De'ot* 9 (2001), 16–20 (Hebrew).

131. Based on my interview with Rabbi David Brodman, Kiryat Ono, June 13, 2014.

132. Interview with Rabbi She'ar Yashuv Cohen, Haifa, February 21, 2012.

133. A similar problem cropped up when Pope Francis invited the president of Israel, Shimon Peres, and the president of the Palestinian National Authority, Mahmoud Abbas, to the Vatican to pray for peace there. Peres was happy to accept the invitation, but at the request of Chief Rabbi David Lau, they had the prayer in the garden.

Epilogue

1. Laurie Goodstein, "Pope Says Church Is 'Obsessed' with Gays, Abortion and Birth Control," *New York Times,* September 13, 2013.

2. Jospeh Cardinal Ratzinger, "Mass 'Pro Eligendo Romano Potifice,'" Homily of his Eminence Card. Joseph Ratzinger, Dean of the College of Cardinals, Vatican, http://www .vatican.va/gpII/documents/homily-pro-eligendo-pontifice_20050418_en.html.

3. Commission for Religious Relations with the Jews (CRRJ), "'The Gifts and the Calling of God are Irrevocable' (Rom. 11:29): A Reflection on Theological Questions Pertaining to Catholic-Jewish Relations on the Occasion of the 50th Anniversary of 'Nostra Aetate' (no.4)," Vatican, http://www.vatican.va/roman_curia/pontifical_councils/chrstuni /relations-jews-docs/rc_pc_chrstuni_doc_20151210_ebraismo-nostra-aetate_en.html.

4. Benedict XVI, "'Grace and Vocation without Remorse': Comments on the Treatise *De Iudaeis," Communio* 47 (2018), 168.

5. Benedict XVI, "'Grace and Vocation without Remorse,'" 171.

6. Benedict XVI, "'Grace and Vocation without Remorse,'" 177.

7. Benedict XVI, "'Grace and Vocation without Remorse,'" 183.

8. Benedict XVI, "'Grace and Vocation without Remorse,'" 175–176.

9. The Conference of European Rabbis and the Rabbinical Council of America, "Between Jerusalem and Rome: The Shared Universal and the Respected Particular. Reflections on 50 Years of Nostra Aetate (February 10, 2016)," https://www.kirchliche-dienste .de/damfiles/default/haus_kirchlicher_dienste/arbeitsfelder/judentum/Dokumente /Between-Jerusalem-and-Rome.pdf-ed1a73a7403877577cc5ef69dafb582a.pdf.

10. Zvi Yehudah Kook, "Igeret 71," in *Zemah Zvi* (Jerusalem: no publisher, 1991), 179.

Acknowledgments

I am deeply grateful to the many friends and colleagues who read various parts and versions of this book in different stages of its composition. I am indebted to Aviad Kleinberg for accompanying me in thinking and structuring this project from the moment of its inception, over years of intense work and close friendship. Marc B. Shapiro provided me with a great richness of sources and saved me from many errors and embarrassments. John Connelly, Gavin D'Costa, Menachem Fisch, Jonathan Garb, and Israel Yuval read and evaluated the entire manuscript in its different stages of evolution, and their suggestions have greatly improved it. I am grateful to Philip A. Cunningham, Sergey Dolgopolski, Adam Gregerman, Elad Lapidot, Christoph Markschies, Omer Michaelis, David Nirenberg, Yehiel Poupko, Philipp Gabriel Renczes, Ishay Rosen-Zvi, Peter Schäfer, and others who provided valuable comments and advice. Itamar Ben-Ami assisted me significantly in preparing the English manuscript for production, and the editorial team at Harvard University Press was instrumental in bringing the manuscript to completion in the best possible way.

I am grateful to my children, Lavi, Boaz, and Dror, and my partner, Tomehr, who made room for this project and accepted it as part of the family, and to my parents-in-law, Judy (RIP) and Avery Jochnowitz, for their continuous support. Last but not least, I would like to thank my mother, Esther Pelled, and my father, Shakhar Pelled, who were my companions and beloved interlocutors from the beginning of this intellectual journey to its end.

Index